M000238105

Male Confessions

Male Confessions

INTIMATE REVELATIONS AND
THE RELIGIOUS IMAGINATION

Björn Krondorfer

STANFORD UNIVERSITY PRESS
STANFORD, CALIFORNIA

Stanford University Press
Stanford, California

© 2010 by the Board of Trustees of the Leland Stanford Junior University.
All rights reserved.

No part of this book may be reproduced or transmitted in any form or by any means,
electronic or mechanical, including photocopying and recording, or in any information
storage or retrieval system without the prior written permission of Stanford University Press.

Printed in the United States of America on acid-free, archival-quality paper

Library of Congress Cataloging-in-Publication Data

Krondorfer, Björn.
  Male confessions : intimate revelations and the religious imagination / Björn Krondorfer.
    p. cm.
  Includes bibliographical references and index.
  ISBN 978-0-8047-6899-3 (cloth : alk. paper) -- ISBN 978-0-8047-6900-6 (pbk. : alk. paper)
  1. Confession in literature. 2. Christian literature--Male authors--History and criticism.
  3. Masculinity--Religious aspects--Christianity. I. Title.
  PN56.C67K76 2010
  809'.933826562--dc22

                              2009035055

Typeset by Bruce Lundquist in 11/14 Adobe Garamond

to my daughters Zadekia and Tabitha
who, one day, may wonder
if the man they know as their father
is the same man who wrote this book

Contents

	Acknowledgments	ix
1	Introduction: Male Confessions	1
INTERLUDE	*On Mirrors*	29
2	The Confines of Male Confessions: On Ancient Vainglory and the Postmodern Gaze	34
INTERLUDE	*On Testimony*	72
3	Non-absent Bodies and Moral Agency: Confessions of an African Bishop and a Jewish Ghetto Policeman	74
4	A Perpetrator and His Hagiographer: Oswald Pohl's Confession	100
INTERLUDE	*On Tears*	132
5	Sons of Tears: Displacing the Intimate (Female) Other	135
6	Not from My Lips: From Annihilation to Nation Building	161
7	On Spirit and Sperm: Eroticizing God, Sanctifying the Body	190
8	Outlook: The Power to Name Oneself into Being	231
	Notes	239
	References	269
	Index	287

Acknowledgments

This book has been in gestation for over ten years. I penned the first thoughts on male confessions and the religious imagination in between the births of my two daughters, shortly after I cut the umbilical cord of the firstborn and shortly before I knew we were expecting a second child. Today, at the end of the process of writing this book, my daughters have become teenagers, and I have grown with them. I am no longer the same man I was back then, yet I am the same in so many ways. A book like this grows with one's own changes, intellectually and emotionally, internally and externally. It has also evolved because I have had the good fortune to meet many gentle and thoughtful people who have helped me understand the ambiguities of life that flow into any confessional narrative.

Other than the humbling yet ever rewarding experience of parenting, my life is guided by the challenge of love, and the loving challenge, of being in a long-term relationship. Together, we have learned about friendship, love, and the vicissitudes of commitment. We have learned to appreciate endearments and endurements, entrancements and entrenchments, and what it means to be gendered beings. My deepest gratitude, hence, goes to Katharina von Kellenbach. She has also read two of the chapters, offered invaluable feedback, and provided important resources on the trial case of Oswald Pohl, whom she has investigated in her own research.

I want to thank Philip Culbertson for his encouraging words after reading select parts of my manuscript. Philip and I have exchanged correspondence on issues of masculinity and religion over the years, and we have revealed to each other some confessional secrets of our own. Stephen Boyd was a careful reader of an earlier version of the manuscript, and I want to thank him especially for our conversation on the necessity of risking vulnerability and the ethics of responsible self-disclosure. Norbert Reck read the chapter on gay confessional writings and offered a clear-sighted critique of some of its shortcomings. With him, I have talked for years about masculinity issues as well as the twisted discourse on culpability and complicity in postwar Germany. My thanks also go to Amy Shapiro for her thorough reading of an earlier draft of Pohl's conversion story. Steve Paulsson, Dorota Glowacka, and Annamaria Orla-Bukowska helped me with issues concerning the Polish language and Polish-Jewish culture. Jay Geller was kind enough to share his knowledge of Jewish autobiographies. Robin Bates gave me important advice on film. Martin Leutzsch and Gabrielle Jancke made me aware of the German research on *Selbstzeugnisforschung* (research on testimonial literature), especially as it relates to confessional writings by perpetrators in an international context. I also benefited greatly from advice through conversations and e-mail correspondence with Tom Driver, Scott Haldeman, Mark Masterson, Stephen Moore, and Donald Capps. Ruth Ost's keen eye prevented a few blunders, and Janet Butler Haugaard provided invaluable editorial feedback at various stages of the manuscript. I owe each and every one of these friends and colleagues a sincere and heartfelt thank-you.

I received institutional support from my college, and my special thanks go to Provost Larry Vote. Without receiving a research sabbatical in 2007, I might not have been able to complete this book. I am also thankful to Ralf Wüstenberg, chair of the Institute of Protestant Theology at the Freie Universität, who welcomed me during my sabbatical year in Berlin.

Over the years, I have had opportunities to present ideas contained in this book at various conferences and meetings. In the mid-1990s, I discussed for the first time my thoughts on male confessional writing in a working group on masculinity at the Society for Values in Higher Education. In 2001, I presented an early version on the confessions of Calel Perechodnik and Augustine in the "Men's Studies in Religion Group" at the American Academy of Religion. Parts of Oswald Pohl's perpetrator testimony I presented in 2006 at the International Conference on "Memory, History and Responsibility" at Claremont McKenna College, California. In 2007, I introduced the concept of male "confessiography" in Glasgow, Scotland, and I want to thank Heather Walton and Allison Jaspers for inviting me as keynote speaker to their conference on "Sexing the Text." The same year, I was able to elaborate on the issue of religion and remasculinization at the conference on "Religion and Gender" at the Böll Foundation in Berlin. In 2008, I discussed my thoughts on radical orthodoxy and gay theology at the "Netzwerk Geschlecht und Theologie" in Zürich, Switzerland. I want to thank Tania Oldenhage for the invitation. From each of these occasions, I have returned with deeper insight into the complexity of the material.

Parts of this book have been previously published but are presented here in thoroughly revised and expanded form. Chapter 2 has it origins in "The Confines of Male Confessions: On Religion, Bodies, and Mirrors" (in *Men's Bodies, Men's Gods*, ed. Björn Krondorfer [New York: New York University Press, 1996], pp. 205–234), and Chapter 3 is based on "Revealing the Non-absent Male Body: Confessions of an African Bishop and a Jewish Ghetto Policeman" (in *Revealing Male Bodies*, ed. Nancy Tuana et al. [Blooming-ton: Indiana University Press, 2002], pp. 245–268). Segments of Chapters 4 and 5 have appeared in "A Perpetrator's Confession: Gender and Religion in Oswald Pohl's Conversion Narrative" (online *Journal of Men, Masculinities and Spirituality* 2/2 [2008]: 62–81) and in "Textual Male Intimacy and the Religious Imagination" (*Literature and Theology* 22/3 [Oxford University Press, Sept. 2008]: 265–279).

One of the anonymous reviewers compared this book to an "innovative exhibit" of a "good museum curator" who creates "new ways of seeing works previously known but not comprehended in the same way." I want to thank this reviewer for suggesting this lovely image and invite the reader to take a stroll through this exhibit to see anew the tradition of confessional writings by men.

Male Confessions

CHAPTER I

Introduction

Male Confessions

"I have become a problem to myself," writes Saint Augustine in the fourth century. "I shall nevertheless confess to you my shame, since it is for your praise."

"I have made the first and most painful step in the dark and slimy maze of my confessions," writes Jean-Jacques Rousseau at the beginning of modernity. "It is not crimes that cost me to speak, but what is ridiculous and shameful."

"I am disconcerted by an irritating tendency to blush," writes modernist Michel Leiris in the twentieth century.

"Finally I want to tell You what is meant only for Your ears," writes Calel Perechodnik, a Jewish ghetto policeman, to his wife already killed by Germans. "I have deceived You."

"The moment of transformation filled me with an ardent love," writes Oswald Pohl after his conversion to Catholicism and shortly before he is hanged as a Nazi war criminal.

"I no doubt wanted the sperm of Jesus, the mark of his unfailing affection, to cover me and save me just as his holy blood did," writes Donald Boisvert in the twenty-first century.[1]

. . .

Voices of men from different centuries and different historical situations, men struggling to give testimony to themselves: they confess. They do so in writing, and they search for an audience. They confess their sins, their shame, their shortcomings, their deceptions, their desires. They confess because they imagine a dialogical "you": God, a wife, the public, other men. They confess because they feel an urge to share with us their intimate selves, because they have sinned, because they have experienced a transformative moment, because they want to be forgiven, or because they are self-absorbed and self-interested. This book is about these and other men trying to give a truthful account of themselves.

The field of associations evoked by the amorphous title *Male Confessions* reaches from questions of faith to pornography, from voluntary admissions of sins preceding a religious conversion to coercive techniques of police interrogations.[2] The citations at the beginning of the chapter echo such ambiguity: Augustine seems to speak from within a framework of faith, whereas Boisvert seems to pursue an ecstatic fantasy. Pohl seems to tell of a successful conversion of his old sinful self, whereas Perechodnik seems driven by a guilt for which he wants to atone. The religious imagination plays an important role in these confessions. And where the religious imagination seems absent—as in the case of men like Rousseau and Leiris, who adopt a decidedly antireligious stance—we can learn something about the modernist loss of religious perspective, bringing into sharper profile the kind of questions pursued in this book.

If this book about confessions neither refers, in any narrow sense, to statements of faith nor to pornographic eavesdropping (after all, "male confessions" might be the title of a gay porn movie), what is it about? It is about confessions as a mode of self-examination. It is also about men. It is about men opening their intimate lives and thoughts to the public through the form of confessional writing. As public documents, these writings tell us something about the interior struggle that men are willing to share with a larger audience during particular personal circumstances and in particular moments of history. As texts, they speak to the sincere attempts of men to lay bare aspects of themselves that would otherwise have remained hidden.

A Gendered Reading

No study, so far, has undertaken the task of examining confessions by men as a particular style of gendered writing and of subjecting the latter to a reading that pays attention to issues of religiosity and masculinity. *Male Confessions* makes a first foray into this complex territory. The terrain is difficult to negotiate because I am bringing together four areas—men, religion, gender, confessions—which are, each for its own reasons, complicated and highly contested. I do not seek, however, to clarify the various theoretical and methodological claims on definitional authority for any of these four areas. Rather, *Male Confessions* is more humble in scope and ambition while, at the same time, no less daring in the complexity of its arguments. I wish to demonstrate that men are able to talk about themselves intimately, but I also want to examine critically the limits of such intimate male talk. On the one hand, I want to take seriously the vulnerability exposed in male self-disclosures and learn from those who dared to walk down this path. On the other hand, I offer a critique of the religious and gendered rhetoric employed in such discourse.

The religious imagination, I will argue, allows men to talk about their intimate selves, their flawed and sinful selves, without having to condemn themselves entirely or to fear self-erasure. When I refer to the "religious imagination" in the context of male confessions, I have in mind how men, given their personal religiosity in a given historical circumstance, imagine religion and how they call upon the "religious" to articulate themselves in a self-examining mode. By foregrounding the religious imagination rather than other forms of religious sentiment and practice (such as liturgy, worship, devotion, or doctrine), I am not evaluating these men's spiritual understandings against a perceived religious orthodoxy. Instead, I ask whether the religious imagination facilitates (or obstructs) intimate self-disclosure. These men do not have to be doctrinally correct in order to play with the religious imaginary in their attempts to take account of themselves. Calling upon, and resorting to, religious language offers them escapes from the confining circularity of male self-absorption. Believing in the possibility of a transcendental Other and harboring hopes for redemption, both of which widen the imaginary horizon, enable men to self-examine and to grant others a look into their hearts. In view of something grander than one's own mortal being, some men feel sufficiently secure to expose a vulnerable self. Religion may not be the only venue that enables men to open their souls to the eyes and ears of an Other, but in the history of Christianity, and its subsequent developments of practices of the self in the Western world, the religious imagination has played a crucial role.

To say that men are gendered beings is tautological, yet I need to re-state it right at the beginning of this book since this simple insight gets so easily overlooked and forgotten. Men are not naturally destined to be norm-setting creatures but are people caught within their own rules of learned behaviors and acquired attitudes.[3] At stake is that unacknowledged male gender perspectives within religious discourse have all too often been claimed as normative. Once authorized as norm, religion has legitimated and enforced privileges of certain men in the name of universal truth. To counter such universalizing assumptions, I propose to read texts produced by men from a critical and consciously male-gendered perspective. Almost paradoxically, this is an exercise in simultaneously confirming a shared ground of "male" experience (however unstable and shifting it might be) while disentangling notions of normative masculinity from the variety of men's lives. In other words, a consciously male-gendered reading is a cri-tique of hegemonic masculinity and heteronormativity (and the concomi-tant social privileges bestowed upon men of certain classes) without giving up the category of "men" altogether.[4] It is at once an acknowledgment of difference (and we always need to ask, "difference from whom?") as well as an awareness that such differences may not exist in any essential or natural sense but are constituted by way of articulating oneself in contradistinction to (often fictionalized) others.

A critical and consciously male-gendered reading, then, assumes a *male difference* without claiming that men constitute a homogeneous whole. Put simply, but no less thorny in its implications: men are men, but not all men are equal; men become men by articulating their distinctiveness from women; men become "straight" by distinguishing themselves from "devi-ant" male behavior; men become heteronormative by mistaking *sameness* of discrete groups of men as *universal*; men become "real men" by reiterating the fictions they have helped to construe about the other.[5] Male confessional writings, as we shall see, do not only render men vulnerable but also reinforce and strengthen their identities. They function, so to speak, as articulations of male subjectivity, creating a "new" man in response to a crisis, to a realization of wrong-directedness, or to a transformative moment or conversion.

Confessional writings do not, however, constitute a mere continuous re-making of the male self.[6] They are more than a series of reiterative performances.[7] Confessional writings also open up the possibility of questioning what is perceived as normative masculinity, creating alternative spaces for men to reveal something about the variety of their intimate lives, of the complexity of motives, and of the embarrassments of clandestine deeds and thoughts.

Dominant ideals of manliness and masculinity can be undone by critical and self-reflective investigations, and the confessional genre, in which men demonstrate their willingness to remove their public masks in order to reveal a hitherto unknown intimate self, seems to be one cultural instance in which such "undoing" of gendered assumptions might be possible. Confessional writings, thus understood, can constitute a transformative "moral space" for men orienting themselves anew.[8] The religious imagination plays an important role in creating occasions for men exposing their intimate vulnerabilities, occasions on which men can name themselves into being beyond normative masculinity.

Male Confessions in the Context of Men's Studies in Religion

With this book, I wish to contribute also to the nascent field of men's studies in religion.[9] This field can be described as a subdiscipline within the larger body of transdisciplinary gender studies. Its organizational home has been primarily at the American Academy of Religion, particularly the "Gay Men's Issues in Religion" group (founded in 1988) and the "Men's Studies in Religion" group founded two years later. In 2004, "men's studies in religion" made its debut entry into the archive of encyclopedic knowledge:

> MEN'S STUDIES IN RELIGION is part of the unfolding concern within religion to address the effects of gender and sexuality upon religious faith and practice. As a new field of scholarly inquiry, it reflects upon and analyzes the complex connections between men and religion, building upon gender studies, feminist theory and criticism, the men's movement, and the increasing number of subdisciplines in the academic study of religion. Methodologically, men's studies in religion is an open field; its object of inquiry is "men" as gendered beings in relation to religion. . . . The task of men's studies in religion is to bring gender consciousness to the interpretation and analysis of men in relation to any aspect of religion. (Krondorfer and Culbertson 2004, 5861)

This description, by and large, still holds true, but I would now call this field of inquiry *critical* men's studies in religion. This subtle shift indicates that this project is not about a positivist and heteronormative reading of men's presence in religious traditions but, instead, a critical reading of the privileged performances of male gender within those traditions.[10]

"The writing of a religious man," Culbertson and I write in the entry for the *Encyclopedia of Religion*, "is not the same as the scholarly study of a male author's gendered text and context" (2004, 5862). When this insight is applied to confessional texts created by men, it should be apparent why a study of male confessions cannot remain gender neutral and why it refrains from excising from such texts ontological and universal insights. The confessional texts I examine are all written by men, but it takes a critical approach to point to—and, in some cases, to unearth—the genderedness of the writing subject and the genderedness of the narrative protagonist and the consumers of such texts.

Culbertson and I identify male confessional writings as one of the literary subgenres of religious discourse worthy of further exploration.

> The religious traditions have accumulated a wealth of spiritual journals and autobiographies, mystical journeys, and confessional testimonies written by men. They constitute a vast source for examining individual as well as collective presentations of the male self. Bringing a gender-conscious perspective to these texts yields critical insights into the male psyche and forms of male embodiment, intimacy, and sexualities.
>
> The literature reflecting on men's spiritual and autobiographical voices often blends scholarly analysis with a more personal and existential style. The borders between critical analysis and an envisioned spiritual renewal are intentionally porous. Areas of concern in the Jewish and Christian traditions are issues of embodiment, sexual theologies, and the deconstruction of traditional masculine roles. . . . Another aspect of men's studies in religion is to reflect critically on confessional modes of male discourses on religion. Still an underutilized approach, most of this work is located within the Christian tradition, largely due to the lasting influence of Augustine's (254–430 CE) *Confessions* and the thought of the French philosopher Michel Foucault (1926–1984) . . . [who] mapped out an influential theory about the Christian monastic roots of the modern concern over sexual practices, desires, and politics. . . . A Foucaultian framework helps analyze religious men's desire for intimate self-revelations; at the same time it can be used to investigate both subjugated and liberating knowledge of male sexualities as revealed in confessional, spiritual, and autobiographical writings. (Krondorfer and Culbertson 2004, 5863)

This book picks up the threads sketched in this entry. It examines select confessional writings as "individual presentations of the male self," which—

because of their meta-individual implications—also constitute a collective response to a need particularly felt by men. Battles with male identity, embodiment, relationality, and intimacy speak through these writings. They show that men are endowed with styles of expression that speak to their specific perceptions of the world, conveying differently gendered experiences of growing up, of social roles and affective expressivity, of bodily metaphors and incarnated knowledge. A confessional text offers a window into male interiority, into a man's way of perceiving himself within the constraints and possibilities of his environment.

Confessional writing, I suggest, is a gendered activity. First, writing itself—that is, the ability to articulate a self and the access to means of preserving the written word—is a privilege based on education, social status, and felt entitlement to a public hearing. For a long time, it was primarily available only to men. Second, disclosing one's intimate self in written form is attractive to men because it differs from actual face-to-face encounters with intimate others. In real encounters, the outcome is less predictable and more difficult to shape and control. Third, the act of confessional writing appeals to men because it is pervaded by a tinge of adventure. It is a titillating activity. It fills the writer with the invigorating sense of being suspended between risk and control. "Control," because the writer, in and through the process of creating a text, also creates a distancing from himself, others, and events in the past. He remains largely in command of the story he wants to tell about himself. "Risk," because writing for an audience exposes men to public ridicule and censure. Male confessants relinquish the protection offered either by the privacy of direct conversations or by the secrecy of the religious confessional and therapeutic spaces.

Male Confessions, then, neither is a religious and cultural history of confessions in Western Christianity nor does it seek to clarify the debate on how best to define confessional narratives as a literary genre. Rather, this study—informed by the relevant literature of multiple disciplines and attentive to the context of each work examined—relies on three interwoven approaches: an empathetic hearing, intertextuality, and critical-discursive analysis. It does so without claiming to present a comprehensive survey of confessional works relevant to such a study (colleagues can easily point to many more samples); it does not even claim to offer an exhaustive interpretation of the texts selected. Rather, the book follows up on some signals and traces that confessional texts have left for us as contemporary readers. It wants to draw attention to what some men in their confessional writings have said or have failed to say. It creates linkages between seemingly unrelated texts in order to suggest similarities across space and time. It aims at stimulating our interest in and curiosity about fresh questions about normative and resistant behavior among men. And it will indicate a few conceptual trajectories for a reading that aims at understanding men through their self-representations and show how both the religious imaginary and gendered rhetoric affect these representations.

Confessiography

Male Confessions is, as previously mentioned, an amorphous title open to interpretation. Hence, I need to briefly clarify the use of my terminology. I also propose to use the term "confessiography," a neologism that best describes texts in which men, in a mode of self-examination, have attempted to reveal themselves to themselves and to others.

In the long history of confessional practices and their associated broad semantic field, a number of seemingly incongruous pairs have been fused: confessions are voluntary or coerced, secretive or self-revelatory, sensationalist or guarded, therapeutic or inquisitorial, public or private, religious or sexual. "From the desert communities of primitive Christianity to Dante's total vision of humanity, from the pulpits, stakes, and confessionals of the Counter-Reformation to the alcoves and stages of court society, the confessional *dispositif*[11] will prove to be one of the essential networks that defines subjects and societies," writes Matthew Senior in his literary study of confessional discourse (1994, 7). Peter Brooks picks up where Senior left the chronological summary: "From the thirteenth century, when the Roman Church began to require annual confession from the faithful, it has become in Western culture a crucial mode of self-examination; from the time of the early Romantics to the present day, confession has become a dominant form of self-expression, one that bears special witness to personal truth" (2000, 9). Confessions, these brief sketches make clear, occupy an important place in Western culture. As a practice, they have profoundly impacted how we define the self in relation to law, truth, religion, sex, power, and the Other. "Western man has become a confessing animal":

> [T]he confession became one of the West's most highly valued techniques for producing truth. We have since become a singularly confessing society. The confession has spread its effects far and wide. It plays a part in justice,

medicine, education, family relationships, and love relations, in the most ordinary affairs of everyday life, and in the most solemn rites. . . . One confesses in public or in private, to one's parents, one's educators, one's doctor, to those one loves; one admits to oneself, in pleasure and in pain, things it would be impossible to tell anyone else, the things people write books about. One confesses—or is forced to confess. (Foucault 1990, 59)

It is not coincidental that we associate, at one and the same time, such diverse concepts as religious truth, personal authenticity, or sexual secrets when we hear the term "confession." Changes in the religious understanding of the self in early modernity, especially the Reformation and Renaissance, but also technological advances like the printing press, facilitated the transformation of the practices of penitential and auricular confession in Christianity into a secularized and interior mode of confessional writing and reading. The privacy of the printed word (written in private and read in private) enabled not only the search for an authentic male self (all the way up to psychoanalysis) but also the production and consumption of pornographic material. Jeremy Tambling puts those changes of the confessional mode into the larger context of literary and economic developments, in which, as he argues, the self began to constitute itself (as reader and writer) through the autonomy of texts. Religion had its share in these developments, but secular events contributed as well, such as the rise of the novel and the spread of erotic literature. "The private space—that which permits pornography to be read—and the economic ability to buy books and make of them a commodity, so that a man can project an image of himself through his library—these things come together [in the seventeenth century]. . . . The self produced *through reading* is confessional, acknowledging textual authority; that produced *by writing* confesses too, and the links between the 'rise of the novel' and Protestant confessional autobiography are documented" (Tambling 1990, 96, 98; emphasis added).

The broad historical and cultural spectrum of confessional texts and practices that spans from the religious confessional to inquisitorial legal practices, from the modern novel to psychoanalytic investigations or pornographic whispers, informs my project but does not take center stage. This spectrum supplies, so to speak, the background music for the study of texts that I propose to call "confessiography." In analogy to autobiography, *confessio/graphy* is the *graphein* (Greek, "writing") of the confessing self.

I ascribe to "confessiographies" a shared quality, which—notwithstanding the difficulty of drawing precise boundaries—makes them different from a number of other confessional instances. First, a confessiography is a written text; hence, it does not refer to the practice of oral confession (I shall say more about this difference later). Second, the term "confessiography" does not refer to the vast archives that document the emergence of the subject/ subjected self in Western history (say, in medicine, law, or psychoanalysis), and neither does it have in mind denominational *Bekenntnisschriften* (confessional/credal statements).[12] Third, confessiographies have a kinship to autobiographies, memoirs, diaries, novels, or poetry, but they are not the same.[13] An autobiography, for example, can limit itself to the recounting of fame and fortune without opening a window into male interiority; a memoir can be a very personal narrative without showing a male self in need of renewal; a diary, which can be revealing in utmost detail (like listing the daily food one consumes), may have never been intended for public consumption. What, then, makes a text a confessiography? It is the sincere attempt of a male confessant to investigate himself in an introspective and retrospective mode, often triggered by some rupture in his life and followed by a transformative experience. Confessiographic writings are characterized by a certain intensity and sincerity in the search for authenticity without shying away from exposing layers of intimacy to the public.

The confessional impulse can be found, of course, in a number of hybrid texts: an intimate diary, an autobiographical novel, a tell-all memoir, a confessional poem,[14] even religious scholarship shot through with autobiographical disclosures. If, as Foucault says, modern man has "become a confessing animal," we ought to expect to find modes of self-examination in many genres. "In an increasingly secularized culture," Brooks writes, "truth *of* the self and *to* the self have become markers of authenticity, and confession—written or spoken—has come to seem the necessary, though risky, act through which one lays bare one's most intimate self, to know oneself and to make oneself known" (2000, 9; emphasis in original). Insofar as hybrid texts carry markers of confessiographic quality as described earlier, they can also be considered material to be included in a study of male confessions. The boundaries are fuzzy. Perhaps we would best conceptualize confessiographies—and I will use this term interchangeably with "male confessional writings," "confessional texts written by men," and so on—less as a *genre* and more as a *quality*.[15] We encounter such quality in written documents in which men have made an effort at revealing intimate, tender, shameful, or hidden aspects of themselves.

A close reading of select confessiographies constitutes the core of this book. Because Augustine's shadow looms so large in the history of confessional texts—for many a model, a mirror, an echo—his own *Confessions* will be a steady companion throughout these pages. Two other key documents in this study are the lesser-known deathbed confession of Calel Perechodnik (1996), a Jewish ghetto policeman who perished during the Holocaust, and the equally unknown confessional conversion story of Oswald Pohl (1950), a high-ranking Nazi perpetrator who reconverted to Christianity while in Allied internment after the war. Because complicity and culpability are among the questions guiding my gendered reading, I have chosen texts written by a Jew and a German, respectively—a choice informed also by my long-standing interest in Holocaust studies.[16] By introducing material that can be identified explicitly as perpetrator and victim testimony, I aim, on the one hand, at heightening our awareness of the issues of complicity and resistance and, on the other, at blurring the lines of rigid moral demarcations.

The blurring of lines—between revealing and hiding, between self-examining and exculpating, between sexual exposure and moral witness, and between the scholarly and the intimate voice—extends to a group of texts examined in the book's last chapter. There, I will look at writings by contemporary American gay theologians who, in their scholarly research, open themselves up to the eroticization of the spiritual male body.

All of these works (Augustine, Perechodnik, Pohl, gay theologians) are contrasted, supplemented, and augmented by cross-references to a diversity of other documents. Some of them are "iconic" among confessions of modern men, such as those of Jean-Jacques Rousseau and Michel Leiris, whereas others are introduced as tiny sparks from the history of Christianity and, to a lesser extent, Judaism, such as hagiographic accounts of the desert fathers, a confession of a Hasidic Jew, or confessional fragments of contemporary male theologians. What they all share in common—despite their many differences—is that they tell us how our lives, men's lives, are filled with contradictions, vagaries, indecisions, limitations, blind spots, turmoil, and unresolved business; and how male confessiographies, in their partial and partisan ways, bear witness to a boisterous, tarnished, and fragmented vitality.

The Sigillum and the Public Witness

Written confessions are monological; oral confessions, dialogical. Or so it seems. Confessions in general involve "a narrator disclosing a secret knowledge to another, as a speaker to a listener, writer to reader, confessor to confessor" (Foster 1987, 2). In a confessiography, this relationship is between writer and reader, a relationship mediated by a text. The writer, it would appear, is clearly the *confessant*, the one who makes a confession. But does this make the reader the *confessor*, the one who hears a confession? Or does the text itself take on the function of the confessor? Or is the confessor the imagined Other in the text, like God in Augustine's *Confessions*? Augustine's seemingly monological self-examination is, after all, also a dialogue with an imagined divine partner.

The confusion regarding the *confessor* in confessiographies is echoed in the semantic ambiguity of the word itself. In the English language, a confessor can refer both to a person who *makes* a confession and one who *hears* a confession. A confessor can be the sinner but also the priest. A confessor is also someone who can publicly acknowledge two different things, either faith or crimes/sins. Furthermore, a confessor can refer to a person who remains steadfast in his or her faith in times of adversity, witnessing it under the threat of torture. Hence, a confessor is also related to saints and martyrs (see Castelli 2004, esp. chap. 2). Such ambiguity says something about the complicated nature of confessions. The fact that a confessor can occupy two seemingly opposing roles may point to a spiritual kinship between the one who makes and the one who hears a confession. Confessor and confessant may occasionally be interchangeable.

For clarity's sake, however, I will consistently employ the term "confessor" when referring to a person *hearing* a confession and "confessant" when referring to someone *making* a confession. In this book, we will mostly contend with confessants, that is, with men avowing publicly their faith, sins, faults, or desires. However, confessors will not entirely absent themselves from this study and appear occasionally as a confessant's collaborator and hagiographer.

I will return to the question of whether confessiographies are essentially monological or dialogical in a moment. First, however, it is important to acknowledge the difference between *confessionals* and *confessiographies*, that is, the apprehensive relation between oral and written confessions. To understand the difference between them is significant for how we conceive of the intimate secrets shared in the confessional mode.

Auricular confessions have a long history in Christianity, from canonical penance in late antiquity to the medieval penitentials, from the obligatory yearly confessions demanded by the Fourth Lateran Council (1215) to the launching of the confessionals at the Council of Trent during the Counter-Reformation in the 1550s.[17] It has often been noted that the confessional mode of religious practices has morphed into its secular counterpart, namely, psychoanalysis. "Psychoanalysis, one of the most conspicuous inventions of the twentieth century, offers a secular version of religious confession: it insists on the work of patient and analyst—comparable to confessant and confessor—toward the discovery of the most hidden truths about selfhood" (Brooks 2000, 9). We may hesitate, though, to claim unswervingly that the religious and the psychoanalytic confessional modes are twins or siblings and that they pursue basically the same goal, only under different historical circumstances. Perhaps they are related in the manner of distant cousins. But whatever kinship metaphor we are tempted to use, one would have to blind oneself if one were to deny a family resemblance between them.

An important element of auricular confession is the transferential dynamic involved in confessing sins in exchange for receiving (religious) absolution or (psychological) relief. Such transferences rest on the trust that revealed secrets remain protected from the public. The person to whom one confesses must keep the revealed secret a "secret." He or she is obliged to the *sigillum*, the seal of secrecy without which oral confessions would be unable to operate. Within the culture of the religious confessional, it is the priest— and within a therapeutic confessional culture, the analyst/therapist—who hides from the public what is revealed within the protected space of dialogical secrecy. The person to whom one confesses is not really "human" but represents a transpersonal entity.[18] "The confessant addresses his or her *pater peccavi* not just to the priest but most essentially to a transferential father in heaven," writes Senior, while "the analyst allows himself to be a surrogate for the real father so that the analysand can reenact forgotten traumatic events and gain mastery over them" (1994, 10). Priests and therapists are not truly human listeners. Rather, they are signs or representations of a greater power, which, in the religious imagination, is God, and in the psychoanalytic situation, the Unconscious. The priest imbued with divine power is an intermediary for the sinful self; the analyst/therapist with his quasi-magical power is a neutral guide for the traumatized self's recovery.

Notwithstanding the potentially coercive nature of inquisitorial moralism of the religious confessor and, equally, notwithstanding the potentially misleading nature of the therapist's inquisitive speculation, oral confession promises to restore the individual.[19] Its restorative power lies in the listener's pledge to guard the content of the confession from a potentially hostile, noncompassionate public. Because this transpersonal listener is not the confessing self's intimate other (friend, wife, lover, parent) but operates as an impersonal channel, he or she is freed from the obligations normally required by law or social regulations. Even under threat of death, the priest/ therapist is not supposed to reveal what he has learned from the confessant/ patient.[20] This kind of extraordinary power bestowed upon the listener by social agreement allows the individual sinner or patient to reveal, unravel, and then reconstitute the self. Oral confessions imply "a listener, however impersonal—an interlocutor to whom the confessional discourse is proffered" (Brooks 2000, 95). Religious or therapeutic interlocutors allow the burdened individual to say *I* (or discover the *I*) even in the most uncomfortable places of one's hidden acts and thoughts. Confessions are "a situation in which the speaking *I* necessarily implies a listening *you* who can in turn become the *I* while the speaker becomes *you*. . . . Saying *I* implies and calls to a responsive *you*, and in this dialogic, transferential relation consolation and self-definition can be found" (Brooks 2000, 95; emphasis in original).

Such a dialogical relation constitutes the core of auricular confession. It "invites attention to the ear" (Tambling 1990, 73). Here, the safety and protection guaranteed by a listening other, who is personally, legally, and emotionally unattached to the confessing individual, are essential for the private self to reveal itself to itself—via the detour of an imaginary that is more potent than the *I* of the confessant/patient, and also more potent than the *You* of confessor/therapist. The operative referent is God or the Unconscious.

Confessiographies, however, function differently. Here, the secrets poured out on paper do not seek the sheltered privacy of the *transpersonal other* (as in the confessional) but address themselves to the *public other* of the imagined reader. "Confession is a relationship within a self and between the self and God, but in its ideal form . . . it is also public declaration" (Coles 1992, 50). The act of writing replaces the oral/verbal transaction. In confessiographies, the same pages bear traces of the virtuous avowal of faith, the admission of crimes, and the expectation for absolution—addressed publicly to no one in particular and, in the same instant, to everyone. The question, then, of whether confessiographies are monological or dialogical cannot be answered easily. Their monological character rests in the solitary act of writing (which bears the danger of solipsism); but as a public act, they always address somebody and thus remain dialogical in their rhetorical structure.

A number of replacements are performed in confessiographies: the impersonal listener of the confessional is replaced by an ideal reader as public witness; the *sigillum* is relinquished; an imagined dialogical *I* and *You* materialize in a text that is not transient but fixed and preserved; the hidden self is revealed not in face-to-face conversation but through the detour of the imaginary of the power of the written word. Instead of being sheltered by the *sigillum*, confessiographies rely for protection on rhetorical and strategic textual operations. The text, thus, has an oppositional, if not contradictory, task: to make available private intimacies for public consumption while, at the same time, to shield the confessing self from being consumed, harmed, or socially obliterated. It is thus questionable whether a written confession—hampered by the epistemological and affective difficulty of revealing while simultaneously protecting—can ever reach the same degree of self-effacing truthfulness as in the ideal situation of auricular confession.

However we are inclined to answer this last question, we will discover in the following chapters that, on the one hand, men are willing to give testimony to themselves in the name of truthfulness and authenticity but that, on the other hand, they have created texts that bear witness to how difficult it is to remain truthful and authentic. Confessional texts can hide as much as they can reveal. Total self-disclosure is impossible, not least because—short of self-erasure—the confessing self must also shield itself from hostile reaction.

How do men protect themselves in confessiographies? In lieu of the assured safety of oral confessions, the material preservation of a crafted text must mediate the danger that accompanies intimate self-disclosure. Such textual mediation is far more fragile than the assurances one receives through the *sigillum* of auricular confession. Why, then, do some men risk ridicule and social ostracism by taking up a pen and fixing words on paper as public testimony rather than opting for the safer route of a transpersonal listener? Why do they choose durable matter on which to confess (paper/ink/manuscripts) over the spiritual transience of the therapeutic or religious confessional that leaves no documentary trace?

I am not asking these questions in order to prepare a psychological profile of a certain male personality prone to confessional writing. I will neither engage in an archeology of the male psyche in order to unearth a repressed male secret nor track down genealogically the origins of modern man's wish to reveal himself. Rather, I will look at the possibilities that the confessional mode offers to men and also examine the recalcitrance of the material: that is, the difficulty of men testifying to themselves truthfully.

"I have become a problem to myself," writes Augustine, "and that is my sickness" (*Confessions*, 10.33.50).[21] Like other male confessants, Augustine does not keep his problem to himself but publicly acknowledges his own failings. We need to remind ourselves that Augustine is not obliged to reveal his inner battles, which he diagnoses as sickness. That he is a "problem to himself" Augustine could have hidden from others—and even from himself. Or he could have shared it with an entrusted other under the *sigillum* of secrecy. Instead, in a monological fashion, he engages in a conversation with himself in full public view—a self-scrutinizing, in which he seems to assume both the role of patient and healer. He diagnoses his own sickness with the aim of restoring his (spiritual) health. But whether—in his twin role of patient/doctor—he has enough distance to diagnose himself truthfully is a question worth asking.

To accuse Augustine of mere solipsistic circling, however, misses an important point that the church father is trying to make. It is, after all, religion—his religious imaginary—that allows him to report on himself in intimate detail. What does Augustine say? Let us take another look at the sentence quoted earlier, which I did not cite fully. It actually reads: "*In your eyes* I have become a problem to myself, and that is my sickness" (emphasis added). The imagined dialogical You in Augustine's *Confessions* is always God. Augustine, so to speak, imagines seeing himself through the eyes of God, and with this perspective, he begins to gain knowledge of himself. God is essential in order for Augustine to gaze at himself truthfully. Augustine approaches himself both from above and from deeply within, turning introspection into the universal.[22] In Augustine's own perception, he makes his confession primarily to God—God is his partner in this intimate conversation—and only secondarily to the public.

For us as contemporary readers, such an explanation may not be satisfactory. Many of us no longer share Augustine's religious universe and his theistic certainty. Yet we as readers are invited to enter Augustine's world, to partake of the interiority to which he grants us access. The moment a male reader enters into such a text, he enters into a dialogical situation, becoming simultaneously a *co-confessant* (who identifies with the narrator and seeks with him absolution) and a *confessor*, who in empathy with the writer grants him absolution, or in judgment denies it to him. Today, as social creatures living in a secularized "singularly confessing society" (Foucault), we may be less friendly toward Augustine's work than he had wished for from an ideal reader. We may not be able to desist from thinking that Augustine, despite his claims to the contrary, really panted after public recognition—just as many modern men do. God, in such a modernist view, is employed only as a figure of speech; God is but a rhetorical move on Augustine's part in order to hide a different motivation: namely, to achieve "fifteen minutes of fame," as artist Andy Warhol provocatively and incisively described the attention span granted to the modern subject. "[I]n an age when for many, God is dead," Coles writes, "Augustine's confessing self now appears in a different light. The effects of confession as a mode of being must open themselves to questions that were concealed as long as being itself was unquestionably thought to be designed by God and Christianity was considered the only true story of the world" (1992, 172).

Augustine's world no longer exists. It is no longer retrievable, and we read his *Confessions* differently than he may have intended them. Consequently, as contemporary male readers, we need to recognize, and perhaps lament, the loss of a religious certainty that enabled men like Augustine to place their flawed and intimate embodied selves within a larger universe. At the same time, we are encouraged to embrace our modern and postmodern difference that allows us to approach these texts with new questions.

Postmodern Sensibilities

To signal our postmodern difference as contemporary readers, I want to call attention to four clusters of questions that guide my empathetic listening to, and critical investigation of, male confessiographies.

SEDUCTION, COMPLICITY, AND GENDER

In the language of current gender analysis, we can describe male confessional writings as a privileged and gendered performance. "Privileged" because they are produced by men who not only possess the technical skills to do so (for example, it assumes literacy and education) but who also presume that their self-revelations muster sufficient public interest. "Performative" because these men do not write a private diary but perform a public act. They feel entitled to a public hearing, and they speak with a voice that is sufficiently intact. "[T]he fact that I present myself and take your time implies that I think it might be interesting," Derrida reflects on his own confessional discourse (2005, 24). At the beginning of a confessional performance[23]—at the very moment when the text, hardly set in motion yet, is already imagined being read by others upon its completion—these men already know of their own subjectivity, which provides them with a grammar to talk about themselves.

Women in history have not enjoyed the same opportunities for such privileged (writing) performances. Robbed of access to education, to a public voice, and to subjectivity, some women scholars have argued that they cannot even take part in the kind of confessional memory work performed by men. Shoshana Felman, for example, theorizes "that *none of us, as women, has yet, precisely, an autobiography.* Trained to see ourselves as objects and to be positioned as the Other, estranged to ourselves, we have a story that by definition cannot be self-present to us" (1993, 14; emphasis in original). Without subjectivity, no story of the self can be told. Without a sense of self, there is no *I* that can confess to the past not owned. Felman continues, "Insofar as any feminine existence is in fact a traumatized existence, feminine autobiography *cannot be* a confession" (16; emphasis in original).[24] Because trauma radically alters and disrupts a person's sense of self, women cannot engage in the confessional mode. Trauma is an antidote to confession. A woman's trauma "can only be a testimony: to survival" (16).

If Felman's gender claims were correct, then the existence of male confessional texts would lead us to conclude that men, who are capable of producing written confessions, have not been seriously traumatized in the same way. If trauma is antithetical to narrating the self, the gravity of experiences that urged confessing men to reveal hidden aspects of themselves in writing—the wounding they received, the shame they felt, the wrongdoings they committed—could not have plumbed the depth of self-shattering harm that marks traumatized people.

Have men who preserve their confessions in writing never been traumatized? We may hesitate to embrace too quickly the exclusivity of such a claim. After all, one could make the case that there is a temporal chain of events. It is conceivable that a man is capable of composing a confession only *after* he has freed himself from the source of his trauma. In this instance, it is not that he has never been traumatized but that he is *no longer* traumatized. His written confession would testify to a trauma successfully resolved.

Felman's insight, however, is important to remember. It prevents the male reader from becoming seduced too easily by male-authored confessions. We need to keep in mind, for example, that what a text presents as a grave wounding of the male self might, in some instances, be better understood as a veiled self-pitying rather than the result of trauma. Or what might seem, at first glance, a courageous act of self-revelation may turn out on closer inspection to be a rhetorical move of self-aggrandizement. Or confessing men may claim to be rebellious risk takers but play it safe after all. They may claim to abdicate narrative control but, less visibly, stay in command of interpretive patterns. They may convince us of their sincere regrets regarding a sinful past and sway us into granting them absolution, but we may continue to suspect that they are urged on by a need for self-exculpation. Or male confessants wish to come across as chastened and humbled creatures but cannot escape the clutches of vanity.

There is always the risk that we, as readers, will be seduced by the pleasure that a text provides when it professes to reveal an authentic self.[25] The intimate nature of confessiographies makes it possible for the reader to identify with the personal battles of the confessant. The occasions when men take off their masks in public are rare enough that, precisely for this reason, they are so seductive. As an intimate and wounded male self is laid bare, the male-identified reader is tempted to take the male writer's words at face value. Hence, lending an empathetic ear to a confessional text can lure the listener into complicity with the author's presentation of himself, thereby denying that the confessional text itself may constitute yet another form of masculine masquerade (see Benthien and Stephan 2003). We need to remind ourselves that confessional writings are carefully crafted products. The implication of Felman's cautionary insight is to remain vigilant about the seductive rhetoric of a confessional text. A critical distance—a hermeneutics of suspicion—is what we, as male readers, have to bring to male confessiographies.

In a "confessional relation," writes Foster in *Confession and Complicity in Narrative*, the reader "consents to listen, and thereby he enters the evasive discourse of the narrator, tracing a path that inevitably misses the encounter with truth" (1987, 4). The confessing author plays with the reader's desire to know about the life of the former, and the reader likes to be pleasured by the reading experience. It is this desire to know, Foster argues, "that the writer can use to gain complicity of the reader," and thus the reader becomes "complicit with the motivations of the writer" (12–13). Seduced to give credence to the personal integrity of an autobiographical work, we may become oblivious to the possibility of being subtly manipulated.[26] We may forget to ask about what and who are missing in a text. We may neglect to ask whether male and female readers are differently seduced by a male confession. Or we may forget to ask with what perspective a reader, independent of his or her biological sex, identifies. "[Women] have unwittingly been trained to 'read literature as men,'" laments Felman, "[and] to identify, that is, with the dominating, male-centered perspective of the masculine protagonist, which always takes itself—misleadingly—to be a measure of the universal" (1993, 5). Similarly, Margaret Miles in *Desire and Delight* writes, "I always read [Augustine's] *Confessions* as a man":

> I have been seduced, enchanted, ravished by this text. Augustine's autobiography remains for me crucial . . . [and] it is no exaggeration to acknowledge that reading Augustine has altered the course of my life and that I continue to be profoundly grateful for his authorship. Yet I am a woman, and I notice in the *Confessions* who speaks and who listens; I detect the myriad ways that the male author's experience informs and gives body to his text. (1992, 136–137)

In order to resist the seductive pull of a male-identified perspective, Miles proposes to apply a gendered reading. "What would it mean," she asks herself, "to give a gendered reading of Augustine's *Confessions*? What if I were to refuse the author's positioning of the reader as a male confidant, privy to his subjectivity because temporarily granted—if necessary—an honorary universal (male) subjectivity?" (1992, 80). It would radically alter our ways of understanding these texts, recognizing the limited particularity of male subjectivity present in such confessions as well as acknowledging the absence of female subjectivity. "A gendered reading, however, reveals the absence of a female subject position in the text; it also makes visible Augustine's extensive use of male sexuality as a primary and pervasive model for human life" (81).

And how about men? To read male confessions as a male reader from a supposedly gender-neutral perspective is nothing new. It would merely reinforce the expectation of the male authors themselves and reiterate apparently objective (but really masculinist) patterns of interpretation. In all likelihood, without a critical gender analysis, men would continue to mistake the presented male perspective as universal. Would they realize that, in most cases, the presence of male subjectivity corresponds to the absence of the female subject? Would they reflect on their own gendered position as one that sanctions male identifications and, in the same instant, acts as if these identifications do not exist? An uncritical reading ensnares men into a double complicity: first, they are seduced to identify with the male protagonist of the narrative (here, the text functions like a mirror); and, second, the mirrorlike quality of the autobiographical narration seduces them to deny the genderedness of both the male protagonist and themselves. Complicity, in this instance, turns into sameness, and sameness becomes confused with the universal. A critical and consciously male-gendered analysis, in contrast, tries to resist this doubly seductive trap laid out for men indulging in the pleasure of reading confessional texts. What might it mean for a man to say, "I always read the *Confessions* as a *man*?"

MALE SUBJECTIVITY, AGENCY, AND RELATIONALITY

Confessional texts require a subject. Witnessing or testifying to oneself is an activity that assumes a subject that is legally recognized and that knows of its ability to act morally and politically. If one does not perceive oneself as a subject, or is not perceived as such by one's social environment, one cannot write a confession. A confessing male writer knows of his own subjectivity, even when, at the time before or during the writing, he perceives himself in crisis. The act of writing in the confessional mode, then, reclaims a subjectivity-in-crisis; it rescues and reconstitutes a subject that perceives itself at the brink of loss and despair. At the completion of a confession, the old self has metaphorically died and a new moral self has emerged. "Men, it seems, write their autobiographies from memory. The act of remembering, however, is also testimony to the death of a 'self.' . . . 'I' am dead; and 'I' survive" (Burrus 2004, 87). Confessiographies are a type of memory work that stabilizes the writing subject in the present.[27] In the unfolding act of the retrospective narration the male self is reinvented, restored, and strengthened. Deconstruction through self-interrogation is also an act of reasserting subjectivity.

The fact that male subjectivity is ever present in male confessiographies is not, in itself, objectionable. To know oneself as a subject is living auspiciously. This right should not be taken away. If anything, it should be spread more generously and democratically across people from all genders, classes, and ethnic backgrounds. Subjectivity becomes problematic only if it is divorced from moral agency. By "moral agency" I refer to the ability to be morally responsible and accountable for one's past and present deeds. Knowing oneself as a subject comes with the responsibility of acknowledging that one is fallible and, potentially, culpable. Insofar as our cultural history recognizes men as being the agents of their own actions, such agency enables them to examine their motives and motivations as well as the consequences of their deeds. Not all men, however, desire to do so.

For some men, professional activity and external productivity are virtues by which they define themselves, and any critical self-reflection would only be frowned upon. Other men are happily quotidian in their life's expectations without desiring spiritual depth. Again, others attain reasonable content-ment through emotional detachment, insularity, and guarded privacy. Given these and other motives and motivations that desist and resist introspective reflections, we ought to cherish the few men who willingly let us peek into their hearts and who wonder aloud why, in the past, they fell short morally, spiritually, or sexually.

Subjectivity and moral agency, hence, are not the same thing. While the confessant as a male subject can be fully present in a text, his moral agency can disappear behind rhetorical maneuvers. One would expect that in texts in which men try to take an honest accounting of themselves a fine sensi-bility toward their own moral acts is deployed—and, certainly, this is the case compared to the neglect of moral reflection in one's day-to-day life. Yet in critical moments even confessional texts use strategies to shift atten-tion away from culpability and complicity of the male self. These evasive shifts are not limited to a specific male confessant—as may be assumed by my choice of juxtaposing, for example, the conversion story of a Nazi perpetrator with the confessional diary of a Jewish ghetto policeman. To be complicit—whether by failing one's moral agency as confessant or by being willfully seduced as reader—is not the provenance of one species of male confessants. As we shall see, such evasions often occur in situations when the confessant's relationship to intimate others is at stake (often to his female companion) and when the particularity of the male body fades away. Rarely is the body of heterosexual male confessants critically investigated as a gendered body.

INTROSPECTION, RETROSPECTION, AND EMBODIMENT

Self-examination in the confessional mode—as long as it is not coerced (as in police interrogations or torture)[28]—is an introspective journey. "Who-ever does not want to fear, let him probe his innermost self," Augustine states in a sermon.

> Do not just touch the surface; go down into yourself; reach into the farthest corner of your heart. Examine it then with care: see there, whether a poi-soned vein of wasting love of the world still does not pulse, whether you are

not moved by some physical desires, and are not caught in some law of the senses; whether you are never elated with empty boasting, never depressed by some vain anxiety: then only can you dare to announce that you are pure and crystal clear, when you have sifted everything in the deepest recesses of your inner being. (Sermon 348.2, quoted in Brown 1969, 432)

For Augustine, self-examination is an inward journey, a bringing to light of the "deepest recesses" of one's being. On the body's surface, there is not much to find, except, perhaps, vanity and other forms of masculine masquerade. But peel away layers of skin, and pulsating and poisoned veins will emerge; still deeper, desires and anxieties keep a hidden life. It is only through the encounter with one's unlikable self that man emerges from that bottom, cleansed and transformed.

The introspective gaze is one of apprehension. Who wants to hurry down a path where you will encounter your unlikable self? Who among men is really that interested in facing his own contradictions and imperfections? Who among men wants to be shamed by discerning a gap between one's ideal and actual self? Who wants to scratch open the scabs of old wounds or to awaken dormant desires? "Whoever does not fear!" is Augustine's answer. Note that Augustine does not claim that a man has to be free of fear—he himself is quite anxious at times, as we shall see—but that a man has to be willing to work with, and get through, his fears.

A good millennium and a half later, Sigmund Freud made an astoundingly similar admission. He, too, went on an introspective journey, even though it was into the world of his dreams, not the heart, as in Augustine's words ("It was in my innermost heart," Augustine says, "where I had grown angry with myself").[29] Freud writes:

I will not pretend that I have completely uncovered the meaning of the dream or that its interpretation is without a gap. I could spend much more time over it, derive further information from it and discuss fresh problems raised by it. I myself know the points from which further train of thought could be derived. But considerations which arise in the case of every dream of my own restrain me from pursuing my interpretive work. (Freud 1958, 120–121)

Whereas Augustine eventually realizes that the deepest recesses of his inner being ultimately remain inaccessible to him and are known only to God, Freud similarly admits that he had reached the furthest extent to which he could explore his own interiority. Like Augustine, Freud does not claim defeat at this realization but emerges a little more humbled, yet proud of the courage of having proceeded as far as he did. "If anyone should feel tempted to express a hasty condemnation of my reticence," Freud admonishes his readers, "I would advise him to make the experiment of being franker than I am" (1958, 121).

Given such family resemblance between the saint and the analyst, it seems a little rushed in judgment, if not a little haughty, of Freud to claim that "in [religious] Confession the sinner tells what he knows; in analysis the neurotic has to tell more" (Freud 1959, 189).[30] Both Freud and Augustine, it seems, have probed the extent to which modes of self-examination could take them. We, too, would do well not to adopt too quickly a male posturing that belittles what these men have achieved or to accuse them of not going far enough. It is tempting to confuse the relative ease with which we can consume their confessions as readers with the hardships that went into creating them—the "tears and blood of uncontainable memory [that] ink the page" (Burrus 2004, 88).

The perceived threat of the *introspective gaze* is, however, eased and mediated through the *retrospective gaze* characteristic of the confessional form.[31] In distinction, for example, to a mere autobiographical reporting of one's accomplishment, a male confessiography sketches a movement from the past to the present, a movement that speaks of a transformation of an old to a new self. Often this transformation is urged on by the religious imaginary, whether through a particular eschatological expectation, a conversion experience, or an imitation of a religious model or pattern. When writing a confession, the new self is already in place, and from a position of a newfound stability, it is relatively safe to describe retrospectively the deviant or heretic paths one once walked. If introspection contains some danger, retrospection assures safety.

When male confessants claim that they have left their sinful selves behind, they still inhabit their bodies in the present. Their bodies remind them of the past, of the desires they once felt and of the wrongdoings they once committed. Their embodiedness, however, forces them to live in the here and now. They still need to eat, drink, sleep, seek shelter, negotiate pleasure, manage human relations, and fend off allegations. In some cases, confessants find freedom from sexuality, yet they still deal with the body's unruly desires. In other cases, they embrace sexual liberation but still encounter stubborn residues of repression. Some male confessants remain under physical threat (their bodies targeted for annihilation), whereas others adopt a nihilistic attitude, proclaiming the meaningless banality of the flesh. What male confessants have to say about their bodies past and present will be a recurring theme in these pages.

AUTOBIOGRAPHICAL INSERTIONS

The last of the four clusters of questions that signal our contemporary post-modern sensibility concerns autobiographical insertions. Examining other men's attempts at revealing themselves intimately, I will occasionally inter-rupt the flow of my scholarly prose with my own autobiographical voice. I owe it to these men—as well as to the contemporary reader—not to stay a "closed book" myself but to make transparent some of my personal doubts, battles, motivations, and experiences. A gendered reading, as proposed in this book, downright begs for abandoning a position that proclaims objec-tivity, neutrality, and control. As a critic, I have my own confessional needs and desires (see Veeser 1996), and as a male critic of other men's confessions, I cannot abstain from disclosing my own gendered practices and experi-ences. They belong to this book, enriching and complicating it. Through the fragmentary evidence of my own trepidations shine the contours of the confessiographic mode.

I am not the first religious studies scholar inspired to insert a personal voice into his or her criticism.[32] In patristic studies, for example, Virginia Burrus has interrupted her interpretations of people like Augustine, Greg-ory, and Jerome with her own autobiographical fragments. In *The Sex Lives of Saints* (2004) she explores the presence/absence of female biography in early Christian treatises and hagiographies: "Oddly enough, I was reading the following gossipy passage in one of Jerome's letters while sitting veiled under a hair drier at a beauty salon, eyes lowered demurely to the little red book on my lap: 'In those days lady's maids used to arrange her hair, and her poor head, which had done no harm, was imprisoned in a head-dress crammed with curls. Now it is left alone and knows that it is sufficiently cared for when it is covered by a veil'" (2004, 88). Synchronically, Burrus's reading of Jerome's letter coincides with her own cosmetic practices of "fem-ininity" across several hundred years, and it makes her think of her own subjectivity and the loss of the female voice in ancient manuscripts. What Jerome tries to veil (here, woman's hair), Burrus unveils for the reader. This kind of confessional intervention of scholarly criticism is, when applied to my project, like a lifting of the veil from the impersonal face of the male critic—as if to say, "Look, he has a body, too, and also a lived experience that informs his way of reading!"

To insert one's own voice comes with a number of difficulties and potential traps. The confessional voice may make public what is appropriately private, assign too much significance to what is trivial, betray the trust of others in the name of authentic self-disclosure, seduce the reader into confidentialities when analysis fails, or remain caught in vanity under the guise of unswerving self-scrutiny. "The only way out of the infinite regress that threatens attempts to write about masculinity is to make the gesture of reflexivity itself the subject of preliminary enquiry," Middleton writes in *The Inward Gaze*, and "much of the impetus towards a better understanding of masculinity by men has come from . . . confessional material" (1992, 12, 21).[33] Indeed, the dilemmas encumbering one's own autobiographical voice are no different from the analysis of other men's confessional texts.

In "True Confessions and Weird Obsessions," Stephen Moore calls such insertions "personal criticism" and defines it as an "autobiographical performance within the act of criticism" (1995, 21).[34] My own confessional interventions are also a performance, with the task of demonstrating that it is feasible for male scholars to disclose a little more of themselves—despite the fact that these performances are always insufficient, always lacking. As a performance, my autobiographical voice does not seek to simply illustrate a particular point of my analysis through the use of a personal anecdote. Rather, these insertions constitute counterpoints, or points of resistance, to the confessional texts I examine. Functioning like a mirror vis-à-vis my critical analysis, they interrupt the academic prose in creatively suspenseful and dialectical ways. They reveal how I—like other confessing men—search for words as I search for meaning.

My autobiographical voice will be visually distinguished through the use of *italics*. This is not a new technique; others have used it before.[35] Moore, for example, when analyzing male biblical scholarship, prints his scholarly voice in regular font. "Personal criticism is a form of self-disclosure, but needless to say the degree of self-disclosure, of self-exposure, varies wildly." In his confessional italicized voice, he says: "*Personally, I want [the critics] to perform, and to perform well. . . . [I]ncreasingly I want to be entertained even as I am being informed. I want to be moved, amused, aroused, absorbed*" (21). Like Moore, I, too, aim at offering a criticism that enchants, inspires, and irritates, and the interplay of academic and confessional prose hopes to achieve it. When I speak confessionally, however, I want to avoid falling into the trap of self-pity, self-absorption, and banality. Whether my fragmentary revelations will reach these self-set targets and whether they meet the tastes of my readers, I do not know. To the potential heckler, however, who is feared by all male confessants, I say with Freud: "I would advise him to make the experiment of being franker than I am."

Conclusion

Having thus delineated the circumference of this study, to examine confessions through a consciously male-gendered lens against a rich cultural and literary background imbued with religious significations remains a taxing challenge. Would such a study do justice to the literary analysis of the confessional genre? Would it satisfy the demands of the historian of religion, who understands the practice of confession and its textual documentation primarily within specific historic settings? Would it inspire any Foucauldian reader or entice a cultural studies person who, with a penchant for popular media, might miss a chapter on the confessional turn in television talk shows and on the Internet? Would it irritate the social ethicist whose heart is with those who suffer from coerced confessions, such as victims of political torture? Might it disappoint those who are engaged in feminist and queer debates about theology and religiosity? Would spiritually inclined gay men find enough food for thought in these pages? Would my criticism dishearten those heterosexual men who have put personal and scholarly efforts into reforming their ways of thinking about themselves and religion?

I ask these questions because *Male Confessions* wishes to address itself to people of such diverse perspectives, yet I fear the judgment of the experts in any of these disciplines. My expectations and anxieties, then, are not so different from those of the confessing men who are the object of my study. They, too, have expressed fears of being misunderstood, of indulging in (unmanly) trivialities, and of exasperating the reader with their autobiographical revelations. To counter their fears, these men have variously appealed to the goodwill and patience of their anticipated audience. Like them, I also imagine my ideal reader: he or she would approach my work with an empathetic ear and, along the way, pick up a few morsels of intellectual sustenance and inspiration.

The fact that some men have chosen the confessional mode to take account of themselves should not prejudice us either way. Neither should we assume *with* these men that they write from a genderless, universal perspective—we need not be seduced to such complicity by their autobio-graphical disclosures—nor should we hold their gender *against* them and assume that, only because they are men, they try to trick or coerce us into a perspective alien to ours. In this sense, this book is less about *proving* a particular point (say, about the nature of man; about the genre of confes-sion; or about the power of religion) and more about *probing* different lay-ers of meaning that we can discover when lending those texts an attentive ear. Written confessions, after all, want to be read and heard. So let us try to listen to them.

INTERLUDE *On Mirrors*

Spiegel: noch nie hat man wissend beschrieben,
was ihr in euerem Wesen seid.
Ihr, wie mit lauter Löchern von Sieben
erfüllten Zwischenräumen der Zeit.

Mirrors: never yet has anyone described in knowing ways
what you are substantially like.
You, as if filled with nothing but sieve holes
Interstices of time.

RAINER MARIA RILKE[1]

Confessional writing is a turning to oneself, a turning to one's own past, an autobiographical compulsion to face oneself, a face-to-face encounter with one's life as if it were a mirror. Mirrors, material or metaphoric, may be the beginning of a search for oneself, an incentive for putting on paper what otherwise might remain hidden to oneself. Confessional narratives, in turn, can serve as mirrors for others to see themselves reflected in them. Mirrors and confessions are related to each other, but their relationship is apprehensive, if not antithetical.

In Rilke's poetic imagination the mirror itself, the inanimate object, is described as possessing an enigmatic essence. The mirror's mystery is independent of the person who engages in the act of seeing, in the act of becoming a witness to oneself. For Augustine, on the other hand, it is man who is a mystery to himself. "Without question, we see now through a mirror in an enigma, not yet face to face" (10.5.7). It is man who tries to see himself face-to-face yet deceives himself so easily in front of a mirror's sieve holes. Mirrors without divine depth present an image of man caught in pretense and vainglory. If Rilke's modern ontologizing lyrics inspire our flight into poetic disembodiedness, Augustine's *Confessions* of late antiquity testify to the torments of an embodied self.

A mirror is surface and depth, metaphor and matter, replica and trickster. Its material substance, consisting of a layer of aluminum deposited on a sheet of glass and of a sealed backside, is complemented and counteracted by its essential quality, which seems to remain punctured as a sieve. A mirror is metaphorically porous, pointing inward and outward, and centered on a surface that invites spatial and temporal confusions. We can gaze into mirrors with narcissistic rapture, pained inquisitiveness, or the confidence of a new convert. We may see only the external layer of our skin reflected in a mirror's cold and glassy surface, or we may follow its inward spatial quality that seems to lead to forgotten pasts, making us aware of the scars engraved into our bodies by too many years of living. Or we may imagine the reflection of our face pointing outward, moving, like a visual projectile, away from the surface toward us, and even behind and beyond us: we see a future, not a past. We might delight in what we see, we might despise what we see, or we may not even recognize ourselves. Mirrors are tricksters: they prod us into reading into our body's present reflection the regrets of the past and the hopes for the future. Mirrors: what are you substantially like?

This is Rilke's question. My concern in this book, however, is not the mysterious essence of a lifeless object but the lived experiences of the male subject. Men in their gendered subjectivity are the protagonists here, men who perform the act of gazing at themselves and of writing in a confessional mode.

Mirrors and confessions: Augustine, the confessing male protagonist par excellence, mentions the enigma of the mirror twice, referring in both instances to Paul's letter to the Corinthians (1 Cor. 13:12). "Of your eternal life I was certain, though I saw it in an enigma and as if in a mirror" (8.1.1; also 10.5.7, quoted previously). Mirrors, seemingly reflecting an accurate picture of who we are, deceive and imprison us. They trick us into believing that what we see is how we are seen by others, whether by humans or God. But this is not so! Even on the simplest level, a mirror image is always a reversal of how an other sees us: what is left is right, and what is right is left (the reversal becomes obvious when comparing a photographic portrait with one's mirror image). Face-to-face with my likeness, I believe myself able to take account of myself. The mirror image, however, is not so much an essence but, at best, a substance filled with nothing but sieve holes of *Zwischen-räume der Zeit* (literally, intermediate spaces of time). The mirror image with its simulated spatiality is filled with the problematics of temporality. We *now* see through a mirror, but we are *not yet* face-to-face.

Augustine's mirror-as-enigma addresses the relationship between himself and God, and not a "face-to-face" encounter between man and man. This is significant, and I will return to it later. For the moment, I want to explore briefly the idea of the face-to-face encounter with one's own mirror image—and this is not entirely in violation of Augustine's intention, since his sentence occurs within the larger context of why becoming a witness to oneself is both difficult and yet of "profit" (10.3.4). We *now* see through a mirror, Augustine writes, but *not yet* face-to-face. The sequential ordering suggests that mirrors are, at best, of temporary value or, worse, an impediment in face-to-face encounters. The enigmatic quality of the mirror is linked to the difficulty of writing confessions. Mirror images can reveal something about oneself, and they might motivate a person's introspective quest. Ultimately, though, they are insufficient, for they do not constitute a strong enough Other that would make it possible to transcend one's ontological confinement while searching for a self that has not yet come to the fore. To be radically transformed, the self needs an Other more powerful than any mirror image can provide. Why? Because mirrors attract the narcissistic gaze. The one who gazes remains arrested in visual solipsism, in a posture of postmodern amorousness with oneself, in which the self is not so much revealed as it is restated in the flatness of its surface. "Many a time the mirror imprisons [men] and holds them firmly," write Dada artists Marcel Duchamp and Man Ray in "Men Before the Mirror," a short text accompanying a collection of Man Ray's photographs (1934). "They are absorbed, separated from reality and alone with their dearest vice, vanity."[2] The solipsistic flat self—the "sinful" self of Christian confession narratives—does not seek depth, does not seek to be shaken in its existential grounding, but wishes to confirm itself in the present in the hope of defying aging and dying.

In his *Confessions*, Augustine testifies to the power of deception that hinders man from coming face-to-face with himself. He berates the mental and physical resistance to changing the enslavement to one's past self. The tortuous battle is well described in a passage of Book 8, shortly before Augustine's final conversion to his new, Christian self:

> You [God] took me up from behind my own back where I had placed myself because I did not wish to observe myself, and you set me before my face so that I should see how vile I was, how twisted and filthy, covered in sores and ulcers. And I looked and was appalled, but there was no way of escaping from myself. If I tried to avert my gaze from myself . . . you once again placed me in front of myself; you thrust me before my own eyes so that I

should discover my iniquity and hate it. I had known it, but deceived my-self, refused to admit it, and pushed it out of my mind. (8.7.16)

Here we encounter a man resistant to observing himself from a perspec-tive outside his own confinement. Augustine stubbornly resists a face-to-face encounter with his spiritually sick self. He wishes to hide behind himself, his face turned away from himself, but he is forcefully taken "from behind" his own back and placed "before" his own face—by a power, Augustine says, not his own, but God's. And what is the eventual result? The prolonged and anguished battle with his vile self finds rest in God's embrace, and Augus-tine can proclaim: "Then I turned to myself, and said to myself: 'Who are you?' I replied: 'A man'" (10.6.9).

Augustine may have "human" in mind when he writes, "Tu quis es? Et respondi: *homo*" (10.6.9; emphasis added), but a gendered reading of his *Confessions* would still reveal that "man" is the true subject of the confes-sional battle. The *Confessions* document the birthing of a new man; as a confessional document, it also strives to be a model for others. It is almost with a sigh of relief when Augustine, toward the end of the *Confessions*, can finally reveal the purpose of his efforts of public self-disclosure. "So what profit is there, I ask, when, to human readers, by this book I confess to you who I am now, not what I once was?" (10.3.4). "A brotherly mind," he continues, "will love in me what you teach to be lovable, and will regret in me what you teach to be regrettable" (10.4.5). The detailed and intimate investigation of the self has turned into a public role model for others.

Contrasting Rilke with Augustine, I am shifting attention away from the inanimate object of mirrors (as if the mirror is to be faulted for its enigma) to the male subject who is actively engaging in an act of seeing himself anew. The enigma is man, not the mirror. Such shift in focus—the aware-ness of "man" as a gendered subject—is an important step in the investiga-tion of texts that bespeak men's efforts at revealing their intimate selves. The problem is, of course, that Augustine, and centuries of confessional male writers after him, have spoken and written in a normative and authoritative voice that equates "man" with "human," thus concealing the genderedness of the male experience. Although man is in the center—and anyone in his orbit is measured by and compared to him, to the one whose experiences are universalized—he remains, as gendered subject, invisible. He appears and disappears simultaneously. He is like Foucault's "man erased, like a face drawn in sand at the edge of the sea."[3] The substance of man as a consciously gendered being seems to be as enigmatic as the sieve holes of Rilke's mirror. In a playful variation, we can rephrase the poet's stanza by substituting "men" for "mirrors":

> *Men*: never yet has anyone described in knowing ways
> what you are substantially like
> You, as if filled with nothing but sieve holes
> Interstices of time

Men as enigma: Do male confessants reveal who they truly are? Are confessional writings mirrors in which other men find themselves reflected? I will begin my investigation into male confessiographies by asking how men write about their intimate selves and how they speak about their bodies. I will also ask to what degree the act of writing is itself an act of intimacy or whether it is merely a public performance. In the next chapter, our guides will be Augustine of late antiquity, Rousseau of modern Enlightenment, and Leiris of (post)modernity.

CHAPTER 2

The Confines of Male Confessions

On Ancient Vainglory and the Postmodern Gaze

When men confess, they have already lived a life that they are now willing to abandon and whose changes they are willing to share with a public. To a certain degree, confessants, whether religious or agnostic, have already detached themselves from a lived past. Confessions are a pouring out of personal memories and thoughts and may originate in a state of being confounded, of being disturbed by the way we have arranged ourselves with our lives. Etymologically, the term *confusion* derives from the Latin *cum* (together) and *fundere* (to pour), and carries the meaning of "pouring out together," "mingling," of being "overwhelmed" and "perplexed." In order to manage our confusion, we confess.

Confusion may compel us to confess, but confessing is not the same as confusing. The act of confessing (or, if it occurs over a prolonged time, the *process* of confessing) is a recollecting of memories that emerge from within us, although as confessants we assume a position that appears to be outside and beyond the immediate moment. Confessions impose a new order onto experienced chaos. A confession is an interpretation of the past, a reenvisioning of our lives, a reinvention of ourselves.

Confessiographies share many characteristics with autobiographical writings, but the latter do not have to adopt the former's nostalgic perspective and transformative claims.[1] Autobiographies can be motivated by the urgency of the moment (a person recuperating after having fallen from public grace), they can be released in response to the public demand to know about a life of fame and fortune (artists, corporate and military leaders, infamous criminals), or they can emerge from an overtly political context (as part of an election campaign). Autobiographies can be written with the awareness that changing the circumstances of one's life is either not desirable (because the author enjoys a privileged position) or not feasible (because of political oppression, social dependency, mental inability). In confessiographies, by contrast, the confessant invites the public to become witness to the new meaning he has attached to his life. The Latin *confessare*, a composite of *cum* (together, fully) and *frateri* (to acknowledge), conveys the public and dialogical dimension of "acknowledging together," that is, to talk about one's life publicly. Confessional writings are a testimony to a transformation of an old self to a new self that requires an other as public witness. Its appeal is based on the fact that the confessant is trusted to have "fully acknowledged," that is, has attempted to reveal himself truthfully. In its best tradition, confessing is the result of a newly grasped awareness of and about the self that is shared with others.

Does male confessional literature display such awareness? Many men have been successful in publicly sharing and communicating their religious, spiritual, political, or sexual conversions and transformations because patriarchal traditions have provided them with the means to do so. Have they equally succeeded in fully acknowledging their lives? Or have they produced texts that differ little from the self-deceiving sieve holes of Rilke's mirror? The privileges men have enjoyed in Western cultures may have locked their confessions into a narcissistic meditation, blinding them to the fate of others.

I have ambivalent feelings about male confessions: I like to read them, but I also get impatient with men pouring out intimacies in navel-gazing and self-pitying terms. On the one hand, I wish that men would talk intimately about their embodiedness and spiritual selves, and on the other hand, I am easily frustrated with, occasionally even bored by, the narcissistic longings of the male ego exhibited in confessions. Tempted to confess myself, I fear that I might merely make public a private confusion.

Conflicting voices have inhabited my body self in the past. As an adolescent, I fantasized leading a monastic life or, short of that, becoming a hedonistic millionaire (though with a heart). The appeal of simple dualisms: asceticism versus debauchery, religion versus body, spiritual paucity versus creative excess! I remember well when these competing desires left me confused. The battles of Hermann Hesse's fictional male protagonists and alter egos spoke to these coming-of-age conflicts. Later, as a university student, I struggled to learn the language of church and theology, often feeling pressed to repeat the voices of theological teachers rather than find my own. Mimicry was to prepare me for the ministry. Clothing myself with these voices promised institutional authority and security—"my preference was for the ministry, for I fancied myself as a preacher" (Rousseau 1953, 34)—but at the price of neglecting my emotional and intellectual growth.

I started to explore dance and art. I loved playful exuberance and found comfort in liminal spaces. Later still, I became lover and husband, father and teacher, immigrant and citizen: a symphony and cacophony of whispers and demands, sobs and laughter, stammering and verbosity. Should I ever feel tempted to confess, which one of these voices would do the confessing? Do I have perspective on myself?

Perspectivity and Redemption: Augustine and Leiris

In his *Confessions*, Augustine, despite the obsessive scrutinizing of his motivations and deeds, still has the privilege of perspective. It is the privilege of knowing himself in relation and in opposition to the divine, a perspective that permits him to escape the danger of solipsism. The *Confessions* provide a narrative dynamic in which it is "God who turns Augustine around and Augustine who is answering" (Caputo and Scanlon 2005, 5). Augustine exuberantly praises God before he reveals any intimate details about himself. Only after he finishes glorifying God does he proceed to talk freely about his bodily needs and desires. "You are great, Lord, and highly to be praised. . . . Man, a little piece of your creation, desires to praise you, a human being bearing his mortality with him" (1.1.1). These opening lines frame Augustine's *Confessions*. The account of intimate details is placed into a proper cosmic order. Whatever intimacies Augustine reveals, they are ultimately a small thing compared to God's immeasurable power and wisdom.

Once the stage is set, a stage from which God is not yet expelled, Augustine is ready to introduce the carnal necessities of his existence. "So I was

welcomed by the consolation of human milk. . . . For at that time I knew
nothing more than how to suck and to be quietened by bodily delights"
(1.6.7). The privilege of a divine perspective enables him to portray the delights of human flesh, even the sucking of his mother's milk.

There are ample textual examples in the history of Christianity that use an earthly,
bodily language. I did not know them when growing up in postwar Germany. I won-
der why German Lutheranism, the tradition into which I was confirmed, restricts
the acquisition of a body language beyond sitting in pews. It would have been un-
thinkable to speak about lactation in the same breath as about faith and church. But
Augustine did it.

   In my twenties, I needed to distance myself from church and theology, leaving be-
hind what I experienced as a body-repressive politic. Theater and dance helped me to
fully inhabit my body. Yet the separation of sensuality from spirituality continued to
exert its influence. For many years, for example, I got uncomfortably tongue-tied when
pious people asked me about my endeavors as performer, or when artists asked me
about my religiosity. To articulate publicly the relation of expressive movements and the
expression of faith did not come easily. I can diagnose my discomfort as a lack of mental
integration; it does not change the fact that I am a child of a particular historical mo-
ment in Christianity.

Augustine's sudden turn to descriptions of physical intimacy may surprise
those readers who have had no prior exposure to the *Confessions*. Accus-
tomed to characterizing Christianity as a dualistic tradition that devalues
body as matter but exalts spirit and mind, the bishop's reminiscence of his
mother's milk is startling.[2] We need to reaccustom ourselves to the idea that
Christianity talks about the body, and it does so persistently, from its early
roots in late antiquity to the medieval ages, from European Thomistic scholasticism to nineteenth-century American Protestant health reforms, from
mysticism to contemporary Christian men's movements (see Shaw 1998;
Bynum 1987; Griffith 2004; Culbertson 2007). Christian thinkers may not
have pleasing things to say about the body. Yet in their theological discourse they often speak vividly about the delights, filth, rottenness, pleasures, health, temptation, sins, and punishments of the flesh. "And the

beleaguered devil undertook one night to assume the form of a woman and to imitate her every gesture, solely in order that he might beguile Antony," Athanasius writes about the fourth-century Egyptian ascetic. "[The devil] placed his confidence in the weapons *in the navel of his belly* [and] advanced against the youth. . . . The one hurled foul thoughts and the other overturned them through his prayers; the former resorted to titillation, but the latter, seeming to blush, fortified the body with faith" (1980, 34; emphasis in original). Subjecting the body to ascetic control meant having to acknowledge the intimate realities of the flesh. Antony wanted to conquer not only titillations but also the instinctive reaction of blushing, for as long as he blushed, he still felt ashamed, caused by desire he had failed to control. To know how far one could push the body's boundaries, whether abstaining from food or channeling one's sexual drive, meant to plumb the depths of human desire in the forms of lust, gluttony, and greed.

We can read the ascetic praxis of early Christian men as a lifelong performance that required them to discipline their bodies. Documents of and about early Christian martyrs and saints do not lack in dramatic quality, except that their stage is not a modern theater or television studio but the desert, the hermitage, or the Roman arena. Their lives were infused with a spiritual theatricality whose emotional appeal, from a modern perspective, is (almost) incomprehensible. It was performed with such sincere conviction that its theatricality had to be denied and read as a divine mandate. At stake was not admiration by the public but God's love.

During the years I performed onstage, I was most intrigued by ideas emanating from Antonin Artaud's "theater of cruelty" (1958) and Jerzy Grotowski's "poor theatre" (1969). In order for contemporary theater to be of any importance, it had to become an all-consuming, sacrificial act. Grotowski speaks of the "holy actor" who does not "exhibit his body, but annihilates it, burns it, frees it from every resistance to any psychic impulse [and] sacrifices it" (1969, 34). Holy actors are to undergo a rigorous training, in which they learn to transgress and transcend the social and physical limitations imposed on the body. To me, these ideas were liberating. I also intuited that Grotowski's holy actor might not differ that much from the Christian male ascetic, but I lacked the knowledge and maturity to articulate this semblance. Ascetics renounce earthly desires to uncover the spiritual possibilities of the body; the practical consequence of their

idealism is a continuous struggle with and against their embodiedness. Likewise, the modern holy actor subjects his body to a discipline that counters social and aesthetic norms, undergoing ascetic-like training to explore the body's aesthetic possibilities. Both the male ascetic of antiquity and the holy actor of modernity get to know their flesh and bodily fluids more intimately than men who merely employ their anatomy in pursuit of career, pleasure, and health. Spiritual and artistic experimentations with the male body stand in contrast to its modern utilitarian use.

Physical self-sacrifice in pursuit of loftier goals: holy actors and religious ascetics are driven by a male ideology that resists normative ideals of masculinity. Yet they remain caught in a strongly gendered, solitary belief system, a kind of spiritual machismo. It is no coincidence that Grotowski relied on Ryszard Cieslak, a male actor, who most exhaustively embodied his sacrificial ideal of "poor theatre."[3]

I wonder whether ascetic discipline appeals to men—as it occasionally appeals to me—less because it renounces the body but because it promises seclusion. Are men attracted to asceticism because it allows them to keep relational intimacy at bay and to find deeper pleasure in a solitary existence?

When Augustine writes his *Confessions*, the excessive physio-spiritual practice of the desert fathers has already become a distant memory. Augustine and his friends of the late fourth century did not hear of Antony, the ascetic master of the late third century, until, one day in imperial Milan, a fellow African by the name Ponticianus tells them a "story of Antony the Egyptian monk, a name held in high honour among your [God's] servants." Instilling amazement and surprise in Augustine about "the greatness" of Antony (8.6.14), Ponticianus continues to "speak of the flocks in the monasteries and their manner of life well pleasing to you [God] and the fertile deserts in the wilderness." "Of these," Augustine admits, "we knew nothing" (8.6.15).

The story of Antony inspired Augustine and his friends to contemplate briefly an ascetic life for themselves. In the end, however, Antony's life remained just a story to them. The Egyptian desert merely occupied a place in their religious imagination and did not represent an option they truly wanted to pursue. Antony became a model for contemplation, not imitation. More accurately, it was the *narrative* about Antony that served as a model for contemplation. Augustine recalls how Ponticianus continued: how, while staying in Trier, one of Ponticianus's friends was "set on fire" when he found "a book in which was written the 'Life of Antony.'" While reading, this man was "filled with holy love and sobering shame . . . [and] began to think of taking up this way of life and of leaving his secular post in the civil service." But "in pain at the coming to birth of new life"—Ponticianus concluded his account—this man "returned his eyes to the book's pages. He read on and experienced a conversion *inwardly* where you [God] alone could see and, as was soon evident, his mind rid itself of the world" (8.6.15; emphasis added).

When Augustine recalls what Ponticianus's unnamed friend had experienced, it is clear that he identifies with him. Like him, Augustine realizes that being reborn as a Christian no longer requires the ascetic body discipline of the desert fathers. Instead, *reading* the fathers' inspirational stories is all that is needed for conversion. For Augustine, it is no longer the ascetic practice itself, no longer the actual encounter with a desert saint, not even a pilgrimage to the Egyptian wilderness that moves him. Twice removed from owning Antony's experience (he only hears a story about someone reading a book about Antony), Augustine is inspired by a story. It is words, a *text*, that set Christian men "on fire." Antony's external rigorous physical discipline is replaced by Augustine's serene posture of reading that, in turn, leads to an inward spiritual conversion. Such inward gazing is a turn of the self to "radical reflexivity," which Augustine "bequeathed to the Western tradition" (Taylor 1989, 131).

Augustine finds spiritual sustenance in the discipline of reading and writing (whereas he is often disappointed by real people).[4] He wishes his written *Confessions*, like Athanasius's narrative account of the "Life of Antony," to be of equal service to other men. Confessional texts are models and mirrors that inspire inward conversions and offer pathways to God. For Augustine, the practice of radical asceticism is replaced by radical reflexivity. Reading and writing become a new anamnestic device and a path toward redemption.

Augustine's recollection of the encounter with Ponticianus directly precedes the passage in which he describes how much he defied God's attempt to make him see himself face-to-face: "But while [Ponticianus] was speaking, Lord, you turned my attention back to myself. You took me up from behind my own back where I had placed myself because I did not wish to observe myself and you set me before my face" (8.6.16). Augustine keeps resisting the face-to-face encounter with his own appalling self; only with the help of God (and the text) is he able to do so. He opens himself to the reality of God neither by absconding into the desert nor by gazing at his mirror image but by being drawn into a textual world. Equipped with postmodern sophistication, modern readers may ask whether it was first God or the text that allowed Augustine to see himself, or whether God and text must be seen as an inextricable unit with respect to the process of self-discovery and transformation. However, for the moment, it is evident that for Augustine the written word is of exceptional importance and that the story of Ponticianus illustrates the divine power of texts. Shortly thereafter, Augustine converts (8.8.19).

The act of writing the *Confessions*, then, can be interpreted as Augustine's innovative way of giving testimony to the Christian faith. To declare in public "Christianus sum" (I am a Christian) no longer required the martyr's blood or the dried-up shell of the desert monk.[5] Being set ablaze by word and text alone was sufficient.

As much as Augustine admired and proclaimed the power of the word as a path toward God, he also feared its commanding sway. He understood, from his own experience as a skilled rhetorician, the hazards of sophistry and casuistry, which would lead the believer astray. Still, the right words were therapeutic. "Writing of the *Confessions*" was "an act of therapy" (Brown 1969, 65), a kind of talking cure, as Margaret Miles implies in her study of Augustine (1992). Indeed, Augustine healed his self-diagnosed restlessness through language: "our heart is restless until it rests in you" (1.1.1). His talking cure, however, did not unfold in a series of verbal conversations with a confessor but through introspective and solitary contact with paper.

Focusing on texts, Augustine's writing of the *Confessions* contributed to the domestication of the eccentric performances of ascetic men outside the control of imperial religion that Christianity was about to become.

Still, Augustine talked about his mother's milk; I would not.

Augustine feared that his intimate revelations would lead to ridicule: "Proud people will laugh at me" (4.1.1). Although he employs personal disclosures with great deliberation, and hence seeks to forestall some of the anticipated scorn, the bishop—after returning from Milan's imperial urbanity to the North African province—had the courage to make the intimate body the site of inspection and introspection. What gave him the strength to do so? It was his firm conviction that a power existed far greater than him, far greater than his accomplishments and his likeness in a mirror, and far greater than the mother who gave birth to him. God offers perspective on a (male) self. Augustine could talk about his mother's milk only *after* praising God in the opening of the *Confessions*. Acknowledging the sucking on his mother's breast was intimately linked to the praising of God. The clairvoyance with which Augustine confessed man's dependency on biological necessities corresponds to the strength of his confession of faith. Augustine found the courage to speak about his mother's milk because he knew himself to be ultimately nourished by God.

When we compare Augustine's *Confessions* to Michel Leiris's *Manhood: A Journey from Childhood into the Fierce Order of Virility* (first published in 1939 in French as *L'Age d'homme*), the wide gap between antiquity and modernity becomes evident. "I have just reached the age of thirty-four, life's mid-point," the French poet, anthropologist, and museum curator informs his readers in the opening paragraph of his work.[6] "Physically I am of average height, on the short side. I have auburn hair cut short to keep it from curling, and also to prevent the spread of an incipient baldness. . . . My eyes are brown, the edges of the lids habitually inflamed; my complexion is high; I am disconcerted by an irritating tendency to blush, and by a shiny skin" (1992, 3; see also Brée 1980, 202). Leiris, who broke with the surrealist movement when he began to work on *Manhood* in the 1930s, exposes the agonies of being and becoming a man. It is a modern version of male self-scrutinizing that places a body self at the center. The male subject is wrapped in physical self-consciousness.

As opposed to Augustine's, the first thing the reader learns about Leiris's life concerns his physiognomy ("a straight nape" and "a broad, rather bulging forehead"), his habitual gestures ("sniff[ing] the back of my hand"), his chief activities ("literature"), his sex life ("sexually I am not, I believe, abnormal [but] have long tended to regard myself as virtually impotent"), and his "disgust of pregnant women" (1992, 3–5). From the very beginning, *Manhood* is hopelessly entangled in a solipsistic perspective on the body. Leiris sings a hymn to the male body—to a body that is not beautiful, powerful, or sacred but homely, impotent, and mundane.

This body knows no sin. While sin is thrown out of the window of enlightenment, a man remains in a room in front of a mirror without depth and perspective.

Writing about the male body is distressing. It is, after all, my body, and my body resists being written about. It/I become painfully self-conscious precisely at the moment I want to write about my body—a fairly trivial and repeatedly observed phenomenon. I feel the sensations in the tips of my fingers, the slight burning in my eyes, my tense shoulders. My body that needs to perform the techné of writing becomes an object outside myself, an image disconnected from the person that is thinking and writing about it/me.

What is the value of such solipsistic circling? How can men escape it? Would a divine reality that is still in place for Augustine help men transcend their self-centeredness?

Leiris's accounting of his physical likes and dislikes takes up approximately the same space that Augustine uses to extol God in the opening paragraphs of his *Confessions*. Contrary to Augustine, who prepares the reader and himself to consider the physicality of a man's life by first establishing a divine perspective, Leiris tightly organizes his opening passage around the description of his body but concludes with a metaphysical allusion: "I should like to set down here, in a few lines, what vestiges I can gather of the *metaphysics of my childhood*" (1992, 6; emphasis in original). Not only does Leiris's body precede all metaphysics but the metaphysics Leiris has in mind does not leave the realm of the immature self. It is the metaphysics of childhood, of nostalgia.[7] The point of departure is no longer God but the infantile past, not the superego but the id—and it is no coincidence that Leiris credits Freud's influence on the composition of *Manhood*.[8]

"Without question, we see now through a mirror in an enigma, not yet face to face" (Augustine 10.5.7). I mentioned previously that Augustine's reference is not a solipsistic gazing into a mirror but an anticipated relationship with God. Man cannot fully know himself but must be known from a power outside: this is one of the insights toward which the *Confessions* is working from the very beginning. Augustine picks up on Paul's wording: "For now we see in a mirror, dimly, but then we will see face to face. Now I know only in part; then I will know fully, even as I have been fully known" (1 Cor. 13:12). He finds in the apostle's letter scriptural evidence for his own experience: that knowing oneself fully is impossible in the here-and-now. To "fully know oneself" is a gift, a promise, that must wait until the time that God and man can see each other face-to-face.

The profound realization of the *Confessions* is that, despite all confessional efforts, the male self can never fully grasp itself. Self-analysis must remain incomplete, must wait for its final completion at the end of all days. Does this make the act of confessing obsolete? No. It only puts it in perspective. A man traveling down the confessing path must remain cognizant of the relative success of his enterprise. For this reason the converted and mature Augustine—after he has cured himself from the sicknesses of his old self—insists that even his Christian conversion does not result in full knowledge: "Accordingly, let me confess what I know of myself. For what I know of myself I know because you [God] grant me light, and what I do not know of myself, I do not know until such time as my darkness becomes 'like noonday' before your face" (10.5.7). Conversion is not a magic bullet for self-understanding.

The twentieth-century Leiris, who places himself among "writers of confessions" (1992, 22), lacks such perspectivity and, hence, lacks redemption. Whereas Augustine draws up a theological position of omnipotence and eternity outside himself, which enables him to talk freely about his mother's milk, Leiris construes his self around the aging male body, which has no perspective on itself, except for its childhood. Leiris's body knows no salvation. His mirror image is a "sign of irreparable sorrow," conveying "a sense of loss" (Enterline 1995, 1). His body is subject to an inevitable process of disintegration. "On the far side of that abyss lies my early youth toward which, in recent years, I turn as the only happy period of my life, though already containing the elements of its own disintegration, and all the features which, gradually deepening into wrinkles and lines, give my portrait its likeness" (Leiris 1992, 6).

Voyeuristic Gazes and Male Intimacies: Leiris and Rousseau

In the safety of my bathroom, I look into the mirror uninhibitedly, not just for cleaning and shaving my face but also for trying to discover signs of aging. The more time I spend at home—to prepare for class, do daily chores, write, clean, read, or cook—the more often I check myself in the mirror. Home provides protection from the public gaze and hence permits the private gazing at myself. I do this to take a break, gather my thoughts, or fight a feeling of emptiness. When my work takes me into the public arena, mirrors become immaterial, because the public itself becomes a social mirror. I feel confident in my existence when I see myself reflected in others: the public as an extension of the male self.

Photographic and mirror images are not the same: they reverse sides. In photographs, I see myself as others would see me: "your right, my left." In mirrors, left remains left. When my face is marked by a scratch or a zit, I notice this reversal. What on a photograph appears on the right (from the viewer's perspective), I have seen in the mirror on the left. Of course, I can abstract from myself and project myself into my mirrored face, in which case "I" would look back at me. Then, the scratch on my left side would be right, just as in the photograph or as any other person would see me.

Do modern confessions function analogously? Once put into writing, the confessional text stares back at the confessant. I no longer know whether it is I who does the looking or whether it is the written and remembered "I" that looks back at me. "Even if I confess myself," Derrida muses, "I am confessing another one" (2005, 25). There was, for example, a large mirror in my grandmother's house. As a child, I would slowly approach it with my eyes fixed on my body and then quickly look behind the mirror in order to catch my image. I am tempted to use this childish game as a paradigm for modern confessiographies: the effort of men to construct and hold on to an image of themselves.

Are confessions, which turn private thoughts into public property, an attempt at breaking out of the mirror's solitude?

Leiris interprets the world through his body and insists on a metaphysics of childhood. Indeed, a contemporary male confession would strike us as incomplete if either body or childhood were missing.[9] Yet both the scrutinizing of our carnal activities and the search for childhood patterns that influence our adult lives are signs of the modern affliction of self-gazing.

When Leiris begins *Manhood* with a description of his "auburn hair cut short to keep it from curling," we must assume that he writes these lines in front of a mirror. How else would he have been able to present his physiognomy in such graphic detail? "I loathe unexpectedly catching sight of myself in the mirror . . . [and] I seem humiliatingly ugly to myself each time" (1992, 3–4; also Porter 1991, 124). It takes courage to portray one's body with an authenticity that transgresses bourgeois expectations of decency.[10]

Leiris has this courage. But he is not the inventor of a new autobiographical style. "From Montaigne's *Essays* to Rousseau's *Confessions* through Stendhal's journals to the modern confessions of Gide, Jouhandeau, and Genet, the great writers of France have been concerned to a singular extent with the detached presentation of intimate feelings" (Sontag 1992, viii). Leiris does not present his male obsessions with passion but gazes at them analytically and with detachment.

I discovered my first zit while standing in front of a mirror, awed by the growth on my skin, just beneath the nose. When I squeezed it and the white pus squirted out, I had a strong bodily sensation, like ejaculating—though at the time I had not yet experienced the spilling of semen. I was not repulsed and only now am embarrassed by the words I use to recollect this memory. I thought of an eruption, of something that had been contained and was now thrust forward. I experienced my still boyish and angelic-looking face as undergoing a tremendous change, witnessing something aggressive, destructive, and liberating. I felt a step closer to adulthood.

Rousseau, the other grand confessant, avows in the opening paragraph of his 1782/1789 *Confessions* "to display to my kind a portrait in every way true to nature, and the man I shall portray will be myself" (1953, 17).[11] Rousseau, who desacralizes the religious confession, no longer places himself within the universe of revealed religion, like Augustine, nor does he struggle with disciplining his body, like the early Christian ascetics.[12] He articulates modernity's self-centeredness: *portrait, man, I, myself.*

"Rousseau's example," writes Brooks, "[is] decisive for the modern confessional tradition" (2000, 73); he does not direct his "invocations . . . to God, but to his fellow man" (Moseley 2006, 7).[13] Rousseau's *Confessions* are written with reference to, but above all in deliberate opposition to, Augustine's *Confessions* (see Hartle 1983; Kelly 2001, 303, 305). What makes Rousseau's *Confessions* modern is man's self-awareness of his subjectivity and his solitude: the source of his strength (subjectivity) is also the cause of his anxiety (solitude). In contrast to Augustine's probing, the "test of the 'true confession' is not only the revelation of sin and crime [but] the confession of abject, unavowable, 'unhealthy' behavior and inclinations" of the solitary self (Brooks 2000, 73; also Marcus 1994, 196–198). Exposing oneself to public view requires from the modern, self-centered subject more courage than from a man knowing himself to be resting in God's grace. The societal mirror is all there is for the solitary self, and this condition leads to pure anxiety, both in the form of self-abasing behavior and the potential devastation wrought upon the self through social ostracism.[14] Rousseau— as is well known to readers of the *Confessions*—exposes himself literally to unsuspecting women in dark alleyways (he shows them his naked behind) and, when caught by a "man with a sword," can extricate himself only by pleading "mental derangement" (1953, 91).[15] Exposure usurps social respectability, and the self can be rescued only by claiming to be an "idiot," in its double sense of being a mad man and a private man (the ancient Greek *idios* means "private").

"I am alone in the universe" (Spender 1980, 117).[16] To ease their anxiety, modern male confessants will ask others to join their heroic venture of self-exposure. Leiris wishes as his ideal reader a "neighbor" who is "less a judge than an accomplice" (1992, 157), and Rousseau announces on the opening page of his *Confessions*: "So let the numberless legion of my fellow men gather around me, and hear my confession. . . . But let each of them reveal his heart . . . with equal sincerity, and may any man who dares, say: 'I was a better man than he'" (1953, 17). The modern confession Rousseau sets in motion becomes "an act of defiance and challenge to one's fellows, designed to implicate them as equally guilty of shameful acts, equally in need of the courage to confess" (Brooks 2000, 73). Without a divine safety net, multiple solitary male selves—a horde of brothers, really—confess equally to abject behavior.

At times, Rousseau's casual style is surprisingly postmodern. He recalls various episodes not because they hold special meaning but simply because they happened. "I do remember once having made water in one of our neighbour's cooking-pots while she was at church" (1953, 21). The image of young Rousseau peeing in a pot while the owner is at church conveys his mundane treatment of both body and religion. He does not scrutinize his motivations and does not analyze in depth the childish episode—unlike Augustine before him (who would have interpreted the scene in the light of man's ontological sinfulness) or Freud after him (who might have diagnosed his peeing as Oedipal aggression).[17] Indeed, Rousseau's reminiscence of peeing in the neighbor's pot follows his admission of having stolen "fruit or sweets" (1953, 21) for no particular purpose, thus deliberately evoking a parallel to the famous passage of Augustine's theft of pears as a youngster (Kelly 2001, 314). But while Augustine tires his readers with pages of scrupulous self-reflection, Rousseau concludes laconically: "And that is a brief and truthful account of all my childish misdeeds" (22).

Northrop Frye calls Rousseau's *Confessions* a "modern type" of Augustine's invented "confession form" (1957, 307).[18] Truth is at stake for both Augustine and Rousseau. Reading their confessions today through a consciously male-gendered perspective, we become witness to the struggle of two male confessants trying to reveal themselves intimately under different discursive conditions. "I have only one thing to fear in this enterprise; not that I may say too much or tell the untruths, but that I may not tell everything and may conceal the truth" (Rousseau 1953, 170).

Yet, with respect to their perspectives on the world, Augustine and Rousseau bear little semblance. Had Augustine reported the peeing episode, he would have used it to explain to his readers how all rationales for justifying such deeds fell short, thus illustrating how such a foolish act is nothing but a symptom of humanity's postlapsarian condition. Not so Rousseau. For him, the body has its own trivial needs and worries. These can be exasperated in a religious environment but are spiritually insignificant. "Now I have made the first and most painful step in the dark and miry maze of my confessions," writes Rousseau. "It is the ridiculous and the shameful, not one's criminal actions, that it is hardest to confess" (1953, 28). When, for example, Rousseau remembers being accosted as a young man by a pederast in a religious convent, he reports this incident with indignation but without moralizing outrage.

> He resumed his caresses [and] tried to work up to the most revolting liberties and, by guiding my hand, to make me take the same liberties with him. I broke wildly away with a cry . . . for I had not the slightest idea what it was all about. . . . [A]s he gave up the struggle I saw something whitish and sticky shoot towards the fireplace and fall on the ground. (1953, 71)

Emotionally confused, Jean-Jacques reports the harassment to adults. He gets angry only at their explanations, which he finds too dismissive of his experience. Augustine may have used the occasion to talk about the nature of sin, but the lesson Rousseau learns is to guard himself in the future "against the attentions of pederasts" (1953, 73). His body is no longer the battleground for the torments of sin and the glory of repentance. His bodily memories merely signify the failings of otherwise good people.[19]

As a boy, I was once sexually harassed by a museum guard in front of Greek statues in the Louvre, and another time cornered by a man in a train station in Paris. Like Rousseau, I did not fully grasp what was happening but had enough sense to get away before being humiliated. I was more confused than ashamed. I remained silent and learned how to be more careful in the future. The incidents had no religious significance.

Rousseau, like his French compatriot Leiris, wants to expose intimate details: "Since I have undertaken to reveal myself absolutely to the public, nothing about me must remain hidden or obscure" (1953, 65). He wants to be transparent like a mirror.[20] But unlike Leiris, Rousseau still seeks the reader's empathy. To mitigate misunderstandings, he supplies a chronology of dates, places, stories, explanations. "I was born at Geneva in 1712, the son of Isaac Rousseau, a citizen of that town, and Susanne Bernard, his wife" (17). Philippe Lejeune ridiculed such autobiographical prose as the misguided effort to fill out a "questionnaire sent by a punctilious administration." The autobiographers are born, present "a family tree [and] one or more first memories; next they go dutifully to school; they make the first discovery of everything they should, while drawing a spicy, compassionate, or incisive picture of the family milieu; the crisis of adolescence comes along; and so on" (1989, 235). Rousseau's work is more complex than Lejeune's parody, but it falls to Leiris to deliberately counter such prose.

Leiris does not present a chronology of his life but writes about a man (himself) who, out of a sense of confusion, desires to confess without hiding things considered to be repulsive and trivial.[21] Leiris confronts the reader with a self-loathing mentality that speaks through his graphic descriptions of his body, his sexual preferences, and his misogynist relations to women. *Manhood*, Leiris declares in a 1961 interview, represented a risk. "It entailed displaying my own deficiencies. As a rule a man tries to puff himself up like a cock" (quoted in Pilling 1981, 65).

Language that describes private bodily functions is sometimes more abhorrent than the activities themselves. For example, I cringe when reading Leiris's description of his

habitual gestures—"to scratch my anal region when I am alone" (1992, 4)—though I
perform, like most men, similar gestures at home.

Because reading remains a private act, my embarrassment is well contained. Were
someone to reveal such intimate obsessions in a conversation, I would blush. It is easier
to write about zits in a confessional mode than to speak about them publicly.

Susan Sontag called *Manhood* an "exercise in shamelessness," a "sequence of
self-exposures of a craven, morbid, and damaged temperament" (1992, ix).
Roger Porter praised it as an "open wound" and a "courageous act" (1991,
125). Germaine Brée concluded that it is "certainly the most intensively
fascinating volume in Leiris' sometimes tedious autobiographic itinerary"
(1980, 204). Leiris himself, though concerned about shame and courage as
well, is ultimately more intrigued by the arbitrariness of reconstructing one's
life. He does not shy away from tediousness.

> Hence it occurred to me to write these pages, primarily a simple confession
> . . . with the goal of liquidating, by formulating them, certain obsessions
> whose weight oppressed me. . . . [But] even as I write, the plan I had devised
> escapes me, and one might say that the more I look into myself the more
> confused everything I see becomes. (1992, 14, 83)

Leiris gazes inward and becomes confused. Such disorientation he shares
with Rousseau. But whereas the latter's *Confessions* leave the impression that
his confusion motivates him to confess (Rousseau is variously confused by
his emotions, his memory, or feelings of dissonance),[22] Leiris's confessions
remain caught in confusion. Does Leiris really see his inner self? Or does he
merely observe the mirrored surface of his body?[23]

I can relate to Leiris's struggle. The more I try to grasp my body, the more it escapes
me. Looking into my past or seeing my likeness in the mirror does not seem to solve the
dilemma. Perhaps modern men are cursed by the same predicament that women in
antiquity supposedly encountered: according to a misogynist belief reported by Aristotle,
a mirror into which menstruating women gaze becomes spotted (see Rank 1971, 66).
Spotted mirrors as sieve holes: they obscure the real presence of my body.

Because *Manhood* remains arrested in negative narcissism, it is also highly voyeuristic. Leiris not only turns the reader into a voyeur but, above all, gazes voyeuristically at himself. The entire perspective of *Manhood*, like the opening description of a mirrored body, is one in which the French man looks at himself through the reflections of mythological figures,[24] women, infantile wounds, dreams, and fantasies. Everything, including his body, is used as an object through which he can expose himself.

Gazing at the mirror image of one's body—searching for time lost, for signs of decay, for affirmation of the self—is an exercise in hermeticism. Mirrors confine. Sontag perceptively remarked that Leiris wishes "to convince himself that this unsatisfactory body—and this unseemly character—really exist" (1992, xi). He is, by no means, alone. Chuck Barris, a television icon of the 1970s, opens his *Confessions of a Dangerous Mind* with a paragraph that could have been lifted right out of *Manhood*: "It was June 1980, and I was standing in front of a full-length mirror studying my body. What I saw didn't please" (2002, 1). To the degree that mirrors make people conscious of their bodies, modern confessants are body conscious. Leiris is also disrespectful of his embodied self. "This lack of esteem or respect for himself is obscene" (Sontag 1992, ix).

Leiris cannot embrace his carnality. "The autobiographer's lived experience of his body," Shirley Neuman writes about *Manhood*, "disappears, yet again, into the metaphysics of the disembodied 'voice' of masculine autobiography" (1991, 163). Leiris's embodied self is defined in solipsistic rather than relational terms.[25] *Manhood* deceives the reader into believing that it is an autobiographical revelation of a male embodied self, but, in fact, it is a disembodied gazing at a male body. Many male confessions are infected by the same disease.

In contact improvisation, a modern dance form, people are in physical contact with each other or, when they are apart, remain fully attentive to the other's presence. Contact dancers explore the range of movement possibilities by conceiving themselves in relation to other bodies: giving and receiving weight, leading and being led, lifting and being lifted, real and imagined contact. Empty space between moving bodies is filled with present attentiveness. Contact improvisation is intimate, at times erotic, but not sexual. I always enjoyed it because I was able to give of myself, to reveal myself nonverbally,

thus breaking through the solitary walls of the disembodied posture of male confessional writing. Fully in my body, I was equally responsible for the other person's presence: an embodied revelation in relation to an other that eludes the male self-gazing.

Leiris's *Manhood*, Rousseau's *Confessions*, the Dadaist manifesto "Men Before the Mirror": they all illustrate how important mirrors have become to male confessants in modernity, beginning with the Renaissance. According to Gusdorf, the invention of nondeforming mirrors coincides with the wish of Renaissance men to see themselves directly, without the mediation of a divine gaze, thus leading to the emergence of a solitary male autobiographical self (Gusdorf 1980; also Moseley 2006, 29; Marcus 1994, 156–158). Whereas in the Middle Ages theological mirrors "play[ed] up without pity the slightest faults of the moral personality," Renaissance man wanted to see himself "without a taint of the transcendent" (Gusdorf 1980, 34). The modern male subject does not look for God but, like Rousseau, finds himself reflected in societal mirrors (see Spender 1980, 116), or, as in Leiris's case, looks at the surface of mirrors, which reflects back the contingencies of his body. The restlessness of the adolescent Rousseau (1953, 90) is not reconciled in God but is thrown into a "darkness" that entombs the Rousseau of age and leaves him without orientation (544).

Wounds and Vanity

Heterosexual male theologians of the twentieth century rarely identify themselves with their bodies. They talk about the pain of the crucifixion, the joy of resurrection, the torment of sin, and the glory of salvation. They do not, however, make their bodies the site of God-talk. Tom Driver's "Tub Water and Holy Ground" is an exception: "The theologian soaked in the bathtub. . . . Tired limbs and untoned muscle spoke to him. 'Wash us,' they said. . . . It was not a prayer to God but an instruction to himself. . . . Well, he had the gospel in his soul. . . . Where he seemed not to have the gospel was in his body" (1977, 1–4).

Driver's bathtub theology, which challenges preconceived notions about the production site of Euro-American theology (the ivory tower, the altar, the desk, the pulpit), runs the risk, as in Augustine's and Rousseau's cases, of being ridiculed. What good can come out of a bathtub? Martin Luther's mental breakthrough at the *cloaca* (or so it is said) is a reminder of the "explosive" significance of doing theology at profane places (see Erikson 1962). Similarly, when Driver touches neglected parts of his body and explores theological possibilities, he seems to drag the glorious heights of theology to the trivial grounds of washing his thighs. But from his thighs rises again—though without phallic erection—a theological reflection on sin, forgiveness, salvation, touch, healing, and God. The body is no longer a fountain of sin that requires divine salvation but a ground for therapeutic healing.

Driver locates his emotional woundedness in his thighs, and that discovery motivates him to do theology. Healing, for him, cannot be found in professing an otherworldly God but in recovering childhood wounds inscribed in his flesh. In this regard, Driver has more in common with Leiris than with Augustine. "He felt that if his body's longing for salvation could not be answered then he did not have the gospel at all" (Driver 1977, 4). To still this longing, Driver focuses his attention on the thighs, which have, in the past, offended him. "Too soft and too white. Too much useless flesh" (7). What men often desire and fear in a woman's body (the soft, white, useless flesh), the theologian discovers hanging on his own legs.

I locate my woundedness in my shoulders, chest, and pelvis, each carrying a different meaning: somebody watching over my shoulders, someone pressing against my chest, something locking my pelvis. In theater workshops I learned to relax my muscular tensions, dared to breathe and scream, and discovered the pelvis as the center of expressive movements. If spirituality denotes an experience of wholeness, then movement improvisation gave me a glimpse of spiritual life. Interstices of time were not sieve holes but filled with possibilities neither willed nor random: overflowing with movement, moved by the moving presence of others, nothing forced, just a gift.

Eventually, Driver finds redemption in the bathtub. After recalling the biblical thighs of Jacob, the thighs of girls riding on his shoulders at a pool party, or the unselfconscious kicking of his feet during angry outbursts, "he lifted his left leg and stepped out onto the floor. Then the other leg, and reached for a towel. . . . He dried first his thighs, massaging the backs of them and feeling the muscle under the fat. His legs felt new. While there was plenty of fat and he had to stand with feet wide apart to dry the inner softness, still each thigh had more muscle than he had supposed" (1977, 27).

Is the discovery of muscle Driver's redemption? Fat as the source of alien-ation, muscle as a promise of salvation? The imagery is peculiarly gendered. Offended by the feminized softness and uselessness of too much flesh, the discovery of muscle revitalizes his energy and renews his sense of masculinity. The bathtub episode comes to its conclusion. "His foot pressed the soil. His thigh pushed it there. . . . He was full of an energy that has no name" (28).

Driver does not preach the renunciation of carnality—in part, it seems, because he rebels against an American Puritan autobiographical style (see Couser 1979; Tambling 1990, 97). By touching his thighs, Driver goes be-yond the confines of a detached male self-gaze. When men touch themselves tenderly and consciously, they may be on the right path toward reaching out to others and treating them with similar care and nurture.

Driver's bathtub theology must be appreciated for its risk taking. Similar to Augustine's case, a theological framework allows him to ponder the fleshi-ness of his thighs. Yet we can also ask whether Driver would have written about his body without legitimating it theologically. What would have hap-pened had he described the cleaning and touching of his flesh without doing theology? As radical as Driver's bathtub theology may strike us, the religious frame also protects against accusations of vanity. Is the theological perspec-tive a distancing device that allows religious men to relate to their bodies?

Occasions for heterosexual men to speak publicly about their bodies often have a utilitarian purpose: a physical pain, a political aim, a medical problem, a theological justification. Straight men can talk about broken bones and war scars, abortion rights and AIDS research, prostate cancer and sexual ethics. Talking or writing about our male bodies without a "legitimate" reason, however, is viewed as narcissistic, vain, obscene. What would be the point of describing the difficulties of my sexual awaken-ing? Who would want to know that I did not masturbate until I was twenty years of age and only after I had had sex with my first girlfriend? I recall those old anxieties as if they happened yesterday, but I am not sure what their significance is today. I empa-thize with Leiris's admission that "the anecdotes I am telling here do not . . . represent anything crucial or exceptional for me; I offer them simply because they come to mind apropos of this idea of injury—a wound inflicted on a man with whom I identify myself" (1992, 77).

Any description of physical intimacies can be attacked for its vanity and in-consequentiality. "Impatient readers will perhaps be bored" (Rousseau 1953, 170). Even Augustine, who would have been among the first to renounce the modern exhibitionistic pleasure in body trivia, struggled with the problem-atics of vanity (see Asher 1998). Yet any (post)modern arbitrariness is counter to what the fourth-century theologian would have wanted to convey—and that, perhaps, makes him once again attractive, yet inaccessible, to modern sensibilities. In his *Confessions*, Augustine talks about his body because he pursues a larger spiritual agenda. He acknowledges the reality of carnal plea-sures and addictions that, however, do not produce happiness. True happi-ness lies in the surrender to God, beyond the body, beyond the self.

Augustine skillfully plays with the voyeuristic curiosity of the reader but at its peak switches to a dispassionate prose. He titillates the reader's imagi-nation only to frustrate it a moment later. "Each time he evokes the 'torrent of pitch which boils and swells with the high tides of foul lust' [II.2], it is quickly followed by philosophical or theological reflection" (Miles 1992, 26). A moral lesson can be learned from each activity of the male body—this is Augustine's rationale for revealing intimate details.

I am angry at Augustine because he stirs me in a direction where I begin to take my body seriously, only to be told that such a venture is pointless, if not outright foolish, for true happiness lies in a beyond-the-body relationship with God. I am also envious of men like Augustine because I no longer have the theological certainty of a perspective larger than myself.

Most confessants display some doubt about the relevance of their private disclosures and are wary of being criticized. "I must present my reader with an apology, or rather a justification, for the petty details I have just been en-tering into" (Rousseau 1953, 65). Without a perspective of a transcendental Other, Rousseau (let other men say, I was a better man than he) and Freud (let other men be franker than I am) can only admonish their readers not to mock them but first show the same courage of revealing their souls. But Au-gustine, too, expects his audience to have little patience with his trivialities, so he calls on God's mercy to stall ridicule: "Allow me to speak: for I am ad-dressing your mercy, not a man who would laugh at me. Perhaps even you deride me but you will turn and have mercy on me" (1.6.7). Pleading with his (male) readers to lend him an empathetic ear, he writes: "But what edification do they hope to gain by [my confession]? Do they desire to join me in thanksgiving when they hear how, by your gift, I have come close to you, and do they pray for me when they hear how I am held back by my own weight? To such sympathetic readers I will indeed reveal myself" (10.4.5).

Now that the Augustinian universe is no longer in place, what is it that men talk about when they talk about their bodies? Revealing one's intimate self is dirty business, and getting habituated to public revelations of this kind may become tedious and monotonous.[26] The modern trend to reveal our innermost intimacies may have created a discourse in which intimacy becomes ultimately irrelevant. Why reveal myself if intimacy is no longer a value? How can Rousseau's peeing, Driver's thighs, Leiris's homeliness, or my zits be of any interest to the public? Or, as one of my heterosexual colleagues in religious studies once told me in an academic conversation, "What do I do with my anus if it has no significance anymore?"

Writings about "intimate experience," Spender states, "are indiscreet," "too interested in themselves," and "not important to others." Confessing men are "immoralists, exhibitionists, pornographers" and "egomaniacs." Yet we need the dirty business of self-revelation: "We cannot afford altogether to despise anyone who—for whatever reasons—is the humblest und ugliest servant of truth" (1980, 118). This, indeed, is the modernist project that began with Rousseau. "If I am to be known I must be known in all situations, good and bad" (1953, 373)—here lies the seed for conceptualizing truth as public transparency of the private self, a truth linked to the modernist obsession with memory. And so Rousseau adds: "I am well aware that should these memoirs eventually see the light of day I shall myself be perpetuating the memory of an incident of which I intended to suppress all traces" (372).

With Leiris, however, we enter the postmodernist phase of male confessions since the truth he conveys calls into question the significance that one attributes to personal reminiscences. It is left to Leiris not to apologize for writing about trivial details. "I attach no excessive importance to these recollections from various stages of my childhood. . . . [There is] a certain arbitrariness in the choice of facts I am recording" (1992, 14, 87). The real, and perhaps intended, scandal of *Manhood* is not the revelation of intimate details but its stubborn affirmation of the trivial.[27] Leiris does not care about an empathetic reader. He does not want the reader to attach meaning to the childhood memories of his injured body or to the loathing of his impotent adult body. The body simply is. The discomfort we may feel when reading *Manhood* may have less to do with the graphic depiction of his wounds and more with his professed disinterest in a larger order.

I am angry at Leiris for taking up my time with self-exposures that provide no vision beyond his petty injuries. With Susan Sontag I am tempted to say, "Who cares?" (1992, ix). I am also envious of men like him because I rarely allow myself the pleasure of publicly indulging in my injuries.

The "petty details" for which Rousseau apologizes and the trivialities and arbitrariness that Leiris affirms are part of a posture of male confessants that has potential entertainment value. Modern technology and commerce have seized this potential, morphing confessions into a consumer good. Popular "confessional" television shows cajole people to reveal long-held secrets to the point of self-humiliation, and the Internet seduces people into breaking through the barrier of isolation and solitude through confessional statements—to the point of actual self-destruction.[28] Culturally speaking, today we are eons away from those aspects of the medieval confessional that were administered with care and compassion, perhaps best expressed in Jean Gerson's (1361–1429) admonition: "Let the sinner accuse himself humbly and not derisively, honestly and not deceitfully, purely, directly and sincerely, avoiding irrelevancies; and above all discreetly, so that he does not reveal those who were his companions in sin."[29] The (post)modern confessional culture, instead, has become largely indiscreet and irrelevant, pulling intimate others into public acts of self-humiliation and shaming. Of course, no one wants to return to the coercive and inquisitorial practices of the ecclesiastical courts and religious confessionals, but we need to be equally wary of modern media and technology that introduce a new coerciveness in the name of individual freedom and sexual liberation.

The Pleasure of Danger, the Danger of Pleasure

How dangerous is it to engage in confessional writing? Are men afraid of trivia, of being laughed at, of losing academic credibility or public honor? In confessiographies, men expose intimate memories of their woundedness.

"After a year of work, tears and healing I began trying to write a book about what had been happening," John Lee writes in *The Flying Boy: Healing the Wounded Man* (1987, 79). Men generally regard the opening up of one's intimate self as a perilous activity; hence, they either despise the confessional work of their peers or praise it as an act of courage.

Separating my critical from my personal voice protects me. Surrounding my self-revelations with academic discourse, I seek shelter from the public. In the interstices of scholarly prose and confessional insertions, I hide. It occurs to me that my strategy resembles Lejeune's vision for his scholarly work On Autobiography. *"I chose to work, academically, on autobiography," he writes, "because in a parallel direction I wanted to work on my own autobiography. . . . As soon as I write . . . I share the desires and illusions of autobiographers, and I am surely not ready to renounce them"* (1989, 132–133).

"Let us grant once and for all," Leiris admonishes his readers in his 1946 preface to *Manhood*, "that to write and publish an autobiography does not involve, for the man who undertakes such a thing . . . any danger of death" (1992, 159).[30] This is somber advice for male confessants who exaggerate the danger of intimate self-disclosure: it does not lead to death. Even though Leiris compares the confessional writer to the *torero*, it is only the latter who exposes himself to "bodily risk," whereas the former faces merely "moral risk." Because both enter a competitive struggle accompanied by the danger of wounding, the confessant's commitment "to tell the whole truth and nothing but the truth" (160) can be compared to the agon of the bullfighter.[31] Such agon, however, is a controlled danger, since confessional writing follows, like a bullfight, certain rules. Hence, Leiris can write that the danger that the confessional writer invites is "directly proportional to the rigor of the rule he has imposed on himself" (160). And whatever the danger is, many male confessants are compensated with public acclaim for their initial fear of being ridiculed, and their work occasionally acquires canonical status.

Since male confessants may fear the agon yet willingly submit to it, should we conceive of the ability to interpret and reenvision one's life as a privilege rather than a risk? If one aim of confessiographies is "to manage the body" (Neuman 1991, 138), then to write them offers men a safe means to make contact with their bodies. For many men, is must be easier to *write* about one's carnal obsessions, fantasies, and dreams than to *talk* about them in conversation with spouses, friends, companions, or colleagues. "In private conversation," Rousseau laments, there is "the necessity of always talking. . . . This unbearable constraint would be enough in itself to disgust me with society. I can think of no greater torture than to be obliged to talk continually and without a moment for reflection" (1953, 114–115). Men more willingly reveal their secrets in confessional texts than in conversations with intimate others. Contra Neuman's claim that confession "remains an intimate and private discourse" (1991, 138), written confessions actually try to escape from the privacy of social discourse and seek out the monological safety of paper, even though such monologue is written with a public audience in mind. In confessiographies, the act of writing, then, functions as a buffer between private and public discourse. The written form mediates intimacies. It transforms inarticulate experiences into speech, body into voice. Written confessions are a relatively safe way of acknowledging the woundedness that men may not otherwise admit—those "various recollections relating to *wounded men*" (Leiris 1992, 64; emphasis in original). In the solitary act of writing, there is no immediate other to dispute the retrospective construction and interpretation of the male self.

Such uninterrupted reconstruction must be regarded as pleasurable. There is a pleasure in the danger of recollecting one's wounds and flaws of the past. "Such were the errors and faults of my youth," Rousseau muses. "I have related the story of them with a fidelity that brings pleasure to my heart" (1953, 257).

I am flooded with memories: moments of sexual prowess and impotence, failed friendships with men, aborted affairs with women, playfully wrestling with my father, consoling my daughter's tears, suffocating sensations during worship, my eroticized passion of the Passion narrative, the pelvis as center of creativity and anxiety, the calmness of sitting meditation, my voice that never seems to find the right pitch for Christian hymns.

In my not-written confessions, I would address issues that I would not share otherwise with colleagues, friends, not even my spouse. They concern incidents of social,

*emotional, and sexual embarrassment—moments of shame where I felt powerless, vul-
nerable, and exposed.*

The writing of confessions can be pleasurable, regardless of the agon and of
the risk of public ridicule. Beyond the danger to oneself, however, there is
also a danger to others. For example, it is not uncommon for male confessants to misrepresent the other gender. Women repeatedly appear as screens
for male fantasies, as mirrors in which men see only themselves. Or women
disappear altogether in a text, especially mothers and wives. Leiris's con-
temptuous attitude toward his own body, for example, corresponds to his
"whorish" relationships with women: "the eminently inaccessible actresses,"
"the girl who bit my lips," "the girl no longer young but still pretty," "the
whore encountered one night in an American bar," "the cold, arrogant
American woman," "the submissive whore," "the girl who had become the
mistress of my accomplice"—each cartoonish portrait followed by a short
description of sexual activity, no less flattering (1992, 96–97). Women as
mirrors of the male pornographic imagination!

Rousseau's *Confessions* being an exception (numerous women are paraded
in front of the reader's eyes, frequently in relation to his erotic desire),[32]
it is in Augustine's *Confessions* that women disappear almost entirely. The
North African bishop hardly ever mentions his female lover and companion
of thirteen years, though it is she with whom he had enjoyed most of his
sexual life prior to his conversion. Just as the pleasure of sexuality is always
on the verge of vanishing in his text, so are women. Augustine suppresses
lust by banishing the objects of his lust.

Except for his mother, Monica (as legions of readers and scholars have
noticed before!): Augustine portrays her as the pious believer he wants to
become. She stands for a piety he wishes to acquire in order to make forgotten the lust he felt when associating with women as erotic partners.
While other women are presented as objects of his sexual appetite, Monica
is described as helpmate for stilling his spiritual hunger. When finally taking the vows of celibacy, Augustine exchanges his obsessively sexualized
relationship with women for a spiritually intimate relationship with his
mother. At that moment, "he does, and does not, want to see himself reflected in her eyes," as Burrus perceptively muses. "He is happiest to stand
shoulder to shoulder, peering into the still more perfect mirror of an eternal
sameness" (2004, 90). Yet Augustine will not stand shoulder to shoulder for

long—a theme to which I will return in later chapters. Mothers are mirrors, but maternal-filial "sameness" is not what a son can endure for long. It frightens him.

One of the more challenging tasks a therapist once asked me to do as a weekly exercise was contained in five simple words scribbled on a piece of paper: "Become more like your mother."

What makes Augustine's portrait of his mother so unusual is not the spiritualization of Oedipal desires but the fact that he never blames her outright for his spiritual and existential crisis. It may be for this reason that the modern reader is tempted to consider their relationship unhealthy. Blaming one's mother has become commonplace in both psychological and confessional writings, including parts of the men's movement (see May and Bohman 1997). The mythopoetic movement in particular has turned mothers, archetypal or real, into negative mirrors, accusing them for inhibiting their sons' transition from boyhood into manhood, and leaving them deeply wounded and caught in a cycle of sexual guilt and abusiveness. The son, according to the mythopoet Robert Bly, spent long months in the mother's body and "got well tuned to female frequencies." If he is not slowly "retuned" to the "older masculine body" that can revive the "wild man" within him, the young man will suffer emotional starvation. "Women cannot, no matter how much they sympathize with their starving sons, replace that particular missing substance" (Bly 1990, 94).[33]

"Sadly, I was my mother's mirror [but] my mother had not been the mirror I needed and longed for," remembers John Lee as he reflects on his dependency on his female lovers Kim and Laural. "Kim was [a mirror] whereas Laural only was to a degree. Kim showed me to me. . . . I looked into her face and saw my own" (1987, 9). When sons look into the faces of their mothers, and later lovers, they find the image of their own starving selves. In Lee's search for his "feminine soul" and "negated masculinity," women are reduced to mirrors for his wounded and narcissistic self, a mirror that his mother did not provide. A truly Kafkaesque version of male blindness: every female face is man's own.[34]

The relationship with my mother turned particularly painful during adolescence. I was furious when she, on several occasions and behind my back, disinvited girls I wanted to date. She wanted to hold the family together as a closely knit unit. Friends were welcome as long as they did not bond intimately. Then, the "intruder" would be emotionally shunned, sometimes made to leave. My mother's actions left me scarred at the time, but ultimately, she was left with the greater wound: after her children left home, she frequently fell into periods of depression.

Decades later, and only after the birth of my daughters, did I begin to fathom my mother's obsessive and desperate clinging to the image of a happy and intact family. As I am witnessing the growth of my daughters, from the diaper stage to toddlers, from their first day at school to the first driving lesson, I realize how much I see myself in them. My heart aches at the thought of them leaving my paternal embrace and worries.

One of the downsides of men pouring out intimate thoughts is the depiction of the female gender as harmful to the development of the male identity. Because strong women—feminists—have turned gender into a political issue, contemporary man "resists facing, much less sharing [his] feelings about masculinity," Gerzon claims in *A Choice of Heroes* (1982, vii; also May and Bohman 1997, 147). The danger of the intimate pleasure of revealing the male self is its latent misogynism. "The male psyche is in continual danger of being inundated by the feminine sea [like] sandy atolls in a monsoon-swept ocean," Sam Keen writes in *Fire in the Belly*, a self-help book on male spirituality with numerous confessional references. Keen detects a fragility of the male psyche that is "not psychological, not neurotic [but] an ontological fact rooted in our being" (1992, 15)—a view that parallels Augustine's anthropological anxiety around *concupiscentia*. Just as Augustine tries to contain the flood of sexual lust in order to become a spiritually virile man, Keen wants modern men, beleaguered by the "feminine sea," to become "fierce gentlemen" who "discover a peaceful form of virility" (121). In Augustine's case, all women (except his mother) are dangerous; in Keen's case, the peril stems from "ideological feminists" who continue "genderal enmity and scapegoating" (195; see also Bordo 1993, 710).

The pleasure of writing intimately about the male self compels many men to blame women for their woundedness, and it seems that they are chronically unaware of this pattern.

Anus Mundi: A Different Kind of Mirror

I have argued, with Augustine, that confessions are, for men, an important tool for self-reflection. I have also suggested that male confessiographies suffer from narcissistic fantasies, solipsistic gazing, patterns of blame and self-loathing, misrepresentations of women, and other protective and deceptive devices to facilitate a discourse on the male body. Why do men resort to such defensive operations? What are they afraid of?

A deep-seated male anxiety, I believe, is the fear of being shamed—a shaming intimately linked to anxiety about the male body. Talking about men's bodies, my body, touches on forbidden zones. Where the body is permeable, where it excretes and is open to intrusion, it is feared most. Whenever the discourse reaches these regions, heterosexual men react with fury or in silent withdrawal.

To contain these fears, normative ideologies have construed male bodies as closed, dry, and clean. The excreting body belongs to women: open, dirty, dangerous. By homophobic extension, gay male bodies are seen as equally dirty, dangerous, and perverse, and we can include in this list the racist and phantasmic physiognomies of Jewish men, black men, or colonized men. The church fathers saw the female body as "the gateway for the devil," medieval theologians perceived the liquid body as morally debased, Inquisitors feared the invisible power of witches, Victorian anxieties revolved around the *vagina dentata*, and archetypal psychology mythologized women as holes, darkness, void, water. Western culture, it seems, made a persistent effort to transfer male anxieties onto women (and feminized men) and turned the female anatomy into the antithesis of the male body. Women are fluid; men are not. *They* are dirty; *we* are not. In reality, however, the male body endowed with a mouth, ears, nose, skin, penis, and anus is as permeable and liquid as a woman's body (except for menstruation, lactation, and the fluids of childbirth).

The most shamed and shunned area of the heterosexual male body is the anus. Not surprisingly, there are only scant references to it in male confessions. The dread of feces: the anus is an opening that leads deeply into the male body, and from it "primal possessions" emerge (later, the child is taught to classify them as waste and dirt). The homophobic imagination is threatened by this opening: the anus can be penetrated, that is, subjected to sexual violation or same-sex erotic pleasure. In a heterosexual culture, nothing seems farther removed from spiritual significance than this part of the male anatomy (see Krondorfer 2007b).

A well-known joke: One day, the different body parts have an argument about who should be in charge. When the brain, eyes, hands, legs, and the stomach all claim this honor for themselves, the rectum raises its voice and says, "I should be in charge." When, in consternation, the other parts protest, the rectum closes up. Soon, the legs turn wobbly, the stomach queasy, the hands shaky, the eyes watery, and the brain cloudy. Now they all beg the rectum to be in charge. The moral of the story? To be important, you just have to be an arse.

I read this joke as a secular version of Paul's letter to the Corinthians (1 Cor. 12:12–26), where the apostle argues that the more unseemly the body part, the higher the respect it deserves. However socially unseemly, all body parts make up the Christian community, which is envisioned as the body of Christ in its fullness.

Paul called the body "a temple of the Holy Spirit" (1 Cor. 6:19). Yet, claiming the anus as part of God's sanctuary borders on blasphemy. Tom Driver "felt a bit dirty, perhaps subversive of worship" when he made the discovery "that to hit and sustain a high note while singing hymns in church, it helped if he relaxed the anus" (1977, 24). The Gnostic Valentinus went so far as to fancy Jesus' perfectly continent body as unable to defecate (see Meeks 1993, 137). Martin Luther, whose bawdy language counters some of Christianity's pietism, used anal imagery predominantly as a weapon against the devil: "Note this down," he warned the devil, "I have shit in the pants, and you can hang them around your neck and wipe your mouth with it" (quoted in Erikson 1962, 244). The place where a male body dirties itself is profane, obscene, dangerous, and untouchable.

A few men have dared thinking about God and the anus in the same breath, among them C. G. Jung, who confesses to his boyhood fantasy of a defecating God. At the age of eleven years, he underwent psychological and mental torments before he allowed himself to envision God's anal processes and, as a result, to experience "unutterable bliss." One day on his way back from school and suddenly overwhelmed by the sight of the cathedral's roof glittering in the sun, he had these thoughts:

> "The world is beautiful and the church is beautiful, and God made all this and sits above it far away in the blue sky on a golden throne and . . ." Here came a great hole in my thoughts, and a choking sensation. . . . I kept repeating to myself: "Don't think of it, just don't think of it!" I reached home in a pretty worked-up state. My mother noticed that something was wrong . . . [and] I did have the thought that it might help me if I could confess to my mother the real reason for my turmoil. But to do so I would have to do the very thing that seemed impossible: think my thought right to the end. . . . I gathered all my courage, as though I were about to leap forthwith into hell-fire, and let the thought come. I saw before me the cathedral, the blue sky. God sits on His golden throne, high above the world—and from under the throne an enormous turd falls upon the sparkling new roof, shatters it, and breaks the walls of the cathedral asunder.
>
> So that was it! I felt an enormous, an indescribable relief. Instead of the expected damnation, grace had come upon me. (Jung 1973, 36–39)

God's turd as a moment of grace? Does Jung's fantasy offer the seed for a spirituality that is based on embodied experience rather than transcendent principles? Jung's story is only a child's daydream. Grace occurs at the climax of a boy's inner turmoil and not as the result of a man's experience with his mature body. Adult, heterosexual men seem to have trouble relating to their anuses privately and publicly. Today, the medical screening for prostate cancer is one of the few occasions when "public access" is granted.

A Catholic Korean male student once related a dream in my course on religion and psychology. "A family type of dream: My sister was arguing with my wife, as usual. My sister said that my wife is not doing her best to me, as a husband. I was sitting on a toilet, not in the bathroom, but inside a church. I could hear my mother praying to the cross, outside of the church. I felt strongly that I wanted to say or ask something to my sister. But I was very ashamed of being in the church with a naked body."

Women, mother, church, defecation, nakedness, shame—the dream elements reveal a conflicted male identity. The public sharing of this dream rendered the students in my class speechless, and it shamed the dreamer into silence. There was no relief.

Why do anal processes either shame us into silence or become objects of dirty jokes? Children experience pleasure when noticing their first prized possessions. Why do adults not exhibit the same awe? Is it because the anal pleasures of infants are predivine, that is, they are experienced prior to experiencing God, and hence unworthy of mature theological consideration? Is shit too "human"? Milan Kundera may be correct when he writes, "I, a child, grasped the incompatibility of God and shit. . . . Either man was created in God's image—and God has intestines!—or God lacks intestines and man is not like Him" (1984, 245). The biblical conception of man being created in God's image has spurred the religious imagination, from Michelangelo's bearded Father-God to *God's Phallus*, the title of Eilberg-Schwartz's book on the displaced homoeroticized love between Jewish men/Israel and God (1994). Why not, then, imagine a defecating God? "Shit is a more onerous theological problem than is evil," Kundera writes, because man is able to "accept the idea that He is not responsible for man's crimes. The responsibility for shit, however, rests entirely with Him, the Creator of man" (1984, 246; also Carrigan 1991).

To declare God responsible for shit, as Kundera suggests, assumes, of course, an overly naturalistic understanding of God's metaphoric possibilities. The crux, it seems to me, instead lies in the theological bracketing of feces. Shit is putrid matter and as such the opposite of the *logos*, the word. As a bodily waste product it must be kept strictly separated from theology. Defecation cannot be permitted into consciousness because the closed and clean male body is believed to transcend matter. Shit destroys the illusion of the closed male body. What passes the anus smells of decay and mortality, and that is exactly what heterosexual men wish to overcome in their confessional writings. Words are written for eternity; feces decompose quickly. Writing immortalizes; defecating does not.[35] Are men afraid of becoming arrested in the anal phase when imagining the spiritual possibilities of the rectum? Are they afraid of becoming identified with a primal bodily product in which they see no redemption?

James Broughton's *The Androgyne Journal* (1977) is one of those rare confessional texts that explores the compatibility of spiritual and anal experiences. It is a record of Broughton's erotic explorations of divine energies flowing through his androgynous body. Despite some occasional references to Christian symbolism and childhood memories, the bulk of the five-week-long journal concerns Broughton's mature body interacting with a pagan religious imagination. For example, on June 24, his first day in an old wooden cabin near Mendocino, California, he is visited by a woman spirit at night who encourages him to pursue pleasure without shame. "What is your name? I asked her. Are you Andromeda? Annabel Lee? Anima Mundi?" (1977, 10). Step by step, Broughton discovers that to be ashamed of the shameful parts of the male body (nipples, phallus, anus) is wrong. On July 31, near the end of his stay in Mendocino, he sleeps with Mother Earth and reaches an orgiastic peak: "I dug the hole deep, and thrust my penis in. . . . I felt like some sacrificing hero of antiquity. I thought of Sky Father cohabiting Earth Mother to create the world" (67–68).

I respect Broughton's remarkable candidness, though I can't say I like it. He genuinely attempts to treat the male body not as a muscular, clean, iron entity but as an erotic, fluid, and vulnerable organism. His self-exposures touch areas of my own shame, and—though they embarrass and, at times, even repulse me—they make me aware of my own repressiveness.

His journal irritates me for another reason. I become witness to yet another male confession centered on the male, solitary ego: a man gazing at his body as he pleasures it/himself, cut off from responsibilities to others.

The Androgyne Journal is the record of a solitary journey of a modern-day, pagan ascetic. The spiritual adventures of the early Christian desert fathers are replaced by the erotic explorations of a juicy hermaphrodite, the dry male body replaced by an excreting queer body. What Broughton has in common with the early Christian ascetics, though, is solitude. He does not need the presence of other human beings for his erotic-spiritual quest because his androgynous body is self-sufficient: a pair of nipples and a functioning penis are all that is required.

> I could feel the enticing Venus in me. . . . I could make love to her visible bloom till she squirmed and stretched in delight. Then I could be she loving the king in me . . . till he ripened and towered in desire. Finally, it was the royal pair in mutual adoring play, breast and phallus in equally passionate caress. (51)

"Shame is no longer possible [because] my sex is part of the divine whole," Broughton writes on the day he reconciles his genitals with spirituality (46).

A few days later, he becomes aware of his "neglected backside." In a dream, he paints with "symbolic shit," then sets out to paint with real shit. He learns a new, universal truth: "When all colors are blended, the result is the color of shit. Is this what the spectrum of solar light ultimately boils down to? Is the color of Oneness, then, the color of shit?" As he further explores anal processes, he devotes a prayer to shit ("My Lord Sun, teach me how to accept this"); wonders whether he would have the courage to eat it ("a ritual act to acknowledge and experience the end as a beginning"); and, finally, observes and worships a "shit-colored gastropod worm," which he imagines to be a creation of his bowel movement and his earlier union with Mother Earth (53–55, 69–74).

Like other male confessants before him, Broughton takes the risk of being ridiculed. He opens himself up to new bodily possibilities of spirituality. More than any other confessiographic text I have come across, *The Androgyne Journal* removes the theological brackets around feces and puts excrement in the center of an embodied spirituality.

What is disturbing, though, is Broughton's masturbatory narcissism. The (male) androgynous body is nipple and phallus, male and female, Hermes and Venus. Similarly, anal processes are beginning and end, creation and death. "Man, if he but knew himself, is the most sacred edifice on earth. For he contains all the gods and goddesses" (57). In contrast to Augustine's enigma of the embodied self, of never fully knowing oneself outside of God, Broughton solves the anxiety by incorporating God and Goddess into his body. The male body is a self-pleasurable unit, a self-contained cosmos.

The mature man faces his *faeces* and sees nothing short of an entire universe. The male anus as *anus mundi*, a mirror of majestic proportions! Under the male gaze, even fecal matter can turn into spirit.

Closed Bodies, Fixed Eyes

Luther once wrote that God smiles at the father who "goes ahead and washes diapers or performs some other mean task for his child" (1962, 40). Although Luther used this example to emphasize the importance of faith rather than a father's duty to change diapers, the statement points to an issue that is missing in many male confessiographies: the value of relationality. Monadlike, the male self views itself as independent of the web of mutually dependent relations and sees itself mirrored in whatever direction it chooses to look. The male confessant gazes at his body, his lovers, his mother, his gods, and his feces and sees but a universe that is a reflection of himself.

The perception of the male body as a closed body is part of this solipsistic operation. The male body is closed anatomically (dry and clean) as well as relationally (not dependent on others). As a self-sufficient universe, the closed male body is not part of a web of relationships but remains arrested in narcissistic awe. It is not responsible to others. A body that is perceived as not excreting and smelling cannot relate to other excreting and smelling bodies. It is no accident that almost all menial tasks that have to do with the cleaning of bodies are done by women or by colonized and otherwise disempowered men: changing the diapers of babies, nursing the putrefying wounds of the sick, wiping the bottoms of the old, cleaning toilets. The closed, male, normative, heterosexual body does not consider as its primary task the nurturing of those bodies on a daily basis or the removal of the smells of age, sickness, and death.

"Go to any landfill," Sam Keen suggests, "and see the mountain of disposable diapers . . . and it will be obvious that womankind is as compulsive a consumer as mankind" (1992, 197). Laying the responsibility for soiled diapers and the blame for a spoiled environment on the laps of mothers, the male body remains clean and virtuous. It also remains an irresponsible and uncaring body.

A closed body isolates and imprisons man, drying him up spiritually.

I admit that until the birth of my daughters, the prospect of wiping, washing, and nursing other bodies on a daily basis would have frightened me. Only in lovemaking with my intimate partner or in improvisational dance did I experience my body as open and fluid and, at the same time, related to others. Occasionally, my dancing body—a body healthy and able to move—took me to spiritual peaks. I enjoyed the unspoken privilege of not having to think about bodies that cannot move, that spill their fluids uncontrollably, and that require the patient care of others. Would such bodies spiritually enrapture me?

During the birth of my daughters, I supported my wife's back and shoulders, watching the little heads push their way out, blood and fluids gushing forth. When cutting the moist umbilical cord, I felt connected to something larger than myself—a muddled but ecstatic and deeply satisfying experience that I can only call spiritual. Later, when

changing diapers, I felt a similar physical and spiritual sensation of connectedness.
Cleaning my daughters, I was neither disgusted and ashamed nor tempted to worship
anal processes. Occasionally, I was impatient and annoyed by the smell. But more than
anything, I experienced the cleaning as an intimate, humbling, and bonding act of love.

Whether Augustine washed diapers, we do not know. It seems that Augustine was not privy to such a relationship with his son—or, if he was, he kept it hidden from the reader. This is an issue to which I will return in a later chapter. I mention it here only because it illustrates Augustine's apparent inability to (or resistance to) admit shared intimacies with significant others. His unnamed lover and his child hardly receive mention in the *Confessions*. To gain a close bond to God, Augustine is ready to pay the price of abandoning earthly intimacies. Consequently, his loved ones disappear in the text and thus from public view. For contemporary men, who, "beyond patriarchy,"[36] wish to bond physically and emotionally with intimate others, Augustine's *Confessions* are, in this regard, a dimly lit mirror. Reading the *Confessions* would not set postpatriarchal men on fire but make them burn in agony.

This, of course, is our problem, not Augustine's. His ideal sympathetic reader, to whom he addresses himself, would understand that his *Confessions* are a mirror with both depth and horizon. Looking backward and inward, men would recognize the vanity of their earthly strife; looking outward and forward, men would acknowledge God as a promise transporting them beyond their own confines. Only the man caught in the mirror's surface, imprisoned to his mirrored likeness, would remain truly unredeemed. Such a man does not seek transcendence—like Leiris, who wishes "to keep my eyes fixed on myself instead of turning them beyond and transcending myself" (1992, 156). Augustine held up the *Confessions* as a mirror to man's vainglory while, at the same time, offering a model for transcending male vanities.

Once Augustine pushes the narrative beyond the description of his past iniquities and beyond his conversion experience, he is eager to explain that the act of confessing is an ongoing process. Even a spiritually reborn man cannot pat himself on the back in a self-congratulating gesture. Men must continue the process of public confession even after a spiritual transformation: "The profit derived from *confessing my past* I have seen and spoken about. But *what I now am* at this time when I am writing my confessions many wish to know, both those who know me and those who do not but have heard something from me or about me; their ear is not attuned to my heart at the point where I am whatever I am" (10.3.4; emphasis added). After acquiring episcopal authority, Augustine continues to scrutinize his motivations. He has taken the vows of celibacy but *now* struggles with erotic memories; he has renounced the pleasures of food but *now* puzzles over the slippery slope between biologically necessary nourishment and luxurious appetite; he has embraced humility but *still* struggles with the temptation of vainglory.

Augustine never declares himself free of temptation since no man is ever fully in control of himself. Man needs God to gain perspective on himself. A confession does not make men perfect but makes them realize that they are flawed and finite creatures in need of divine mercy. This is the message Augustine would like other men to hear. Therefore, continuous self-disclosure as an act of public testimony is, for him, always beneficial.

When I am confessing not what I was but what I am now, the benefit lies in this: I am making this confession not only before you with a secret exaltation and fear and with a secret grief touched by hope, but also in the ears of believing sons of men, sharers in my joy, conjoined with me in mortality, my fellow citizens and pilgrims, some who have gone before, some who follow after, and some who are my companions in this life. (10.4.6)

INTERLUDE *On Testimony*

Confessional writing is a gendered activity. It is an attempt at giving testimony to oneself and (imagined) others, an act of becoming a public witness to one's intimate self. Etymologically, the act of bearing witness is linked to the male sexual anatomy: "testifying" and "testicles" have a common root in the Latin *testis* (witness). Although contested by some scholars, this linkage points—beyond a homophonic similarity—to a strong cultural-semantic connection "between testicles and solemn declarations" (Katz 1998, 191).[1] In a more literal sense, testicles witness male sexual intercourse, virility, and fertility. Transferred to the ritual realm, testicles have assumed a legal function across different cultures. In ancient Greece, for example, "testicles of ritually slaughtered animals" were employed in deciding homicide trials (194). The Torah attests to a similar ritualized legal power of testicles when Abraham demands that his servant take an oath to protect Isaac's lineage: "Put your hand under my thigh [Hebrew, *yarek*], and I will make you swear by the Lord" (Gen. 24:2–3), a ritual gesture that is later repeated between Jacob and his son Joseph (Gen. 47:29). Taking an oath while grabbing the male organ (*yarek*) secures loyalty and patrilineal continuity.[2]

Confessional writings testify to various levels of prowess and impotence of the male subject. As a solemn declaration, they are most persuasive and effective when the confessant successfully conveys to the reader the sincerity of the oath he has taken: "to lay bare one's heart, to write that book about oneself in which the concern for sincerity would be carried to such length that . . . 'the paper would shrivel and flare at each touch of his fiery pen'" (Leiris 1992, 158). There is a fierce energy in the act of confessing—dangerous and seductive. "To expose myself to others," Leiris continues, "was an attempt to seduce my public to be indulgent" (156). At the same time, the male confessant fears his impotence. Socially and sexually frustrated, Leiris threatens to castrate himself (137, 142). A "slight strain in one testicle," he writes, caused him a "sense of impotence" and rendered impossible "any sexual relation with women" (132).

Confessiographies are gendered documents in yet another sense. Although women often engage in autobiographical writing and are, according to Hogan (1991), specifically drawn to the diary, the distinctive quality of confessiographies attracts men.[3] Writing a confession is a relatively safe way of testifying, of making public what before was private, of admitting vulnerabilities and personal flaws, and of acknowledging old sins, wrongdoings, or errors of judgment. What makes it safe is that no other voice can interrupt the flow of the introspective and retrospective construction and interpretation of the male self. What is shared with the public in a self-disclosing process is the meaning the narrator attaches to lived experiences of the past. Those experiences are recounted in order to indicate to the imagined audience—Augustine's "sympathetic reader" (10.4.5)—that the present narrator is no longer identical with the person he used to be or with the choices he once made. The distance created between the confessant's present and past selves grants him a certain degree of immunity. By relying on the preemptory operation of subtle or overt self-accusation, the writer avoids public accusations for his sins committed in the past. "Autohumiliation," Jackson writes, is a "strategy of self-preservation" because "self-mockery aims at reducing the mockers to silence" (1992, 81). The confessant is thus free to seek some understanding and, perhaps, compassion from the reader. "Every confession contains a desire to be absolved," Leiris remarks in his 1946 preface to *Manhood* (1992, 156). The one who confesses "pleads to be forgiven, condoned, even condemned, so long as he is brought back into the wholeness of people and of things" (Spender 1980, 120).

Testis: circumambulating, circumscribing, and circumfessing a seduction that is both feared and desired.

CHAPTER 3

Non-absent Bodies and Moral Agency

Confessions of an African Bishop
and a Jewish Ghetto Policeman

In confessiographies, the male writer establishes a narrative background about already-lived experiences against which he, as present narrator, wishes to be judged and forgiven. Françoise Lionnet speaks of "the dual nature of narrator (the converted self) and protagonist (the sinning self)" (1989, 43).[1] Such doubling and mirroring of the confessant's role demand from the reader particular identifications. Although the popular appeal of a confessional text might lie predominantly in the sinning self, in the end the reader is supposed to side with the converted self and forgive the old self.[2] Hence, confessional texts come with an implicit moral expectation, which a sympathetic reader would willingly accept. "Even the most shamelessly revealed inner life pleads its cause before the moral system of an outer objective life" (Spender 1980, 120).[3]

A moral structure underlies confessiographies. This is true with respect to the narrator, who implicitly claims that his remorseful introspection grants him a new place in society and renews his moral authority, and it is equally true with respect to the reader who is seduced into believing the truthfulness of the narrator's self-disclosure and the authenticity of his conversion. Given such implied morality, it is important to ask about the confessant's subjectivity and moral agency: Does he take on responsibility for his past deeds, or does he employ rhetorical devices that make his failures invisible? In his written testimony, does he perceive himself to be the actor of his life or just a plaything of God and fate? Does he presume male privileges, or does he resist normative expectations? This chapter will argue that the issue of moral agency is intricately linked to the representation of the male body. By juxtaposing the texts of two very different men, Augustine and Calel Perechodnik, it will make an argument about the textual disappearance of male bodies, namely, that the *non-absence* of male bodies in male confessiographies hides moral agency.

Perechodnik and Augustine

Given the focus on perceiving the male self as being capable of asserting a new identity after acknowledging past sins, it is not surprising that confessional writings have been variously praised or criticized as primarily a Christian and Western phenomenon.[4] To assume that men can "turn around" is at the heart of the Christian concept of *metanoia* (repentance) but also present in the Jewish notion of repentance (*teshuva*, lit., "returning"). Men return, rethink, reassemble, and reconstitute the self in accordance with a newly ascertained set of (moral) standards. Such a process of introspection presumes a particular relation between an autonomous self and a telos in history. The male self, capable of obtaining self-knowledge by abstracting from previous experiences, strives toward acting coherently in history, a history that moves toward the fulfillment of a grander or divine design. The Latin root of *confession* already points to these aspects of self-assertion and transcendence: *confiteri* is "not only to admit sins but to praise God" (Asher 1998, 230); it is "affirming speech" (O'Donnell 2005, 218).

Augustine's *Confessions* serve as a perfect example of this literary genre.[5] The North African bishop reflects on intimate details of his life not with the intention of pleasing the audience with profane distractions but with directing their attention to God (thus, the *Confessions* contain, to the dismay of many modern readers, lengthy segments of prayers and praise to God). As an "*architexte* of Western autobiography" (Lionnet 1989, 37, 42), Augustine's self-revelations exemplify the nondivisible task of *confessio peccati* (confession of sins) and *confessio fidei et laudis* (affirmation of faith and songs of praise).[6] "Let me confess," Augustine writes, "what I know of myself. Let me confess too what I do not know about myself. For what I know of myself

I know because you [God] grant me light" (10.5.7). God, who provides an external perspective, is also imagined as Augustine's prime reader.

The twentieth-century testament of Calel Perechodnik, *Am I a Murderer? Testament of a Jewish Ghetto Policeman* (1996), seems to have little in common with this literary tradition of confessions. In the face of impending death, Perechodnik finishes his writing in his hiding place in the Gentile section of Warsaw on August 19, 1943. Given this context, it would seem more reasonable to place his work, which Perechodnik himself had titled "A History of a Jewish Family During German Occupation," among the archival and published body of Holocaust diaries, testimonies, and memoirs rather than in the company of Augustine's *Confessions*.[7] Yet his writing does not easily fit the style of other personal and "factually insistent" (Young 1988, 15) narratives of the Holocaust.[8] Though Perechodnik sees himself, like other Jewish writers during and after the Shoah, as a witness who must recount the horrors so that they will not be forgotten, he is not primarily concerned about chronicling his life or the events around him. Rather, he feels compelled to write because he wants to understand himself. He wants to understand why—after his ordinary life had been ruptured by the Nazi occupation of his Polish town—he had "entered the ranks of the Ghetto Polizei" (1996, 9) and thus become an accomplice to the murderous policy of the Germans. "If I believed in God," Perechodnik writes, "I wouldn't have written this [book] at all" (xxi). In contrast to the African bishop, the Jewish ghetto policeman cannot establish a divine perspective: the imagined prime reader is not God but his wife, who is, when Perechodnik begins his retrospective diary, already dead.

I am a reader neither Augustine nor Perechodnik could have foreseen. Augustine pleaded with God and a male Christian audience in the Roman Empire; Perechodnik pleaded with his (dead) wife and the "democratic nations" (1996, 155) to take revenge on the Germans. The perspective I bring to their confessions is that of a man who was raised Christian in postwar Germany. Augustine stimulates mostly my intellectual curiosity (contrary to what he, as a rhetorician, had hoped to accomplish, namely, to affect my heart), whereas Perechodnik affects me emotionally and morally (though he wishes Germans to be destroyed). When I first read Am I a Murderer? *I felt the immediate urge to respond, first, by telling friends and colleagues about the book and, later, by*

wanting to respond in writing: to express in language the sorrow I felt; to write against my tears.

Perechodnik variously refers to his manuscript as a memoir, a diary, an eternal monument to his wife, a dead fetus, or a second child (1996, 189, 191, 192, 202). But above all, he calls it his deathbed confession. Hence, he is—despite the strong Christian hold on the confessional tradition—writing as a Jew from within Jewish culture. Michah Yosef Berdichevsky, a fin de siècle East European writer and critic, notes for example: "For the most part, Judaism only knows of the *death-bed confessional*: Put your house in order, for you are on the point of expiration! . . . Confession is the breaking of the heart and the reckoning of man with his heart and soul" (emphasis added).[9]

> This is a confession about my lifetime, a sincere and true confession. Alas, I don't believe in divine absolution, and as far as others are concerned, only my wife could—although she shouldn't—absolve me. However, she is no longer among the living. She was killed as a result of German barbarity, and, to a considerable extent, on account of my recklessness. Please consider this memoir to be my deathbed confession. (Perechodnik 1996, xxi)

Perechodnik presents a painfully honest account of what he perceives as his moral failures: his failure to grasp the extent of the German deception of the Jewish people and of the Nazi will to annihilate them; his failure to have courage and foresight; and most important, his failure to protect his wife and daughter from being transported to Treblinka. "There is nothing quite like this in the history of confessions," writes Frank Fox in the introduction to *Am I a Murderer?* "This is not Saint Augustine troubled by his own salvation or Jean-Jacques Rousseau remembering a childhood peccadillo. This is a twentieth-century man bereft of all beliefs, shorn of all human relationships, who begs to be understood even as he confounds us" (1996, x).

Most confounding are the events on August 19, 1942, the day of the *Aktion*, the German euphemism for the liquidation of the ghetto of Otwock. During the *Aktion*, Perechodnik—as part of the Jewish police force—helped to guard the remaining Jewish inhabitants as they were waiting for deportation, his wife, Anna (Anka), and daughter, Athalie (Aluska), among them. Ironically, they were shipped to their death on Aluska's second birthday. Exactly a year later, he finishes the last page of his confessional writing: "Today, August 19 [1943], is the day of my wife's Golgotha. . . . These diaries—

although I wrote in the preface that they should be considered as a deathbed confession—are basically an account placed before You [Anka] on the anniversary of Your death" (1996, 196, 191).

During the eighteen months of his job as ghetto policeman prior to the *Aktion*, Perechodnik comes across as lethargic and cynical (in his own words, "naïve" and "fatalistic" [1996, 14, 191]); after the *Aktion* he is filled with despair, rage, and self-loathing, despite the fact that he sometimes describes himself as being "without feeling about everything" after the loss of his "dearest beings, my wife and daughter" (110).

The events on August 19 offer a key to understanding what drives Perechodnik to write his confessions in his hiding place: guilt, shame, and anger urge him on as much as his despair over having to admit only the most trivial reasons for his choices and behavior as ghetto policeman. "They tell us to load the remaining people into cattle cars," Calel writes about the last hours of the *Aktion*. "O cursed Germans! How wise you are! How quickly we become the obedient marionettes in your hands! We work briskly; the demon of revolt no longer dominates us, not even a feeling of pity for the remaining Jews" (1996, 44). Later, already imprisoned in a labor camp, he asks himself: "Was this the result of a heart turned to stone or a sign of a bad character?" (114).

In contrast to Augustine, who pleads with God (and the reader) for forgiveness of his previous bad judgment and moral failures ("I do not blush, Lord God, to confess your mercies to me and to call upon you. . . . You are present, liberating us from miserable errors" [4.16.31, 6.16.26]), Perechodnik pleads with his wife for forgiveness, a theme that runs throughout his manuscript. He longs for but feels undeserving of his wife's forgiveness—just as Augustine feels toward God. "Am I a murderer, my wife's executioner?" he asks after the *Aktion* (1996, 54), and the concluding sentence of his confession spells it out one last time: "Anetka, have You really forgiven me?" (194).[10]

The Non-absent Male Body

A question may be legitimately asked at this point: What do the confessions of a fourth-century Christian bishop of Roman Africa have to do with the testament of a twentieth-century Polish Jew who died in the Holocaust? From a strictly historical perspective, very little. But as a contemporary reader I was immediately struck by common themes that run through the confessional narratives of these two men. Both contain a sense of revelation (with its core meaning of a dramatic disclosure of something previously not realized). Augustine acknowledges his previous errors of judgment in light of his discovery of the power of a transcendent God, whereas Perechodnik realizes his errors of judgment as his life is increasingly confined by the ubiquitous presence of Nazi genocidal antisemitism. Within these frames, both men report and reflect in personal terms on issues of choice and control, morality and faith, guilt and forgiveness, hope and despair, human failure and the (im)possibility of redemption, and on their relationships to their parents, spouses, children, lovers, friends, adversaries, and God.

Augustine's and Perechodnik's responses to the circumstances of their lives that compel them to write are radically different; yet in their dissimilarity, they are, like mirror images, linked to each other. Whereas Augustine's *Confessions* portray a deliberate spiritual search, in which the body is seen as an obstacle to Christian salvation, Perechodnik's deathbed confession tells of forced flights and escapes, in which the Jewish body is the prime target of destruction.

Whereas the *Confessions* are a narrative of (relative) success, in which the self evolves spiritually through the classical stages of death of the old self, conversion, and rebirth (see Lionnet 1989, 50), the ghetto policeman's testament is a narrative of failure, a modern document of unmaking, of the destruction of the self as an inferior other. Perechodnik can never quite free himself from seeing himself through the eyes of Nazi ideology: in his self-loathing condition, he is colonized by the racist views of the occupiers, literally becoming the other to himself. In Augustine's case, God is the Other: his voluntary submission to God's will triumphs over the desire for bodily pleasures and creates a spiritually reborn, Christian man. In Perechodnik's case, the political will of the Nazis to annihilate European Jews triumphs over the increasingly desperate attempts to keep a Jewish body alive.

Even though I wish to explore the remarkable parallelism between Perechodnik's testament and Augustine's Confessions, *I am aware of conflicting motives: to assess cognitively what had touched me deeply (speaking as husband and father); to venture a comparison between a spiritual confession and a Holocaust narrative (speaking in the prosaic voice of a religious studies scholar and as a Gentile born and raised in Germany); to problematize the discourse on the male body in men's confessiographies (employing the language of a male cultural critic). While I want to convey that the*

self-presentations of Augustine and Perechodnik are relevant to men's experiences today,
I also want to stay alert to the danger that academic writing about the male subject
can easily become a "device of self-distanc[ing]" rather than "self-touching," as feminist
autobiographical criticism has suggested.[11] *I want to stay in touch with my roles as*
man, father, and scholar.

The body plays a key role in the writings of Augustine and Perechodnik. For the former, the issue is desire; for the latter, survival. But the body is not really present, since both men assume a facticity about their body that prevents them from seeing it as gendered. This gender blindness makes their bodies neither fully present nor fully absent. The male body is not absent in their confessional texts but is also not consciously claimed as a gendered body. The failure to grasp the gendered condition of the body robs both confessants of the opportunity to take full advantage of the confessional form. Ideally, confessions could provide men with a safe medium in which to reflect critically and contextually on the following: first, their former perceptions of their gendered body (the making); second, on their determination to change their attitudes toward the body (the unmaking; or, in traditional terms, the act of acknowledging past sins); and third, on their envisioned restoration of the body (the remaking).[12] The confessional discourse on the male body, however, rarely takes its own genderedness into account. Male confessional writings have portrayed male bodies in various ways—as a battlefield of opposing desires, a measure of gauging one's progress over the old self, an object unrelated to one's true self, a manifestation of men's difference from women, or a mirror of one's mental and spiritual condition—but the *body* of the heterosexual male confessant is usually not subjected to critical inquiry.[13] Because it has been viewed for so long as the normative body, its dependence on cultural assumptions, which flow into the making, unmaking, and remaking of the male body, remains obscured.

In light of such gender obliviousness in confessiographies, I suggest that we speak of the *non-absence* of the male body (rather than its presence or its absence). Although the male body is always *in* the text, it is *not present* in the text as a consciously gendered body. It is not even an "absent presence," a concept evoked and explored, for example, in monuments that commemorate people effaced and eliminated in (genocidal) violence. An "absent presence" assumes a consciousness about that which is absent—and especially artists working with the difficulty of material representations of the Holocaust have explored this concept through voids, negative spaces, fading imprints, and melancholic acts of material disappearance (see Young 2000; Apel 2002; Morris 2003). In contrast, the term "non-absence" does not even assume awareness of what is present but not represented. Rather, it points to the narrator's obliviousness to the present void. A non-absent male body is the confessant's obliviousness toward the gendered body's *material reality* (which follows its own set of rules) as well as his blindness to the gendered body's *textual reality* with its own discursive organization.

By speaking of the non-absent male body, I wish to introduce an analytical category to make visible anew the male body in confessional texts. A non-absent male body, I hope to demonstrate, deflects attention from the male confessant as moral agent and gendered subject. To speak of the non-absent body requires reading between and against a confessant's intentional textual disclosures. Miles articulates the dual obligation of critical reading in her study on Augustine's *Confessions*: to be both an "obedient reader" who "endeavor[s] to grasp what [the author] worked to communicate" and a "disobedient reader" who "highlights features . . . considered accidental or incidental to his self-revelation" (1992, 11).

Augustine's *Confessions* illustrate well the non-absence of the male body.[14] Although the body is constantly referred to as the locus of false pleasures that prevent a Christian man from finding true happiness in God, Augustine does not problematize his body and embodied self as a product of gendered desires and expectations. In order to understand such obliviousness, we first need to understand Augustine's view of the human condition after the fall, the postlapsarian condition.

What the *Confessions* implicitly assume is that the postlapsarian male body "naturally" expresses certain desires, which are, interestingly, neither culturally nor metaphysically determined. Desires are neither a product of culture nor of God's original good creation but the result of Adam and Eve's original sin. Because a body in the state of original sin depends on (and hence "desires") what is necessary (hence "natural") for the physical survival of the human race, man left to his own devices is unable to suppress entirely his carnal appetites (food, sex, power, beauty). The male body naturally seeks pleasure in food and sexuality, because they are necessary for survival; the same body seeks power and beauty, because they seem essential to (man's) life. "We restore the daily decay of the body by eating and drinking," Augustine writes about the biological dependence on food, "[b]ut at the present time the necessity of food is sweet to me, and against that sweetness I fight" (10.31.43). With regard to power and beauty, these delights are biologically nonessential but provide pleasures that are as addictive as food and sex. "To entrap the eyes men have made innumerable additions to the various arts and crafts in clothing, shoes, vessels, and manufactures of this nature, pictures, images of various kinds, and things which go far beyond necessary and moderate requirements and pious symbols" (10.34.53).[15]

Augustine, who distinguishes between pleasure derived from biological necessity (food, sexuality) and pleasures dependent on cultural variations (power, beauty),[16] considers these drives not to be part of original creation but interprets them as inevitable restrictions placed on the freedom of humans after the Fall. Just as humans cannot undo original sin and return to a state of innocence by their own will, man cannot overcome his carnal desires without God's mercy. What men can do, however, is commit themselves to struggle against desire, thus preparing the ground for a spiritual rebirth that brings them closer to God. Ultimately, salvation is dependent on God's mercy.

Augustine exemplifies humanity's bleak condition by pointing to the problem of nightly emissions, a physical activity that serves as sign and reminder of original sin.[17] Although nightly emissions are indisputably an issue of male anatomy and sexuality, Augustine presents it as a universalized sign—a telling example of what I call a non-absent male body. At the same time, Augustine is revealingly frank about his own flesh. He admits that he fails to control, even as celibate bishop, the "sensual images" in his dreams, which cause involuntary emissions. He bemoans this dilemma in Book 10 (the first of what some critics have called the "nonautobiographical" books of the *Confessions*).[18] There he no longer writes retrospectively about the sinful self but as present narrator about the converted self. "I have now declared to my good Lord what is still my present condition in respect to this kind of evil [i.e., nightly emissions]. . . . I hope that you will perfect in me your mercies to achieve perfect peace" (10.30.42). Man can control his body only up to a certain degree, and it is up to God to change this recalcitrant imperfection of man's postlapsarian, carnal nature.

By the time my students at a public, liberal arts college reach this passage in the Confessions, *many are frustrated by Augustine's overly conscientious and zealous*

self-scrutiny. They read his confessional statement about nocturnal emissions as one more sign of a guilt-ridden personality, and they frequently advise him postmortem to "get a life."

I, however, find it quite astounding for a man of his episcopal stature to write so intimately about his body. He could have easily remained silent on this point, for no witness could have proven him wrong. Although the spilling of semen is put into the purposeful context of lamenting the lack of control over his sexual organ, he still makes his bodily fluids part of a public discourse on spirituality and is, in this regard, more daring than many modern men, myself included.

As an obedient reader, one can follow Augustine's lead and consent to the ultimate disappearance of the body as it is intended in his confessional project. Just as the *Confessions* aim at the ego's self-effacement in light of God's power and grace (see Asher 1998), Augustine would like to see his body vanish, since it is the body that keeps reminding him of the unredeemed condition of humanity. His body, however, never leaves him. He will have to live with it until the final moment of release from this bondage, the moment of death. Precisely this moment escapes the grasp of all autobiographers. "The total communion with God," Lionnet writes, "can only be achieved at a point and time outside of autobiography, that is, in *death*" (1989, 44; emphasis in original; also Folkenflik 1993, 15). Paradoxically, Augustine tries to persuade his audience of the insignificance of the male body/self by revealing in detail intimate fragments of his embodied self; by doing so, he writes himself into history and, unbeknownst to him, into the Western canon, thus immortalizing his battles with carnality.

A disobedient reading of Augustine's text would reveal more than just an eschatological yearning for a time beyond the soul's earthly imprisonment in a body. Instead, we would notice the non-absent male body at places where Augustine does not want us to see it. Feminist criticism has repeatedly pointed out that Augustine's suppressed male desire reappears, positively, in the form of maternal language about God and, negatively, in the form of a fictive construct of "woman."[19] "What am I but an infant sucking your milk and feeding on you, the food that is incorruptible?" Augustine wonders, imagining not his mother but a nurturing God (4.1.1). But women, with the exception of his mother, cannot be part of his spiritual rebirth, and Augustine's female partner and lover of thirteen years (about whom the reader learns little in the *Confessions*) is but one of the victims of a confessional discourse that is not consciously gendered.

Ironically, the male body is non-absent even when its biological maleness appears to be most present. When, for example, Augustine voices his displeasure over the nocturnal spilling of semen, he describes an activity limited to the male body. Yet he will jump to abstract theological conclusions—a rhetorical operation that is possible only because he presumes the male body to be normative. Rather than examine nocturnal emission as a specific male issue that may require gender-specific responses, Augustine turns it into a generic human predicament that will lead him to articulate the concept of original sin. Not to reflect on the body as a *male* body privileges the male experience as normative, and such neglect has social consequences for gender relations. The result of a non-absent male body is that nonmale bodies no longer fit the norm. Nothing can be learned about spirituality, for example, from the experiences of his female lover, nothing from the ways in which women as erotic partners manage and control their bodies and desires. Their experiences are rendered invisible, dispossessed, or at best, forced to accommodate to the norm.

Choice and Control

Applying gender awareness to Perechodnik's deathbed confession also reveals a non-absent male body, though in a different way than in Augustine's case. For the African bishop, it is the opulence of carnal desires—that is, the inevitable human tendency after the Fall to covet more than is necessary (food, sex, power, beauty)—that leads him to treat the body as an obstacle to moral improvement and salvation. For the Jewish ghetto policeman, it is the scarcity of choices (food, love, power, safety)—that is, the Nazi policy to take away what is necessary for survival—that leads him to commit immoral acts and makes irrelevant any thoughts about bodily pleasure. Against his will, Perechodnik is reduced to the most basic needs. "I did not have the energy to take the rudder in my own hand," he writes a few days after the *Aktion*. "A rapid current and a strong wind pushed all Jews into one direction: to Treblinka. . . . For days on end I lay senseless on my bed; at night I went on duty at the police station" (1996, 64). The experience of dearth and scarcity throbs like a bleeding heart below the surface of the text, and it is difficult to imagine Calel being plagued, like Augustine, by "sensual images" in his dreams. From Perechodnik's perspective, to contemplate the theological/anthropological significance of nocturnal emissions is an indulgence, a luxury. Hence, we do not find the same detailed scrutiny of the male embodied self in his deathbed confession as in Augustine's testimony. Perechodnik's primary concern is his moral failure, not the body, and certainly not a body consciously gendered—in spite of the fact that the physical threat against his Jewish body is an ever-present reality in his life (and for the reader, in the text).

For Augustine and Perechodnik, the relationship between body and morality is enmeshed with two existential concerns: control and choice. How does control over one's bodily needs shape one's moral choices? Augustine responds to this concern by correlating moral freedom with release from bondage to the body. Man's ability to make moral choices increases to the extent that carnal desires decrease. The bishop of Hippo writes to persuade his audience that a man's voluntary commitment to control the body's insatiable appetites (a source of much anxiety for Augustine) is rewarded with moral and spiritual freedom. "You [God] snapped my chains. . . . What I once feared to lose was now a delight to dismiss" (9.1.1). And persuasive he proved to be! He succeeded in blazing a trail into the declining hegemony of the Roman Empire, opening up the option for a new masculine ideal: the celibate man.[20]

Like Augustine, Perechodnik perceives the issue of choice and control central to how the body influences morality. Unlike Augustine, his anxiety is not rooted in the oppositional pairing of moral freedom and bodily bondage but, almost inversely, in the interdependence of bodily freedom and moral agency. External restrictions placed on his body result in a loss of moral choice. Put differently, the more Perechodnik loses control over his physical survival, the more restricted is his ability to make good moral choices. Amid destruction, he writes to curse the "monstrousness of our times" (1996, 114), which has only one objective: a dead Jew.

Morality, body, God: Despite the centrality of choice and control in Augustine's and Perechodnik's experiences, they understand the consequences of their activities in strikingly different terms. Whereas Perechodnik perceives the Nazi encroachment on his *Jewish* body as leading him to act immorally, that is, against his family and community, Augustine perceives his voluntary restrictions of his *Christian* body as leading him to act morally and establish an intimate relationship with God. Perechodnik finds himself in a position where he is forced to sever the ties to his wife and daughter in order to save his body from the Nazi onslaught: "[M]y dearest daughter, you are looking at me through the barbed wire. . . . You stretch out your hands to me, but I have no right to take you. If I do that, I will immediately get a bullet in my head" (1996, 36). In the process, he loses his faith. "If I believed in God, in heaven or hell, in some reward or punishment after death, I wouldn't have written this at all. . . . I don't know how to pray, and as for faith, I have none" (xxi).[21] Augustine, on the other hand, deliberately decides to break away from his lover of many years and other sexual relations in order to save his soul and be socially and mentally free for God. "Lord, my helper and redeemer, I will now tell the story, and confess to your name, of the way in which you delivered me from the chain of sexual desire, by which I was tightly bound, and from the slavery of worldly affairs" (8.6.13). Whereas Augustine volunteers to abandon sexual relations in order to find faith in God, Perechodnik is forced to abandon his wife, Anka, and daughter, Aluska (the fruit of his sexuality), and loses faith in God. Augustine writes to persuade the reader of the moral gain when separating from one's sexual partner(s); Perechodnik writes out of despair over the loss of morality that contributed to the irreversible separation from his loved ones.

Morality, relationships, kinship: Augustine and Perechodnik respond differently to the choices that they can (or cannot) control. Augustine, for example, tries to keep his composure when sending his nameless female partner and lover back to Africa. But the text is suffused with his hurt. "My heart which was deeply attached was cut and wounded, and left a trail of blood. She had returned to Africa vowing that she would never go with another man. She left with me the natural son I had by her" (6.15.25; see also Brown 1969, 88–89; Power 1996, 99–101; Miles 1992, 77–80). His passive role hides, among other things, the fact that it was he who made his lover return to Africa. He shields himself from responsibility. The child he mentions fleetingly is introduced three books later as "the boy Adeodatus, my natural son begotten of my sin," who dies in his teenage years. Augustine, the man of many words, reserves only a few lines for the departure of his female partner and the death of their only child.

The ghetto policeman, on the other hand, is devastated by the loss of his wife and daughter and openly grieves, curses, and vows revenge. "Anko, Anko, let your beautiful eyes gaze for the last time at the heaven, at the sunset. Send me your last greeting—a benediction or a curse," he writes as he imagines her arrival at Treblinka; and yearning for a faith now broken, he continues, "Anka, Aluska, Rachel, and you sisters and brothers of mine, how I would like to say from the depths of my afflicted heart the prayer *El Mole Rachamim* for the repose of your souls. . . . We the sons, brothers, husbands of yours still living, we shall avenge you with blood. Amen" (1996, 50–51).[22]

When I first encountered Perechodnik's deathbed confession, my youngest daughter was two years old. No wonder that Calel's description of the final moments with his two-year-old Aluska affected me deeply. During the Aktion, *the Germans had deceived the Jewish ghetto policemen into believing that their wives and children would be spared. However, when all Jews were loaded into the cattle cars, the Germans started to separate the remaining children: they were not to be released. "Beside myself, I grab Aluska, blood of my blood, bone of my bone, and I place her to the side. She stands alone, hungry, sleepy, surprised. Maybe she does not understand why the father, always so good to her, leaves her in the dark. She stands and does not cry; only her eyes shine, those eyes, those big eyes" (1996, 45).*

I am fighting tears when reading this passage. I grieve. I can say to myself: I am not living in the ghetto; I am not Jewish; I live in the rural parts of Maryland where my daughters are relatively safe; I grew up as a German in a country of onlookers and perpetrators. But these rationalizations don't help. At this very moment I remain most strongly identified with Calel's confession, and I hurt. What he experienced, and then put into words, is a primal scene, which cuts through time and space, through cultural and religious differences, and renders insignificant my intellectual reservation about identifying as a German with Jewish victims of the Shoah. Calel's experience speaks to me because it speaks to my worst fears: a forced separation and abandonment of my daughters while looking on helplessly.

Perechodnik's biblical lament, "blood of my blood, bone of my bone" (cf. Gen. 2:23), is not echoed in the *Confessions* when Augustine describes his son's death. From the bishop's throat—he, who so masterfully knows how to weave into his text numerous biblical quotes and references—no inconsolable moan escapes. "I contributed nothing to that boy other than sin," he declares, crediting God, not his lover, for raising the child to become "a fine person," with an "intelligence [that] surpassed that of many serious and well-educated men. . . . Who but you [God] could be the Maker of such wonders?" (9.6.14). Does Augustine really not mourn Adeodatus's death, a man whose grief abounds when he tells of the loss of male friends and of his mother, Monica? His displayed equanimity may not persuade us. As appointed bishop of Hippo, he might have chosen to downplay his emotional attachment to his son, for he was a reminder of his own sinful past, another obstacle to the father's spiritual rebirth. Known for the employment of rhetorical devices (see Power 1996, 97), he may have used the occasion of Adeodatus's death to pursue his larger narrative agenda: to show how God's love and mercy helped him to detach himself from previous affections. On the other hand, such an apologetic reading of Augustine may be wishful thinking on the part of fathers whose hearts would be broken when parting from their children. As long as one believes in the possibility of a gentle subtext (in which Augustine remains a loving father but cannot admit it due to narrative reasons), the reader is not left with Augustine's cruel distancing from his child—so different from Perechodnik's cri de coeur, "blood of my blood, bone of my bone."

Collaboration, Resistance, and the Question of Gender

As obedient readers, we may despair with Perechodnik over the loss of his loved ones and the cruel choices he was forced to make, or we might be confounded by his decision to abandon his daughter and wife in order to save his own body. One might hesitate, however, to reproach him for his gender blindness. If one's survival is at stake, any discourse on the gendered subject and male embodiment seems largely academic. Perechodnik focuses on describing and examining his behavior as a *Jew* under Nazi assault, not as a Jewish *man*.

Cognizant of the Shoah, one may be willing to overlook the fact that his confession does not address and problematize the male body. Reading it through the construct of the non-absent body, however, reveals how moral agency and some (albeit limited) privileges are rendered invisible. What privileges did Perechodnik have in times of genocidal assault? For example, he had the option of joining the ghetto police. This was open only to men. Calel had a choice to accept or decline this opportunity. He could have refused to join, as did other men, and thus escape the accusation of not possessing a moral backbone. His wife, Anka, on the other hand, never had such a choice and, as a consequence, would not have found herself in the position of assisting in the deportation of her daughter and husband. We would have to imagine Anka's deathbed confession—had she had a chance to write one or the wish to do so—as significantly different from her husband's. It is in this light that gender, far from being the latest academic fad,[23] must be addressed even in situations of life at the extremities, such as the Shoah.

A disobedient reading of *Am I a Murderer?* needs to take another look at the non-absent male body. Rarely the focus of Perechodnik's reflections, and constantly at the brink of disappearing behind his anguish over the loss of moral choices, his body is nevertheless present in the form of the Nazi threat to annihilate it. It is a negative presence, a body in the process of annihilation; or, as Perechodnik remarks, a body to be "utilized as a valuable raw material—for example, as natural fertilizer or as fat" (1996, 15). In the context of such unprecedented genocidal violence, we can speak of Perechodnik's body as *doubly non-absent*: historically, his Jewish body is the target of annihilation, its presence one of gradual destruction; textually, his male body disappears as a gendered body in his own writing.

To theorize a doubly non-absent body in Holocaust narratives written by men would open the door for a careful gender analysis without violating the experience of victims and survivors.[24] Rather than pitch the study of the Holocaust against gender studies, we need to remain aware of the assault on the male body as primarily a *Jewish* body (and thus remain empathetic with what is at the core of Holocaust narratives: the destruction of Jewish people and culture) but also stay alert to the Jewish body as a *male* body, that is, to the genderedness of the writing subject and his experiences.

In Perechodnik's case, the concept of the doubly non-absent male body opens the possibility of approaching a central ethical concern posed by his deathbed confession. Is he a collaborator, an accomplice, or a repentant sinner? Is *Am I a Murderer?* a testament to collaboration, opportunism, or resistance? The book invites such questions, tempting people to provide quick answers. Jewish ghetto policemen were widely despised by the ghetto population during the war as well as by Jews who survived the Shoah. They stand accused of voluntarily aiding the Nazis in their dirty work for base motives (such as greed, selfish will to survive, etc.). In the afterword of *Am I a Murderer?* Paweł Szapiro, the editor of the original Polish publication, calls Perechodnik a perpetrator. To publish "a public confession" of a "perpetrator," he writes, can be "read as a display of shamelessness . . . rather than proof of an authentic penitence" (Szapiro 1996, 215). Perhaps it is not even prudent to publish such a document, Szapiro continues, for it may violate "the sanctity of the victims" (215) and cause ignorant or anti-semitically inclined people to conclude that Jews were helpmates in their own destruction. Given these objections, the publication of the original record of a Jewish ghetto policeman is a breathtaking moment in the historical documentation of the Shoah.[25]

It would be difficult, however, to read Perechodnik's deathbed confession as the document of a corrupt soul. Despite the fact that Perechodnik volunteered for the ghetto police, one would be hard-pressed to argue that he acted out of his free will. We can accuse Perechodnik, as he accuses himself, of being deluded and deceived willingly by the Nazis, at least to a certain degree, but not that he exhibited the mind of a perpetrator. "I was, after all, a policeman, one of the most prominent," Perechodnik writes about his position before the *Aktion*. "I was also a personal friend of the Ghetto Polizei commandant . . . and I believed that I could feel completely secure about myself and my family" (1996, 22).[26] And later: "It is interesting that every catastrophe in history is foreshadowed; there are always some signs . . . [but] rarely does anyone believe them" (28).

Like other Jews, and especially those employed in the ghetto self-government, Perechodnik held on to the belief that there was some logic behind the apparent randomness of Nazi occupation policy. The Nazis offered plenty of deceptive evidence to make Jews believe in some reasons behind the early arrests and deportations, until it was suddenly too late to resist. Only after the *Aktion* does Calel understand the full extent of his delusion. "You see, Anka," he admits in the final pages of his work, "I was terribly afraid of death—not before the Otwock *Aktion* but after it. Before the *Aktion*, I was a fatalist. . . . But I never imagined that You would perish and I would remain alive" (191).

The efforts to stay alive, which consumed most of Perechodnik's waking hours after the *Aktion*, can be interpreted as a willful act to resist the Nazi intention to annihilate his body. His body was to vanish from this earth, just as would any sign of the despised Jewish culture. Resisting such violence, Perechodnik did more than just keep his body alive: he started to write his confessions, for whose preservation he made careful arrangements. Against the threat of imminent annihilation, he added another Jewish sign: a written document. If his body wouldn't survive, which would make it impossible to personally carry out revenge, his written testament might at least have a chance to be preserved and to persuade others of the necessity of retribution.

> Then—on May 7 [1943] to be exact—I decided to write down these events. Maybe they will be preserved and in the future will be handed down to Jews as a faithful reflection of those tragic times and will persuade democratic nations to absolutely destroy all those Germans, to avenge the innocent deaths of millions of small Jewish children and women. (155)

Perechodnik harbored few illusions about his physical survival. "I know now that sooner or later I will share the fate of all the Jews in Poland," he writes in the opening paragraphs of his preface. "A day will come when they will take me into a field, command me to dig a grave—for me alone—order me to remove my clothing and lie there on the bottom, and kill me. . . . I have seen so many executions that I can just close my eyes and see my own death in detail" (xxi). Without expecting to be able to protect his body, he nevertheless continues to write, uncertain even about the fate of his manuscript. He writes against the almost certain disappearance of both his body and his words (by contrast, Augustine wants his body to disappear but is confident that his words will survive). Is it possible, then, to suggest that Perechodnik's introspective writing constitutes an act of resistance because it testifies to the author's refutation of his dehumanization and "desubjectification" by the Nazis?[27]

To call his deathbed confession an act of resistance is, however, troubling, for it neglects the question of what Perechodnik did in order to keep alive, at least long enough to make his writing possible. Perechodnik himself is aware of this dilemma. His living body is a testament to his immoral choices, so his body is the source of his moral anguish. He is alive partially because he helped the Germans put others to death. To be alive and able to write betrays his active (though limited) participation in the murder of Polish Jews. Even when he contemplates his own dying, as in the passage quoted previously, the vivid details of his imagined death (dig a grave, remove clothing, lie on the bottom) betray his complicity. He knows all these details because he has seen and heard them as a policeman.

As readers, we have, in the end, the privilege of knowing more than the author does. In a letter dating from 1950, Genia, Perechodnik's short-term, young lover in their common hiding place in Warsaw, tells about his final hours: weakened by typhus, hunger, and despair, Calel perished during the

Warsaw uprising—very likely by using cyanide pills.[28] His confessional document, however, was preserved.

The doubly non-absent body (external threat against Jewish body; textual disappearance of gendered body) expresses the reader's uncertainty about how to judge Perechodnik and his writing, oscillating between the extremes of calling him victim or perpetrator. Did he collaborate or resist? Perechodnik displays "neither heroic nor quiet virtues," writes Istvan Deak (1997). "Who can blame him?" Because Perechodnik is constantly exposed to an external threat against his body, his anguish, despair, loss of moral choices, and "relentless self-exposure" (Ezrahi 1980, 64) may sway the reader to empathize with this young husband and father, this hunted and haunted twenty-seven-year-old man, who is plagued by his conscience and who hopes against hope to get another chance—not for another life but for revenge.[29]

The internal, textual disappearance of his gendered body, however, reveals another side. Here, the non-absent body allows Perechodnik to render invisible some of the responsibility he carries for his decisions. Perechodnik, we must assume, spoke truthfully,[30] but he may not have told us everything, or, as Szapiro points out, "could have written more" about certain events (like the work of the Jewish police in the Otwock ghetto).[31] In some instances, Perechodnik displays a tendency to blame *all* Jews for failing to act rather than focusing on the specific role of the Jewish ghetto police and on himself. He writes, for example: "Then, as now, I ascribed the entire blame for all of our misfortunes equally to German sadism as well as to the Jewish religion and traditions" (1996, 151)—a sweeping claim that helps to divert attention from his own actions. Elsewhere he claims that "there was no Jew who loudly cursed his executioners before his death. They were all passive, resigned, without hope for life" (79)—contradicting his many accounts of desperate creativity by which Jewish men and women tried to outmaneuver the Germans. His wife, for example, is specifically upset about her husband's failure to make arrangements for his family's protection, such as obtaining a *Kennkarte*, which would have given them temporary relief. Most women, like his wife, were burdened with taking care of the children and the elders, whereas some men, especially functionaries in the self-government, to which Perechodnik belonged, had access to better means of survival (food, information, protection, larger freedom of movement, etc.). Whenever Perechodnik moves to generalizations, he renders some of his responsibility invisible.

A last, harrowing story may shed some light on my argument that a non-absent male body deflects attention from the author as moral agent and gendered subject. The night before the execution of Jews caught after the *Aktion*, Perechodnik, guarding the condemned, finds a little girl who resembles his daughter, Aluska (who by that time had already been deported).

> I took her from her mother . . . sat her on my knee, cuddled her, and thus we passed the night. When I heard that the [German] gendarmes were arriving, I understood that I had to part with her. My charge, whose name I did not know, cried loudly and did not want to be returned to her mother. She sensed that death awaited her on the other side of the screen. She tightened her arms around my neck, and I had to forcefully tear myself away. When I returned her to her mother, I felt as if I killed the child with my own hands. (74)

In this heartrending scene, Perechodnik comes across as a gentle father figure as well as an accomplice to the execution. Since he blames himself for the latter, he is also the repentant sinner. The story unfolds in a manner that seems fated from the start, offering no alternatives of behavior. It sounds as if Calel had no choice. We have to remind ourselves, however, that Calel presents himself in this passage as fully present in his body when he comforts the child. He actively seeks her out and cuddles her. His body, however, disappears the moment he abandons her, and he quickly switches to a passive role: "I understood that I had to part with her." As he returns the girl to her mother, he assumes again the duty of a policeman, who leaves his "fatherly" body behind. The failure to act as a protagonist at that very moment produces a guilt-ridden chronicler of the event.

This episode can be read as Perechodnik's missed chance to redeem himself. Having lost his own daughter earlier in similar circumstances, he could have tried to do something for this other little girl. But as before, he remains awkwardly inactive, his language hiding some of his culpability. "You stretch out your hands to me," he writes about his daughter in a puzzling phrase already quoted (recalling Augustine's use of the passive voice when describing his lover's lone departure to Africa), "but I have *no right* to take you" (36; emphasis added). Why not? Why does he not have this right? Perechodnik could have taken his daughter's hands, just as he could have held tight the other girl in his arms in the morning when the Germans returned—and suffered the consequences. He has a right to take his daughter and hold the other girl, but it comes at the price of putting his own body in harm's way.

His rhetorical phrasing expresses a moral understanding fixated on duty. Certainly, short of a miracle, Perechodnik could have saved neither Aluska

nor the little girl. He could, however, have done what he laments no other
Jew did: take the child's hands in the morning, curse the German gen-
darmes, throw himself against them, and take a few with them into the
grave dug for Jews. His genuine attachment to the little girl lasts only until
the moment his own body is at stake. His lament is also the grief of the
melancholic chronicler.

*My judgment is harsh. I may not have acted differently than Calel did; and had I
acted like him, I am not sure I would have had the courage to preserve my behavior in
writing. I would have hoped that all memory of such vicious choices would vanish with
my own death. Perechodnik decides against such forgetfulness: he writes. He writes and
makes himself vulnerable to accusations by future readers. "I have decided to write this
diary not to justify myself but to give truthful testimony" (75). Without a chance to re-
make himself—the classic ending of a Christian confessional narrative—he is left with
the awareness of his unmaking, which leaves me, as reader, in the midst of his moral
dilemma, without any easy resolution.*

In the paragraph that immediately follows the story about the little girl,
Perechodnik does what Augustine has mastered to perfection in the *Confessions*, namely, jumping from recounting a specific life experience to raising large and abstract questions. "I hear her voice till today," Perechodnik
writes about the little girl he cuddled before her deportation. "My own
thoughts as well: Is there a God? Is there some higher justice that rules this
world? If so, why is it silent?" (74). These are legitimate questions, yet one
wonders about their timing and placement in the text. Does it not divert
attention from himself as moral agent? What if he had asked: "Where was
my courage? For someone in my position, would there have been a way to
act justly this morning in Otwock? Why did I not cry out?" A shift away
from male embodiment toward abstract reasoning is a move toward self-
distancing, a device that can be located in the confessional texts of both
Perechodnik and Augustine. Such rhetorical devices (regardless of whether
employed deliberately or not) help confessing men cope with the guilt they
are willing to admit retrospectively—though these devices also hide the full
extent of their culpability.

Writing as Birthing

Despite all their self-scrutinizing, self-loathing, self-accusation, or even self-effacement, male confessants remain in a position more privileged than the loved ones they write about. Augustine sends his lover back to Africa; Perechodnik does not intervene when his family is deported. Their texts, however, have survived. Writing a confession requires a subject capable of the act of writing, and the written product opens an opportunity to immortalize the author. Confessional writing is a chance for men to be reborn, a male rebirthing in the form of a text. The non-absent male body draws into its imaginary reverse-gendered scenarios of birthing.

The *Confessions*, which "recount Augustine's own salvation history" (Power 1996, 18), are structured as a movement toward the moment when Augustine is ready to be reborn in the Christian faith, the typical gesture of conversion narratives. Eventually, the Christian male believer will be reborn spiritually. A cathartic process is presented as a period of the self's uncertainty and tribulation (pregnancy), which is followed by an eventual transformation (rebirth). Men free themselves from the shackles of their carnal bodies, thus moving from death to life. Man's own natural birth and his natural nourishment by his mother's milk must eventually be replaced by a spiritual rebirth and divine nourishment. One of the key moments that concludes Augustine's transformation is the mystical rapture at Ostia with his mother, Monica, shortly before her death. More will have to be said about his mother later; suffice it to say here that the shared vision at Ostia is not only an homage to his pious mother but also a final replacement of her as a measuring rod for her son's spiritual progress. As a reborn man, Augustine no longer needs the mother who had once given birth to him.

The *Confessions* are a testimony to Augustine's new birth, but even more so, the *Confessions* are also his child, the product of his spiritual union with the Divine. After his conversion and after the death of his mother, the now celibate Augustine is empowered to give birth to spiritual children, namely, a text. This new generative power may further explain why his biological son, Adeodatus, can disappear in the text. He is recalled only as a brief, dispassionate memory: the *Confessions* have taken his place.[32]

Perechodnik, too, conceives of his confessional text in the imagery of birthing. Whereas Augustine's narrative is optimistic, moving toward salvation, Perechodnik's confession is desperate, moving toward (earthly) damnation. The image of a spiritually reborn man is replaced by an image of a stillborn. "I had to beget a dead fetus into which I would breathe life," Perechodnik writes. "These diaries are that fetus—and I believe they will be printed one day so that the whole world will know of your suffering. I wrote them for Your glory in order to make You immortal" (1996, 191–192). The You in Perechodnik's text is, as we already know, his dead wife. Unlike Augustine's addressee (God), Perechodnik's You cannot promise eternal life. There is no rapture, just rupture. His wife is already dead, and as an act of final gift giving, Perechodnik places his deathbed confession before her "on the anniversary of Your death" (191). The Jewish ghetto policeman and his wife can no longer have a child; thus, he calls his manuscript a "dead fetus."

Perechodnik's manuscript, however, is more than just a dead fetus. He also calls it his "second baby" and "second child, born in death pains" (192), and he goes to great effort to preserve it. He entrusts the manuscript to a Gentile Pole, instructing him to "carry out faithfully my testament of revenge" (202). As self-effacing as Perechodnik might be, he also wants his words to survive. "I only know that I will be needed as a witness after the war," he writes in the final pages. "If my memoir fulfills that role, I can die without regret" (201). What he could not do for his wife and daughter, he tries to do for his manuscript: secure its survival. He proclaims that writing the diary will make his wife "immortal" (192). As today's readers, however, we see him immortalizing his own words more than he did his wife. He has built a self-deprecating monument to himself. Perechodnik lived on not through his flesh-and-blood daughter but through his textual "second child."

The different births—a Christian spiritual child and a Jewish dead fetus—witnessed in the *Confessions* and *Am I a Murderer?* mirror the differences of the circumstances the two confessants faced. The former is a document of remaking, the latter of unmaking; one celebrates an experience of rapture, the other bemoans the experience of rupture. Yet in both cases, a text is born, while real people—namely, Augustine's lover and son and Perechodnik's wife and daughter—disappear without their words being preserved.

Power, Accommodation, and Resistance

The privilege of the writing subject does not automatically translate into an experience of power and pleasure. As a matter of fact, both Perechodnik and Augustine experience and perceive themselves as being powerless. In Augustine's case, it is man's lack of control over bodily desires and the need to acknowledge a far greater and transcendent power, the presence of God; in

Perechodnik's case, it is his lack of control over basic bodily needs because of the overwhelming power of the Nazi presence. The two confessants employ various rhetorical devices to communicate their sense of powerlessness to their readers, but sometimes their rhetoric renders invisible their culpability, as we have seen previously in select examples (hiding behind generalizations and abstraction; switching to a passive tense and role). As critical readers, we suspect that Augustine and Perechodnik accommodate to their respective environments far more than they are willing to admit. But we cannot forget that different things are at stake: Augustine's *Confessions* are about spiritual rebirth, and Perechodnik's deathbed confession is about physical survival. Behind the semblance of rhetorical strategies, we see a Christian bishop who remains the protagonist of his narrative, paradoxically against his wish to make God the protagonist (a dilemma he articulates in his qualms about false pride and vainglory),[33] and a Jewish ghetto policeman who never seems to be the protagonist of the events he chronicles, although he accuses himself, and now stands accused, of being one.

I tend to respond emotionally to Perechodnik, intellectually to Augustine. This difference is linked, among other reasons, to the degree to which each writer controls (narrative) power. Augustine reveals his culpability but does so skillfully and guardedly. He remains in control of his confessions. As far as his intention is concerned, by the end of the book the ideal reader has no choice but to acknowledge the power of God. Perechodnik, on the other hand, reveals himself to the point that he denies himself the power to control the reader's judgment. As opposed to Jewish post-Holocaust writings on the Shoah with "maximal autobiographical content and minimal autobiographical self-revelation" (Moseley 2006, 471), Perechodnik's deathbed confession is "maximal" self-revelation, rendering him unprotected from harsh verdicts. Since, in the end, it is up to the reader to judge his culpability, Perechodnik is left vulnerable—and I am simultaneously drawn to, and frightened by, the risk that Perechodnik takes.

Perechodnik rescinds some of the male confessant's privilege and power of reassembling and reconstituting the self retrospectively. Yes, he remains gender oblivious, hiding the full weight of his culpability, but he has, far more than Augustine, given up control in the process of narrating the self.

Perhaps Perechodnik's risk taking can become a model for male confessiographies today: confessional writing not as an act of reinscribing power but of resisting it.

Is such resistance possible? Foucault's critique of the Western obsession with producing truth through confessions, thereby establishing and maintaining power through knowledge, questions any such attempt. "The obligation to confess," Foucault writes, "is now relayed through so many different points, is so deeply ingrained in us, that we no longer perceive it as the effects of a power that constrains us" (1990, 60). Any confessional act, in this view, already accommodates to power.

The question remains: Do male confessional revelations reinscribe social norms, or do they offer opportunities to resist norms of conformity?[34] We may not find unequivocal answers, but we can state that Augustine and Perechodnik do not only accommodate to but also resist the circumstances of their time, and in both cases their embodied selves, imbued with moral ambiguity, play a central role. Augustine resists the societal expectations to seek a career in Roman society. After he has forcefully separated from his lover (at the cost of leaving him with a bleeding heart), there seems little standing in the way of his entering the Roman heartland. He, the North African teacher of rhetoric, has successfully established a network of important friends in imperial Milan and is newly betrothed to a young girl of the Milanese upper class. Just then he renounces all sexual pleasure and, with it, social prestige. "The effect of your [God] converting me to yourself was that I did not now seek a wife and had no ambition for success in this world" (8.12.30).

Perechodnik resists the genocidal violence directed against him as the ultimate other by keeping his Jewish body alive, at the cost of witnessing and participating in the destruction of his loved ones. Civilization is experienced as rupture, and history is divorced from any notion of redemption. There is only one movement: from life to death. A genocidal ideology of purification seeks to turn the Jewish body to ashes and fertilizer, as Perechodnik remarks repeatedly. He "sacrifices" his wife and child to fend off the assault against his Jewish male body. In the end, he perishes in a bunker during the Warsaw uprising.

For Augustine, his *restlessness* moves him to take account of himself through the act of confessional writing: "our heart is restless until it rests in you" (1.1.1). For Perechodnik, his *recklessness* compels him to write: "[My wife] was killed . . . to a considerable extent on account of my recklessness" (1996, xxi).[35] Restlessness can be redeemed; recklessness, not.

Returning to Africa as an avowed celibate, back to the margins of Roman society, Augustine succeeds in anchoring the image of a new man into the Western canon—a man of God who works within society. The *Confessions* eventually become a classic Christian model for the internal, spiritual re-making of man. Cramped into his final hiding place, Perechodnik's last days are spent under "demolished houses, in bunkers, and in sewers."[36] No image of a new man can emerge from these dark and putrid places, only Perechod-nik's portrayal of modernity's violent unmaking of a Jew. Let us hope, then, that this document of unmaking becomes, like Augustine's *Confessions*, part of an enlarged canon and does not fall into oblivion.

"Then no one will shed even one tear on my nonexistent grave. I don't deserve it" (Perechodnik 1996, 202).

CHAPTER 4

A Perpetrator and His Hagiographer

Oswald Pohl's Confession

A normative model of Christian confessional writings assumes a repentant sinner who is willing to confess his sins (*confessio peccati*) and reaffirm the Christian faith by praising God (*confessio fidei et laudis*). It is an act of giving testimony both to a self once chained to sin and to the renewing, universal power of God.

"Man, a little piece of your creation," Augustine writes in the opening paragraph of the *Confessions*, "desires to praise you [God], a human being 'bearing his mortality with him,' carrying with him the witness [*testimonium*] of his sin and the witness [*testimonium*] that you 'resist the proud'" (1.1.1). Faced with his own mortality, man gives testimony to his past transgressions, to his vainglory, and to a power greater than himself. Garry Wills argues for a close link between confession and testimony, stating that the Latin *confiteri* means "to *cor*roborate, to *con*firm testimony."[1] Augustine bears public witness to his sins precisely because he can testify to God. With a perspective external to himself, the sinner is offered the possibility of stepping outside his own sinful self and of recognizing—at the risk of public shaming and ridicule—the need to undergo a spiritual and moral transformation. A confessing sinner moves from the old Adam to the new Adam, from the old sinful and physical self to a new and spiritually cleansed self. The "man of dust" becomes the man closer to "heaven" (1 Cor. 15:42–49).

This, at least ideally, is what Christian confessional writings as public testimony are supposed to accomplish. Compelled by the awareness of the ubiquity of God and divine grace, the sinner has taken it upon himself to render himself vulnerable by exposing his shameful past to others, namely, to God and the public, so that a reconciliation and transformation can occur.

Are genocidal perpetrators capable of giving public testimony that follows such an ideal type of Christian confessiography? This is the question I want to pursue in this chapter by using the example of a Nazi perpetrator. Oswald Pohl's *Credo: Mein Weg zu Gott* (*Credo: My Path to God*) is the attempt of a high-ranking German National Socialist to offer the public a confession story. Since Nazi perpetrators, after 1945, rarely gave public testimony in which they admitted wrongdoing and guilt, *Credo*, as a written confession, is the exception to the rule. Though it was not uncommon among accused Nazi war criminals to (re)convert to Christianity after 1945 or to renew their church membership while in Allied captivity, they rarely *publicly* repented. Admittance of former Nazi perpetrators into the Catholic or Protestant churches in postwar Germany did not translate into public testimony. *Credo*, hence, deserves our attention.

But is it a genuine confession? Exploring the issue of whether a male genocidal perpetrator is capable of revealing his innermost self in a mode of repentance and self-purification, I engage in a close reading of *Credo*'s religious rhetoric within the larger political discourse of postwar Germany. I hope to show that *Credo* exemplifies a confessant's inept moral reckoning that is embedded in a conservative religious imagination and in a society's postgenocidal discourse. This chapter, then, widens the critique of male confessiographies by including a political dimension.

Confession and Conversion

Pohl's *Credo* is not only a confession but also a conversion story. This is not too surprising since confessions and conversion stories often converge. The confessional self is also a converted or reconverted self.[2] The conversion of the agnostic, the skeptic, the cynic, or those who have otherwise strayed from a righteous path testifies to the belief in the effectiveness of the confessional moment. Within the Christian economy of redemption, the person with the most to gain from a confession is the one furthest removed from God. The righteous man does not need to confess, but the sinner does. The righteous does not feel compelled to produce a written confession, or, if he were to do so, such work would fall on deaf ears. The drama of conversion and confession narratives is built around the most unlikely contender, for it is he who provides evidence of the undeserved mercy of God. In pre-Enlightenment times, this drama demonstrated the theological truth of the compelling and unsettling power of faith and divine grace; in modern times, this drama appeals to the sensationalist appetite for private revelations and reaffirms a confidence in the human potential for self-healing. Bereft of a theological dimension, modernity's public confessions can also be spectacles—staged events satisfying voyeuristic desires.

The dramatic suspense is based upon the assumption that public confessions are agonizing processes into which people are drawn by an irresistible force both internal and suprapersonal (hence also the proximity to martyrologies; see Castelli 2004). The more abusive the power and pride of the former self, the more shameful the recovery of the new self; the more illicit the pleasures then, the more painful the healing now! Almost against his will, the sinner is pushed into a moral reckoning. His soul descends into the hell of self-examination, and the "I" undergoes a metaphorical death before it can emerge purified and cleansed.

What better conversion story, then, could be hoped for than the spiritual confession of a Nazi perpetrator? It would epitomize the ultimate culture war—or, for some, cosmic war— between the forces of spiritual good and the forces of an immoral, anti-Christian evil. Such a confession could restore the belief in an ordered universe that was severely ruptured by National Socialism (NS) and the Holocaust. A confessing Nazi perpetrator would cease to be feared as *Herrenmensch* (master race) and *Übermensch* (superhuman) and, instead, could be embraced as a humbled and domesticated repentant sinner, now disarmed and nestled in the bosom of *ecclesia*. The church could appropriate the exemplary confession of a repentant Nazi as proof of Christianity's victory over the evils of materialism, modernism, secularism, and human hubris, whereas a more secular-minded populace with its taste for private exposures would feel reassured in its belief that a spark of genuine kindness resides in all human beings. In times of moral relativism, the juxtaposition of darkness and light that lies at the base of a perpetrator confession would signal the transformation of absolute evil into a beacon of hope.

Did Oswald Pohl produce such a confession? *Credo* was written and published in Germany in 1950, five years after the Second World War ended. On the surface, this work seems to satisfy the church's ambition for having successfully reconverted a lost sheep among Nazi perpetrators. It also feeds on the popular hunger for an authentic confession of a high-ranking Nazi "monster." But as we will see, *Credo* ultimately fails on both these accounts. Due to its stilted and conventional style, it did not seize the popular imagination, and today it is largely unknown outside a circle of specialized historians. *Credo* also fails as a heartfelt confession despite its pretense of being one. It has no literary merit, is of little theological value, and even the authorship of many passages is questionable. Why, then, bother? Because it documents the difficulty of culpable men to account for themselves. *Credo*'s peculiar religious rhetoric veils a perpetrator's agency and culpability.

How cautious must we be when approaching a male confessant who is not just an ordinary sinner but a genocidal perpetrator? Is it possible for such a perpetrator to purify himself through the cathartic process of publicly giving testimony to his sins, of professing his faith and praising God? Did Pohl really render himself vulnerable to his readers and to God? Or did he simply exploit the genre for apologetic purposes? On one level, *Credo* is a political document that puts a conversion story into the service of attempting to reintegrate the confessing sinner into society. Hence, *Credo* must be read as the Christian confession of a Nazi perpetrator during a transitional moment in Germany's restoration period.[3] On another level, *Credo* requires the critical reader to double-think: however flawed and pathetic, *Credo*'s authenticity as a perpetrator confession may paradoxically rest in its disingenuousness. This is a point to which I will return in my concluding arguments.

From the Mouth of the Perpetrator: I Believe

Pohl describes the crucial moment of his religious transformation in the following words: "I was shaken to the depth of my soul. My eyes were able to see with more clarity than before: They gazed into a new world. Before my inner face, something marvelous passed by. Credo!" (*Credo*, 53).[4] This is the measured rhetoric of a conversion story typical of the Christian confessional form: Credo / I believe. The soul is in profound crisis and compelled to undergo a radical transformation; as a result, the sinner discovers with unambiguous clarity the essence of what truly counts in the world—true faith in the love of God. Indeed, as readers we may want to ascribe such pious sentiments to Augustine, who, in the early books of the *Confessions*, deplores the state of his soul: "Such was my heart, O God, such was my heart. You had pity on it when it was at the bottom of the abyss" (2.4.9). After his conversion—when Augustine was in his thirties, but not writing about it until his mid-forties (see Brown 1969, 163)—the Roman African bishop could speak with confidence about God's love: "My love for you, Lord, is not an uncertain feeling but a matter of conscious certainty. With your word, you pierced my heart, and I loved you" (10.6.8). The soul is lifted from the abyss; the crisis turned into love of God.

Pohl takes his cues from Augustine. Modeling his own experience after the confessional narrative of late antiquity, he writes:

> The moment of transformation filled me with an ardent love. It is love that counts. Indeed, love is the essence and main objective of Christianity. Everything else is only a means to an end. Sermons and the gospels, sacraments, fasting and praying—all of them are meant to educate us toward love, to kindle love within us, to nourish, complete, strengthen, purify, and fortify love: the true love for God and our neighbors. (*Credo*, 57–58)

Stripped of their context, these words do not raise any suspicion. There is a happy ending to a soul's crisis, the goodness of which would be hard to refute. Pohl, the former sinner, who has found a new love for God, calls us into moral responsibility for our neighbor, thus giving the story a saintly quality.

Has Pohl become a deeply caring and religious man after he had been led astray by Nazi ideology? The rhetorical predictability and conventionality of the previous passage contests such a conclusion. The words come across as rehearsed and lifeless, chipping away at the credibility of the professed transformation. The external markers characteristic of a good conversion story are placed too deliberately: A crisis precipitates a man's willingness to acknowledge his past blindness, followed by a transformative moment that allows for the clarity of a new vision. There is a schematic feel to this progression, as if Pohl wanted to make sure that his readers would make no mistake about how to interpret his experience. Who is this man who has thus confessed?

On February 12, 1950, in the War Crime Prison of Landsberg am Lech (Bavaria), Oswald Pohl officially converted to Catholicism. Born in 1892 into a Protestant family, he grew up in a home of "true religiosity" following the "evangelical-reformed faith tradition" (*Credo*, 17). Pohl belonged to a generational cohort of men for whom the Great War of 1914 and the

Versailles Treaty of 1919 were decisive political events that shaped their affective national identification. Most of the founders of National Socialism belonged to the same cohort of 1918 (the 1918ers): Adolf Hitler, Heinrich Himmler, Hermann Göring, and Rudolf Hess.[5] Pohl served in the German navy during the First World War. Afterward, he signed up for law school but abandoned his studies when the navy hired him for a position in financial administration at the rank of an officer. Pohl had been part of the National Socialist movement since the early 1920s, and in 1925 he became an active member of the SA (the Storm Troopers or Brown Shirts).[6] He joined the SS (Schutzstaffel; Defense Corps) in 1934 through the recruitment efforts of Himmler, chief of the SS and the Nazi terror apparatus. During this period, he left the church and became *gottgläubig* (God believing), a Nazi term indicating that he had abandoned Christianity. Himmler had been impressed by Pohl's administrative and organizational skills, and Pohl soon moved up through the ranks, eventually becoming the head of the Wirtschafts-Verwaltungshauptamt (WVHA), the Economic-Administrative Main Office of the National Socialist regime. Here, Pohl was responsible for organizing the industrial production within the concentration camp system, building and supervising a complex administrative web among the SS, the armament industry, and private firms (see Allen 2000, 2002). Between 1942 and 1945, Pohl oversaw the entire workforce of concentration camp inmates, including the economic utilization of personal possessions of the exterminated Jews, such as their clothing, gold teeth, and hair. Arrested in 1946, he was sentenced to death at the Nuremberg trials in 1947. After several failed appeals for clemency, he was executed in the Landsberg prison on June 7, 1951. Pohl was among the last seven Nazi war criminals hanged by representatives of the American government in Germany. If *Credo*'s goal was to pardon and rehabilitate Pohl, its mission failed.[7]

Older even than my grandparents, Pohl is far removed from me, sharing neither a generational nor geographic proximity. He had been born in Germany proper—according to Nazi ideology he was a Reichsdeutscher—*whereas my grandparents lived at the margins of Germany as ethnic Germans. In the Nazi terminology, they were* Volksdeutsche. *My Protestant maternal grandmother grew up in the German population of Siebenbürgen (Transylvania/Romania). She later joined her husband in the far northeastern corner of Germany, near the East Prussian city of Königsberg (today in Russia),*

*where my mother was born. My father was born into a devout Catholic family of
Sudetendeutsche, the German minority of the newly formed Czech Republic after 1918.
Before the First World War, my paternal grandparents belonged to the multiethnic and
multilingual Austro-Hungarian Empire.*

*The degree to which my families of origin were partially complicit with aspects of
the NS regime and ideology remains a contested issue in our family.[8] Pohl's biography,
in contrast, is the story of a high-ranking perpetrator. He would have been loathed
by my grandparents and parents, regardless of their own checkered history of partial
nonconformity and partial complicity. The degree of his culpability makes him different from the kind of compromised men I am personally familiar with. Disconnected
emotionally, I approach his biography as a scholar.*

In the preface to *Credo*, Pohl's confessor, Karl Morgenschweis, the official
Catholic prison chaplain of Landsberg am Lech and fellow German, writes:
"On February 12, 1950, the former general of the Waffen-SS Oswald Pohl
was received into the Catholic Church in the war crimes prison (W. Cr. Pr.)
Landsberg with the approval of the Hochw. Bischöfl. Ordinariates [espisco-
pate] of Augsburg according to the necessary proviso of canon law" (9). In
the summer of the same year, Pohl, with the help of Morgenschweis, published *Credo*, his seventy-five-page conversion story. The title page bears the
name of the author as "General der Waffen-SS A.D. Oswald Pohl."[9] Nine
thousand copies were printed with the imprimatur of the church in Munich
on July 7, 1950.[10] Published by a small Catholic press (Alois Girnth in Lands
hut), *Credo* was not the marginal product of a Nazi rogue but a work authorized by different levels of the Bavarian church hierarchy. Pohl dedicated the
book to his confessor, Morgenschweis, expressing his "deep gratitude" to the
man, "who, in love, has brought me home to the Triune God."

Credo is preceded by a six-page preface by Morgenschweis, in which
the prison chaplain identifies the narrative as an exemplary conversion/
confession story. He attests to Pohl's steadfast and manly character and
creates an unwavering interpretive and theological framework. *Credo* then
proceeds through four chapters, which do not constitute a memoir but an
account of Pohl's religious and moral self-questioning. The mélange of select
autobiographical details, theological and political musings, and various citations of Catholic authorities is largely apologetic in nature. *Credo* concludes

with two poems and a brief biography (the latter put together by Pohl himself), each of them listed in the table of contents under a separate heading: "Solace" (*Trost*), "Finale" (*Ausklang*), and "Biography" (*Lebensdaten*).

Each chapter has a distinct flair and character. In "Protestant Youth and Years of Travel," Pohl traces his Protestant upbringing within the context of the First World War. With sentimental simplicity, Pohl asks larger religious questions about God and Christianity: "How can Christianity claim to be the only true and hence redemptive religion on this earth? . . . Who, after all, is Christ? . . . Who is this 'God'?" (18–19). If there is an organizing principle behind these haphazard thoughts about religion and recollections of his youth, it is the juxtaposition of that which had guided him in the past (God, the Bible, his mother's piety) and that which is troubling him as a young man returning from the war in 1919: skepticism, religious dissatisfaction, and a growing distance from Christianity. Interwoven into his personal reminiscences and religious musings are—typical for his generational cohort—his military experience of the Great War.[11] The chapter actually opens with a memory at the dawn of the First World War, in "the summer of 1913" (17), when he, as a twenty-one-year-old sailor of the German navy, had landed at a small island in the Pacific Ocean. There he came across military graves of young German sailors who had lost their lives during an indigenous uprising. Apparently, it made a deep impact on him. At the end of the war—"behind me the shattering experience of the First World War and the collapse of our *Volk* [people]" (22)—he had become a skeptic. Biblical words no longer gave him direction but had become empty and "foreign" (22).

In chapter 2 ("Between Faith and Disbelief"), Pohl gives an account of his professional career in the SS. The chapter is not intended as a résumé but an interpretation of his decision to leave his secure position in the navy for Himmler's SS. Pohl does not hide the fact that he had supported National Socialism from early on but portrays himself as a task-oriented man of the military (*Berufssoldat*) who was "politically untrained and inexperienced" (29). The chapter is a balancing act between, on the one hand, taking pride in his career choices and, on the other, trying to remain blameless in regard to the murderous NS policies. He seeks to present himself as a professionally respectable man and, at the same time, politically innocent. Religious discourse helps him perform this straddling act. His career decision to join the SS is embedded in a discussion about the tension between faith in the Christian God and in the Nazi *Gottgläubigkeit* (30–31). *Gottgläubig* (God believers) was a Nazi category, which SS members especially adopted to indicate their religious classification after they left the Christian churches (see Steigmann-Gall 2003, 219–220; Nanko 1993). Pohl had become *gottgläubig*, he writes, after he had given in to Himmler's "pressure" (28) to work for the SS. Pohl claims that he never quite believed in the category *gottgläubig*; it had just been a formality for his personnel files. "True religious feeling, when it saturated a person, did not suffocate even underneath the black uniform [of the SS]" (34). In 1936, he left the Protestant church as part of the wave of *Kirchenaustritte* (leaving the churches), following the examples of Reinhard Heydrich and Himmler.[12]

Although chapter 2 tries to establish a sense of respectability and blamelessness, the next chapter ("Return to God") indulges in a rhetoric of victimization. Now a prisoner in Landsberg, Pohl wonders about the extent of his guilt but never admits having played an instrumental role in the extermination of Jews and other people deemed undesirable. Instead, the chapter opens with the ominous sentence, "Then came the atrocious year of 1945." In Pohl's perception, the true catastrophe of 1945 was the "collapse of Germany and the total victory [*totale Sieg*] of the Allied forces," which "brought me to the victor's tribunal . . . and to the gallows as a 'war criminal'" (39). This opening line is remarkable since no word is said about the victims of Nazi terror or about Pohl's brutal industrial utilization of concentration camp inmates. Rather, Pohl sees himself as a victim of the victor's justice. Consequently, the term "war criminal" appears in the text only in quotation marks in order to express doubt over the American jurisdiction.[13] Pohl does not deny that Nazis committed crimes but alludes to them only vaguely. He feels partially responsible for the "moral morass" (42) and "moral failure" (45) of the Nazi ideology but maintains that he is personally innocent of any crimes. "I had never beaten anyone to death," he writes, "nor did I encourage others to do so." Instead, "I energetically opposed [any] inhumanities, provided I learned about them" (43).

What allows Pohl to even consider the question of guilt in chapter 3—however incomplete and flawed—is the religious frame within which it is couched. He slowly comes to accept the spiritual truth of the Catholic faith. What begins with the "atrocious year of 1945" ends with the praise, "Credo in Deum" (I believe in God)—the final words of the third chapter (49).

"In the Bosom of the Only True Catholic Church" is the last narrative chapter.[14] Here, Pohl describes his spiritual homecoming. The longest of the four chapters, it is the least autobiographical, perhaps mirroring the dual structure of Augustine's *Confessions* with its autobiographical books (1–9) and the concluding, more philosophical books (11–13).[15] It is a pastiche of moralizing proclamations, Catholic dogma, and theological citations (especially of Catholic theologian Karl Adam).[16] Autobiographical insertions no longer dwell on the past but are very much in the present, centering on the official conversion, the moment when "I made my life's confession to our prison chaplain . . . and experienced the zenith of my life" (66). Pohl presents himself purified, calm, and resigned. He is beyond the passions and follies of this world and has put his trust entirely in the Catholic Church and God. The famous line from the opening of Augustine's *Confessions* (1.1.1) is deliberately placed in the text: "You have made us for yourself, and our heart is restless until it rests in you" (69). A little later, in another conscious reference to the confessional tradition with its dual nature of confessing sins and praising God, the chapter's very last words read, "Te Deum laudamus"—God, we praise you (70).

A Hagiographer's Ambition and the Prodigal Son

It is fairly certain that Pohl did not write *Credo* by himself but must have—despite Morgenschweis's claims to the contrary—received active help and support from his confessor. Not only are there drastic stylistic differences—most obvious between the personal reminiscences of chapter 1 and the more sophisticated theological references of chapter 4—but it is also unlikely that Pohl's theologically untrained, thoroughly nationalistic and bureaucratic mind could have penned passages that so deliberately present a Catholic worldview and so obviously model themselves after the Christian confessional convention.

How heavy-handedly Morgenschweis guided Pohl's writing and how scrupulously he may have edited or doctrinally embellished Pohl's draft are difficult to determine.[17] It is safe to assume, however, that the two men consentingly collaborated from the very beginning. Such an alliance does not diminish the value of *Credo* as a perpetrator confession. Conceptually, Christian confessions are not mono-authored texts but the result of dialogical situations. In the confessional, such dialogue transpires orally between the confessant and the confessor, whereas in confessional writings, dialogue occurs between the self and an imagined Other, as, for example, between the sinner and God or the public.[18] *Credo* as a written text must be approached as the creative product of confessional conversations between

Morgenschweis and Pohl. Therefore, the validation of its authenticity is not dependent on determining a single authorship. Confessions are a dialogical project, wherein a confessor gets intimately involved in the confessant's journey. It takes both to arrive at a truth. What Pohl and Morgenschweis present in *Credo* is a truth that both men consented to in writing, and they felt confident enough about it that they proceeded to share it with an audience outside their spiritual pas de deux.

Morgenschweis is very conscious about publicity, and in the opening page of his preface he repeatedly addresses the public nature of Pohl's testimony. Morgenschweis acknowledges that Pohl's actual conversion (*Bekehrung*)—before *Credo* was written—"caused a great sensation in the *public*," and he expects that the now available written conversion story (*Bekehrungsgeschichte*) will also "cause a great sensation." Morgenschweis states that Pohl wanted to use "this writing to make *public* his acceptance into the Catholic Church," "to renounce *publicly* his previous religious and ideological profession [*Bekenntnis*]," and "to declare *publicly* his belief [*Bekenntnis*] in the Catholic Church" (9; emphasis added).[19] As these phrases reveal, the prison chaplain insists from the very beginning on two important points: that *Credo* belongs to the tradition of conversion narratives [*Bekehrung*] and that, as a confession [*Bekenntnis*], it is truly a public testimony. As the public confession of a perpetrator, then, *Credo* is more than an introspective search. Indeed, we may be better served to read it as a staged performance with a "confessional script" that allows "perpetrators to reinvent their past through narrative" (Payne 2008, 19).[20]

It is reasonable to assume that Pohl and Morgenschweis had different motives for bringing this testimony to the attention of a German readership. Morgenschweis probably hoped to promote Catholic faith and to reinforce the claim that the church always kept its moral integrity, even in times of corrupt and corruptible secular powers, of which Nazism was as much a bad instance as communism and modernism.[21] Pohl, in contrast, probably hoped for clemency leading to his eventual release and social reintegration. This hope was not far-fetched, given how persistently the Protestant and Catholic churches in postwar Germany kept appealing to the Allied forces to grant political amnesty to Nazi war criminals—appeals that were repeated by many West German jurists and parliamentarians after the founding of the Federal Republic in 1949.[22]

Pohl's desire to be pardoned is never made explicit in *Credo* but is resolutely expressed elsewhere. Two days before his execution, Pohl wrote a letter to Retired Admiral Gottfried Hansen, who apparently had intervened on his behalf by contacting the German chancellor and General Eisenhower.[23] In a tone of self-serving and self-pitying defiance, Pohl writes:

> You can hardly imagine the feelings that your speaking up for me aroused in me. For the first time in the five years of solitary confinement (of which four years were spent on death row), helping hands extend themselves through the barred window. I could only fold my hands in prayer and thank the Almighty for this sign of his mercy. . . . Two weeks ago, our "liberators" had almost hanged me for the second time! And this remains a grave danger. . . . The American high commissioner has decorated me with additional invented "responsibilities." . . . The whole game at U.S. courts is geared only toward sabotaging . . . the request for granting a genuine appeal.[24]

Pohl and Morgenschweis do not have identical interests, but their motives and motivations richly overlap. Like Pohl, Morgenschweis must have hoped for clemency. He, too, wished to see his prodigal son reintegrated into German society. To this end he kept defending Pohl's reputation even long after his execution, claiming that only false accusations had brought him to the gallows. Pohl "was not responsible for the concentration camps and the annihilation of Jews," Morgenschweis is reported to have said in 1965.[25] Conversely, Pohl was indebted to his confessor and hence may have had a true investment in conveying his gratitude to the Catholic Church, which had accepted him despite his crimes. Most important, both men felt content with the written product of their interaction and were willing to present *Credo* as public testimony to a German audience.

If *Credo* is not a mono-authored text and contains conflicting voices, is there still compositional unity? Would Morgenschweis's preface have to be treated independently from the chapters attributed to Pohl? I don't think so. The chaplain's six-page preface is an indispensable part of *Credo*. Neither is it a theological coming to terms with Pohl's war crimes and his crimes against humanity (for which he was found guilty at Nuremberg three years earlier) nor does it critically assess the credibility of the conversion experience. Instead, the preface establishes a theological and ideological framework that directs the reader's gaze rather forcefully to a partisan interpretation. The confessing sinner is portrayed in a sympathetic light, his religious experience unquestionably elevated. Pohl is described by Morgenschweis as a "man full of energy, willpower and vigor." He is a military "officer from top to toe," a man of a "highly cultured mind and heart [*hohe Geistesbildung und Herzensbildung*]," upright, honest, and truthful." "Pohl," Morgenschweis reports, "lives like a monk in his cell, in prayer and sacrifice and where, whenever possible, he works and studies." He is a man "filled with the ardent love of Christ," who, as a new convert, has "entirely succumbed to God" and awaits "his fate" with calm composure. His poise is "testimony" to his "*Haltung*" (attitude),[26] "which is the fruit of his total inner conversion to God and his homecoming to the Catholic Church" (12–13). Descriptions like these authorize an image of a converted perpetrator dimly painted in the colors of a Christian saint.

Morgenschweis is not only Pohl's confessor but also his hagiographer. If part of the ancient and medieval hagiographer's task is to render the extravagant and sometimes excessive lives of saints palatable to the Christian laity by revealing God's miraculous work and the human virtuousness of a saint's amazing deeds, then Morgenschweis's task is to normalize the extraordinary evil of a Nazi perpetrator by humanizing and Christianizing him. "As priest and pastoral counselor," Morgenschweis argues, "I have the holy duty to portray Pohl in just the way I have seen him as his spiritual father and soul-guide in the several years of direct intercourse [*Verkehr*] with him" (12–13).[27] Morgenschweis portrays Pohl as his spiritually intimate other. The term "intercourse" (translated literally but correctly from the German *Verkehr*)[28] offers a linguistic clue for the intimacy of the devout exchange between confessor and confessant, between spiritual father and prodigal son, between hagiographer and saint.

The preface to *Credo* thus aims at communicating to a postwar German audience the civility and respectability of the confessant ("the image of the converted Pohl is still obscured in the opinion of many people"; 12). Morgenschweis's hagiographic ambition is to normalize the perpetrator. The saintly qualities of Pohl do not reside in any past miraculous deeds but in his present ordinariness. As hagiographer, Morgenschweis has to convince his audience that the true miracle of Pohl's conversion is his human decency, in spite of the Allied trial that condemned him to death for his part in the Nazi crimes. Since Morgenschweis and Pohl are in this project of normalization together, the preface cannot be separated from *Credo*. It is a thematic preview of the chapters that follow.

In the social code of postwar Germany, Anständigkeit *(decency) played a key role in the rehabilitation of complicit and culpable men. "Sei anständig!" (be decent), or "den Anstand behalten" (hold on to your decency): these behavioral admonitions ruled a*

*child's life in the 1950s and 1960s. I recall such phrases in situations of a child's ability to
publicly embarrass or annoy authority figures. To "behave decently" meant for a child to
show respect. My parents used this code to restrain their children, but they also let us loose
and frequently sided with us when older people hurled these reprimands at us. What
I did not know then is how closely related the code of "decency" had been to efforts of
reintegrating former Nazis. The platitude "im Grunde war er ein anständiger Mensch"
(fundamentally, he was a decent human being) was part of the apologetic arsenal on
behalf of former perpetrators. It was used to silence the querying of a person's past.*

As a child, I experienced the admonition to be anständig *as an issue of authority,
age, and fear. I remember when "old men"—men of approximately Pohl's generation—
yelled at us children. Disgruntled and perpetually angry, these men would yell at us
because we were too loud or unruly, or because we violated an unspoken code of decency, or simply because we were kids enjoying ourselves. In adolescence, we called them
"Nazis." Later, I regretted such name-calling. Still later, after studying the biographies
of political cohorts of NS perpetrators, I think our adolescent protest might have intuitively gotten it right: these men could have been Nazis or, in any event, had been
marked by a poisonous mentality.*

Morgenschweis cannot divulge that *Credo* is the result of a shared effort.
On the contrary, he must insist—as he does—that Pohl "has written the
conversion story himself" (9) and that Pohl himself, on his own accord and
without undue external influence, longed to convert to Catholicism. "Pohl
came to his conversion solely under the influence of God's grace. I have in
no way prompted him to do so. The desire emerged from within himself"
(10). Morgenschweis needs to insist on Pohl's independent decision making
and authorship in order to uphold the integrity of the conversion. Hagiog-
raphers cannot allow the reader to confuse the genuine desire of the confessant with their own hagiographic ambitions, for otherwise they would risk
being accused of writing fiction rather than reporting truth. The exemplary
character of a conversion/confession rests in the volition of the sinner, not
the coercive power of the pastor/confessor. However much this assertion is
rhetorical, it is an illusion that must be maintained. The credibility of *Credo*
is thus dependent on the belief that Pohl came to his faith by his own desire
and through God's grace alone. Indeed, the public testimony of a convert

would be an inopportune moment for a confessor-cum-hagiographer to take personal credit for his pastoral guidance.

The chaplain's main task is to frame correctly the experience of the repentant sinner, and he does so theologically through the form of a conversion miracle and, politically, through a normalizing discourse that trivializes guilt. In the 1950s, postwar West Germans felt they were ready to move on with their lives, yet they needed to figure out how to integrate their totalitarian and genocidal past with the current democratic and economic reconstruction efforts (cf. Schwarz 1989). Especially vexing was the problem of the personal guilt of individual Germans, which philosopher Karl Jaspers had raised as early as 1946 in his famous essay *Die Schuldfrage* (*The German Question of Guilt*, 1947). How should a democratic society handle the thousands of people who had been active perpetrators or complicit in genocidal crimes? These people were, after all, colleagues, teachers, peers, friends, neighbors, and family members. "Large parts of the German society showed solidarity with the '*Betroffenen*' [the Nazi convicts]," Frei concludes in his study on how the Federal Republic dealt with its past between 1949 and the mid-1950s. In those early years, Germans were "obsessed" with applying to themselves the alleged Allied accusation of "collective guilt" (1999, 397), while, in the same breath, vehemently repudiating it. As a countermeasure, they exhibited a "desire for self-rehabilitation: A society, which, after all, could credit itself with first successes in regard to economic and political reconstruction," wanted to "exonerate itself" (401–402).

The publication of *Credo* occurs right at this time. It expresses the wish for self-exoneration and seeks solidarity between convicted Nazi perpetrators and German society at large. If it could be shown that a high-ranking Nazi leader, like Pohl, was able to abdicate Nazi ideology and replace it with a new morality, it might encourage other Germans to put their trust in the national reintegration efforts. Pohl, in this narrative and symbolic configuration, is Germany's prodigal son—on both a religious and a national level. He is the unfaithful son who had gone astray, squandering Christian morals, but now returns as a spiritually purified man to his father, that is, to God and the Catholic Church. On this level, Pohl resembles Augustine, whose *Confessions* have also been interpreted through the biblical motif of the prodigal son (see Robbins 1983; Ferrari 1977; Breyfogle 2003, 41). As unfaithful son, Pohl also squandered Germany's proud national inheritance but now returns as a decent man to his father/land. On this level, Pohl resembles other perpetrators of massive state violence who publicly confess in a politically reconfigurated society (Payne 2008; Gallagher 2002). As a self-rehabilitated man, Pohl is the national embodiment of a denazified but still conservative morality—a morality closely aligned with the values of West Germany's democratic beginnings. It is geared toward normalizing Germany's rightful place among nations.

I sometimes felt the urge to please the old men who had yelled at us children. I wanted to show them respect by submitting to their authoritarian unpredictability. I felt that I was in the wrong and they were right. I wanted to return as prodigal son. At the same time I knew how different I was from them and that I would never be able to appease "den Zorn der alten Männer" (the wrath of these old men)—unless I was willing to cripple my own growth. Submitting to them would have meant to swallow their poison. The behavioral code of decency demanded acceptance of their venomous ideology. To become a "prodigal son" to these "prodigal sons" of the newly democratic nation would have meant to forgive their unacknowledged moral failures and to step into the shoes of their anger.

The period of seeking normalization by pushing for a general amnesty for Nazi perpetrators and accomplices has lately been criticized as "cold amnesty" (Friedrich 1994) and "grand peace with the perpetrators" (Giordano 1990, 11). But in the 1950s, the cultural milieu dictated different sentiments. Shortly before his execution, Pohl received an apostolic benediction from the pope (though somewhat by accident).[29] Pohl himself, however, did not benefit from the partial amnesty and sentence reduction that U.S. High Commissioner John McCloy granted a large number of Nazi convicts in January 1951. He was hanged. His confessor and hagiographer, Morgenschweis, however, received several public awards, including the Order of the Federal Republic of Germany in 1952, the Decoration of the German Red Cross in 1958, and, from the Vatican, the honorific title of monsignor in 1959.[30]

Confessing Guilt, Denying Culpability I: The Hagiographer

In the political climate of postwar Germany, the vexing question of guilt was key to social integration, and both Morgenschweis and Pohl knew they had to address it. If, however, one were to expect from the spiritual confession of a Nazi perpetrator a candid and full account of his culpability, *Credo* disappoints. Pohl, as prodigal son, is portrayed as a decent German man for whom there ought to be a place in the new moral order of an emergent democratic nation. As we will see, his Christian conversion points not only to the superiority of the Catholic Church over the hubris of this-worldly powers but also to the steadfast character of the German people.

Both Morgenschweis and Pohl carefully avoid any admission of severe wrongdoing, although they do not deny that Pohl held a high position in the NS regime. Pohl writes that he "built up the administration of the Waffen-SS" (*Credo*, 28), but he does not name the WVHA directly. At his trials, however, Pohl insisted that people had to report to him as the head of the WVHA. In his closing words at the Nuremberg trials in September 1947, for example, he emphasized that he was the "creator" and "engine" of the WVHA and ultimately responsible for it (quoted in Schulte 2001, 43).

Morgenschweis never mentions the crimes for which Pohl is sentenced to death. He never calls him a perpetrator, and nowhere in his preface does he accuse him of any specific guilt. Aware of some dissenting voices among a German chorus that favored clemency, he elevates Pohl to sacrificial victimhood.[31] The publication of *Credo*, Morgenschweis writes, might "evoke perhaps a few protests and contrary opinions," but the reader should realize that the imprisoned Pohl "followed God's call even at the price of extreme sacrifices" and "developed a rare eagerness for prayer and a sacrificial spirit" (9, 11–12). It is quite possible, Morgenschweis admits, that Pohl, like other Nazis, might not have turned to the Catholic Church if "God had not burdened them and our whole *Volk* [people] with the grim fate of a total collapse of a totally anti-Christian power."[32] Today, Morgenschweis continues, "many of the former comrades are even wearing the Catholic habit" (10). What distinguishes Pohl, however, from all the others is his disciplined sincerity about his newfound faith. "When God calls," Morgenschweis quotes Pohl approvingly, "then everything else in life has to take second place, even one's own family" (11). Pohl's abdication of his own family is supposed to demonstrate the convert's firm character and Christian resolve. What stands out for today's reader, however, is its clichéd and authoritarian tone. After all, Pohl had been guided by a similar principle of duty and obedience throughout the Nazi regime, except that then his absolute devotion was not to God but to his superior Heinrich Himmler and his work at the WVHA.[33]

Morgenschweis continues: The new convert is "ready to confess guilt, where guilt is, and to repent for this guilt" (13). What this guilt consists of, however, the confessor does not tell us. The text remains intentionally vague. The strategic advantage of such elusiveness is twofold: Politically, the prison chaplain does not have to declare his position in regard to the serious charges of the American court—"these words should therefore not be seen as judgment about the judgment that the court at Nuremberg passed on him" (12). Theologically, the specific guilt of a Nazi perpetrator is made to disappear behind the general condition of human sinfulness—not unlike Augustine's and Perechodnik's inclination to generalize and universalize in order to hide specific responsibility. Read within the context of the teachings of original sin, nonspecificity implies that the perpetrator's guilt does not differ essentially from that of any ordinary (Christian) sinner. In a postlapsarian world all humans are sinners. Pohl might be guilty, but so is everyone else.

The phrase "ready to confess guilt, where guilt is" thus eludes culpability. It neither denies nor affirms any wrongdoing. In this manner, Morgenschweis avoids a scolding by the American forces (under whose supervision he works in the War Crimes Prison) without having to assent to the Allied accusations. Pohl is guilty of something (like all human sinners), but not necessarily guilty of those things that others have said about him (such as the American charges of crimes against humanity). With respect to repentance, then, Pohl must establish a spiritual rapport with God but is not obligated to admit to the criminal charges of his accusers. The sinner is willing to repent for his "true" (read: universal) guilt but not for the alleged guilt as a Nazi perpetrator for which he is on death row. Since the ground for Pohl's confession is not the legal court but God, cooperation with the judicial system to determine the exact nature of his culpability is deliberately obstructed.

Morgenschweis, of course, does not interpret Pohl's defiance as a character flaw but as strength of his *Haltung*,[34] which has led him to accept the Catholic faith. A spiritual confession that surpasses judicial justice is not seen as a weakness of the concept of repentance but as a strength of Christian forgiveness. In the concluding paragraph of the preface, Morgenschweis praises *Credo* as a "contribution to *reconciliation* and *peace*. . . . May it become a blessing for many, especially for his family and his former comrades! May it also reconcile those who are still living in *hate* over the injustice inflicted on them by a system that the former General of the Waffen-SS had served" (14; emphasis added).

According to the confessor, the (former) perpetrator is willing to reconcile, whereas the victims continue to live in hate. Readers today—after decades of education about the severity of the crimes of the Holocaust and other genocides—must be baffled by the audacity of Morgenschweis's claim: spiritual integrity is granted to the perpetrator; moral ignobleness, only to the victims. Such theologically grounded moralizing exposes a dark side of the Christian concept of forgiveness (see Kellenbach 2006, esp. 279–288). The hagiographic frame tips the moral balance in favor of the individual perpetrator. The affective-political message cannot be mistaken: the reader's empathy is directed toward the perpetrator-cum-confessant, while the trauma of victims is ignored. Five years after the liberation of the camps, it is the Nazi perpetrator who seeks reconciliation and peace, while the former victims and survivors continue to live in hatred. The perpetrators have transformed themselves into prodigal sons and good Christians, while the (Jewish) victims stagnate in their hate.[35]

Morgenschweis's apologetic argumentation is by no means original but repeats a fairly standard moral discourse on guilt and forgiveness cultivated after the war in conservative circles inside and outside the German churches. Those "conservatives stressed the powerful message of God's forgiveness. . . . The [faith] confession was not meant to be made to the Jews or other peoples grievously mistreated by Germans . . . but to God who was angry with German disloyalty" (Hockenos 2004, 70; also Kellenbach 2006; Kleßmann 1993; Greschat 1990; Löhr 1990). Such theological reasoning fed a political morality in which Germans saw themselves as victims of Allied injustices, such as the carpet bombing of civilian cities, the forced expulsion from the East, the delayed release of German POWs, the imposed jurisdiction in the Western zones, and the much-criticized American denazification and reeducation campaigns (see Moeller 2001; Frei 1999, 54–69; Vollnhals 1992; Krondorfer 2006, 108–110). Despite the national and personal humiliations suffered under the alleged hypocritical justice of the Allied victors, the German people, Morgenschweis implies, possess the moral fortitude to stretch out their hands in gestures of peace and reconciliation, whereas scornful victors and victims, who should have had enough time to let go of their resentment, continue to act against Germans with vengeance. A strong message contained in *Credo*, then, is directed toward the Allies: Show that you can exercise "true" justice! Show that you can be moved to generosity by Pohl's transformation from a Nazi to a morally upright, decent human being!

Confessing Guilt, Denying Culpability II: The Confessant

Pohl's perception of his own guilt essentially follows his confessor's contentions. Pohl never admits culpability; he universalizes and spiritualizes guilt, claims personal innocence (but not ignorance), and stakes out a moral high ground. Pohl's discomfort with the whole question of guilt is indicated by putting quotation marks around the word "*Schuld*" (guilt). He cannot avoid the term altogether but does not want to be too closely associated with it. Switching to a passive voice when reporting on ignominious autobiographical details is another way of avoiding culpability. Pohl, like Augustine and Perechodnik, frequently turns to passive linguistic constructions when recollecting unresolved business—a strategy regularly pursued in confessional performances of perpetrators. The passive voice corresponds to "the perpetrator's need to disempower himself" (Vetlesen 2005, 217) and thus to minimize his moral agency during acts of wrongdoing.

In *Credo*, for example, Pohl downplays his decision to join the SS administration. Although historical evidence reveals a very eager man ready to pursue his professional ambitions under Himmler's directives,[36] *Credo* portrays Pohl as having been pressed and pestered (*bedrängen*) by Himmler to leave the navy and join the SS organization. It was a very difficult decision, Pohl writes, "to take on" this task. Once "I accepted Himmler's *Auftrag* [orders, task] I got *unsuspectingly* into an organization that eleven years later was to be branded 'criminal'" (28–29; emphasis added). Pohl repeats a similar passive formulation in *Credo*'s attached short biography: "For almost a year, Himmler pursued me with his offer to set up the administration of the Waffen-SS. In February 1934, I gave in. It was the most serious decision of my life! It brought me eleven years later as the head of the Economic-Administrative Main Office before the tribunal of the victors and the gallows" (75).

Pohl does not claim total ignorance, and in the chapter "Return to God," he wonders aloud about the whereabouts of his "conscience" at a time when "the methods of the National-Socialist state authority took on apocalyptic forms. . . . Many things did not remain hidden from me, even if I personally did not take part in them" (40). This is the closest the former head of the WVHA comes to admitting culpable knowledge. Not surprisingly, he does not linger on this insight but quickly declares his personal blamelessness. In subsequent paragraphs, he trivializes his personal knowledge of the (unmentioned) crimes by pointing to the "conscience of all the many others," who had remained "silent." The lack of conscience is true "not only for Germany

[but] everywhere" (40): "Inhuman acts—'crimes against humanity'—have regrettably not been limited to isolated occurrences during times of war. In view of the planetary events after the cessation of weapons-based hostilities they have become the dreadful traffic regulations [*Verkehrsmethode*] of human society" (41).

Pohl—in a move typical of postwar Germans defending themselves against criminal charges—can entertain only the vaguest notion of his own culpability by instantly pointing to the guilt and moral failures of others. As the previous quotation demonstrates, not only does Pohl imply that inhuman acts were merely "isolated occurrences" during the war (when, as a matter of fact, he oversaw the systematic exploitation of millions of slave laborers) but he also points the finger at the Allies, who are in power after the war and, according to him, govern with equally inhumane rules.

The pointing of fingers at the guilt of others: I have witnessed this time and again in conversation with Germans who lived through the Nazi regime. They point to the shared guilt of the Allies, the severity of the military advance of the Soviet army, the bombing raids by the British, the marauding Moroccan soldiers of the French occupation force, the expulsion of Germans by Poles and Czechs, the American-led efforts of postwar trials and denazification, as well as to the inhumanity performed by all nations, not just Germany. In comparison, the newly emerging pacified West German democracy did not look so bad.

Pohl does not need to specify that he has the Allied forces in mind, especially the Americans, when he points fingers. For *Credo*'s intended audience, this would be self-evident, and calling the Americans by name directly would have been counterproductive. Pohl is still dependent on their goodwill for clemency. A direct confrontation would not only hurt his chances but also contradict *Credo*'s intent to portray the new convert as a serene and composed man.

Earlier, however, Pohl does not mince words. In a letter written in 1948 from prison to a friend, he summarizes his fate with the following words: "I was 54 years old, had served unimpeachably my fatherland for 33 years, and was [regarding my person] not aware of any crimes." He concluded the letter with the broad claim that the American prosecution "lacked any objectivity. . . . Driven by blind hate and plain vindictiveness, the goal of the prosecution, which was dominated by Jewish representatives, was not to determine truth but to annihilate as many adversaries as possible."[37]

Such sentiments, of course, could not have been expressed in *Credo* since it tries to foreground Pohl's faith-induced tranquility. Plenty of textual fissures indicate, however, tensions between, on the one hand, an image of a man who, with the help of divine love, has surrendered to his God-given fate and, on the other, Pohl's old loyalties to his militaristic, totalitarian, and nationalist mentality. In the fourth chapter, we read, for example, about the spiritual nature of humans: "The more a person knows about himself, or thinks he knows about himself, the more he disappears to himself as a unified whole and clearly definable entity. . . . Herein lies the deepest meaning and the greatest riches of salvation: to lift up the rationally endowed creature [*Geschöpf*] from the infinite distance of his ontological powerlessness [*Seinsohnmacht*] and from the abysmal forlornness of his sin to divine vitality, and thereby enable him to join in the work of salvation" (53, 65).[38] The eloquence of such religious-philosophical musing stands in striking semantic contrast to other passages, where a cruder and remarkably different understanding of Christianity emerges. There, Pohl ponders, for example, the "totalitarian claim" of Christ's teachings (19), portrays his awakening to the Catholic faith as a "frontal breakthrough" (*Frontaldurchbruch*), and speaks of the "new armor of faith" that helped him in his "battles" with doubt (58). "After all, no one will blame an old soldier for being highly impressed by the strong love of order and authoritative leadership of the Catholic Church by which it distinguishes itself from all other Christian denominations: Order, unity, leadership and obedience all rest in the sphere of the military" (60). These sentiments seem to mirror more closely Pohl's soldierly mind. Only a most credulous reader today would be seduced into believing that one and the same person could have penned these simplistic understandings of Christianity as well as the ornate theological musings quoted earlier.

Morgenschweis's hagiographic interventions help to present a benign version of the new convert. At times, it seems that Pohl's old self has to be artfully subdued, for it pushes itself repeatedly through the surface of the text. Pohl retains enough of his own voice that the old self never quite disappears. The tension between these two representations of Pohl is never fully resolved in *Credo*. A German reader of the 1950s sympathetic to Pohl's fate might believe the presented portrait of a converted self; a cynical reader will discredit the story as political opportunism or, simply, fake.

Pohl explicitly states that he did not convert out of "tactical reasons" and that his transformation from an "SS general to a faithful Catholic" was not an "escape to the church . . . in order to play a trick on fate" (66–67). If this were to be true, could we assume that he acknowledges culpability? Truly transformed by faith and at ease with fate—as *Credo* repeatedly claims—he ought to be ready to accept personal guilt.

But is he? Pohl repeatedly turns the question of guilt into an occasion for blaming others, thereby minimizing his own culpability. He blames the Allies, the Protestant church, and his former comrades and employees at the WVHA.[39] On only two occasions does he struggle with guilt in slightly more sustained ways. In chapter 3, he discusses his personal guilt as it relates to criminal guilt, and it is on this occasion that he consistently puts "*Schuld*" in quotation marks. In chapter 4, he reflects theologically on guilt, sin, and suffering as part of God's plan. Whereas in the first case he rejects culpability, in the latter he confesses guilt and sin only in universal terms. The "misery" he now suffers is a divine test for "purification" (68).

Ideally, a male confessant would grasp the opportunity to stand morally naked in front of God (and his imagined audience), but Pohl misses his chances to admit his former wrongdoings and take a first step toward repentance. As such, he is quite different from Perechodnik, the victim of Nazi genocidal antisemitism, who, after admitting complicity in the murder of his own people and family, had rendered himself naked in his deathbed confession. Perechodnik had abdicated control over his reader's judgment, exposing his moral failure to the point of reckless self-effacement, with no redemption in sight. Pohl does not seize the moment to confess guilt for his participation in crimes against humanity and, instead, tries to control his readers' affective and moral verdict. "I do not feel called to examine the political ideology [of National Socialism]," Pohl writes. "I was tormented only by the share of my personal 'guilt'" (43). Wondering whether personal blamelessness "releases me from 'guilt'" (43; recall that he claims never to have killed a person), he refuses to answer his own question. The potentially self-interrogative query is neutralized by an accusatory counterquestion about his former Nazi comrades: "What happened to them?" (43). Venting his anger against fearful and "professional" witnesses,[40] he concludes that only an ethically weak ideology could have produced such men. National Socialism failed as an ideology because it did not produce loyalty. It was weak because it had cut off its ties "to the depth of the soul and the transcendent" (45). National Socialism could not keep its promise, and therein, according to the convert Pohl, lies "the moral failure especially of the higher echelons." "To this development I contributed by support- ing National Socialism. This, at least, is my co-responsibility, hence 'guilt'" (45). Pohl admits only that he had erred in judgment about the power of a human ideology. Not recognizing this error "made me neither less 'guilty' nor guiltless" (45–46).

These few passages are the extent of *Credo*'s admission of personal guilt. It is never linked to the atrocities Pohl had administered as part of the Nazi bureaucracy. The only sin admitted is his support of an ideology that created disloyal men. That former Nazis did not stand by their old con- victions proved the ideological failure of National Socialism. No wonder, then, that Germany lost the war. In other words, Pohl does not feel guilty for having participated in a genocidal nightmare but for having contrib- uted to an unrealistic dream of Germany's grandeur. "I believed in the victory of my fatherland until the catastrophe" (42). In prison and under the confessor's guidance, Christian faith makes him discern the delusional nature of this dream.

Credo testifies not so much to the transformation of an old to a new self as to a male confessant embracing a new power. It does not testify to the transformational power of confessions but to an exchange of powers. The (delusional) belief in the power of National Socialism is supplanted by a (sobered) faith in the power of Catholicism. The fact that in chapter 4 Pohl generally acknowledges "all guilt and all sins" and, equally, all his "misery and sufferings" (68) does not change the flawed nature of this confession. Pohl does not bare his soul to the reader but clings to a new authority to expel the ghosts of the past.

Younger generations of German men tried to expel the ghosts of the past differently. These men were too young to be culpable in any legal and political sense, but they were raised during the Nazi regime and drafted as teenage soldiers in the last two war years. They became good democrats in West Germany (and good socialists in East Germany). Like my father. Like my mother. After forced to abandon their childhood homes in the Eastern territories, they were young and flexible enough to adjust to a new geography and new political system. In our new home in West Germany, my parents showed no

sympathy for Nazi perpetrators. They felt betrayed by them and showed no patience for their grandiose posturing during the war and their self-pitying posturing after the war.

My parents are not free from the past—how can they be? But they have struggled to understand their involuntary place in history. The older they get, the stronger they hold on to particular interpretations of their experience. Many of their views I do not share, but they never became like those "old men" I feared as a child.

Self-Pitying Blindness (A Failed Confession)

Unter mein bisheriges Leben habe ich entschlossen einen Strich gezogen.[41] I resolutely drew a line under my former life. What was good in it, I have taken with me as uplifting memories to the born-again life. What was bad in it, that which caused the negative balance, my numerous sins, I presented to God in prayer and fasting. (*Credo*, 67)

Christian theology has too often blurred the distinction between the human sinner in general and people who perpetrated large-scale violence. If confessing a genocidal crime were no different from confessing sexual impropriety—because the perpetrator knows himself to live under the same fallen human condition as everyone else, and hence in God's grace—then we would end up with a "universal night in which everything is equally black" (Moltmann 1992, 126). Does the writing of a confessing self have to proceed differently when the sins to be repented reach beyond the pale of Rousseau's theft of a ribbon or Augustine's seemingly trivial stealing of pears from a neighbor's tree (2.4.9)—the deliberate "much ado about almost nothing" episode (Burrus 2004, 81)? What if the sins exceed the dilemmas of lust, temptation, desire, appetite, or randomness that Rousseau and Augustine bemoan throughout their *Confessions*? What if Augustine's "hellish pleasures" of the "shadowy jungle of erotic adventures" (2.1.1) were replaced by the "hellish" realities of the concentration camp universe?

The tendency to universalize sins "makes people blind to specific, practical guilt" (Moltmann 1992, 126). *Credo* suffers from precisely such blindness and elusiveness. No specific instances of guilt are confessed, yet Pohl with the help of his hagiographer imagines himself to be forgiven and saved by God. He declares that his conversion allows him to draw a final line, a *Schlussstrich*, under his old life, but he hastens to add that not everything from his former life needs to be abandoned. He wants to retain the "good" (though he fails to tell what the "good" consists of). Neither does the conversion compel Pohl to cooperate with the Allies in determining the degree of his culpability nor does he take responsibility for the harm inflicted on the victims of his WVHA policies. In Pohl's perception, the Allies and victims remain his adversaries because they refuse to be witnesses to his born-again life.[42] The Allies keep persecuting him with trumped-up charges; the victims continue to live in hate. Because neither Allies nor victims give credibility to his claim of having found closure to his former life, they cannot participate in God's grace and reconciliatory power.

In regard to severe wrongdoing—the kind of "culpable wrongdoing" that Claudia Card defines as "evil" because it produces "foreseeable intolerable harm" (2002, 3)—an ethical line must be drawn between an ordinary confessing sinner and a confessing genocidal perpetrator. In the end, *Credo*, as a conversion narrative, is guided more by political and ecclesiastical self-interest than by a desire for self-interrogation. The male confessant does not render himself vulnerable but seeks spiritual and political amnesty through recourse to a religious experience. In this sense, *Credo* fails as a model of male self-revelation, although it may not, paradoxically, fail as a perpetrator confession.

Why does it fail? Because the confessant Pohl—like most genocidal perpetrators—continues to hide his moral agency. This failure is not just Pohl's individual weakness (but surely it is that, too) but goes to the very nature of genocidal crime itself. As opposed to regular crimes, including murder, for which "normatively speaking . . . the *individual agent* must be held accountable," the individual disappears in the collectivity of systematic, large-scale annihilations (Vetlesen 2005, 260; emphasis in original). In the violent dynamics of genocidal situations, perpetrators perceive themselves as lacking individuality. "The perpetrator," Vetlesen writes in *Evil and Human Agency*, "would frequently attempt to *deindividualize* his particular victims" as well as obliterate individuality of the in-group perpetrating the deeds. "Genocidal logic subscribes to a notion of agency as collective" (2005, 260; emphasis in original).[43] Given this logic—as analytical explanation, not moral exoneration—Pohl might be incapable of recognizing the severity of his actions. He certainly fails to see the intolerable harm that he inflicted on the slave labor population in the concentration camps. As he writes his confessions in the Allied prison cell, he gives no notice to the victims of his administrative SS policies—just as they were invisible to him as head of the WVHA.

Pohl, however, is vain enough not to entirely relinquish the pride in his professional accomplishments at the WVHA. He claims individual agency when it concerns his career but not when it concerns the harmful results of his work. As a matter of fact, perpetrators, who find themselves on the defensive, often claim individual agency with respect to the logistical, administrative, and technical skills they acquired and exhibited at their former jobs but do not claim moral responsibility for the consequences of these skills.[44] "Planners of collective, large-scale evil present *self-sacrifice* . . . as *moral virtue*" (Vetlesen 2005, 260; emphasis in original). Pohl claims precisely this kind of virtuous behavior.

> In front of the [prison] gates stayed my life, which had guided me without any patronage or "connections" from a simple son of the working class to the highest positions in the military trade: through diligence, pragmatic level-headedness [*Nüchternheit*] and sacrifice for a cause, to which I devoted myself in enthusiastic idealism from the beginning. My life's work was smashed. (*Credo*, 39)

Self-praise intermingles with self-pity: against the odds of social class, Pohl attributes his success to his self-sacrificial, hard work and his steadfast character, only to see it all destroyed in 1945. It is a fitting example of what Vetlesen calls "the perverted type of morality that is cultivated by organizers of collective evil" (2005, 260). Such self-acclaimed virtuousness remains thoroughly egocentric, with no room for compassion for the victims. Because in Pohl's perception his idealism demanded sacrifices of him, he fails to see the thousands of people he sacrificed for his cause. While sitting on the "plank bed of my dark and cold cell," he laments his own miserable existence but not the innumerable wounded and dead as the result of his WVHA orders. "I was overcome by an icy loneliness and bottomless desertedness as if I were 'in a dry and weary land where no water is'" (*Credo*, 39).

Quoting the Psalms,[45] the previous phrase evokes biblical images of the lost sheep and the prodigal son. Like a martyr of old, Pohl is languishing in prison for his idealism and ideological convictions. *Credo*, however, carefully avoids any obvious parallelism between Christian martyrs and Pohl. Such a comparison would not only contradict *Credo*'s claim of a credible conversion (unlike Pohl, Christian martyrs were persecuted *because* they already professed Christ; they did not convert in prison), but it could also potentially backfire. Despite the widespread German calls for clemency and amnesty in 1949 and 1950, Pohl could not be portrayed as a national martyr. There was not enough support for presenting the Nazi leadership in the light of martyrology. This became evident when the majority of the German press responded with restraint to the news of Pohl's eventual hanging in 1951, a few months after *Credo*'s publication. One newspaper commented that the Landsberg gallows "were not the cross of Golgotha," and a popular Protestant newspaper echoed a similar sentiment when it expressed a "simple human compassion" for the hanged prisoner but hastened to declare that "certainly no heroes or martyrs ended up on the gallows of Landsberg."[46]

Credo does not portray Pohl as a martyr, but its rhetoric inches up to a concept of confession more generally understood as "confess[ing] faith in Christianity in spite of persecution" without "suffer[ing] martyrdom."[47] Within such suggestive imagery, Pohl is not the one who persecuted others: he is the one persecuted! Compassion is elicited for Pohl, not his victims: "He [God] poured over me the whole wretchedness of life: slander, humiliation, physical and mental abuse, earthly judgment and gallows" (67).[48] Self-pitying, Pohl laments his current imprisonment and the squandering of his earlier self-sacrificial devotion. The perpetrator's lack of shame and culpability corresponds to the complete absence of compassion for others.

Authentic Disingenuousness

Pohl did not accept the teachings of the Catholic Church without some internal resistance. After all, to be measured by the standards of a new morality produces anxieties, and Pohl as former head of the WVHA is not free of them. He writes:

> My fate has taught me something else. The teachings were quite bitter, the methods of the gallows barbaric, but extremely curative. In the purgatory of this extreme dejection I was purified to receive the true faith in God. . . . The moment of transformation filled me with a longing love. It is love that matters above all. (*Credo*, 57)

Can these words be trusted? It is important to restate that Pohl actually converted to Catholicism and that he must have believed in some kind of personal transformation. He had been shaken up to some degree by reading his life through the lens of a newly acquired belief system. His changes were also credible to Morgenschweis, who, after a period of religious instruction, administered the eucharistic sacrament and welcomed him into the church. Analyzing *Credo* critically does not call into question the conversion itself. It clearly took place, and we must assume that a certain amount of sincerity transpired between Pohl and his confessor to which we as readers are not privy.

In my critical reading, then, what is at stake is the public dimension of this confession-and-conversion narrative, and not what might have privately transpired between confessor and confessant—since the latter is not accessible to anyone outside Pohl and Morgenschweis. In other words, what draws my attention to Pohl is not so much the fact that he converted—after all, other Nazi perpetrators rediscovered God after the war and rejoined the churches. Rather, it is the idea that this perpetrator felt called to produce a public confession. How should we evaluate a confessional writing produced by a man, who, after all, is not just an ordinary sinner but a genocidal perpetrator? Can the evil of genocidal acts be poured into the confessiographic form the same way as Augustine's sin of stealing pears?

A peculiar dynamic between empowerment and disempowerment drives *Credo*. Pohl disempowers himself in two ways: by denying agency for his own culpable actions in the past and by portraying himself as victim in the present. The narrative follows a chronological pattern. In the past (chapters 1 and 2), the full agency of the male self had been variously impeded: Pohl just fulfilled his duties, he was duped by his superiors and disobeyed by his inferiors, and he had to suppress his true feelings. In the present (chapters 3 and 4), the male confessant is not fully in control of agency because he is victimized, suffers in prison, and is treated unjustly (by the Allies). The passivity and self-pitying that accompany this narrative pattern amount to a certain self-feminization—if by "feminization" we understand not a representation of real women but a cultural code that stands in contrast to traditional views of masculinity. It is a cultural code to which men like Pohl had subscribed before the end of the Nazi regime. It is precisely this turn to a feminized passivity—the self-pitying and self-victimization—that allows men like Pohl to briefly expose their souls. Small concessions and incomplete confessions slip through tiny cracks in the manly facade of (former) perpetrators. Religious language lends a hand in presenting a male self in need of care and compassion—an admission of emotional dependency, which, for men socialized and politicized in the Great War and its aftermath, was no small feat.

Strangely enough, the temporary feminization of their gendered persona also empowered these men. It enabled them to turn the postwar situation to their advantage and reclaim moral authority. A "softer" male self—suffering yet receptive to the new morality of the early 1950s—was a ticket to the possibility of clemency and social reintegration. *Credo* plays with these potentialities, even if, at the end, Pohl was not awarded another chance. To a small extent, the confessional model allowed Pohl to open his soul to public scrutiny. His minor admissions should not, however, be mistaken for an acknowledgment of culpability. Precisely that which is most desperately needed from a perpetrator of massive state violence, namely, the public recognition of his full culpability, is absent in his testimony.[49] In *Credo*, each instance of a partial recognition of guilt is predictably followed by some mental or rhetorical retraction. In this sense, *Credo* falls short of the demands that the genre of public confessional writing exerts on men. Emulating Augustine's *Confessions*, it never reaches its height and depth, either in terms of literary and philosophical sophistication or in terms of a man's willingness to open his heart and soul without reservation. Pohl does not render his sinful self naked to the public eye and, hence, to judgment.

Credo's apologetic discourse seeks to protect its male subject. Instead of employing the confessional form in order to account for the extraordinary culpability of a perpetrator, it rehearses certain narrative conventions and inserts external markers of the confession tradition in order to persuade the reader of the credibility of Pohl's transformation. Must we therefore conclude that *Credo*, as a confessiography, presents nothing but a deliberately disingenuous effort for no purpose other than seeking a strategic advantage in the debate about political amnesty and church-supported clemency? I don't think so. On the one hand, the pathos of self-pitying, feminization, and self-victimization moves religious sentimentalization and audacious political counterclaims to and fro, widening the credibility gap. On the other hand, such pathos does not simply demonstrate the inauthenticity of *Credo*. Just the opposite might be closer to the truth: we need to seek in exactly this kind of pathetic discourse the *authentic* language of a perpetrator. It is authentic precisely because it is disingenuous. When perpetrators testify, witness, or confess publicly, we need to expect a text full of contradictions, tensions, and fissures simply because it might be impossible for genocidal murderers to fully acknowledge their culpability if they were to continue living a "normal" life (see Krondorfer 2008c). Pohl did not morally despair over the hurt he had inflicted on others. If anything, he felt sorry for himself and was clinging to his own life. The seemingly disempowering language of self-pity reempowered him as a newborn, decent man. He became, in Morgenschweis's words, a "complete Catholic" who "serves today God and Christ and His divine love in the world" (*Credo*, 14). The disempowered, yet remasculinized male confessant is fraudulent and authentic at the same time.

Te Deum Laudamus

God, we praise you. With the Latin phrase *Te Deum laudamus*, the main narrative of *Credo* concludes. It is, of course, yet another deliberate reference to Augustine, but this does not change the fact that we are dealing here with an authentically disingenuous perpetrator confession rather than a genuine confession. The latter requires a male confessant making the best possible effort of rendering himself vulnerable to himself as well as to the public eye and, possibly, to God. It requires an *unmaking* before a credible *remaking* can be achieved. Submission to judgment outside the control of the male confessant is crucial.

Relinquishing such control means to confess *all* grievous sins, which, in the case of genocidal perpetrators, translates into publicly confessing culpability for all acts of abetting and committing atrocities. Granted, no confession of guilt can be total and complete, since no confessing self can perform the ultimate act of self-erasure. The confessant always (re)constructs himself in the process of confessing. *Credo*, however, is lacking any sustained effort of soul baring. Augustine writes in a commentary to the Gospel of John that "to testify (*confiteri*) [is] to speak out what the heart holds true. If the tongue and the heart are at odds, you are reciting, not testifying" (quoted in Wills 1999, xvi). In *Credo*, tongue and heart are at odds. Hence, Pohl's confession, in light of Augustine's admonition, is a "reciting." By and large, Pohl and Morgenschweis *recite* a litany of already-practiced arguments that are part of a discourse by and about perpetrators. They repeat them, rehearse them, modulate them. What *Credo* adds to this chorus is that it deliberately clothes itself in the style of a Christian confessiography.

Te Deum laudamus brings the narrative part of *Credo* to an end, but it does not yet end the booklet. Two religious poems and a one-page summary of Pohl's biography follow. The poems are thematically suggestive of Pohl's interior disposition, portraying the desolate state of a prisoner whose only comfort is God. The first poem, "Solace" (*Trost*), by Ruth Schaumann, addresses the divine refuge Pohl is seeking in the face of human hostility. The first stanza reads:

> In der Menschen Hände gabst Du mich,
> in mich selber aber gabst Du Dich!
> Mögen sie mich greifen und zerschleißen,
> mögen sie mich halten und zerreißen,
> wenn Du bleibst, so bin auch ich.

You put me into the hands of humans,
but into myself You gave yourself!
May they seize me and wear me out,
may they detain me or tear me apart
if You remain, so also am I.

To find solace by submitting to God's omnipresence in the face of unjust suffering at the hands of humans is the poem's main theme. It also conjures up the Passion of Christ, thus obliquely and subtly suggesting a parallel between Pohl and Christ. The fear of abandonment, which also speaks through these lines, is echoed and amplified in the second poem. Here is how it begins:

When you are fully abandoned
do not lament for a moment.
Only then can you grasp yourself
can you return to God.[50]

The return to God promises an end to all human agony. But whose agony is it? It is Oswald Pohl's agony. Identified in these poems (as throughout *Credo*) as a lonely man, who has been fatefully abandoned and persecuted by humans, Pohl is the one deserving empathy. This is no cri de coeur of a man who is overwhelmed by the magnitude of his accumulated guilt. It is a pathetic plea of and for a man who perceives himself burdened by fate.

No doubt, these poems are deliberately placed at the end of *Credo*, and it matters little whether Pohl or Morgenschweis selected them. They were intended for a postwar German audience, which was expected to identify with Pohl's newly embraced moral decency and to participate in the pardoning of a high-ranking Nazi as an act of German self-forgiveness. Pohl's victims, in turn, were erased. They were invisible to him during his criminal deeds as head of the WVHA as they later remained invisible in his confessional text. The few times victims are circuitously mentioned in *Credo*, they are portrayed as bearers of hate and vengeance. Their erasure, it seems, is not an occasion to praise God but an occasion for tears.

On Tears

I closed [my mother's] eyes and an overwhelming grief welled
into my heart and was about to flow forth in floods of tears. But
at the same time under a powerful mental control my eyes held
back the flood and dried up. The inward struggle put me into
great agony. Then when she breathed her last, the boy Adeodatus
cried out in sorrow and was pressed by all of us to be silent.

AUGUSTINE, *Confessions*

[Augustine] says he has to do so in *writing*, precisely, after
the death of his mother, over whom he does not deplore the
fact of not having wept, not that I dare link what he says
about confession with the deaths of our respective mothers
. . . for my mother was not a saint.

JACQUES DERRIDA, "Circumfession"

Men, it seems, first write their autobiographies by giving
testimony to the death of an Other, a woman.

VIRGINIA BURRUS, *The Sex Lives of Saints*

I cannot conceive of love save in torment and tears . . . [and]
nothing moves or attracts me so much as woman weeping.

MICHEL LEIRIS, *Manhood*

Overwhelming grief and sorrow disintegrate a person; the act of writing, in
response, is an attempt to restore the ruptured universe. Between the moment of psychophysical devastation and the mental restoration through the
logos, the agon/agony of tears.

Tears resist language. At the boundaries of the body, they express that
which language fails to articulate. Weeping, the male confessant gives in to

the realization that he is not in control. He fights tears because he fears being drowned by a flood, by a death-resembling anguish, which would leave him wordless, without a language that would help to anchor him in this world. A man-in-sorrow who forcefully tries to hold back those lacrimal fluids is clinging to the illusion that stability can be found in his pre-ruptured world. But this world, or, better, his perception of that world, is irretrievably lost. To maintain his illusion, he stoically silences himself as he needs to silence those who dare to cry out in public. In this state of agony, Augustine observes himself with great accuracy: The loss of an intimate other (his mother) leads to the silencing of another intimate other, his son (9.12.29). It also leads to self-alienation, as Augustine soon realizes. Resisting tears will not bring back that which has been irretrievably lost, and in the privacy of his bedroom he eventually surrenders to the "flow of tears" (9.12.33).

Real men don't cry, but male confessants often do. Are confessing men crybabies and mama's boys? The platitude that men are less prone to weeping than women has been repeated in modernity so often that it has attained a facticity that seems irrefutable, thus veiling plenty of evidence to the contrary. Historical and autobiographical texts paint a different picture: Augustine weeps, and so before him the desert fathers and after him the fathers of monasticism; the Byzantine fathers in the East do it and also Gregory the Great in the West; St. Francis of Assisi weeps (his blindness in old age, it was said, was caused by an excess of tears) and also Ignatius of Loyola, whose autobiography is inundated with crying episodes; Dante weeps in the fourteenth century and so do the melancholic men of the Renaissance; even the deconstructionist philosopher Derrida reveals his proclivity for weeping when "circumfessing" around Augustine's *Confessions*.[1] "Male crying is everywhere," Lutz writes in his work on the cultural history of tears. In the waning years of the twentieth century, "even action stars like Mel Gibson, Sylvester Stallone, and Bruce Willis" have teared up on-screen. "The desired male is once again becoming the man who cries" (Lutz 1999, 189).

On the other hand, there is, undeniably, a strong trajectory in Western philosophical and medical-spiritual thinking that demands that men control their passions in order to occupy the positions of householder and free citizen. Aristotle's misogynist reasoning is one of the more obvious places to find a pseudobiological explanation of gendered differences: "Woman is more compassionate than man, more easily moved to tears, at the same time is more jealous, more querulous, more apt to scold or strike." In the nineteenth century—to cite a later instance of this trajectory—William James argued that a "dry-eyed, healthy-minded" religion had to be differentiated from the weeping "medieval saints" and "neurotic weepers" of the religion of the "sick souls."[2] Modernist men, like Leiris, "repress a desire to weep" (1992, 20), or they mock the sentimentality of tears, like Man Ray, whose 1932 photograph *Larmes* depicts tears like "plastic pearls" affixed to the cheeks of his female model (see Lutz 1999, 37–38, 279). Tears are construed as a bodily signifier by which one can differentiate between women and men, emotionality and rationality.

Weeping signals loss of control, enslavement to (com)passion, and endangerment of a healthy masculinity. Such a view was embedded in the larger Hellenistic understanding that a man's task was to control his passions (such as anger, sorrow, lust). Men losing control were in danger of becoming like women and slaves or, later, hysterics and neurotics. Both the social and symbolic orders are inextricably entangled, one reinforcing the other, pulling men into the sexual rule of the father that operates as much on metaphoric and literary levels as on the restrictive level of the *oikonomia* (household/economy). Men in power, who became enslaved to their emotions, could lose their manliness and their male privileges, whereas, in contrast, men enslaved to political and economic oppression (such as slavery, class, colonialism) were not permitted to choose their sexual relations and were denied a masculinity granted to the elites. Hegemonic and dominant men had to continually ensure and enforce their place in the symbolic order, whereas oppressed and marginalized men lived in submission to or rebellion against that which the social order denied them.

Social slave or metaphoric enslavement: These systems were tearing and pulling, weaving and reknotting the fabric of relationships within the political, sexual, religious, and affective ordering of the universe. The effects of these privilege-based, gender-enforcing systems are real. Culture-specific surveys taken in Europe and America—two political geographies that saw the emergence of a new ideal of tough manliness in the nineteenth century—suggest that men cry five times less than women and that 45 percent of men never weep (see Lutz 1999, 185; Benke 2002, 22). But no less real are the cultural and textual instances in which we find men "crying everywhere." When male confessants confess to weeping, they resist the order of the householder and the fiction of stoic masculinity.

CHAPTER 5

Sons of Tears

Displacing the Intimate (Female) Other

Male confessiographies tell of tears caused by the grief over intimate others or the wounding associated with them. Do male tears reveal the confessant's deep attachment to loved ones? Do their tears veil a clear perception of intimate others? Or do tears of grief displace the intimate other? As we shall see, male vulnerabilities, to which confessional writings testify, do not necessarily translate into a deepening of relationships with intimate others. Men's confessional language frequently fails the reality of the intimate other, who is silenced, replaced, or rendered invisible. It is this intimate other to which I turn in this chapter.

The Internal Intimate Other

Distinguishing the "external" other of confessional texts (the implied, anticipated, sympathetic reader) from the "internal" other in confessional texts (such as wives, children, mothers, and lovers) can be helpful. It clarifies the confessant's differing relations to the people he wishes to address and to the people about whom he speaks. It is the difference between *to whom* he speaks (external) and *about whom* he speaks (internal). In both cases, the confessant engages in an act of imagination and fictionalization of the other—imagining, for example, the external other as a fictionalized ideal reader, or fictionalizing the internal other (for example, a lover) through imagined dialogue. Of course, the lines of separation between internal and external other can be blurry. For example, the imagined listener, to whom a confessant addresses himself as an *external* other, may be God, as in Augustine's case, but God is also Augustine's *internal* other. Vice versa, the intimate partner, about whom a confessant writes as an *internal* other, can be his wife, as in Perechodnik's case, but she is also the *external* other to whom he addresses himself in an imagined direct speech. Despite this blurring, drawing a distinction between external and internal others in confessiographies heightens our awareness of the confessant's interdependence on flesh-and-blood people during his life. Of particular interest to me are the people who are part of the confessant's circle of familiar and erotic intimacy, such as spouses, lovers, parents, children, and friends (as opposed to, say, a confessant's intellectual relations to his mentors, colleagues, and adversaries). How do these intimate internal others appear and disappear in male confessiographies?

In preceding chapters, I have shown how male confessiographies variously negotiate instances of vulnerability and protection by addressing themselves to *external* others. For Augustine, the external other is God, and the *Confessions* constitute a consciously composed yet guarded model for the faithful that is intellectually intriguing and emotionally complex. For Rousseau, the external other is the unsuspecting public, and his *Confessions*, with their ambition for "total transparency" (Brooks 2000, 161), articulate the emergence of the modern self's hubris to reveal one's internal and external life "absolutely to the public" (Rousseau 1953, 65). Leiris renders himself naked to the reluctant public eye by ridiculing and trivializing himself with utter sincerity. For Perechodnik, the external other is the democratic nations that may take revenge, yet the self-effacing reckoning with his own moral failures leads to a narrative loss over controlling the reader's judgment. Finally, Pohl's *Credo* manipulates a postwar German audience into a sympathetic hearing through a strategic recitation of confessional rhetoric.

Male confessants, however, also speak about their loved ones, those internal textual figures to whom these men are intimately related. As readers, we have no direct access to these internal intimate others, since our knowledge of them is always mediated through a text presented by the male narrator. Reading about them puts us in a position seemingly equivalent to that of a confessor in the religious or therapeutic confessional. Ideally, we would listen nonjudgmentally and let ourselves be seduced into believing what is presented to us. As opposed to the confessional, however, contemporary readers can no longer engage in a direct conversation with the confessant. We cannot ask him any questions, cannot clarify ambiguities, and cannot articulate a doubt we may have. The male confessant has revealed himself through creating a dialogical and transferential relation through texts, through the detour of the imaginary of the power of the written word, which aims at publicity, not secrecy. What is left is the text with which we can engage.

In confessiographies, the issue of privacy and publicity is perforated in multiple ways. As readers, our private reading experience draws us into bearing witness to a private confession, but the medium, through which it is communicated, is a public document. As opposed to auricular confessions, which guard the secrets confessed from a potentially hostile and noncompassionate audience, written confessions invite the public gaze. In our private reading experience today, we bear witness to a man's public testimony of the retrospective presentation of his intimate, private life. For example, when Augustine privately surrenders to tears, this event is not truly private because his written testimony invites the public to peek into the church father's bedroom (as we shall see later) in order to witness his state of lacrimal dissolution. In the religious confessional, Augustine's testimony would have been shielded from the prying eye of the community, but not so in his *Confessions*. There, he opens himself up to public scrutiny.

A confession of my own: Just when I was beginning to outline this chapter, an unexpected crisis erupted in my marriage. A love and companionship of twenty-five years was at the brink of sudden dissolution. I lost all ground under my feet, felt a grayness descend upon me that obstructed my ability to write, erasing all pleasure in words. The wounding I received turned rage into grief—into a lamentation without words, into a stream of tears for days and nights on end. Struck by the treachery of love, all vitality seemed sucked out of my body, and I lay listless on the couch.

Wounded, I started to rethink my initial ideas. They no longer held together in ways that, earlier, seemed to make up a valid and consistent argument. In the midst of a crisis, experience taught me better. The thrust of the earlier argument rested on the assumption that the wounding, of which male confessional texts bear traces, would have to be located in the lives of women, and that male confessants concealed the harming they themselves had inflicted by erasing the memory of female companions. Now I needed to open myself up to the possibility of a wounding of men, perhaps an injury that men could manage only through an act of confessional writing.

A wordless grief locked as physical pain into my body, a pain that shrank the vast universe to a size barely beyond the boundary of my skin, but it also gave me perspective. I needed to look at myself again, anew, and from an angle of profound distress—and "from a hidden depth [of] profound self-examination . . . I let my tears flow freely" (Augustine 8.12.28).

There is, of course, a simple alternative to the urge of writing confessions: Talk directly to intimate others! Open your soul and heart to children, lovers, partners, wives, friends, or parents in candid conversations. Do not write about them; talk to them. If direct conversation is an alternative option, we realize that confessional texts can operate on the level of displacement. They displace conversations that, in many cases, these men could have had with real flesh-and-blood intimate others.[1] Displacement implies that various transformative and transpositional operations occur: intimate bodies become ciphers and, in turn, texts become bodies—or, more accurately, texts become memories of intimate bodies. These textual "bodies" can be created, born, nursed, caressed, and devoured; in turn, they can feed and nourish the reader. We have already seen that the completion of confessional manuscripts is sometimes conceived of as the birthing of new children, when, for example, erotic intercourse is no longer desired (Augustine), no longer possible (Perechodnik), or when a confessional text emerges as the product of spiritual intercourse between confessant and hagiographer (Pohl). Given these symbolic displacements, the act of confessional writing looks like verbal intercourse with an intimate other, from which this other is excluded. The delicate liveliness of actual dialogue is exchanged for the safety of a solitary discourse based on letters and words. Are men afraid of the actual encounter with intimate others? Is there a wounding on the part of men that impedes the soul's opening to those others? What do male confessional texts say about these intimate others? How are we to understand that which is said, muted, or displaced?

Wounds and tears: In this chapter, I will trace the harm, silence, and abandonment in which the intimate other is entangled in texts that men have left as public witnesses to themselves. As we shall see, some acts of confessional writing are grounded in and motivated by a deep anxiety over the wounding related to intimate others, thus impeding and compromising face-to-face conversations. As a result the confessing *I* is drowning in memories resistant to language: in tears. In other instances, the disappearance of loved ones seems to be an intentional disavowal of the intimate internal other in order to make possible an uninterrupted reconstruction of the male self. Here, language fails to paint a full picture of the male confessant's embeddedness in loving relations.

Weeping Saints

Augustine weeps. As a matter of fact, tears feature prominently in his *Confessions*. He speaks about weeping already in the early parts of Book 1, when he reconstructs his own infancy by observing other babies. When he did not receive instant gratification of all his infantile wishes, he "would revenge" himself upon adult caretakers "by weeping" (1.6.8). Weeping, here, does not connote innocence but coerciveness—a coercion not intentionally willed by the infant but anthropologically necessitated.[2] Mostly, though, Augustine speaks about maternal tears or about tears of agony over the dying of another person (a male friend in Book 4; his mother in Book 9). He wonders whether tears are a sign of false human attachments or a gift of God to humanity.

I conceive of tears as a gift—a gift of psychological maturity. I often wish I could express them more openly in public: the same old, same old lamentation of and about men! "Oh, how sweet are the tears of joy and affection, and how my heart feasts on them!" Rousseau wails. "Why have I been permitted to shed them so seldom?" (1953, 550). Occasionally, I tear up at inopportune moments. Sentimentalized movies on transatlantic flights make me cry. A slight tinge of romantic sadness in these paltry movie plots bring tears to my eyes, which I hide from passengers cramped into their seats next to me.

I rarely think of false tears. I question, though, the almost tears of a self-pitying nostalgia that frequently overcomes me at the waning of a year, when I indulge in leafing through traces of the past: photo albums, diary entries, or poems written years ago. I begin to feel sorry for a self I can no longer retrieve. It is a longing to return to a past no longer available, to a golden age that never was.

Tears of grief come into sight at the boundary of the body. They are an interior condition manifesting itself as sign on the surface of the skin, a physical admission of the collapse of the mental ordering of the world, a speechlessness that threatens religious confidence. Augustine's tears mirror the instability of his spiritual and social struggles with his masculine self. Restlessly, he moves at boundaries: geographically, between the margins of the Roman Empire (Thagaste and Carthage in North Africa) and its center (Rome/Milan); socially, between the elite status that upper-class Milan society is ready to bestow upon him and the vows of poverty of the new Christian ideal; spiritually, between the Manichees and Scripture;[3] internally, between the addiction to false pleasures and his conflicted admiration for his mother's piety; erotically, between the "vain trifles and the triviality" of his "old loves" who "tugged at the garment of [his] flesh" (8.11.26) and the "chaste Lady Continence" (8.11.27); finally, in terms of gender, between a sexually active, reproductive householder and the spiritual virility of a celibate man. Augustine is a torn man, moved to tears when at wits' end, uncertain about their meaning. Tears, he knows, can be coercive and deceptive like surface markers of the false pleasures of lust promised to him by eroticized female partners, or of the false pleasures of cultural and intellectual divertissements (like theater or rhetorics).[4] Tears, however, are also the physical manifestation of a sincere interior struggle. When Augustine discloses those tears he has shed in private, he embraces, affirms, and declares a new masculinity that valorizes interiority and humility.[5] The new Christian masculine ideal permits the expression of a rightly guided male vulnerability—not a mourning over the loss of false pleasures but a realization of the sincerity of human grief, consoled only by the promise of God's grace.

This, in any event, is the position that Augustine advances when writing his *Confessions* and that allows him to admit the flowing of tears. At first he is unable to weep at all at his mother's funeral: "When her body was carried out, we went and returned without a tear. Even during those prayers which we poured out to you . . . not even at those prayers did I weep." Eventually, though, he finds relief "alone upon my bed" and grieves openly in memory of her in the presence of God: "I was glad to weep before you about her and for her, about myself and for myself. Now I let flow the tears which I had held back so that they ran as freely as they wished" (9.12.32–33).

His tears run freely, but Augustine remains afraid of the ridicule other men would heap upon his weeping. He therefore insists on the sincerity of tears. Men may not "get it," but surely God would not misunderstand:

> My heart rested upon [my tears] . . . because it was your ears that were there, not those of some human critic who would put a proud interpretation on my weeping. And now, Lord, I make my confession to you *in writing*. Let any-

one who wishes read and interpret as he pleases. If he finds fault that I wept for my mother for a fraction of an hour, the mother who had died before my eyes who had wept for me that I might live before your eyes, let him not mock me but rather . . . let him weep himself before you for my sins; for you are the Father of all the brothers of your Christ. (9.12.33; emphasis added)

Several significant issues are compressed into these few sentences: fear of the male critic who *reads* his confession; consolation by God who *hears* his confession; the ability to *write* a confession; the uneasy yet symbiotic relationship with his mother; the reestablishment of the rule of the Father. We will need to say a few things about each of these interrelated themes.

WRITING CONFESSIONS / DESPAIR

Tears of grief resist writing. Before Monica's death, Augustine had experienced intense grief as a young man, when one of his beloved male friends died (Book 4). The loss maddened him so much that he lost perspective of himself and the world around him. "So I boiled with anger, sighed, wept, and was at my wits' end. I found no calmness, no capacity for deliberation. . . . There was no rest in pleasant groves, nor in games or songs, nor in sweet-scented places, nor in exquisite feasts, nor in pleasures of the bedroom and bed, nor, finally, in books and poetry. Everything was an object of horror" (4.7.12). No words, no sex, no books, no other pleasantries would relieve him from being drowned in sorrow. "Hence the mourning if a friend dies, the darkness of grief, and as the sweetness is turned into bitterness the heart is flooded with tears" (4.9.14). Tears overwhelm and render him speechless. It is only years later that Augustine, when writing the *Confessions*, finds words to express the grief of the past in deeply touching poignancy. Now, as he recalls and retells the episode of his youth, he wonders: "Why do I speak of these matters?" And he responds to his own query: "Now is the time not to be putting questions but to be making confession to you" (4.6.11). Temporal and affective distance from the event enable him to confess in language what earlier only tears could express. The flow of tears is replaced by a flow of words.

"Weeping," Lutz writes, "often occurs at precisely those times when we are least able to fully verbalize complex, 'overwhelming' emotions, least able to fully articulate our manifold, mingled feelings. We recognize in crying a surplus of feeling over thinking" (1999, 21). Augustine had experienced a surplus of feeling when mourning his friend's death. Later however, at the time of his mother's death (Book 9), he has arrived at a different emotional and spiritual place. As a new convert, he is no longer sucked into the vortex of pure, speechless agony. Grief no longer pulls him down to a place of no return, of no perspective. It no longer consumes him in unbounded ways as in his youth. Now, as a mature man, he quickly realizes that he needs to express his grief viscerally before he can find his way back to words.

Overall, Book 9 shows an older Augustine who is more conscious about the grieving process. Having found peace in God, he is able to observe himself with more assuredness, no longer plagued by the disorienting restlessness of his youth. He admits to staying dry-eyed and detached during his mother's funeral until he recognizes how much his heart is filled with the "bitterness of sorrow" (9.12.32), a sorrow from which he is relieved only when permitting himself to cry. The all-consuming "sweetness-turned-into-bitterness" triggered by his friend's death in his youth ("I had become to myself a place of unhappiness in which I could not bear to be; but I could not escape from myself" [4.7.12]) has become an adult man's "bitterness-of-sorrow" over his mother's death for "a fraction of an hour" (9.12.33). He allows himself to shed tears over Monica's death in the privacy of his bedroom. Only after he is viscerally relieved of his emotions is he able to put his confession into writing. Because God offers a wider perspective and consolation, Augustine recovers quickly after her death and with less effort returns to the artistry of words. Writing, not weeping.

MATERNAL SYMBIOSIS / GRIEF

Before Augustine is able to weep for his mother, his mother wept for him many times. "By my mother's tears night and day sacrifice was being offered to you from the blood of her heart" (5.7.13). This woman worries about her son's spiritual condition with such an abundance of tears that Augustine can't help having his impatience slip through a text that otherwise tells a mostly consistent story of his admiration for Monica's steadfast piety. While he was a student in Carthage—after he had left his hometown of Thagaste—and while debating Manichean thought, his mother's close emotional attachment to him expresses itself in unrestrained sorrow and in dreams. "For my mother, your faithful servant, wept for me before you more than mothers weep when lamenting their *dead children*" (3.11.19; emphasis added). This statement is shot through with narcissistic pride, anxious sarcasm, and hyperbolic sincerity. The comparison to "dead children" is significant. On the surface, Augustine inserts it to highlight his own spiritual deadness, but he also manages to present, underhandedly, a woman who weeps about her *living* son more than other mothers lament their *dead* children. We hear the exasperated sigh of a boy needing to escape from suffocating maternal clutches.

Augustine can neither stop nor control his mother's overbearing weeping. And he is not alone. Even a "bishop brought up in the church," a mature man, becomes seriously aggravated at Monica's insistent begging to extend pastoral care to her son. "She pressed him with more begging and with floods of tears," to which, "irritated and a little vexed," the bishop responds: "Go away from me: as you live, it cannot be that the *son of these tears* should perish" (3.12.21; emphasis added; see Burrus 2004, 83).

The son of tears can't resolve the symbiotic bind. What Augustine, in his filial bond, fails to accomplish, he delegates to God: "You [God] heard her and did not despise her tears which poured forth to wet the ground under her eyes in every place where she prayed" (3.11.19). Augustine needs the Father to stabilize the wet ground left by the mother.

Tears of intimate others make me anxious when they seem to demand something of me. I react adversely to such a pull and am no longer open to the need of the other.

If any tears overwhelm me, then they are those of my mother. She cries frequently, and more so as she is aging. When she hears of a virus I have caught, her good advice is overbearing ("each time she saw me ill, no doubt dying like her son before me" [Derrida 1993, 117]), and when she knows of my anguish, she falls into a misery of her own. She can spend sleepless nights and weep for her son ("for 59 years I have not known who is weeping, my mother or me" [263]). She defends her torments as an act of maternal compassion, but I feel robbed of my own grief and I distance myself.

Like mother, like son: Boundaries between Monica and Augustine are as porous as lacrimal anatomy. When the body can no longer absorb tears, usually through the puncta and ducts leading to the lacrimal sac, they overflow the eyelids.[6] Exceptional quantities of tears caused by strong emotions cannot be drained by the body, just as the surplus of emotions regarding the mother-son relation overflows the textual boundaries of Augustine's reminiscences. Tears demonstrate, and stand for, the intimacy between Augustine and Monica, an intimacy that causes anxiety, pride, and grief.

Augustine must escape such a maternal hold for the sake of his own individuation. At the age of twenty-nine, he secretly leaves Carthage and sails to Rome, but he can do so only by deceiving his mother, who had begged him not to go or else to join him on the journey. "I lied to my mother—to such a mother—and gave her the slip" (5.8.15). His mother, in reaction, does what she does best. After her initial shock and angry bout, "she was crazed with grief, and with recriminations and groans she filled your [God's] ears. . . . As mothers do, she loved to have me with her, but much more than most mothers. . . . So she wept and lamented" (5.8.15). Augustine sketches Monica again as a woman grander and more demanding than other mothers, a mother who will not easily give up. Augustine's flight from Carthage puts their symbiotic relationship to a serious test, but it cannot resolve it. His escape is short-lived. Less than two years later, Monica rejoins him in the imperial city of Milan and does not move from his side until her death at the Roman harbor town of Ostia: "When she was aged 56 and I was 33, this religious and devout soul was released from the body" (9.11.28). It is only then that he will weep for her.

How do men resolve the anxiety and wounding caused by symbiotic dilemmas between mothers and sons? It is a question not foreign to modern men. Let us listen to two confessional fragments written in quite distinct mental and geographic places. One is Yitzhak Nahum Twersky's "Confession of My Tortured, Afflicted Soul," penned in 1910 in the form of a letter by a twenty-two-year-old Hasidic Jew in Shpikov, Ukraine.[7] The other is Philip Culbertson's "Mothers and Their Golden Sons: Exploring a Theology of Narcissism," published in 2006 by a sixty-year-old American practical theologian residing, at the time, in New Zealand.[8] Like Augustine, both men struggle with the ties that bind them to their mothers.

Twersky, who is part of an established Hasidic dynasty, pours out the troubles of his young heart in a confessional letter to Yiddish writer Jacob Dineson in Warsaw. He testifies to his conflicted soul caused by the backward restrictions of his Hasidic environment, a world he loves and abhors. "I have been consumed by an innermost need to correspond with you, to reveal to you all that is hidden in my heart, to unburden before you all that is concealed and confined in my soul," he writes to Dineson. "All my life is one long chain of suppressed desires, concealed ideas, shattered cravings and wishes" (Assaf 2006, 15). Twersky yearns to liberate himself from the religious restrictions, but, as in Augustine's case, it is—in his perception—his mother that holds him back.

> As difficult as it is for me to sever the thread of my life, as helpless as I am in that respect, nothing would hold me back, nothing would withstand my burning passion, the fire of my aching soul, and I would indeed have taken such a step. . . . Nothing would prevent me—save just one hidden power in my soul which is stronger than all these combined, which holds me back with tremendous force and will not loosen its grip—the power of compassion. This feeling . . . is what will not allow me to carry out my plan—my compassion for my beloved mother. (28)

The symbiotic tie makes it impossible for Twersky to sever the umbilical cord. "I imbibed piety with my mother's milk, I was reared on the well-springs of Torah and Hasidism," he writes, reminiscent of Augustine's blend of maternal and divine nourishment, "and no foreign spirit penetrated our home to dislodge me, God forbid, from my place" (20). But later, a different spirit takes possession of him. The burning passion that afflicts him is over-powered only by compassion for his mother. This mother, however, is not just a helpless figure, depending on her son's compassion, but also a force that threatens to emasculate him. "As long as I am here under my mother's authority," he writes, "I can do nothing. I stress, always *my mother*, not my father, for my father is cold-tempered and will not feel such pain. But my mother—she is warm, feeling, a person, and I must take her into consideration" (30; emphasis in original). In contrast to his coldhearted father, the mother, who restrains him, seems to be like him. There is a mutual, mimetic desire. The burning fire, which compels Twersky to escape, is fed by the same passion that his mother exerts as authority over him. Had he left her, he states, she would have said the following words: "This one too, my son, in whom I have put all my hope, he too has become a disappointment, and so what is left for me in life?" (30). The imagined threat and the fantasized guilt imposed by her immobilize the son. And here the letter ends. But what the letter cannot tell us, we know from other sources today: Twersky never abandons the Hasidic world. In 1926, he is appointed rabbi, and in 1942, he and his family perish in the Belzec death camp.

The issue of mimetic intimacy between mothers and sons is also addressed by Culbertson, who reflects on his filial bond to his mother. "I am sixty years old, have known I am gay for most of my life, and have never told my mother." After this opening line, he continues:

She must know. She must know, as well, that she does not want to know.
. . . My inability to share one of the foundational parts of my identity has
deprived us both of opportunities for deeper intimacy, blocked by secrets and
a modicum of deceit. When I am with her, I am never quite fully present,
because part of me is walled-off from her. (Culbertson 2006, 210)

Similar to Augustine, Culbertson closely links intimacy and deceit. Even
among adult men, there is a wish to let mothers know about the secrets
of their intimate lives while, simultaneously, erecting walls of separation,
lest the son be misunderstood or devoured by a mother's love, ambition,
and worry. The mother, after all, is a son's first audience: she "believed in
us before the greater public did" (Culbertson 2006, 228), even when the
mother, as in Derrida's case, never reads "a single sentence" of her son's work
(1993, 233; see Clark 2005, 224). Eventually, the mother will be exchanged
for larger audiences. When writing their confessions, men idealize and fear
the (unknown) readers as much as their mothers. They seek approval from
both. Writing confessions can be a gesture of love toward the mother—a
mother nonetheless dispossessed because her physical presence is displaced
by a text.

Mimetic desire for the mother can be articulated the moment she is no
longer perceived as a threat to a son's individuation. If she is no longer a
danger, the son can even imitate her. Augustine, for example, weeps like her
at the moment of her death. "He mourns a much-loved woman," Burrus
writes, "grieves like a woman—reluctantly, and also excessively, with ambivalence" (2004, 82; also Miles 1992, 84).[9] Postmodernist Derrida confesses his
mother ("'I confess' means 'I confess my mother'") when she is still "alive"
but is no longer able to "identify me, to recognize me, to name me, to call
me" (2005, 26). Culbertson, the gay son, imitates his mother in drag, but
it takes him until his sixtieth year to confess in writing his mimetic desire.
Movingly he describes how he ventured "into the world of drag," how he
"painted [his] nails in just the same way [his] mother had . . . [in] the same
color [his] mother always wore," and how he, in his new drag identity, "put
on stockings" the same way that his mother did (2006, 223, 225). "Internally," Culbertson writes, some men work at "'being' our mother, instead of
'merely' having her" (225). The "golden sons . . . destined to be special, different, highly individuated over-achievers" are "wounded sons of wounded
mothers" (228–229). Certainly, the relationship between Augustine and
Monica fits this description as well: wounded by her husband's temper and
her worries about an unsteady child, Monica has ambitious dreams for her

son, always plotting to advance him socially and spiritually. We can safely add Augustine, the son of tears, to Culbertson's list of golden sons.

GOLDEN SONS

Men who fit the description of golden sons are inclined to seek approval through extraordinary deeds bent toward religious narcissism. Short of such deeds, they may write self-exploratory, self-disclosing texts. "Confessional practice," Tambling muses, "seems strongly linked to the mother" (1990, 25).[10] They seek through the act of confessional writing an imagined reader worthy of their idealized mother. To them, text matters; it *is* matter, is mater/mother. The text not only nourishes the son but also enables him to nourish his readers. The male confessant dislodges his mother and takes her place. "He makes something new of himself," writes Burrus of Augustine. "Writing, he reads. Sucking, he feeds. He feeds us. We eat him. We are eating him, reading him now. We are eating, reading *her* now" (2004, 86; emphasis in original).

Unlike Augustine, a man of late antiquity, Culbertson, a child of postmodernity, knows that he is narrating his mother, that is to say, he is aware that he fictionalizes her in a text that can never give her a prime voice. "[A]ll these women are 'usable fiction,' *textless texts* into whom someone else's narrative and meaning are read" (2006, 209; emphasis in original). He exhibits, with other modernist confessants, a tendency toward "double self-reflexivity" (Gill 2006, 8), which not only knows about the impossibility to tell it all but also declares that one knows about the fragmentation and fictionalization that go into confessional writing. Yet Culbertson, too, chooses the detour of a confessional text to communicate with his mother. He prefers to confess publicly to the (unknown) reader—whom, by the way, he fears, as Augustine does, as "hostile" (228)—rather than talk to his mother directly and in private. As public witnesses of this detour, we will never know whether Culbertson's mother will read his text, and hence we will never know whether she will learn about her son's gayness and drag performance. This will remain the true secret of Culbertson's confessional fragment! As readers, we witness the son's intimate reflections on gay/drag and mimetic desire, and thus we become seduced by, and complicit in, the confessant's narrative choices. Whether his mother knows as much as we do remains, however, the text's true enigma. In other words, through the detour of a confessional text Culbertson tells us more than he tells his mother, though he truly wishes he could tell her directly. He, like Augustine and other confessing men, holds substitutionary conversations. Culbertson, at least, is aware of this conundrum. Augustine, on the other hand, remains oblivious to it, and Monica remains a "textless text." Monica is the measuring rod of her son's spiritual development, a signpost, eventually sucked dry at the moment Augustine is reborn as a Christian man.

DEATH OF THE MOTHER / GUILT

Yitzhak Nahum Twersky, the nostalgically rebellious son, only fantasizes his escape from his mother. The young Hasid is prevented from any action since he imagines both the social death his mother would experience upon his secret departure and the guilt he would suffer from causing a betrayal of their symbiotic relationship—a relationship marked by a common passion. He does not act beyond writing about his afflicted soul. His confessional letter is his (aborted) action. "A sacrifice I am, a sacrifice to my mother's altar" (Assaf 2006, 28).

At the age of about thirty, Augustine, in a rebellious moment, tries to escape the clutches of his mother. Unlike Twersky, he actually deceives Monica when he flees across the Mediterranean Sea to Rome. Like Twersky, he is plagued by guilt, which expresses itself in the form of imagined threats. The passage in which Augustine describes his escape is filled with images of water that contain mythic power. Maternal tears are brought into close connection to the destructive force of the ocean and the saving grace of baptism:

> I lied to my mother—to such a mother—and I gave her the slip. Even this you [God] forgave me, mercifully saving me from the waters of the sea, when I was full of abominable filth, so as to bring me to the water of your grace. This water was to wash me clean, and to dry the rivers from my mother's eyes which daily before you irrigated the soil beneath her face. (5.8.15)

Guilt-ridden, Augustine imagines dire consequences for having deceived his mother. As he crosses the sea, it is not the maternal flood of tears that threatens to drown him but the Mediterranean itself. Although Augustine grants only to God authority over the sea's natural inclination for calamity, the fear of shipwreck and drowning reads like a surrogate act of maternal wrath. After all, Monica and God always seem to work in tandem, each pushing and pulling the reluctant Augustine toward his salvation. What the waters of wrath threaten to do (death without salvation), the baptismal waters of grace will eventually accomplish: a reborn man. Baptismal water washes Augustine clean—his rebirth—and also dries the tears of his mother:

her death. His conversion makes his mother's tears superfluous. Once she stops weeping, she disappears. The suffocating, perhaps even nightmarish menace of her tears coincides with the son's liberation, which is his individuation and salvation.

Two subjects make my mother weep predictably: the death of her own mother and the loss of her childhood home near Königsberg in East Prussia. In the winter of 1944/1945, when the Soviet army had already encircled that city, my mother was sent by her mother on a journey across war-torn Europe, alone, at the age of seventeen. She was among millions of other Germans. Her story introduced a collective experience of loss and grief into our home, a narrative of national trauma invoked repeatedly in postwar Germany. My mother left behind a childhood landscape she would miss for the rest of her life.

She and I can hardly talk about these memories. Her tears, which regularly accompany these stories, drown any critical assessment and make me restless and anxious. Her weeping demands something of me I cannot give. It may be simple compassion she needs, perhaps a voucher for the innocence of her generation. I read her tears as unfinished business, a personal suffering that hides the unfinished business of a nation's crimes. Her stories present a youth full of innocent joy. Yet, behind her rural home, cattle cars passed by. At least on one occasion, a train came to a stop, and Soviet POWs stretched out their hands from behind narrow, barb-wired windows, begging her and her siblings for water. Such brief reminiscences of horror are like flickering images interrupting the flow of a story about a wholesome and happy home. When they surface, they are quickly covered up by tears. Her tears—and the memories they conceal—will stop flowing only when her generation finally finds peace, taking with them an era in which the unspeakable . . .

Augustine writes hyperbolically that rivers flowed from his "mother's eyes . . . irrigat[ing] the soil beneath her face" (5.8.15). The image conjures up the power of female deities both to fertilize the earth and to flood and destroy the crop. Monica as natural mother fertilizes the spiritual soil on which her son can grow spiritually, but she can also drown him. She also possesses masculine strength: "My mother stayed close to us in the clothing of a woman but with a *virile* faith" (9.4.8; emphasis added).[11] With her death, however, the situation changes. No longer the golden son, Augustine becomes the son of tears, weeping like his mother. Monica's devouring presence and potential destructiveness are neutralized. Her proclaimed piety—as reported through the mouth of Augustine—is transferred to him after her death. By reversing agency—he now weeps for her—he continues in her tradition. He tries, so to speak, to put "her clothes on." It is a kind of emotional drag performance. He wants to *be* her. But he can't stay there for too long. He becomes *her* only in a brief transient act of mimetic intimacy. As a converted man, he adopts and simultaneously usurps her position.

Writing his confessions, Augustine must resolve a number of conflicting affections: unable to disavow his mother and her piety, he temporarily becomes her; threatened to be devoured, he must abandon her maternal body and move beyond her; afraid of being emasculated, he must emerge as a revitalized man. His mother has to die for him in order for him to become a virile man under a new system of validation and valorization. Had she not passed away naturally, she would have had to die textually at this point of the confessional narrative.[12] Augustine is ready to move on, without her. He continues her weeping, but it is a qualitatively different weeping: a weeping not marred by the female despair displayed by a natural mother but the controlled weeping of a son under the consolation of a divine Father.

Not coincidentally, Monica, who cries tears in the quantity of rivers, will die by the bank of a river. "While we were at Ostia by the mouths of the [river] Tiber, my mother died" (9.8.17). Although this textual link is not consciously willed by Augustine, the metaphoric connection still makes perfect sense. Monica dies, and the river of tears finally dries up; Augustine weeps for her, and the river continues to flow—but this time, it no longer overflows its banks. Its devouring force is tamed. Under divine consolation, the filial flow of tears after her death has become a rightly guided lacrimal lamentation "for a fraction of an hour" (9.12.33).

THE RULE OF THE FATHER / CONSOLATION

When Monica dies, Augustine tries to get some relief in a public bath. "I decided to go to take a bath, because I had heard that baths, for which the Greeks say *balaneion*, get their name from throwing anxiety out of the mind" (9.12.32). Augustine evokes again the mythic and metaphoric qualities of water, adding the public bath to his list of rivers, ocean, tears, and baptism. He seeks healing, but the waters of the bath do not console him.

As a matter of fact, they seem to have little effect at all: "But I confess this to your mercy, father of orphans, that after I bathed I was exactly the same as before. The bitterness of sorrow had not sweated out of my heart" (9.12.32).

The fact that the ancient bath—despite the therapeutic power attributed to it—cannot console his grieving heart sounds less surprising once we recall that the bathhouse is associated with Patricius, Augustine's biological father. Whereas tears stand in metonymically for the mother, the public bath conjures up the father and the sexual economies of the household. Earlier in the *Confessions*, it is in the public bath that Patricius, only a catechumen, witnesses the bodily sign of his son's awakening manhood: the stiffening of his penis:

> I was in my sixteenth year . . . [and] the thorns of lust rose above my head, and there was no hand to root them out. . . . Indeed, when at the bath-house my father saw that I was showing signs of virility and the stirrings of adolescence, he was overjoyed to suppose that he would now be having grandchildren, and told my mother so. His delight was that of the intoxication which makes the world oblivious to you, its Creator, and to love your creation instead of you. (2.3.6)

The sexual sign witnessed by his natural father feeds expectations of the continuity of the social order. These hopes are placed in oppositional terms to the reproductive discontinuity expected by the spiritual Father, God.

Patricius plays only a minor role in his son's life. He "is lost to us. Augustine, a man of many significant silences, will pass him over coldly . . . and will mention his father's death only in passing" (Brown 1969, 30). Patricius dies when Augustine is eighteen years old, and what is left of him is quickly overtaken by Monica's maternal care. By the time Augustine returns to the bath after his mother's death, now already a converted and reborn man, nothing remains of Patricius. "I confess this to your mercy, *father of orphans*, that after I bathed I was exactly the same as before" (9.12.32; emphasis added). Why, we may wonder, does Augustine call God, at this point, a "father of orphans"? The curious phrase contains a triple dispossession of Patricius: Patricius is absent as father (Augustine is orphan after his early death); Patricius is replaced by Monica through her overbearing maternal care of their son; and finally, Patricius's paternity is erased by God as father-of-all-orphans. His paternity and presence are reduced to the faintest echo, a memory in the process of its erasure.

When the mature Augustine returns to the public bath after his mother's funeral, he no longer finds cure and consolation in a space once occupied by his father (and his old sexual self). But neither can he find narcissistic comfort in his mother's tears. Both the paternal rule of the *oikonomia* and the maternal control through overbearing tears are surpassed and replaced by the new Rule of the Father. Mothers and fathers as intimate others disappear through the establishment of a spiritual fatherhood that transcends family ties. For the new Rule of the Father to take root, the biological origins of paternity and the spiritual worries of maternity must be expunged. The final textual appearance of both Patricius and Monica happens precisely at the moment when Augustine has reached the end of confessing his sins of the past and when he arrives at his present condition under the spiritual fatherhood of God. He ends Book 9 with the hope that "all who read this book may remember at your altar Monica your servant and Patrick her late husband" (9.13.37): both parents are now relegated to a place of memory, to a time when Augustine had little self-knowledge and no knowledge of God. Weeping over this past has come to an end.

Different kinds of tears are now in demand. "My heart is healed of that wound," Augustine writes as he concludes his thoughts on grief over Monica's death. His earlier-felt, desperate grief is now described in cold, almost clinical terms ("I could be reproached for yielding to that *emotion of physical kinship*"), and from now on he wants to shed different tears. "On behalf of your maidservant, I pour out to you, our God, another kind of tears. They flow from a spirit struck hard by considering the perils threatening every soul that 'dies in Adam'" (9.13.34; emphasis added). Augustine admonishes all other men, who may wish to criticize him for weeping "for my mother for a fraction of an hour," to weep for themselves before God, "for you are the Father of all the brothers of your Christ" (9.12.33). All sons should weep before the Father of all. The maternal flow of tears is supplanted by spiritual tears shed by all sons of one Father—by a horde of equal brothers.

Consequently, Augustine can open Book 10 with a fresh claim to paternity. He is now consoled as someone else's child: "I am a child. But my Father ever lives and my protector is sufficient to guard me" (10.4.6). The new rule is in place.

I love my father. I am his firstborn son. Despite many mutual disappointments, my bond to him has always been affectionate.

MALE CRITIC / FEAR

Augustine, as pointed out earlier, fears ridicule of other men for disclosing his own weaknesses and vulnerabilities. To confess shedding tears over
earthly affairs raises similar anxieties. As Augustine opens a window into a
weeping man's privacy, thus placing the reader into the role of reluctant ob-
server of a man's womanish act, he can be accused of impropriety. Augustine
admits that he is more comfortable speaking about his tears only to God
("it was your *ears* that were there") instead of having "some human critic
put a proud interpretation on my weeping . . . [and] *read* and interpret as he
pleases" (9.12.33; emphasis added). He responds to his fear by wishing the
human critic who mocks him to first "weep for himself" (9.12.33). But he
knows, of course, that praying and confessing to God's ears are safer than
a written confession, the latter exposing him to a potentially hostile public
reception. Still, he chose to abandon the *sigillum* of auricular confession and
renders himself vulnerable to being misread, read against himself, or read
more deeply.[13] Should Augustine have reasons to fear other men? Are his
tears so unique?

"Augustine is not original, but he *is* creative." Augustine is not alone in
his weeping among men experimenting with Christianity as a new spiritual
discipline: "Like Jerome and Gregory, Augustine writes from the perspective of a man grieving" and "like Jerome, [he] writes with tearful ambivalence of a woman" (Burrus 2004, 82, 84; emphasis in original).[14] We can
add the desert father Antony to the list of weeping men, whose anchoritic
life had fascinated the urban Augustine. Antony, too, had admonished his
disciples to weep in the presence of God, but Antony's desert was a harsh
place, from which water was literally absent and symbolically banned.

Of all places, the desert seemed a most unlikely place to permit tears,
since its arid landscape was destined to dry the male body. "Why is your
body dry?" some monks asked Macarius, one of the Egyptian desert fathers of the fourth century. He answered: "A wooden poker which turns
over and over the brushwood in the fire is itself slowly burnt away. So if a
man cleanses his mind in the fear of God, the fear of God also consumes
his body" (Ward 2003, 13).[15] The scorched land and the parched body mirrored each other, each exteriorizing a man's spiritual state of mind, a narcissism reflected in barren soil rather than Ovid's spring.[16] Water of all kinds,
even drinking, was a source of embarrassment, fear, and shame. But from
this desert, weeping men emerged, a tradition later continued in the monastic movement, elaborated among church theologians, and adopted by

medieval women mystics (see Benke 2002; Hunt 2004; Lutz 1999). Tears were allowed to flow freely, and stories of weeping men in the Egyptian desert are told frequently. Antony's hagiographer, the bishop Athanasius, for example, wept publicly when he came across a female actress upon his return from the desert. Fourth-century contemporaries of Augustine also wept, like Evagrius, the theologian of the Christian East, who wrote about the desert fathers and helped establish what some call a "theology of tears" (Hunt 2004, 45). The same is true for Arsenius, an educated man of senatorial ranking in Rome who left for the Egyptian desert. He "kept a cloth at his chest because of the tears that streamed from his eyes." In another instance, Macarius was asked to speak to a congregation, but instead, "he shed tears and said: 'Let us pray and weep, my brothers.'" Sylvanus, after a profound mystical rapture, remained silent and wept despite his brothers' pleas for an explanation. He kept himself isolated in his cell and grieved. Finally, younger brothers craved to weep and feared they were unable to do so: "I hear the hermits weeping, and my soul longs for tears, but they do not come." These examples illustrate that the ascetic men of the desert yearned to weep, which was valued as a visible sign of contrition and of one's longing for God. "The watchful monk works night and day to pray continually: but if his heart is broken and lets tears flow, that calls God down from heaven to have mercy."[17]

Augustine, then, is in good company of other weeping men.[18] He should not fear them. But why is he afraid? What he fears are the recollections of false weeping, like his mother's overbearing tears and other instances of trivial and womanish weeping in the past—all of which are not yet channeled into a safely guarded theological framework.

Compunction: A Spirit Struck Hard

Augustine, the son of tears, stands in a tradition not unknown to Christian men contemplating spiritual life, a tradition that is more fully developed later on. Tears become a sign of mature spirituality, embedded within the concepts of *penthos* and compunction. In compunction, the soul is pierced and wounded by God, a "pricking of the heart, or conscience" (Hunt 2004, 16). Compunction is followed by *penthos*, a subsequent process of intense grief and sorrow over the fallenness of humanity and over the felt distance to God and divine mercy.[19] "The Church Fathers insist that actual tears should be shed" (Hunt 2004, xi). The seventh-century John Klimakos, a theologian of the desert tradition and the Christian East, exemplifies the central place of a "hermeneutic of tears" (Benke 2002, 38). He links tears to natural water, a stream, a bath but also to blood, fire, and heat, which can cause burns, wounds, and pain (40). All of these tears are spiritual: mystical and heroic tears of divine sorrow and repentance, of divine consolation and renewal. Weeping saints and church fathers were admired for their *Tränengabe*, for their *donum lacrimarum*, their gift of tears.

In Augustine's *Confessions*, the spiritual trajectory of compunction and *penthos* is announced but not yet fully elaborated. Augustine struggles. Ante-conversion, his crying and weeping are still earthbound; they point to a loss and not yet to God. During his conversion, "rivers stream" from his eyes like "a vast storm bearing a massive downpour of tears" (8.12.28); crying like his mother, he tastes the power of spiritual weeping. Post-conversion, his tears are poured out to God, and he can write with more tranquility, "You [God] pierced my heart with the arrow of your love" (9.2.3). Still later, when the grieving over Monica's death abates, he speaks of his "spirit struck hard" when contemplating the dangers that threaten "every soul that 'dies in Adam'" (9.13.34). We witness here a transitional moment from personal compunction to universal theology. Augustine's pierced heart is slowly molded into a text that makes authoritative and normative claims.

A wounding inflicted by God makes men weep. Not for nothing did John Chrysostom call compunction "the mother of tears."[20] In contrast, memories of wounds connected to intimate others are more ambivalently recorded in confessional texts. Particularly, weeping over female companions—those with whom one shares bread and bed (*com*, "with"; *panis*, "bread")—does not come easily.

In early Christian hagiographies, traces of wounds received by and inflicted on intimate others have survived. Occasionally, such wounding is named as cause for seeking a spiritual life. Or it is framed as a challenge to such life and becomes transformed through complex spiritual-erotic discourses. One such example we find in the *Historia Monachorum* in a story about Antony and Paul the Simple, written about the time when Augustine completed his *Confessions* (ca. 400 CE).[21] One day, Paul the Simple leaves his home to become Antony's disciple in the Egyptian desert. Antony as spiritual master accepts him only under the condition of total obedience, asking him to perform absurd, meaningless tasks bordering on abuse (total withholding of food and drink; weaving and unweaving baskets; gathering up honey from the desert soil without dirtying it). Paul the Simple dutifully accomplishes them all, eventually gaining his own saintly repute and receiving divine grace.

Before Paul the Simple embarked on his harsh spiritual journey, his heart had been pierced by an intimate other, his wife. "Having caught his wife in the very act of adultery," the anonymous Greek text states wryly, and "saying nothing to anybody, he headed out to the desert to Antony."[22] The emotional injury—the compunction by an intimate other—is the *momentum movens* of the story. "The traumatizing sight of Paul's wife's adultery and all he is leaving behind stays in the mind of the reader" (Masterson 2006, 219). Antony demands from this shattered man obedience to the point of utter humiliation, and we can read Antony's demand as heaping additional abuse upon an already wounded soul. Alternatively, we might see here at work a paradoxical intervention intended to cut Paul the Simple loose from the source of his wounding, from the old attachments to his wife. Antony's exaggerated demands and coercive method, if read in such light, would then correspond to the perceived depth of the initial blow. Paul the Simple's anguish requires a drastic treatment for some healing to occur. Antony might have intuited that a man thus wounded does not need pity but a transformation of pain into a different symbolic order. Masterson's insight that "Paul's new life [is] a reconstruction and replication of the wholeness (though illusory it may have been) that he lost at the moment of his wife's betrayal" (219) speaks to the displacement of an intimate other by a spiritual discipline that seeks intimacy with the Divine, mediated through a third party, another man.[23]

The story about Paul the Simple does not offer any opening into the hermit's "inmost thoughts" (219). We do not hear this man's confessional voice, since the document is a hagiographic account and not a confessional text. But we do find in male confessiographies comparable traces of the wounding inflicted by and on intimate others.

When I was in severe crisis, I did not go to the desert but went to see a male therapist. Instead of a stern Antony who demanded impossible feats, I met with a compassionate Argentinian Jew residing in Berlin and practicing Buddhism. He challenged my perceptions and caringly led me to realizations about my inner turmoil. He said: "Find your grounding." "Let yourself be touched again."

The wounding of and by others recorded in hagiographic accounts can also be found in Augustine's *Confessions*. The departure of his nameless lover of thirteen years comes to mind. Augustine presents the event as a wounding *he* received, but it is *he* who inflicts a wound on *her* by sending her back to Africa in order to pave the way for his intended marriage to a girl of Milan's upper class.[24]

> The woman with whom I habitually slept was torn away from my side because she was a hindrance to my marriage. My heart which was deeply affected was cut and wounded, and left a trail of blood. She had returned to Africa vowing that she would never go with another man. She left with me the natural son I had with her. . . . I was to get the girl I had proposed to only at the end of two years. . . . But my wound, inflicted by the earlier parting, was not healed. After inflammation and sharp pain, it festered. The pain made me as it were frigid but desperate. (6.15.25)

Like Paul the Simple's, Augustine's heart is pierced, and a period of intense mourning begins. Unlike Paul the Simple, Augustine does not seek the desert but, at first, internalizes his pain until, later, he exteriorizes it through the act of writing. The pain remains but is muted. In Augustine's textual recounting, the memory of the forced departure remains suffused with a tension he cannot resolve. On the one hand, Augustine belittles the importance of his unnamed lover by semantically humiliating her and their son ("the woman I habitually slept with"; "the natural son I had with her"). On the other hand, he speaks of blood, wounds, and festering and unhealed pain that render him frigid. Tears are replaced by the metaphoric "trail of blood," and relentless self-pitying takes the place of weeping. Augustine does not shed tears for his lover, though he clearly suffers from the separation. Choosing a passive voice and hiding his agency, he names no guilty party. He does not point a finger either at himself or at his mother, although it is Monica who seems to push him into a legal marriage with the Milanese girl, dictating the removal of her son's lover. "Already a girl was promised to me principally through my mother's efforts," Augustine writes, emphasizing twice how he felt pressured to marry (6.13.23).[25] In his recollection, there are no acting subjects, just tragic figures.

Reconstructing the voice of Augustine's nameless lover is impossible and left only to the literary imagination.[26] Because her reactions are so entirely lost to us, we can only speculate on whether Augustine even "gets her right"—a question different from asking about the truthfulness of his sparse portrayal of her. He may have—beyond presenting his female companion in a self-interested manner—actually misunderstood her! For example, we learn nothing about her feelings and thoughts, but he tells us, oddly, about her vow "never to go with another man" upon her return to Africa. Of all the possible things he could have chosen to tell his readers, why does he share this particular detail?

For the nameless lover to choose a path of continent "widowhood" is a plausible social option for women. Yet one wonders whether her vow might not spring from Augustine's wishful thinking. Knowing her to be without a man may ease the pain of separation, and he may have entirely imagined the vow out of jealousy. Or he may have invented it in order to protect her reputation—a kind of underhanded, retroactive expression of the love of a man who caved in to a mother's pressure. We can also imagine *her* (the un-named lover) promising such a vow in a state of dejection and inconsolable grief. After all, she loses not only Augustine but also the child of her body, Adeodatus. What we know for sure is what we do not know: whether she truly made this vow and, if so, whether she kept it. We can also only specu-late whether she ever recovered from the loss.

A few years later, Adeodatus dies at the age of sixteen. In a short, dispas-sionate eulogy, Augustine praises him for his intelligence but disavows any claim that either he or his (former) lover are to be praised for raising this fine young man. Adeodatus is a "gift" of God, to whom Augustine himself "contributed nothing . . . other than sin." Without tears he recalls the mo-ment of his son's death: "Early on you took him away from life on earth. I recall him with no anxiety; there was nothing to fear in his boyhood or adolescence or indeed his manhood" (9.6.14; see Power 1996, 103). Have Augustine's tears dried up? No; he has not forgotten to weep. Just a few lines further down from the eulogy, he is moved to tears at an unrelated, li-turgical occasion. "How I wept during your hymns and songs! I was deeply moved by the music of the sweet chants of your Church. . . . Tears ran, and it was good for me to have that experience" (9.6.14). Augustine does not tire of telling his readers about his gift for tears, but for his son, he has none.

Augustine has difficulties admitting attachment to his son and his long-term female companion. Love, care, and grief are downplayed and muted. Intimate others, who remind him of a path leading away from God, are best forgotten. "Divine obsession," writes Cioran in his 1937 philosophical tractate on saints and tears, "expels earthly love. One cannot love passion-ately God and a woman at the same time. . . . A woman can save us from God, and God can save us from *all* women" (1988, 50; emphasis added).[27]

For Augustine, this seems to be true enough—even if Cioran's aphoristic thought is not meant as critical commentary on Augustine and thus exacerbates (rather than alleviates) the gender blindness of religious discourse. Augustine's unnamed lover cannot compete with divine eros, and his son Adeodatus, the fruit of his enslavement to sex, cannot compete with liturgical hymns, which are the fruit of spiritual joy.

Can we trust Augustine's proclaimed disloyalty to intimate others? As Miles points out, Augustine teases his reader's imagination by skillfully toying with hedonist ideas (1992, 25–26). Sprinkled across his text are erotic and sexual allusions, like the "hellish pleasures" of the "shadowy jungle of erotic adventures" announced in the opening of Book 2 (2.1.1). Yet Augustine consistently disappoints voyeuristic expectations, and Book 2, consequently, does not conclude with juicy details about his sexual escapades but with a drawn-out discussion about stealing fruit from a pear tree (2.4.9–2.10.18).[28] These titillations actually belie the loyalty Augustine must have felt for his long-term lover. The surviving text veils the possibility that he may have resembled a faithful lover much more than an irresponsible womanizer.

We find a parallel to such rhetorical mystification of women in Michel Leiris's modernist confession. Leiris saturates *Manhood* with unflattering descriptions of his sexual life and equally unappealing images of women. He "studs the pages" with "innumerable femmes fatales," writes Pilling. "The book is full of vaginal images . . . [and] phallic images" (1981, 76). As in Augustine's case, it is, however, questionable how much of the proclaimed eroticism Leiris actually lived and enjoyed. After all, "sexual penetration disturbs him profoundly" (76). It seems that Leiris returns remorselessly to the seeming trivialities of eroticism because he wants to find an appropriate image to express his existential anxiety over a world that either threatens to "devour" him or that remains "pure fantasy" (76). Despite a rhetoric that seems to paint a picture of a libertine and rebellious man, Leiris is loyal to his wife—perhaps not so different from Augustine's unacknowledged devotion to his long-term female companion. "What led me to make demands upon myself," Leiris once remarked in an interview about *Manhood*, "is the fact that I am married, that I love my wife a great deal, and because I know that this book could only upset her."[29]

I love my wife a great deal, which is the reason I cannot write about her. Writing about her would feel like a betrayal of our covenantal trust, however stable or instable

at certain times in our relationship. Like Leiris, I do write for her, that is to say, with her in mind. I communicate with her in and through my writing. I have conversations with her as an internalized companion. Her, more than anybody, I want to please; hence, her judgment I fear most. As the woman I imagine her to be, she appreciates my texts, my monological products. But as the woman reader she really is, she responds critically to my work in direct conversation. The discrepancy is not easy to solve, but unmediated, face-to-face conversations are inevitable for a love to stay alive.

CHAPTER 6

Not from My Lips

From Annihilation to Nation Building

The words "I love" do not fall easily from the lips of male confessants with respect to their intimate others. Their confessiographies display a fundamental hesitation toward intimate female companions. About the wife of Paul the Simple, we only know that she betrayed his trust; in *Manhood*, we learn almost nothing about Leiris's wife; Augustine is silent concerning his lover. In yet other cases, the disappearance of the intimate other comes close to malicious neglect. Here, texts become a device of self-distancing, imprisoning the male self in a circular path of self-centeredness, thus preventing the male from self-touching as well as being touched by others. *Credo* exemplifies such a text: the confessant Pohl is not only out of touch with his culpability but also not in touch with intimate others. We return to him (and the people silenced in his text) in this chapter. But first we take another look at Perechodnik's relationship to his female companions. Whereas the (former) Jewish ghetto policeman writes against annihilation, the (former) Nazi perpetrator confesses his hope to be part of a new nation building. What they share in common with Augustine, Leiris, and other male confessants is that the women on their side are variously muted, disavowed, neglected, fictionalized, and rendered invisible.

All of the women absently present in these writings are complicated textual figures, at once biographically sketched and yet metaphorically strained, narcissistically admired and yet anxiously controlled, repeatedly muted and yet saturated with narrative significance. They are disembodied and dispossessed and yet, in their emptied presence, utilized as necessary building blocks for theologies and nations. Women, who have fed their confessing men literally and emotionally, share, in the end, a common fate: they are consumed and cannibalized, their bodies transformed to divine nourishment and ashen fertilizer. They have become ciphers and words, their ghostlike presence transposed into texts that memorialize their displacement and feed the imagination of future generations.

"*The words* I love *will not fall from my lips*"

While in hiding, Calel Perechodnik struggles with loyalty to his wife. The devotion he shows for his wife, Anka, throughout his deathbed confession rests on an originary act of betrayal: he had failed to protect her and their daughter from being deported to the annihilation camps. In her death, Anka provides him with a perspective from which to lament the misery of the circumstances of his life. *Am I a Murderer?* is a self-accusatory plea for forgiveness, an articulation of a sorrow too large to be endured by any individual, the breaking of a Jewish heart,[1] a process of *penthos* in secular hell, a Jewish *teshuva* and call for revenge. The annihilation of his wife and daughter is a trauma Perechodnik cannot escape, not until he finally submits to the ravages of typhus, or—if we are to believe Genia, his shortterm, eighteen-year-old lover—until he swallowed poison. "I am absolutely certain," Genia wrote in a letter after the war, "that the cyanide pills saved him a great deal of suffering at the last moment" (Perechodnik 1996, 205).

The deep affection Perechodnik feels for his wife is, tragically, linked to her irretrievable loss. After her murder, he wants to remain loyal to her but begins a sexual affair with Genia while hiding in Warsaw. While writing his deathbed confession, in which he imagines himself to be in conversation with his wife, whom he misses dearly, Genia is still alive. She will eventually survive him. Perechodnik has trouble finding the right words for this young lover, trouble admitting what he may have felt for Genia during the last weeks in their common hiding places. He confesses to his dead wife that he made love to Genia but assures her in his imaginary talk that he never loved this young woman: "the words *I love* have not passed between us and will

not fall from my lips" (194). His conflicted prose recalls Augustine's seemingly dispassionate portrayal of his lover at the time of her forced departure
from Milan. One senses an emotional attachment that seeps through fissures in a text that wants to proclaim otherwise.

Toward the end of his manuscript, Perechodnik provides a short account
of how Genia escaped the German *Aktionen* and how she came to live in
hiding with him (and others, including his mother). By and large, it is a
factual account, telling of deprivations, hunger, and despair. Traumatized,
Genia does in her hiding place what Paul the Simple did in the desert:
perform meaningless, repetitive tasks. On Antony's order, Paul the Simple
weaves and unweaves baskets and "unstitche[s] his cloak and . . . sew[s] it
up again" (Russell 1980, 114). Genia knits and unravels sweaters. "After a
while she undid that which she had sewed earlier, making from a camisole
a blouse and from a blouse, a camisole" (Perechodnik 1996, 190). Unrelent-
ing fear for one's life, combined with a relentless monotony of a life in the
underground, turns the hiding place of Genia and Calel in the Gentile part
of Warsaw into a prison and shelter, tomb and womb.

Perechodnik uses gendered imagery of birthing and dying to describe
their underground shelter. There, he "begets a dead fetus" and "second child"
(191–192)—the words he uses to describe the completion of his manuscript.
After nine months of hiding, he also sleeps with Genia: "For nine months
I did not have any sexual relations," he writes. "I avoided [laxity of sexual
morals] with disgust, but after a prolonged period the body did not stand
up to the strain. I had done no physical work, was rested, thought that I
would soon perish . . . in short, on May 13 I slept with Genia" (193–194).
Perechodnik explains his sexual affair not as the result of an affectionate
relationship but biological necessity. It is his *body* that needed to sleep with
Genia, not *him*. His sexual urge is in gestation for nine months, the length
of a pregnancy. Only then does he give birth to a sexual desire for another
woman, a desire he feels so conflicted about that he must confess it to the
ears of only one person: his wife. "Finally, I want to tell You what is meant
only for Your ears. You see, Anka, I have deceived You. After nine months
the organism could not stand it and led me to deceit" (193).

Augustine and Culbertson deceive their mothers; Leiris and Perechodnik,
their wives. They all could have kept quiet, but they chose to confess their
deceptions. Perechodnik claims that his confession is meant for Anka's *ears*
only, and thus gives the allusion of an auricular confession. His claim, however, rings as hollow as Augustine's repeated wish that his self-revelations

are meant for God's ears only. The fact is that both men did not choose the evanescent option of oral confession, which would have left no material traces of their secrets. Instead, by writing, they hoped for a larger audience. "Which of my smaller works could be more widely known or give greater pleasure than my *Confessions*?" Augustine asks with gratification about two years before his death.[2] Perechodnik—not unlike Rousseau envisaging a "numberless legion of my fellow men" to hear his confession (1953, 17)—also imagines fantastic numbers: "I believe that millions will read these diaries" (192).[3] Clearly, Perechodnik did not—despite his claim to the contrary—mean to limit the confession of his affair to his wife. Millions were supposed to read it! Only one person was not supposed to hear that "the words *I love*" did not fall from his lips: Genia herself.

In Perechodnik, we see a man who is compelled to confess because he has difficulties embracing his own agency in critical situations. Earlier, he had failed his moral responsibility when he did not and could not protect his daughter (as well as the other girl he cuddled throughout the night before her deportation). Now, in hiding, he fails to acknowledge his sexual agency while living with Genia. In each case, he responds to these failures with an act of confessional writing. Rather than speak to Genia directly—admitting either that he does not love her or that, on the contrary, he is attached to her beyond mere physicality—he confesses to a person no longer present, namely, his wife, who is alive only in his memory.

> I know that You [Anka] will forgive me. Understand: I can assure You that I will not marry a second time, that I will not have any children, that I will always love You, but, after all, I cannot assure You that I will not have relations. I am only twenty-seven years old. As concerns Genia, I don't understand why she gave herself to me that night, particularly since she offered me her virginity. Maybe she liked me, or maybe she came to the conclusion that she should get along without her hymen in the next world. (194)

Any of these words would have hurt Genia greatly; hence, they need to remain a secret. Had Perechodnik shared them with her, he might have lost the last loving anchor in his life. We can also imagine the opposite: he may have whispered terms of endearment into Genia's ears, words he is not willing to commit on paper! Those unrecorded words were to remain a secret, which he would confide neither to his dead wife nor to his anticipated readership. In the end, we can only speculate. Perechodnik may have simply not understood Genia or not cared enough to understand her. Why, he wonders, did she offer him her virginity?

Like Perechodnik, I am a man who is surprised when a person offers the gift of herself or himself to me. This is especially true for invitations that extend to the realm of the erotic and the sexual. I appreciate the gesture, but, in almost all cases, I decline the offer, even when the attraction is reciprocal. I can list multiple sources for such hesitation: adolescent fears of being embarrassed by sexual intimations; a sense of undeserving the sexual without emotional attachment; spousal loyalty and love; the fear of romantically getting lost in the unexpected; unease over revealing my sexual face to a person I hardly know.

I rarely take the initiative in voicing sexual attraction to a person with whom I am not already romantically related. Rather than make the first move, I am more comfortable waiting for others to articulate a passionate craving. There is cowardice in "playing it safe." My reticence toward actively soliciting pleasure protects a vulnerable self. It also prevents a masculine self from becoming predatory.

In contrast to Augustine's nameless lover, Genia is not entirely without her own words. In a letter written to Perechodnik's surviving brother in 1950, she sketches a more affective relationship between herself and Calel. Genia does not romanticize their relationship, but the few lines we have from her pen reveal a deeply caring bond between them, especially during the tragic last days in Warsaw. Together, Calel (whom she calls Calek) and she "sought shelter under the demolished houses, in bunkers, and in sewers"; they discussed suicide (by acquiring together cyanide pills with the intent to use them); they shared sparse and precious items (food and clothing); and they wandered together around the destroyed city before departing forever. "Oh, what troubled moments these were!" recalls Genia in her letter (Perechodnik 1996, 205). She lovingly describes Calel's weaknesses (he "was least immune to hunger and looked like a shadow") and how she cared for him even to the point of sacrificing her own needs for safety and food. When one day, for example, she received some meat, while Calel hid in a different place, "the knowledge that I was keeping the meat and that Calek was suffering from hunger did not give me peace. The following morning I got up early . . . ran toward Zlota Street [and] at last reached my goal." Afterward, she stayed with him until their final moment of separation. "Calek did not let me return," Genia writes, revealing his attachment to her. In an act of reciprocal loving care, Calel, when realizing he cannot survive the exhaustion of his typhus-ravaged body, asks her to stop caring for him and to leave him for her own sake. "Calek woke me up with these words: 'Genia, you will leave Warsaw, and today.' . . . He collapsed at the last moment; typhus had worn him out utterly. He no longer spoke but cried out he had to perish and that he would not allow me to perish on his account" (204–205).

The sense we get from Genia's description of their bond is far more tender than what Perechodnik had admitted to his dead wife.

Attachment comes with the fear of wounding and being wounded. Leiris speaks of his confessions as "recollections relating to wounded men" but also, surprisingly, as "memories connected with stories of wounded women" (1992, 64, 43; emphasis in original). I have always been afraid of wounding those to whom I am attached. Since I feel safer in the waters of friendship, I turn sexual yearnings into romantic partings, as if a wounding could thus be prevented.

There is another woman in *Am I a Murderer?* especially present in its final pages. Given the many uncanny yet unintended structural parallels to Augustine's *Confessions*, it should not come as a surprise that she is Perechodnik's mother.

In Genia's perception, Perechodnik's mother is part of the little family they formed in their hiding places. In her postwar letter, Genia speaks understandingly of her (unlike Perechodnik himself), although she does not divulge how she and his mother felt about each other. It is clear that they know each other intimately enough that Genia consistently calls her "Mother" and that she cared enough not to abandon her. "Hunger, fear for tomorrow, and, what was the worst, the death of Father so affected Mother that had she a little courage, she would have committed suicide," Genia writes in 1950. "She was very ill to end [sic] of her life. We wanted to join the partisans. Nonetheless, we resigned ourselves to look out for Mother. Hungry and cold, we served time in our prison until 1944" (Perechodnik 1996, 203). For Mother's sake, Genia did not escape to the partisans. Later, when Perechodnik and Genia walked one last time together through Warsaw shortly before his death, they "suddenly stood near the cellar where his mother was hiding. Calek did not want to go inside. . . . We knew that in one way or the other she would perish. In the last moment I ran alone to say good-bye to Mother" (205).

Perechodnik's portrayal of his mother is far more negative. It constitutes another instance in which Calel's and Genia's descriptions of their common bond differ. At times, Perechodnik depicts his mother as unloving, selfish, overbearing, and weepy; at other times, he feels compassion for her situation, her broken heart, and for her attempts to sacrifice herself for him. He blames her for pushing him into Genia's arms and, at the same time, for thwarting their affair. "I also did it [sleeping with Genia] to spite my mother" (194). In Calel's recollection, his mother would have rather given up the hiding place than allow a Jewish man to stay there alone with an unmarried Jewish woman. The question had come up earlier, when Aronek, a fellow Jew in hiding, would have had to stay behind alone with Genia in the hideout in the Gentile part of Warsaw. Mother opposed it. As readers, we assume that she had religious reasons for her stern decision, but her son portrays her more selfish needs. "According to her, it would not have been a misfortune if Aronek had remained in the [Jewish] ghetto and perished— and he did perish." For her, it "would have been worse if he had lived [in hiding] in a Polish neighborhood one on one with a Jewish girl." Later, when his mother's own life is at stake, she changes her mind and allows her son to be alone with Genia. "When I reminded myself of that," Calel remarks scornfully, and "when I saw that Mother, in order to save her own life, was ready right away to leave our hiding place and to leave me alone with Genia, then I showed her in her absence that this did not bite, that no person had died from it" (194). His mother stands accused of Anorek's death as well as of pushing her son into the arms of Genia.[4] Angry with his mother's inconsistency, Perechodnik spites her by sleeping with this young woman.

This is no flattering description of either his mother, Genia, or himself. Perechodnik's confessional account is at the brink of self-erasure yet builds upon blaming the mother. In Calel's recollection, his mother is "of two minds": surviving at all costs or ready to sacrifice herself. On the one hand, "she wants to live and to see the defeat of the detestable Germans"; on the other hand, "the old mother," who presumes, wrongly, that the remaining money will last for the survival of only one, not two people, "wants to sacrifice herself, wants to enable her son to live." In a reversal of Yitzhak Twersky's Hasidic lament, "a sacrifice I am, a sacrifice on my mother's altar" (Assaf 2006, 28), Perechodnik exclaims ambiguously, "Mother, I don't need your sacrifice" (1996, 200). Similar to Augustine's irritation over the flood of maternal tears and worries, Perechodnik expresses not only (narcissistic) gratitude for his mother's willingness to die for him but also his anger for her emotional inconsistency and undue maternal influence. Neither Perechodnik nor Augustine—and here their accounts meet—perceives himself at fault for his behavior toward his female lover. Instead, mothers—as well as the tragic circumstances of life—are blamed. By refusing to assume responsibility, these men leave behind texts that display emotional paucity with respect to the women who may have loved and cared for them deeply.

After Perechodnik completes his manuscript on August 18, 1943, he manages to take up his pen again two months later and write an addendum. He devotes these last pages neither to his wife nor to Genia but to his parents. It is a belated testimony to the parents he wasn't sure he loved: "I do not love my parents—but is this my fault?" (1996, 193). He summarizes the events that led to his father's death after this man had fought for thirteen months for his survival; it is followed by a description of his mother and the "sea of tears that she spilled and is still spilling over the loss of her husband" (199). Since he, like Augustine, cannot weep over his father's death—"not one tear fell from my eye on account of Father's death" (200)—his mother's tears make him nervous. "Should I write . . . of the sleepless nights, or the fact that in the course of a month she aged twenty years?" Or should he write "of the heart of mother and wife that withstood that blow and did not burst from pain" (199)? Perechodnik does not quite know what to make of his mother. Compassionately, he writes how "her tears flowed" and "her shoulders stooped even more" after her husband's death, but he can't resist wondering about the sincerity of her tears: "Now that they took away her husband, she remained without funds. This time she was condemned to death without appeal" (200). Does his mother weep for her husband, the son wonders, or for her own survival? Should he believe his mother's self-sacrificial side or, instead, her selfish side that had sent a fellow Jew (Aronek) to his death? Calel cannot answer these questions, and his words express the failing of a language muddled in emotions. His inability explains perhaps why—according to Genia's letter—he cannot bring himself to see his mother in her bunker one last time before he perishes. Instead, it is only Genia who goes to say good-bye to her. Was Perechodnik afraid that, in this last moment, he might have received an answer to his uncertainty: Does she love me? Do I love her? Weakened, numb, and already half dead, he cannot bring himself to face an answer.

When I am at a loss for words, my wife sometimes finds the right tone to reach my mother's ears and heart. Like Genia, she can be more patient and compassionate with her than I am.

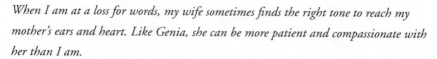

A last word on food and love: Augustine plays with food metaphors in his *Confessions*. He replaces his mother's milk with the nourishing milk of God: "What am I but an infant sucking your milk and feeding on you the food that is incorruptible?" (4.1.1.). In contrast to Augustine's increasingly metaphoric use of nourishment and hunger, in *Am I a Murderer?* scarcity and starvation take on increasing proportions. The hunted Jew is forced to think about food every day. For each new person joining the hiding place—and Genia's arrival is no exception—the food portions, and hence one's life, are at stake. Spiritual nourishment is a luxury Perechodnik cannot afford, but he does indulge briefly in a morbid fantasy. Of his dead wife, he writes: "I know very well that Your body, so many times kissed by me, was burned by the Germans and used as fertilizer. Perhaps out of Your ashes grew potatoes that I am just eating now; perhaps rye grew, from which was made the bread I eat" (Perechodnik 1996, 191). Perechodnik is fed neither by God's body (like Augustine) nor by the Hasidic piety of his mother's milk (like his co-religionist Yitzhak Twersky). Instead, he imagines his wife's body feeding the food he eats. A Jewish eucharistic meal in a time of annihilation? It is, for sure, an image that violates just about all *kashrut* regulations. It is a blasphemous act of love and cannibalism, of a bleak marriage of eros and thanatos. The erotic body he once kissed he now devours to still his hunger. He eats the bread that is his female companion, his *com panis*, the one "with bread."

Centuries earlier, Paul the Simple, traumatized as he was, could no longer feed on his wife's love, could not even taste the honey he was spooning off the desert soil, as Antony demanded of him.[5] Instead, he voluntarily starved his body to be readied for a divine embrace. Perechodnik imagines feeding on his wife as he hopes not for redemption but for revenge. The half-crazed, half-dead figures that populate the narrative of the Jewish ghetto policeman—millennia away from the Egyptian desert—nevertheless have something in common with Paul the Simple: heavy hearted and weighed down by excruciating sorrow, they move like puppets through a nightmarish landscape and perform desperate, repetitive tasks necessary for sheer survival. In comparison, Augustine's pierced heart is no match for such a degree of desperation.

Perechodnik feeds on his wife; Augustine feeds on God. Their confessional narratives, which reflect different religious experiences in history, nevertheless draw from a shared archive of the cultural imagination in order to come to terms with their existential uncertainty and emotional instability. Images of scarcity and nourishment, of feeding and devouring, help them negotiate their anxious states. The images they put out in the world, however, escape their narrative control and develop lives independent from those of their authors. Writing, reading, and feeding interweave. *Reading* Augustine's written *Confessions* is an act of devouring the (displaced) maternal body. In Perechodnik's case, a beloved female body is devoured. Lovingly, he eats her; with him, we read and eat his textual memory of her; we eat *her* as well. Ingesting the trauma, we carry it in our bodies into the future.

In the Bosom of Mother Church

Oswald Pohl is a man who caused the kind of trauma that people like Perechodnik, Anka, and Genia had to endure. As argued earlier, Pohl's confessional testimony, *Credo*, uses religious rhetoric in an attempt to normalize a Nazi perpetrator. Portraying himself as a decent man, Pohl shows little effort in surrendering to the unconditional self-disclosure demanded by the confessional genre. He toys with the latter but ultimately remains walled off. It is not surprising, then, that intimate others are missing almost entirely in his confession. Only a close reading of *Credo*'s gendered subtext will reveal an absent presence of two female figures: his wife, who remains invisible in the text (but is important to the booklet's production), and his mother, whose independent subjectivity is fully expunged.

In 1942, Pohl married his second wife, Eleonore von Brüning, who, given her biography, must have been as convinced a Nazi as her husband (see Koch 1988, 83–91). Heinrich Himmler, a key figure in the Nazi extermination policy, had a not so inconsequential hand in bringing Oswald and Eleonore together, and their marriage ceremony took place in Himmler's military quarters in East Prussia (see Schulte 2001, 40; Schmitz-Köster 2007, 87–90). Eleonore stood by her husband's side after his arrest. The forty-one-year-old Eleonore, writes Schmitz-Köster, is "determined to remain loyal to Pohl. . . . He is her husband, and she would never betray 'a German soldier.' She writes this line in her notes during the first postwar year" (158).

Eleonore contributed four drawings to *Credo*. They are essential to the booklet because they visualize the pathos underlying her husband's confessional narrative. Each drawing illustrates a major theme for each of the four chapters. Three of these black-and-white pictures present a pensive male figure (presumably Pohl), and the last depicts a pastoral scene. Eleonore, who is not credited in *Credo* as illustrator, succeeds in portraying her husband as innocent, victimized, and consoled. Let us take a look at each of her drawings.

The picture preceding the first chapter shows a young male figure in a navy uniform bending his head before crosses marking the burial sites of German soldiers on an island in the Pacific Ocean.[6] It illustrates in a visually condensed form the chapter's emotional and substantive theme, "Protestant Youth and Years of Travel," describing Pohl's Protestant upbringing within the context of the Great War of 1914–1918 and his pondering of grand religious questions with adolescent simplicity. In Eleonore's depiction, the figure still bows his head to the crosses at the grave sites, but he is already an alien in a foreign land. Pohl's religious dissatisfaction and skepticism are cartoonishly indicated by a thick question mark splattered across the drawing.

Eleonore's next image illustrates the title of chapter 2, "Between Faith and Disbelief." We see a stylized figure standing on a path leading away from books and a sword (at the bottom) and toward heavenly planets (top). Pohl is caught between different ideologies and beliefs, partially motionless and inert, yet his arms raised so that his gaze is turned toward the sun. The drawing renders the chapter's account of his professional career in the SS as a spiritual trajectory. Obvious Christian symbols are absent and replaced by a neo-pagan cosmology, especially the sun, which Nazi propaganda had appropriated as symbol for national hope and renewal.[7] On his way toward the astral constellation, Pohl is a small, shadowy figure—not really an individual but a cutout. The silhouette captures well the chapter's central narrative concern: Pohl does not hide the fact that he had supported National Socialism from early on but portrays himself as a small cog in the wheel, as a "politically untrained" man of the military (*Credo*, 29). His career decision to join the SS, he claims, did not diminish his moral sincerity. On the contrary, it was the fault of a corrupt church that made him question Christian faith, pushing him into the arms of Nazi *Gottgläubigkeit* and leading him to abandon the Protestant church in 1936.[8]

Illustration for chapter 1 of *Credo: Mein Weg zu Gott* (Landshut: Alois Girnth, 1950).

Illustration for chapter 2 of *Credo: Mein Weg zu Gott* (Landshut: Alois Girnth, 1950).

Illustration for chapter 3 of *Credo: Mein Weg zu Gott* (Landshut: Alois Girnth, 1950).

Illustration for chapter 4 of *Credo: Mein Weg zu Gott* (Landshut: Alois Girnth, 1950).

In her third drawing for the chapter "Return to God," Eleonore assumes the perspective of someone peeking into a dark and barren prison cell. A figure on a plank bed is holding his head in his hands. The entire picture is framed by a thorny wreath decorated with one small rose—no doubt a symbolic representation of the rosary and, possibly, Christ's crown of thorns. In this chapter, Pohl—now a prisoner of the Allies in Landsberg—wonders aloud about the extent of his guilt without ever admitting culpability. The drawing augments and echoes the chapter's ominous opening phrase, "then came the atrocious year of 1945." Seeing himself as a victim of the post-1945 victor's justice, he remains blind to the victims of his brutal policy. Since Pohl had "never beaten anyone to death" (43), why then—so the unspoken message of this picture—does he deserve to languish in this cell?

Eleonore's fourth and final drawing depicts a pastoral setting of a shepherd in a black habit who is surrounded by a flock of sheep, cradling a lamb. It is a metaphoric transposition of the religious metaphor of the chapter's title, "In the Bosom of the True Catholic Church." Text and image are about Pohl's spiritual homecoming. Autobiographical content is reduced to a minimum, while the focus lies on Pohl's conversion: "I made my life's confession to our prison chaplain . . . and experienced the zenith of my life" (66). The converted perpetrator is depicted as an innocent lamb in the arms of a shepherd—open to metonymic representations of his confessor Morgenschweis, of Christ, of Mother Church, or all of the above. The follies of this world no longer trouble Pohl because he has put his trust entirely in the Catholic Church. The deliberate textual insertion of Augustine's heart that "is restless until it rests in you" (69) is visually reinforced in this picture: Pohl has found rest in the arms of his confessor and the church. We will return to this drawing in more detail later.

These drawings are no masterpieces. Rather, they bear traces of the "naturalist, idyllic style" of Nazi aesthetics (Schmitz-Köster 2007, 43), which Eleonore must have picked up as a trained commercial designer. The lack of artistic merit, which corresponds well with the scant literary value of her husband's text, is compensated by Eleonore's skill in distillation. She manages to condense visually the psychodynamics of *Credo*'s religious-political rhetoric, thus reinforcing the booklet's core sentiment: Pohl is to be imagined as a lonely, contemplative, and decent man whose soul does not find peace until it rests in God.

The fact that *Credo* does not credit Eleonore as illustrator is surprising given that she was trained as a graphic designer and remained loyal to Pohl after the war.[9] Her own biography is anything but uncomplicated. She was born in 1904 to Richard Holtz and Hedwig Müller, and her father died shortly after her birth. After some schooling in housekeeping and stenography, she arrived in Berlin at the age of seventeen and eventually obtained a secretarial position at the Walter de Gruyter publishing house, where she later worked as a graphic designer. Shortly after starting her formal education at the Hamburg school of arts and crafts and working as a freelance designer, she met her first husband, Karl Mass (fifteen years her senior); in 1933, she married her second husband, Rüther von Brüning (twenty-eight years her senior). After the birth of her second child, von Brüning died. A love affair with Ludwig Gniss led to yet another pregnancy, but after the breakup, Eleonore decided to give birth to her third child, Heilwig, in a home of the *Lebensborn*, an SS organization for "Aryan" mothers of "pure blood," where she eventually met Oswald Pohl. In 1937, she joined the NSDAP.[10]

Not a word about Eleonore's life is found in *Credo*. Her husband does not talk about her anywhere in the text. Not credited as an artist, she also disappears as a wife in the confessional narrative. She is entirely absent. And something else disappears from sight: her complicity! Even though Eleonore assists in constructing the myth of a respectable Nazi, of a decent man led astray by forces beyond his control, her Nazi persuasions are never scrutinized in public. She actively contributed to shaping an image of her husband as an innocent soul incorrectly condemned by the hostile victors, but because of her absence, her female collaborative support is concealed.[11] She disappears as a creative individual, as supportive wife, and as a person responsible for her ideological conviction. Robbed of her female subjectivity and her moral agency, she cannot even become culpable.

Benign paternalism creates the fiction of a woman who is not capable of culpable deeds. A pro-feminist men's movement and post-patriarchal male scholarship that see no fault in the other gender carry vestiges of such paternalism. I, too, am tempted to keep women blameless, innocent, eternally victimized, and in need of care by an enlightened masculinity, although I know that women are denied their subjectivity and moral agency when they are deprived of the ability to commit grave errors, to be complicit, or to accumulate guilt.

Male confessants frequently blame mothers and mute their lovers. These are un-praiseworthy textual operations, but they do not render women guiltless. Even when female figures perform disappearing acts in male confessiographies, we must keep in mind women's moral subjectivity. Because they disappear in male texts does not mean they are innocent in life.

Eleonore is not the only intimate other who disappears in Pohl's confessional rhetoric. There is also no word on his father and none on his seven siblings; his children and his first (divorced) wife are not mentioned either. Constructed as a man's spiritual self-examination intended for public consumption, *Credo* leaves no room for any private talk about relatives.

Autobiographies usually locate the male protagonist within his family of origin and mention, at least formally, socially important dates relating to his family of choice, such as marriage or the number of children. Given that *Credo* is not an autobiography but belongs to the genre of conversion narratives, not mentioning family members is not entirely unwarranted. Conversion stories focus on the individual readying himself for undergoing a spiritual transformation. Still one wonders why Pohl does not weave his children and wives into his story, if only to exploit family values to score moral points. Portraying himself as a loyal family man could have humanized his public image. *Credo*, however, remains silent on this account. One could even argue that his children and wives deserve an appearance in the text simply because they all helped Pohl survive in hiding for over a year after the war. Arrested on May 27, 1946, Pohl kept in contact with them as much as possible under prison restrictions. Especially Eleonore, given what we can read into her drawings, must have felt close to him.

The complete absence of intimate others in *Credo*—especially of Pohl's former and current wives—calls for further explanation. On one level, the nonappearance of female companions may simply demonstrate once again that religious male confessiographies generally resist the incorporation of women because the latter are perceived as a hindrance to a man's spiritual rebirth. Women disrupt a man's immersion in spiritual self-examination. They are omitted, displaced, or relegated to the margins of a text because they embody the realm of the trivial—that is, of home and bed, both of which obstruct the spiritual sphere a confessing man seeks to enter. On another level, it is conceivable that Pohl's confessor, Morgenschweis, also had an interest in silencing Pohl's wives. After all, Pohl's divorce and second marriage rubbed against Catholic moral teachings. Rather than complicate the image of a true Catholic convert, it might have been easier for Morgenschweis not to open this can of worms. At the time of the writing of *Credo*, the German churches tried to curb what they perceived as the sexual licentiousness of the Nazi era and of the immediate postwar years. "In the early to mid-1950s," Dagmar Herzog observes, "an abrupt shift toward far greater sexual conservatism" occurred in West Germany, spearheaded by the Protestant and Catholic churches, with "Christian spokespersons often present[ing] sexual propriety as the cure for the nation's larger moral crisis" (2005, 101, 73). In such a climate, Morgenschweis would have been ill-advised to shout from the rooftops improper sexual behavior of his spiritual client, especially since Pohl had no inclination to annul his marriage to Eleonore, which he had entered under the banner of Nazi *Gottgläubigkeit* rather than the tutelage of the church.

Given the textual absence of his wives and of other close family members, it is all the more astounding that one woman is occasionally acknowledged: Pohl's pious mother. Why does she enjoy such privilege?

It is, for sure, a limited privilege his mother enjoys. She is never called by her name and is painted in a monochromatic fashion. She is a "self-sacrificing mother" who modeled for Pohl an "inner piety"; she is a "pious mother" who installed a "religious fervor" in her young son; she is a "simple but infinitely caring and pious mother" who created a "paradise" in his childhood (*Credo*, 17, 21, 42). The maternal typology is plain to see: as mother, she is the guarantor of Pohl's humanness, the paradise from which he was expelled, and she is the seed of a piety to which he eventually returns. Unmistakably, she is modeled after Augustine's mother, Monica, who similarly represents a steady Christian piety. "From his earliest references [in the *Confessions*]," writes Kim Power, "Monica is the ever present and significant figure who mediates the gifts of God to Augustine" (1996, 77). As models for piety, these maternal women are textually bereft of all sexuality; as biological mothers, they are half carnal, half archetypal (see Hawkins 1990, 242). They are harbingers of the eventual arrival and triumph of the ultimate spiritual Mother—"our mother the Catholic Church" (9.13.37), as Augustine writes after his mother's burial.

In at least three respects, *Credo*'s first chapter is crudely modeled after the *Confessions*, and Pohl's Protestant mother holds a symbolic key in it. First, when young Pohl is away from home (and mother) for the first time during his travels with the German navy, he is exposed to the "restless and sinful hustle and bustle of the large Asian ports and trading centers luring with excitement" (17). A knowing reader recognizes at once a reference to Augustine's student years in the Roman African port of Carthage, where "all around me hissed a cauldron of illicit loves" (3.1.1). Second, when Pohl wavers between his dutiful Bible reading in his youth (which is related to his mother's piety) and the increasingly stronger pull of the Stoics, Voltaire, and Nietzsche, he emulates Augustine's elaborate philosophical struggles between, on the one hand, his attraction to Platonism and Manicheism and, on the other, his eventual understanding of the superior wisdom found in biblical scripture. In Pohl's text, however, names like Voltaire are just dropped like popular signposts without even so much as a hint of intellectual engagement. Third, Augustine's *Confessions* also serve as a model in regard to mothers: Pohl's nameless mother is introduced, like Monica, as a representation of a stable piety. Each mother is a measuring rod for her son's moral corruption and distance from God. At the end of chapter 1, Pohl has abandoned the Protestant piety of his mother and is about to go astray. Appropriately, Pohl concludes the chapter by declaring his existential sense of loss: "I was entirely caught in myself, in the shameful hopelessness of [thinking] that I can handle my inner battles myself" (*Credo*, 23). Similar sentiments of loss of self in contradistinction to maternal piety are expressed throughout Augustine's *Confessions*: "What was my state of mind?" Augustine wonders early on. "It is quite certain that it was utterly shameful and a disgrace to me that I had it" (2.9.17). Later, Augustine writes: "I had departed from myself . . . [and] could not even find myself, much less you [God]" (5.2.2). And still later, when already in Milan: "I had no confidence and had lost hope that truth could be found. . . . [Yet] my mother, strong in her devotion, had already come to join me" (6.1.1).

Whatever one can say about the parallelism between *Credo* and the *Confessions*, we cannot forget that the former only replicates opportune Augustinian themes and that Pohl is never moved to explore himself in any comparable depth to Augustine's soul searching. The same is true with respect to their mothers. For Pohl, his mother is no more than a trace, devoid of name, personality, flesh and blood. As a disembodied figure, a "textless text" (Culbertson 1998, 2006), she stands in for the virtues of piety and Bible reading, and, as such, stands against the ills of modern secularism.[12] Without a life of her own, her portrayal does not come close to the restrained complexity of Augustine's portraiture of Monica. Of course, Monica is also

an "idealized figure" (Brown 1969, 164). She is "Augustine's eternally unfinished business" (Burrus 2004, 77) and is "redolent with the imagery . . . of
Mary," "based on the template of the ideal Roman mother" (Power 1996,
91, 71). Monica is never fully fleshed out, but Augustine, who returns to her
portrait after his own conversion, eventually adds a few "rough edges of real
life." No longer just an exemplary model, Monica is described as somewhat
flawed and "deliberately sinful" (Paffenroth 2003, 144–145). She is "subtly
transformed . . . into an ordinary human being, an object of concern, a
sinner like himself, equally in need of mercy" (Brown 1969, 164; also Miles
1992, 81–87). Pohl's portrayal of his nameless mother, in contrast, remains
entirely flat and monotone. What remains of her are a few empty and clichéd markers: pious, caring, simple. If Monica is already a trace, then Pohl's
nameless mother is but a trace of a trace. There is no memory of her.

The mothers of Pohl and Augustine will not have the last word but are
eventually replaced by a mother far greater than any real woman can ever
become. In the famous vision at Ostia, after Augustine's conversion, Monica
and her son experience a moment of shared spiritual ecstasy (9.10.24). Their
shared vision seems to indicate that mother and son are finally on equal
footing: Augustine has ascended to the level of maternal piety, while Monica, whose steadfast faith had just been a little shaken by Augustine's added
short biography, descends to the level of her son's (former) weaknesses. Augustine relates, for example, how his mother battled an addiction to wine.
Son and mother, however, are not on equal footing, and no lasting equality
is established. Since Augustine needs to leave his mother behind and move
on, the narrative placement of the Ostia vision suggests that their shared
experience is less about a moment of spiritual equal opportunity and more
about Augustine's permanent replacement of his mother. Newly converted,
Augustine no longer needs Monica's maternal piety as measurement. "With
her goal accomplished," writes Power, "she literally has no further purpose
in life" (1996, 89). As bishop of Hippo, *he* now speaks for the church. Monica, the natural mother, has been exchanged for a female *ecclesia*.[13]

Similarly, Pohl's mother is no longer needed after her son's postwar conversion. Halfway through the text, she simply disappears. She represents a
sentimentalized memory of Protestant piety, which must be supplanted the
instant her son is cradled in the "bosom of the only true Catholic Church."
In the economy of redemptive gift-giving the Protestant natural mother is
exchanged for a Catholic spiritual mother.

Homosocial Bonding, Remasculinization, and Nation Building

Only after Pohl's mother vanishes in the text does a male-male intimate exchange surface in *Credo*. Two men—the perpetrator/convert and his confessor/hagiographer—bond over the mother's disappearance. The text purged of the natural mother (and of other women), Pohl now takes on a passive-receptive, feminized role vis-à-vis his relationship to a "forcefully" manly Morgenschweis:

> I now opened my heart to the Catholic prison chaplain. Had the eloquently forceful man of God earlier loosened the dried soil of faith through his stirring sermons, he now planted his seeds of divine revelation into the seed-craving land. My whole being changed under his leadership. . . . [Like] a powerful torrent, the Good News, as taught by the only true Catholic Church, flooded me. (49)[14]

The strongly gendered imagery requires some comments. In this sexually charged passage, the prison chaplain as confessor spiritually inseminates the confessant's starved but now lubricated soil and soul. Pohl as perpetrator finds himself on the receiving end of this male exchange, the one in need of spiritual impregnation. Pregnant with spirit, Pohl gives birth to a confession narrative. Not unlike the generative power of Perechodnik and Augustine, Pohl's testimony to a newfound faith is his new child, a child born out of spiritual insemination. In addition, and perhaps more important, Pohl is not just giving birth but is given birth to: he is born again. His new mother is the church, who ensures his homecoming and nourishes him at her bosom.

Eleonore's fourth drawing captures well the dynamics of this sexual-spiritual exchange. We see a male shepherd wearing the black habit of a priest. Surrounded by sheep, he cradles a lamb in his arms. No doubt, Pohl is the small, lost sheep, and Morgenschweis, who stands in symbolically for Mother Church, is holding the prodigal son in his/her arms. The perpetrator and his hagiographer have created a new family bond that gets by without real women. Intuitively—and perhaps enviously—Eleonore zoomed in on the religious sentiment of this male-male enclosure. Biological mothers and sexual female companions are no longer needed. The presence of any woman would only disrupt the pastoral tranquility of this scene. The homosocial embrace paves the way to Mother Church.

Homosociality as an enabler of spiritual transformation has a long tradition in the Christian practice of seeking God. Like Paul the Simple, who left his wife after he caught her in an act of adultery, many men in the early centuries of the formation of Christianity abandoned their social obligations and family ties and banded together in homosocial communities, which excluded any female presence. Yet intimate homosocial bonding also raises anxiety among heterosexual men about same-sex allegations and temptations. Hence, safeguards must be put into place (spatially, metaphorically, discursively) that claim homosocial communities to be sex-free zones in order to avoid any insinuations and charges of same-sex activity.

The homosocial bond between Pohl and his male confessor, which Eleonore's drawing expresses so vividly, must have raised Pohl's anxiety as well. With his military mind and his male socialization during the Great War, we must imagine Pohl detesting all attempts at feminizing him (or, worse, sodomizing him). In *Credo*, this anxiety is negotiated through the process of conversion, showing Pohl caught in a balancing act between his old martial masculinity and a new, softer male self in need of care. To increase his chances of clemency, Pohl could no longer hold on to an old masculinity linked to a corrupted and corruptible Nazi ideology. A softer male was needed. Such a soft male, though, is always in danger of becoming womanish. One way to solve this dilemma is to ban all women from the text. In order to protect the male confessant from becoming "like a woman," female intimate others have to play disappearing acts in confessional narratives.

If this reasoning is somewhat plausible, then the role of "women" is largely compensatory. On the one hand, their presence as an (erotic) other dispels accusations of homosexual desire; on the other hand, their textual disappearance makes possible the emergence of a homosocial bonding, which mediates the transformation of the male self.[15] Paul the Simple, for example, can forget his wife only through his obedient, eroticized bonding to Antony (see Masterson 2006), and Augustine contemplates forming a homosocial male community just at the moment he forces his female companion to depart to Africa (6.14.24). As golden son, Augustine not only leaves his lover but also dispossesses his mother (and her tears) in order to embrace God and the new rule of the Father.

Oswald Pohl, however, is neither a desert monk nor a golden son. Contrary to Augustine, he cannot dispossess a mother who is never really present; contrary to Paul the Simple, he cannot leave a wife who loyally stands by his side. Pohl does not volunteer for the desert because he, as a man denying his culpability, is not devastated by trauma. In many ways, Pohl's confession

is a masquerade: a make-believe contrition and a pseudo-Augustinian posturing. He is a phony saint who does not embrace the monastic hardship
of the desert but complains about the misery of his imprisonment under
Allied control.

*I am not culpable like Pohl. I don't even have to wrestle with uncertainty over partial
complicity with the NS regime, like my father's generation. I am, however, inconsequential in a different way. I often speak admiringly of the celibate queer lives of the
desert saints, who inhabit a desired place of solitude and uninterrupted contemplation
(Krondorfer 2008b). But I would not go to such arid places myself, not even during
dark moments of grief and betrayal. I am not Paul the Simple. I resemble more Augustine. The desert remains a dream, a place of memory, an exotic otherness.*

For Pohl, as for other imprisoned Nazi perpetrators, the world had turned
out to be dramatically different from what he had envisioned only a few
years earlier. The dream of a racially cleansed *Lebensraum* (living space) for
a Greater Germany was reduced to the size of a prison cell.[16] In this new
and limited world, religion began to play a comforting and supporting
role. It negotiated the delicate act of maintaining one's masculinity while
rendering oneself selectively passive and effeminate. Eleonore's drawing of
a lonely man in his prison cell, embroidered by a thorny wreath, epitomizes
the religious consolation sought by postwar German men in crisis: the former *Herrenmensch* (master race) was suddenly in need of care and compassion. Outside the Allied prison cells, German masculinity was in trouble
just the same. With the military defeat and with 4 million German men
dead and close to 12 million in POW camps, men generally had difficulties
readjusting and reintegrating into society in the postwar period—a con-
flict that lasted well into the 1950s (see Schissler 2001b). The lost war, the
denazification program, and the question of guilt were particularly called
upon to explain the deflated sense of the German male, including physical
impotence. One German physician wrote in 1947 that "the male gender
[was] hit harder in its soul by the lost war than the female," while a German psychologist reasoned that "the question of guilt" was deeply dam-
aging to marriages (quoted in Herzog 2005, 86–87). Denazification was
blamed "for the decline in high-quality manliness." "Strong masculinity

was in disrepute," Herzog remarks, "*both* because of Nazism *and* because of its defeat"; in a word: the "straight male egos needed boosting" (2005, 97; emphasis in original).

The boosting of Pohl's ego was an ambiguous enterprise. The path to clemency was sought through conversion to Christianity, but it demanded of Pohl, the soldierly man, to become meek and needy. He had to agree to be (temporarily) feminized. Portrayed as being spiritually inseminated by his male confessor-cum-hagiographer, he had to be open, permeable, malleable. Eleonore's final drawing of Pohl in a homosocial embrace with his confessor must have raised doubts and anxiety about his manliness. A Christian convert looked like a weak and womanish man.

Morgenschweis states with a sigh of relief that his prodigal son Pohl did not have to suffer ridicule in prison because of his conversion. His admission to the Catholic Church, Morgenschweis writes, "became immediately known to his fellow prisoners and former SS comrades. What was feared did not happen: his comrades did not reject him because of this step; they did not greet him with scorn or mockery but, instead, congratulated him" (*Credo*, 10). Was there a danger for such mockery? Since Pohl was not the only Nazi perpetrator finding his way back to the church and employing religious language to exculpate himself,[17] the fear of ridicule by other Nazi convicts is perhaps comparable to Augustine's fear of the male critic, who would laugh at his weeping. Neither man's behavior, however, was entirely exceptional within the possibilities these men had at their disposal. Was Pohl at risk of becoming an object of scorn, or did Morgenschweis exaggerate the fear in order to emphasize Pohl's personal courage and the uniqueness of his conversion?

The case of Karl Brandt, a fellow prisoner at Landsberg, gives some credence to the concerns expressed by Morgenschweis. Brandt, who was sentenced to death by the Allies for his leading role in the euthanasia program,[18] remained a pagan even when in prison after the war. Unlike Pohl, he did not convert or rejoin the church but proudly maintained his anti-Christian Nazi attitude until his death by hanging under Allied jurisdiction. Brandt did not write a confession. But two final letters to his family, which circulated briefly in right-wing circles in the 1960s,[19] give us an insight into this man's thinking. In a blend of religious and political drivel, Brandt exhausts metaphysical explanations for the fate that has befallen him and his fatherland. "One cannot look for the grand meaning, if it is about oneself," he writes two days before his hanging. "How should an all-pervading power

[*Allmacht*]—if it existed—be worried about the well-being of a creature? O, how little it matters." In a letter to his son a month earlier, Brandt writes:

> It is possible that at the end there is disappointment. This, then, is bitter and hurts. But greater is the pain when you'd have to realize that you pushed away your neighbor. Humans remain lonely, somehow. Only rarely, now and then one quietly senses in the other a familiar stirring. . . . This community is what holds together not only human to human but also bonds upwardly to incomprehensible regions. What could this be? Love, faith? A common hope! . . . A home [*Heimat*] shall grow for you [son] and all of you. The soil that devoured our youth, it shall be sacred and remain sacred to us.[20]

In the same letter, Brandt recalls that, in his youth, he was closely connected to the local parsonage and how seriously he struggled "with myself and my God." The passage recalls Pohl's autobiographical reminiscences in the opening chapter. But unlike Pohl, Brandt focuses on the heroic aspect of Jesus' leadership while despising Christianity as a religion. Christ is "a giant," Brandt writes. But concerning Christian believers, he adds: "Hypocrisy and only lies!" He no longer "desires Christianity" and claims that he never found "one Christian, who joyfully armed himself for his last march [to the gallows]. Not one! Only the pagan dies joyfully."

Brandt's pagan affirmation of life, soil, and joyful health is part of a supremacist national masculinity and of the Nazi ideology of worthy and unworthy life. Contrasting his manly attitude with a Christianity for the weak, Brandt asserts that only the healthy and racially pure shall live. Not surprisingly, he ends the letter to his son with a manly assertion: "Confidently and with a firm stride I march into the New Year! I know it is a joy to live, because *everything is life*! You can't dither with the world. . . . Seize life!" (emphasis in the original). Christians are dreary and womanish; only the pagans are strong and manly. Pohl, then, would have reasons to fear ridicule of fellow inmates.

The pagan Karl Brandt may embody the kind of Landsberg prisoner that Morgenschweis had in mind when fearing for Pohl's well-being. As his hagiographer, he makes sure to portray Pohl differently. Brandt, too, found a pastoral caregiver in the Protestant pastor Lonitzer. After his death, Lonitzer swathed Brandt's pagan worldview in Christian rhetoric and administered his Christian funeral. In his eulogy, he sought to reconcile Brandt's ideology with Christianity by featuring prominently the theme of manliness. He praised Brandt's unrepentant mentality and manly defiance in the face of Allied injustice. Brandt, he claimed, found "eternal freedom": no longer "condemned by fate" and no longer a "prisoner of the dark forces of vengeance, hate and lies."

> What he had to say at the threshold to freedom, with lucid defiance and manliness [*mit klarer Stirn mannhaft*], was meant not only for the foreign executioners of this illegal verdict standing before him but also for us all as an obligating legacy, for his beloved German *Volk*, and for history that one day will judge more justly.[21]

On the one hand, the portrayal of Brandt as a victim of the Allies and as a hero of the German people recalls *Credo*'s religious reinterpretation of Pohl. On the other hand, *Credo* makes at least an effort to tease out another dimension of Pohl. By guiding Pohl through a conversion process, Morgenschweis sketches a portrait of a perpetrator who is seeking a religious transformation, showing a man in need of the public's care and compassion—like a child or a woman. Any such attempt is missing in Brandt's case. Lonitzer, the Protestant minister, did not soften the image of his spiritual client but upheld the death-defying illusion of his manliness. Instead of rendering Brandt an effeminate repentant sinner, Lonitzer offers as a parting gift a Christian blessing to an openly unremorseful Nazi criminal.

Pohl must have thought about the kind of reception he might get from his former Nazi comrades, like Brandt, when caving in to the soft ideology of Christianity. Wouldn't it seem odd to see the former head of the WVHA depicted by his wife as a cuddly lamb in the arms of a compassionate male shepherd? Yet it was important to render Pohl's image in a softened light, and Morgenschweis's pastoral efforts and Eleonore's spousal support (through her drawings) worked toward this goal. *Credo* portrays Pohl as powerless and victimized in his relation to the Allies, and passive and receptive in relation to his homosocial bond to his confessor.

Passivity, receptivity, and powerlessness: these characterizations increase Pohl's chances for clemency. They also weaken his heterosexual identity. Pohl knows that he needs to play along with this new image if clemency is to become a reality. But we can imagine him doing so reluctantly. To be portrayed as meek, receptive, and open to a male-male embrace is hard to bear, and the fear of being overly feminized (if not potentially homosexualized) and of having lost one's moral backbone looms ever so large in the background. To counteract such fears, *Credo* must find ways to reassert Pohl's embattled masculinity.

One mechanism for protecting the confessant's manly reputation is to ban the presence of women, and particularly the female gaze, which renders a man symbolically impotent. We do not know for sure why Eleonore is not credited in *Credo*, but we may speculate that her gazing at him through her drawings—a gaze supportive, yet full of pity—might have been more than Pohl (and Morgenschweis) could tolerate. The total disappearance of her presence can be read as an attempt at restraining female power.

Another mechanism for stabilizing an embattled masculinity is to call upon the religious imagination. With the renewed moral voice that Pohl adopts with the help of his confessor, he has a chance to reassert his virtuous manliness. Indeed, Pohl never tires of stating that the attraction of Catholicism lay in its forceful authority. As "an old soldier," he pleads, he should not be blamed "for being highly impressed by the strong love of order and authoritative leadership of the Catholic Church" (*Credo*, 60). Christianity promises Pohl—as well as other culpable men of his political cohort—the gift of a new moral authority, thus remasculinizing him. Pohl's conversion, hence, brings to the fore a larger dynamic: on the one hand, it amplifies the crisis of postwar German masculinity among culpable and complicit men, while, on the other, it offers a solution. Recourse to religious language helps compromised men make meaning of their lives within a context of changed power relations. Pohl fell from power, but as a religious convert in a newly emerging nation he poses as a new man. Remoralized, he is portrayed as embodying the virtues of humility and tranquility; freshly converted, he feels entitled to criticize his accusers (the American Allies) only a few years after Germany's defeat. The initial fear of being feminized through the conversion process is rewarded with a renewed sense of male entitlement. The dictatorial NS ideology is exchanged for ecclesiastical supremacy.

Pohl's testimony thus straddles a fine line between (feminized) self-disempowerment and a masculinist assertion of moral authority. Nestled in the bosom of *ecclesia* and strengthened by his confessor's embrace, Pohl hopes to regain respectability. And respectability is something German men complicit in the Nazi crimes wanted most. It would bring them back into their familial, social, and national surroundings as exculpated, decent men and would secure their place in the rebuilding of the German nation. "Respectability," George Mosse argues, "provides society with essential cohesion." Respectability as a crucial aspect in the construction of modern masculinity is, in turn, closely linked to "modern national consciousness" (1996, 192–193).

The question of Pohl's conversion, then, has relevance beyond the specificity of his case. It illustrates the intersection of religious discourse, masculinization, and nation building. A direction of further research can only be indicated here: it concerns the role of religious and gendered rhetoric in the political transition from a heavily brutalized dictatorial state (Nazism) to an emergent democratic nation (West Germany).[22] For such a transition to happen smoothly, a new understanding of masculinity was required, and segments of the German churches provided a discourse that remasculinized the deflated ego of postwar German men. *Credo* documents such dynamics.

A dire consequence of attempts at boosting "straight male egos" (Herzog 2005) was postwar Germany's silencing of women and the marginalization of victims of Nazi racial policies. In the 1950s, both groups were pushed to the sidelines. A new national cohesion was sought through the exclusion of others. Faith and religion, Anthony Marx claims in a different context, have played a crucial role in "encourag[ing] and enforc[ing]" the exclusion of others in order to solidify "core loyalty to the nation" (2003, 21). According to Marx, the origin of emergent nations rests in the exclusion of others—and not in the idealization of an inclusive "imagined community" (Anderson 1983). In the process of unifying consolidation, emergent nations tend to forget their exclusionary origins. *Credo*, as a confessional document of postwar Germany, is one piece of this puzzle: intimate others (Pohl's wives) and traumatized others (Pohl's victims) are excluded.

Attempting to portray Pohl as a credible Christian convert and respectable citizen bears—beyond his individual fate—the marks of a model character for an emergent nation. From this perspective, *Credo*'s erasure of women's subjectivity and the silencing of victim voices are not accidental. Rather, such erasure is constitutive of the modern reconstructing of an embattled masculinity and nationality.

Calel Perechodnik writes against annihilation; Oswald Pohl writes for the purpose of rehabilitation. Perechodnik assesses realistically that he will not survive the onslaught of Nazi genocidal antisemitism—and he did not; Pohl hopes to escape the justice of the Allies—but he did not. Neither survived, but both men left written testimonies for anyone interested in reading them.

CHAPTER 7

On Spirit and Sperm
Eroticizing God, Sanctifying the Body

Confessiographies are, to a large extent, soul work. Rousseau's wish to make his "soul transparent to the reader's eye" (1953, 169) is echoed by the unlikely confessant Yitzhak Twersky: "That is my confession, the confession of my life, withered and faded before its time, the confession of my tortured, afflicted soul" (Assaf 2006, 31). The struggle of naming one's self into being is, however, always negotiated through the body. The soul's work is read and inscribed into the body, mirrored in it, and practiced through performances of the flesh.

The male body has accompanied us throughout these pages, even when it did not take center stage. We encountered the private body in Leiris's "auburn hair" and "incipient baldness"; in Tom Driver's soft, white, and "useless flesh" of his thighs; and in Broughton's androgynous breast and "neglected backside." We encountered confessional instances that mention intimate exchanges of bodily fluids, such as Augustine's sucking of his mother's milk, Rousseau's involuntary witness of the "whitish and sticky" ejaculate of his molester, or Jung's fantasy of a defecating God. Whereas some of these male confessants theologized their embodiedness (Augustine, Driver), others insisted on the desacralized triviality of their bodies (Leiris, Rousseau). Yet others engaged a new religious imaginary to account for their corporeal experiences (Jung, Broughton). My initial concern that an apprehensive gazing at one's own flesh can lock the male confessant into the mirroring effects of solipsism gave way to an argument for a need of greater relationality. The ability to see oneself embedded within the social and intimate fabric of interdependence became a criterion for measuring the male confessant's avowal, or disavowal, of moral agency—from Augustine's deliberate detachment of intimate others to Perechodnik's embattled self during genocidal assault or Pohl's denial of criminal culpability. The degree to which moral agency is claimed can tell us how credible and trustworthy we should consider a confessing man's claim of a soul's transparency. Moral agency and truthfulness are, in other words, linked to the confessant's ability to open himself up to webs of relational intimacies without drowning the presence of the other.

By returning to the personal dimension of the male body in this last chapter, I do not intend to retrace ground already covered but to shift some of the parameters with which I have operated so far. I want to leave behind—as well as a heterosexual man can do so—the normative world of heterosexuality. Such an exercise begins with the choice of texts to be analyzed, and I will focus here on writings by gay-identified men. We supplant the heterosexual anxiety around masculinity with a sexual and eroticized male body that is to be befriended rather than rendered non-absent. Gay male confessants do not fear intimate homosocial bonds and are comfortable with male-male physical and affective intimacy. Their embrace of the male body is one of pleasurable self-embrace as well as a loving act of relating to another man's body and soul.

One way to go about such a task would be to study gay memoirs as a subgenre of autobiographies (see Chambers 1998; Robinson 1999). I will not do so. Instead, I examine scholarly texts with strong confessional moments authored by contemporary American gay men. The confessiographic *quality* of these texts rests in the confessant's sincere, introspective, and often transformative quest for authenticity that does not shy away from exposing layers of intimacy to the public. At the heart of this chapter are Scott Haldeman, a theologian, and Donald Boisvert, a religious studies scholar. Both men exhibit an openly gay stance toward spiritual and sexual desire; both are on exploratory journeys of discovery in which their religious imagination intersects with the quest for a body-affirmative intimacy.

The Confessiographic Quality of Gay Religious Scholarship

Openly gay theological reflections and gay/queer religious scholarship have steadily gained visibility in academic life over the last thirty years. Though it is difficult to name a particular date as *the* decisive moment in which such scholarship generated public interest—there is no Stonewall for gay theology[1]—one can cite as an important milestone the 1988 founding of the Gay Men's Issues group within the American Academy of Religion, the largest body of American religious scholarship.[2] There, gay scholars found an institutional home where they could explore religious issues through a consciously gay-constructed perspective. The roots of a gay theology, how-ever, go further back in time, growing from earlier apologetic writings (from the 1950s onward) into the liberationist and "unapologetic" paradigms of the 1980s.[3] Since then, the field has seen continual diversification of re-search, including historical, ethical, systematic, liturgical, and comparative approaches. Furthermore, identity politics have shaped debates among and between gay-affirmative, feminist, womanist, and queer voices (see Goss 2002, 239–242; Schneider 2000; Spencer 2004; Krondorfer 2009).

My cautiously optimistic view of the institutionalizing of gay religious scholarship does not deny that a host of resistances had to be overcome on the path toward greater public visibility. Heterosexual scholars, for example, never have to "out" themselves publicly in terms of their sexual preferences, but to be identified as a gay scholar requires a "coming out." What straight men can keep private, gay scholars cannot. To be identified gay means to be identified sexually—as if a label were stuck on one's forehead announcing one's bedroom activities. Even if a gay man never talks about his private life in public, the heterosexual mentality will associate his "coming out" decla-ration with performing particular sexual activities. Such short-circuiting ef-fect of the "gay" label—which reduces the range of human possibilities to a particular sexual practice—functions quite independently of individual life choices, which, after all, can range from celibacy to gay marriages, from the "promiscuous celebration of male beauty" (Long 1997, 280) to "nurturing and sustaining relationships" (Clark 1994, 216).

To be coming out against a long religious and cultural history of silenc-ing, discrimination, physical harassment, and legalized violence means to arouse certain assumptions and biases among one's nongay conversation partners. Minimally, it may force the openly gay man to repeatedly second-guess what the heterosexual other is thinking or imagining. Under such circumstances, one might as well speak openly and publicly about one's intimate life and assign to it spiritual and religious meaning. Indeed, this is a venue that many (but certainly not all) gay theologians have chosen to take. Some speak with pride of the lifestyle in the so-called gay ghettos— urban zones of comfort and security for a marginalized group—whereas others caution against the cloistering effects of such territorial and mental constriction. Critical gay voices argue that the ghetto life is in danger of prescribing a certain gay habitus and of essentializing a particular gay iden- tity, effectively "minoritizing" one's own discourse and curtailing efforts in political networking.[4]

To what extent the heterosexual community should be permitted to peek over the gay ghetto walls and into one's bedroom remains open to debate. There are certainly noncloseted gay religious studies scholars and theolo- gians who, for good reasons, keep their private lives as protected from pub- lic scrutiny as their straight colleagues do and, by extension, abstain from having autobiographical confessions interfere with their research. Others have chosen an audaciously different path and have swung the doors to their closets wide open for anyone to see what is happening "inside." Their research, in turn, is suffused with confessiographic fragments, which trans- gress and transcend disciplinary boundaries.[5] Such transdisciplinarity mir- rors the need to piece together, support, and preserve a wholeness of gay identity that has been seriously fragmented by and disallowed in hegemonic religious discourse. J. Michael Clark, for example, introduces his *Masculine Socialization and Gay Liberation* as a book that "cannot be constructed as if it were merely a traditional academic text" because the issues "require the testimony of our lived experiences" (1992, 4). Boisvert writes that *Sanctity and Male Desire* "constitutes a theological reflection on my life experience" (2004, 7); Robert Goss introduces *Queering Christ* as representing "nearly a decade of reflection as a queer Christian theologian" and remarks that he will "weave narrative details from my own life" into the essays. "Sexual theology," he writes, "involves always the texts of our lives" (2002, xiv, xv). Gary Comstock introduces *Gay Theology Without Apology* as a discussion of Christian traditions on "my own terms, that is, from the point of view of my experience" (1993, 4). Each of these works then proceeds to include au- tobiographical passages as well as personal life stories of friends and lovers.

Such insertions render a scholar vulnerable, and gay writers are particu- larly exposed to potential harm since homophobic and gay-unfriendly re- sponses can turn their intimate revelations against them.[6] Homophobia, however, is not what steers my interpretive interest in this chapter. Rather, my critical reading wants to take seriously the perspectives articulated in gay religious scholarship in which autobiographical insertions adopt a confessional tone.[7] How is intimacy represented? How does it intersect with the religious imagination? How are intimate performances of the body linked to the creation of the gay male self?

Some gay religious scholarship describes in fairly explicit detail sexual desires and practices, especially, though not exclusively, in a genre that I suggest calling "gay devotional" and "gay confessional" scholarship. Goss, for example, describes his own sexual experiences in *Queering Christ*: "With the risk of self-confession, I will use myself as text, not place myself as judge" (2002, 81). Similarly, Clark writes that "self-disclosure has increasingly been a hallmark in the progression of my own work in men's studies" (1997, 316). Others, like Long (1997) and Culbertson (2006), have followed such self-confessional modes, and I now turn my attention first to Scott Haldeman and then to Donald Boisvert.

From Masturbation to Receptivity

Within a span of seven years, Haldeman published two theological essays on the intimate male body, which appeared in edited volumes on the religious dimension of masculinity and sexuality: "Bringing Good News to the Body: Masturbation and Male Identity" (1996) and "Receptivity and Revelation: A Spirituality of Gay Male Sex" (2003).[8] These two pieces are emblematic of an embodied theology that is deeply confessiographic. They also demonstrate, as we shall see, the (post)modern fluidity of male identity. The theological imagination is called upon in an effort to collapse the spiritual and the sexual; sexual practices are, in turn, viewed as essential for the making of the male self. Changes in those practices indicate transitions into new self-understandings, and between 1996 and 2003 Haldeman himself undergoes a transformation that we, as readers, are privy to witness in these two confessional essays.

In "Good News" and "Receptivity," Haldeman exhibits an unswerving commitment to opening up his own bodily practices to public scrutiny and to using these practices as occasions for theological and social-ethical reflections. His general attitude is body positive; his theological stance, liberationist. Without abandoning his critical competency regarding specific embodied male attitudes, his goal is not to condemn or control the erotic male body but to celebrate and expand the sexual and religious imaginary within which men's embodied selves are embedded and grow.

What then are the practices he describes? Haldeman confesses to sexual activities that other men would rather refrain from publicly acknowledging. He masturbates. He finds sexual comfort in being penetrated by another man. He does what has been called, in the medical-moral language of the eighteenth century onward, the unhealthy "self-abuse" of "onanism" (Laqueur 2003) and what church and state have condemned as the perversion of "sodomy," that is, homosexual anal intercourse (cf. Jordan 1997). Describing these practices, Haldeman does not escape into the safety of sparse metaphoric allusions or into a "language of romance" that "risks layering the topic with suffocating gauze" (2003, 221).

> I masturbate. I do it often and in a variety of ways. I do it most often in the shower. . . . Sometimes I linger. Sometimes my touch takes on an urgency that corresponds with a feeling of excitement inside that manifests itself in an erection. Then, I touch myself quite a bit. My penis catches my attention but I feel the pleasure all over from the water, from the soap, and from my wandering hands. . . . Then, my body tenses. My pelvis begins to rock. The muscles in my arms and legs contract. Blood comes to the surface of my body; my chest and face redden. And I come. Release. (Haldeman 1996, 111–112)

> I like playing the receptive role in sex. . . . I experience it not so much as a desire, but as a physical need like hunger or thirst. . . . First, as I play with my lover, I begin to feel a sense of anticipation. He attends to me, and I to him. As he wraps around me, lays upon me, or comes up behind, his erection touches my body, and I shudder. I sense my permeability, abandon notions of self-protectiveness, and I let him cross the membrane of my skin. He enters me. I am full of him, allowing him to touch me deep inside while holding him with my body. (Haldeman 2003, 222–223)

"There you have an account of a despised practice," Haldeman concludes the previous passage. In a caring, direct, and unapologetic tone the theologian and liturgist describes sexual practices that have been condemned, loathed, silenced, prohibited, and punished by religious, state, and medical authorities.[9]

There you have it: accounts of masturbation and the pleasure of the permeability/ penetration of anal sex. They may sit uncomfortably with the reader. Not with all readers, for sure. A gay man may find the authenticity with which Haldeman describes

sexual practices liberating and enticing, or, perhaps, just as natural as the abundant references to heterosexual intercourse in about any popular movie. A conservative religious man, on the other hand, may be shocked and dismayed. A liberal heterosexual man may not mind the description of masturbation but be irritated by gay sex. Speculations about other men's responses, however, get us only so far. It would be better to explore such thoughts and feelings in face-to-face encounters with other men.

I initially responded to these descriptions with embarrassment, perhaps even shame—as if, by reading them, I entered a forbidden zone or participated in a forbidden act. Such is the imagination! It is only in the process of working with and through those texts that these feelings have dissipated.

My journey with Haldeman's essay on masturbation began in the mid-1990s, when I included it in Men's Bodies, Men's Gods *(1996). I liked its boldness, and it fit well into the book's overall intention to forthrightly engage the links between male embodiment and religion. I also knew that I could not have written this essay—too private are some of my bodily practices. Reading "Bringing Good News to the Body" interfered with my sense of privacy, and it is this interference, I believe, that triggered my initial embarrassment.*

Seven years later, when I encountered "Receptivity and Revelation," I worked through a similar process. At first embarrassed, as if eavesdropping on an intimate conversation, I wondered whether I should continue to listen.

Haldeman's language is deliberately nonpornographic. Not intending to offend, he does not use words to incite and arouse or to reject and condemn but to reveal sexual practices experienced as self-love (in the case of masturbation) and, in the case of anal permeability, as consensual acts of mutual lovemaking. Regarding masturbation, he explicitly "encourage[s] masturbation without porn" (1996, 121), and he equally objects to the worshipping of a phallocentric masculinity. Erections, for Haldeman, are not a symbol of phallic prowess but an erotic activity of the penis. Mostly, he describes sexuality in dynamic terms without allocating an objectifying noun to the male anatomy. Hence, a reader who wanted to bring a charge of perversion and obscenity against these passages would be hard-pressed to fault the author for the use of inappropriate language. If Haldeman were once personally conflicted about these sexual practices—an issue he never admits directly but indicates only through his awareness of external hostility—he now is at peace with them. For him, masturbation and sexual receptivity are life affirming. "What religious traditions define as an unforgivable evil is an act in which I find life" (2003, 223).

But does Haldeman really "confess"? One could make the case that his essays lack essential elements of confessional writings and that, as author, he does not so much confess as report. A confession, it seems, requires recognition of one's sinful past and a willingness to do better in the present. If Haldeman does not feel compelled to repent for some deviancy, what is the nature of his "confession"? Has he experienced a transformation that provides him with a retrospective distancing from his former self?

At first glance, Haldeman's revelations are far removed from Augustine's confessional model. Whereas the bishop's *Confessions* are based on deliberate insertions of instances of the intimacies of the flesh in order to demonstrate the vanity of all human efforts, the modern American theologian locates the male self's constitutive core in the practices of the flesh. Whereas for Augustine, happiness cannot be found in earthly pleasures, nor peace in the unruliness of the (male) body, Haldeman feels "at home" (2003, 221) in the risky places of mutual pleasuring.[10] Whereas for Augustine, the male erection is a sign and symptom of humanity's fall from grace, for Haldeman it indicates an experience that is good because it is pleasurable, and, because it is pleasurable and good, it is part of God's good creation. The earthly distractions that Augustine experiences as an obstacle on his path to God are supplanted, in Haldeman's theology, with a holistic understanding of body, soul, and spirit. It is in acts of self-pleasuring and male pleasurable receptivity that God's good news and the divine promise of redemption are revealed and affirmed. "Through our practices we are revealed, just as God reveals her divine self in glimpses of uncontainable glory" (2003, 229).

Through our practices we are revealed! When I first read "Receptivity and Revelation," I wondered whether it was written for men like me. I gave it to my wife to read, with the words: "This is a daring text. Tell me what you think." She read it. She was not perturbed by the description of male-male penetration/permeability. The differences between my wife and me—insofar as one can generalize our reading experiences—indicate that anxiety over sexual receptivity might be more common among heterosexual men than women.

What does my reading practice reveal about my heterosexuality? For one, my initial unease tells me that I am heterosexual—it confirms, so to speak, what I believe I know about myself. It also points to culture-bound anxieties. When a feeling of social embarrassment or sexual shame transpires from a text to a reader—even when shaming is not intended and pornographic imagery not used—we may realize how deeply embedded gender assumptions are within us. I am affected beyond personal intentions to the contrary.

There is the fear of contagion, based on a homophobic panic that considers homosexuality a disease that men, if not careful, can catch like a virus. Hence, the irrational need to protect oneself from gay men, or the demand to socially quarantine them.[11] Contagion, as far as the well-being of gay men is concerned, is far more dangerous than the concomitant fear of contamination. The latter phobia assumes that contact with the gay world—and that includes the reading of gay texts—can morally pollute the heterosexual person. The heterosexual mind fears that reading gay texts—and, by extension, wrestling academically with gay religious scholarship—somehow dirties the reader with the homoerotic visions of gay sexual desire. The heterosexual consumer of gay literature—according to the logic of contagion and contamination—may even become gay himself.

I am—and I can say this with certainty—free of the phantasmic fear of contagion. I am less certain about the fear of contamination, for I occasionally worry about spiteful and snide remarks by heterosexual men concerning my interest in gay religious scholarship. As a matter of fact, one can even read the previous mentioning of my wife as a protective strategy. What better way to reaffirm my heterosexuality than by inserting my wife at a strategic place in my personal commentary on gay theology? Although I do not include her to assure the reader of my sexual identity, it still can be read as sending a clear message: do not confuse me with . . .

Haldeman does not confess to any sinful addiction to sex for which he should plead for forgiveness.[12] He does not subscribe to such a Christian economy of redemption. But he also does not subscribe to modernist versions of confessions, in which one reveals one's dark self to a therapist (in the anticipation of being psychologically restored) or to the profit-driven media that hunt after sensationalist exposures of dirty secrets and, in return,

assure that the narcissistic confessant will feel better after he or she has di-
vulged secrets to the public. Haldeman neither pleads for forgiveness for
sinful behavior nor reveals secrets because he yearns for some cathartic cure.
Instead, he describes a physical reality of desire—and both the reality and
the desire are, for him, of theological value.

> If masturbation is practiced as a conscious ritual of celebration of the good-
> ness of one's flesh as a gift from God, one can regain the sense of bodily con-
> nectedness which leads to a renewed sensitivity to one's own feelings and the
> feelings of others. (Haldeman 1996, 122)

> The practice of being filled has helped me discover things about God. . . .
> We must continue to imagine God in new language that allows her to escape
> any attempts to confine her divine freedom. However, my delight in allow-
> ing my male lover to fill me allows me, analogously, to delight in the inti-
> mate approach of the God who is imagined as male in Scripture. . . . Queer
> love, despised and supposedly unproductive, is, in fact, often gratuitous and
> extravagant like the love of God in creation and redemption, like the kenosis
> of Jesus. (Haldeman 2003, 227–228)

Haldeman's intertwining of theological language with descriptions of
sexual practices is neither traditionally Christian nor modernist-secularist.
Yet the confessiographic fragments reverberate with both Christian and
postmodern sensibilities. With regard to the latter, the presumption that
sexual practices are connected to the constitution of the male self is intimately linked to the emergence of modernity itself. It is already present in
Rousseau's *Confessions*, which, as we shall see later, marks a decisive moment in the history of solitary sex and the self. With regard to Christianity,
Haldeman's ambition to theologize the activities of the flesh is decidedly
antisecularist and has more in common with Augustine's *Confessions* than
with Leiris's *Manhood*.

Does Haldeman confess? To answer the question, we should recall the
dual role of the Augustinian model of confession as a "praising of God"
and "admission of sins." Haldeman praises the possibilities of God, and he
praises the possibilities of the body. Contrary to Augustine, however, he does
not locate sin in the pleasures of the body. Rather, sin is to be located in theologies that fragment and despise the body. It is not to be found in exuberance or *luxuria* but occurs when subjecting the body to restrictive control.[13]
Consequently, redemption is not found in sexual self-restraint but in widening the spiritual and erotic imaginary.

Haldeman's call to explore the spiritual possibilities of the sexual body is, in a peculiar kind of way, allied with the spiritual efforts of the desert fathers of late antiquity. Certainly, a monk's ascetic practice and theological reference system differ dramatically from Haldeman's position, but both support the idea of an "emptying out" in order to be able to receive divine grace. The men of the desert emptied themselves (*kenosis*) in order to be filled with God. The desert is "like an empty cosmic therapy room that is open for the performance of the soul . . . [and] a space for pure projections in which the experience of self and God can be made to emerge" (Sloterdijk 1993, 95).[14] Haldeman, too, claims a kenotic experience: queer love is as extravagant as "the kenosis of Jesus" (2003, 228). It is an emptying of normative control. Metaphorically the desert stands in for the marginal existence that gay men have lived in urban, modern-day America. In contrast to the desert fathers, however, Haldeman's theology—like that of other American gay theologians—is decidedly anti-ascetic. He does not advocate a drying of fluids circulating in and excreting from the male body. Rather, sexual fluids are spiritually significant. In this regard, modern American gay theologians have more in common with the devotional practices of medieval women saints than with St. Anthony.[15] Still, for Haldeman, a kenotic experience remains at the heart of the sexual practice of receptivity. A "posture of vulnerability" (2003, 225) requires an emptying of oneself—spiritually, emotionally, and physically—before the person can be filled again with the immaterial love of God as well as the material love of one of God's creatures: a soul-body filled with spirit and sperm.

Praising God and praising the body are thus intertwined devotional practices that create and affirm a gay identity.

> I am being formed in new ways by practicing this posture of openness and vulnerability, this permeability, this rhythm of emptying and being filled, and this regular, embodied communion. . . . I see a divine self that is more playful and more serious, quite uninterested in notions of purity, and yearning to become a new thing among us. (Haldeman 2003, 225, 229)

Solitary Sex and the Invention of the Self

The sexual and eroticized body, according to Haldeman, is neither sinful nor trivial but a source of meaning that needs to be unfolded and nourished. His theological meditations release him from a mere male self-gazing.

The perspective he thus gains makes his approach resemble the Augustinian model of late antiquity.

A perspective outside one's own immediate needs—that which God-talk can provide—helps to insert into the human longing for egotistical gratification ethical principles of social justice, gender equality, and relationality. These values are explicitly referred to in "Good News." Pleasure is good, but pleasure for the sake of pleasure can also harm and hurt, especially if it comes at the expense of nurturing relations. Masturbation can "result in the deadening of senses and the destructive narcissism of the worship of the self," Haldeman cautions us (1996, 123). Advocating a sexual practice that is neither misogynist nor pornographic, he seeks a "critical praxis of masturbation [that] brings good news to men's bodies": it is an "intentional ritual of worship of the goodness of flesh and our desire to be whole" (1996, 119, 122).

It was only Haldeman's essay on masturbation that irked the editor of a publishing house to whom I had sent the proposal of Men's Bodies, Men's Gods *several years ago. Most presses responded by sending a formal letter of regret, but this editor cited Haldeman's piece as a reason for rejection: "Then there is the issue of explicit language . . . [like] Haldeman's chapter on 'Bringing Good News to the Body'—so what is the point?" Since I have known this editor's otherwise liberal Christian attitude, his response perplexed me, especially since he singled out the issue of masturbation rather than those chapters that explicitly referred to gay spirituality and sexuality. Was the editor's reticence a personal issue, or did it reflect a wider cultural pattern?*

From the eighteenth century onward, the practice of masturbation has been perceived in the West with great unease. Though masturbation had been problematic even before that century—as evident, for example, in the penitential manuals of the fifteenth century, such as Jean de Gerson's *De confessione mollitiei* (*On the Confession of Masturbation*)[16]—it became a serious sexual predicament only at the dawn of modernity. Why? Because the practice of solitary sex, as Laqueur (2003) convincingly argues, could be named as such only when the self emerged as an autonomous being—and such autonomy was greeted with ambivalence. On the one hand, solitary sex was welcomed as the new freedom of the individual; on the other hand, too much autonomy, it was feared, would lead to social anarchy and anomie. Autoerotic sexuality—conceivable as a distinct entity among sexual sins only when the autonomous self emerged—became the lightning rod for a host of anxieties. As a result, the act was vilified as self-pollution, self-abuse, and onanism. Voltaire called it "perverted self-love," Rousseau diagnosed it as "dangerous supplement," and Freud analyzed it as "arrested development" and the lowest "sexual activity of the narcissistic stage."[17]

> Modern masturbation can be dated with a precision rare in cultural history. It was born in, or very close to, the same year as that wild and woolly and profoundly self-conscious exemplar of "our" kind of human, Jean-Jacques Rousseau . . . around the late seventeenth or early eighteenth century. . . . [M]asturbation became so central to the history of the self in relation to the broader cultural history of the last two hundred years . . . [because] modern culture encourages individualism and self-determination and is threatened by solipsism and anomie. . . . Masturbation is the sexuality of the self par excellence, the first great battlefield of these struggles. (Laqueur 2003, 13, 19–21)

Only with the Freudian revolution, Laqueur states, did a cultural change occur. Freud had managed to free solitary sex from its supposed dangers to a healthy sexual development by granting it the status of a primary form of human sexuality. But even in Freud's judgment, masturbation was an immature form of sexuality when practiced by adults. That view did not begin to change until "the 1950s, picking up energy with the feminism of the 1960s and early 1970s, with the subsequent sex wars, and with the worldwide gay movement of the last quarter of the century." It was then that masturbation became "an arena of sexual politics and for art across a wide spectrum of society" (Laqueur 2003, 22).

The post-Freudian appreciation of masturbation as a nonpathological, pleasurable, adult activity is very much at work in "Good News." "Masturbation can expand our sexual vocabulary" and "reawaken our erotic imaginations" (Haldeman 1996, 117). Medieval confessors no longer torment the male soul with detailed questions about whether and how one has touched oneself; eighteenth- and nineteenth-century medical experts no longer warn of the dire consequences of "willful self-abuse" (Laqueur 2003, 15); psychoanalysts no longer counsel their patients to mature in their sexual practices. Now, the modern theologian encourages men to pleasure their bodies without guilt.

Placed within the broader context of the cultural history of masturbation, the unease with which some men respond to Haldeman's "critical praxis of masturbation" becomes more comprehensible. Any reticence to embrace masturbation in public speech can stem from a mélange of traditional Christian teachings on sin, nineteenth-century medical discourse, and Freudian analysis. Likewise, we cannot understand Haldeman's audaciousness without taking the cultural changes of the last decades into account. Without the appreciation of masturbation as a permissible and desirable autoerotic act, he could not have written his confessional theology in the 1990s. "The male gay movement," Laqueur writes, "embraced [masturbation] . . . as a practice in the service of freedom, autonomy, and rebellion against the status quo" (2003, 75).

Haldeman's "Good News" cherishes such freedom, but it does not simply accommodate to the sexual optimism of the post-1960s. It also cautions against darker streaks of sexuality. When Haldeman writes, for example, that masturbation "can be the worship of phallus as a weapon" or "help us recognize our enjoyment of our penises . . . [to] participate in creative social change" (1996, 116–117), he makes two contrapuntal claims: he juxtaposes the danger of phallic symbolization with the liberating practice of the physical penis. Haldeman frequently operates with such oppositional pairs, reminiscent of a Manichean ethical dualism of good and bad, light and dark.

> Masturbation can be a cursory exercise in tension release or an intentional ritual of worship of the goodness of flesh.

> Masturbation can serve as devoted and uncritical worship of a god of war or a god of peace.

> Masturbation can be an exercise in self-glorification or a ritual of self-pleasure that can lead to a renewed awareness of one's sacred embodiment. (1996, 119)

Framed as theological admonition, these binary remarks resonate more with secular concerns of the last two hundred years than with the sex-unfriendly attitude of Christianity, because they echo Rousseau's anxiety over the loss of relationality. Rousseau, as "spokesman of subjectivity," stands at the beginning of the articulation of the modern male self and of the naming of the practice of masturbation.[18] Rousseau, who so "devastatingly plumbed that [modern] solitude and subjectivity" (Kavanagh 1987, 191) and worried whether he could ever "reveal all his guilty secrets" (Brooks 2000, 23; also Riley 2004, 5), confessed to his masturbatory practice in writing. He knew of his autonomous, solitary subjectivity, and hence of autonomous, solitary sex. But Rousseau also worried that the male subject could go astray in his solitude (a condition that is both social and spatial) by separating himself from responsible sociability.[19] He feared that the solitary vice could displace heterosexual intercourse and that masturbators could "dispose, so to speak, of the female sex at their will, and to make any beauty who tempts them serve their pleasure without the need of first obtaining her consent" (Laqueur 2003, 236, 291). Haldeman similarly worries about nonrelationality, declaring that masturbation can be "relationship-denying, frustrating, self-centered" (1996, 118). And when he elaborates that masturbation can "fulfill a man's desires beyond what his current partner can agree to" (120), we hear echoes of Rousseau's concern about the exchangeability—and, ultimately, disappearance—of flesh-and-blood women.[20]

"Masturbation is a moral problem of the modern self" (Laqueur 2003, 249). The question is no longer whether I would deny myself pleasurable self-touch. Twenty-first-century men, like Haldeman and me, no longer dread the nightmarish vision that Laqueur paints of the masturbatory anxieties of men of the Enlightenment, namely, that "hordes of autonomous but somehow complicit individuals" no longer "need each other" and hence turn "on its head the proper relations between self and society" (357). I occasionally wonder, though, whether pleasure is withheld that rightfully belongs also to my intimate partner: "For the wife does not have authority over her own body, but the husband does; likewise the husband does not have authority over his own body, but the wife does" (1 Cor. 7:4). Am I the sole owner of my body's pleasure? How redemptive is the modern idea of sexual self-possessiveness?

Men of the Enlightenment, like Rousseau and Voltaire, ceased to engage the theological imagination other than through their anticlericalism.[21] For them, it is within the social-sexual imaginary that they feared the prison of solipsism. For Rousseau, masturbation was a limitless "dangerous supplement,"[22] because, as a sexual fantasy, it was no longer checked by the social control of real encounters. Haldeman is similarly anxious about the solipsism of the male self, but unlike Rousseau, he engages a liberationist theological paradigm, thus making him a child of Augustine as much as of modernity.

We can now begin to hear more clearly the echoes of the past in Haldeman's ethical reasoning. It is liberationist when seen against the inquisitorial pressures of Christian penitential confessions or when compared to the dire warnings of the medical moralism of the eighteenth and nineteenth centuries. But it is also a celebratory, post-Freudian expression of self-love promoted by sex-positive forms of feminism and the gay movement. Furthermore, it is cautionary not unlike Freud and Rousseau, who, for different reasons, did not dispute masturbation's primary pleasure but regarded it as a socially and sexually immature expression unworthy of healthy adults. Finally, it is post-Foucauldian with its emphasis on masturbation as a "process of self-making" (Laqueur 2003, 69) and identity creation (note the subtitle of Haldeman's essay, "Bringing Good News to the Body: *Masturbation and Male Identity*"). "On the one hand, masturbation can be an isolated and isolating practice, done to fulfill a man's desires beyond what his current partner can agree to and serving as a wall of secrecy between himself and the other," Haldeman states. "On the other hand, masturbation can function as one more expression of a mutual sexual vocabulary" (1996, 120).

Given the cultural history of the ambiguities of solitary sex, Haldeman's disclosure of his masturbatory practices may strike us as less rebellious and revolutionary than at first glance. Nevertheless, his willingness to open intimate practices to the public still remains a courageous act—especially when compared to how little I am willing to share in this regard with my readers.

Donald Capps observed that, recently, American religious culture replaced the vilification of masturbation with the moral disapproval of homosexuality. "Masturbation no longer receives the attention that it formerly received," he writes, and "as a result, those who engage in homosexual acts bear a greater burden as the object of moral disapproval than before." Homosexual behavior has become the "subject of much more moral and theological debate, and is the target of considerably greater moral condemnation than previously" (2003, 249). The editor's irritation over masturbation mentioned earlier, hence, seems rather atypical. We modern men carry within us the combined mentalities of Augustine, Freud, and Rousseau—and also the mentality of the modernist Leiris, who leaves an "intimate offering flowing down the soft gray stone" at the ancient site of Olympia (1992, 28).

There is a final twist to Haldeman's theological reflections on masturbation and on gay male receptivity. Between 1996 and 2003, he undergoes a personal transformation not unlike the cultural shift from masturbation to homosexuality. Though this change does not constitute an act of repentance, it allows Haldeman to gain clarity about his former self.

At first glance, though, no moment of spiritual transformation or conversion is apparent in "Good News" and in "Receptivity." Even the almost omnipresent "coming out" experience of gay American autobiographical literature—which is the structural and affective equivalent to religious conversion experiences—is missing in these essays. Haldeman does not tell a story in which "the old closeted man gives way to the proudly reborn gay," as Paul Robinson writes about the proclivity of American gay men to organize their autobiographies as coming-out stories. Haldeman is not part of the "curious purity of spirit about these American [gay] tales, which have little tolerance for the ambiguity and compromise Europeans seem able to live with" (Robinson 1999, xix).[23] But a significant change takes place in the time span of seven years that separates Haldeman's reflections on masturbation from those on anal permeability/penetration. When writing "Good News," Haldeman is still a heterosexual, married man; when writing "Receptivity," he has become gay. "Sometimes, fantasies are not enough and I ache for the touch of another," he writes in 1996. "At those times I am lucky if my wife is home because sometimes she will join me in the shower or just reach in to touch or kiss me" (111). In 2003, the opening sentence reads: "I am becoming a gay man. This is a lifelong project and a large part of my work in this current phase of my life" (219).

To witness such a transition in the writings of a modern male theologian is remarkable because most religious confessants write retrospectively in order to guard themselves against accusations of inconsistency. It is remarkable also because we, as readers, are privy to witness a change not yet fully known to the confessant himself when writing his essays. We see a vulnerability that still escapes the full grasp of the author.[24] Rather than pure retrospection, there is an unconventional immediacy to Haldeman's revelations. What we witness is a "becoming" of the male self.

On Becoming, Naming, and Performing

Haldeman's confessional directness corresponds with his insistence on "becoming." In order to become a particular male self, one needs to practice it—an insight advanced by Foucault and his followers. This process is less about liberating one's true self than creating and re-creating "the self in its variable relations with itself, with others, and with the world" (Stone 1997, 147). Just as the critical praxis of masturbation became an expression and, subsequently, an extension of the modern self's autonomy and self-sufficiency, the emergence of a gay self is bound to performative practices. "The confession," Radstone observes, "presents the telling itself as the source of self-transformation" and performs its own "becomingness" (2007, 36). The gay self does not exist outside its own becoming.

> Each day . . . I practice my own version of a gay life. I demonstrate my affection to my lover, kissing him goodbye in the kitchen since the porch seems too exposed, reaching carefully for his hand lest the couple behind us in the theater notice, searching out safe places to be together, reveling in each other's bodies at home, seeking yet more intimacy, exploring yet unfound pleasures. . . . In all these things I, like you, practice who I am becoming. I practice being gay as I practice being a teacher, a scholar, a father, a spouse. (Haldeman 2003, 218)

Haldeman does not essentialize gay identity but describes a male identity in the making. The male subject constitutes itself in the "forward trajectory" (Radstone 2007, 37) of its own becomingness through repeated profane and devotional activities and through daily chores and sexual revelations. "[W]e have to work at *becoming homosexuals* and not be obstinate in recognizing that we are" (Foucault 1989, 203–204). By naming a practice and by practicing it, one becomes a gay person. Without such naming, no gay identity. In other words, a man cannot become gay as long as he does not call "gay" what he practices, and unless he practices what he calls "gay," he will not grow into his new identity. If we think such a logic to its end, a man who participates in an erotic or sexual act of male-male intimacy is not gay until and unless he names the activity as such.

I do not know whether Haldeman would agree with my reasoning here, but I believe that his stress on "becoming"—and, concomitantly, on the need of "naming"—motivates him to reveal sexual intimacies. In the case of masturbation, modern men, like Rousseau and Haldeman, are capable of confessing to solitary sex precisely because they have given it a name. Such naming is inextricably linked to the individuation inherent in modernity. Whether we condemn masturbation as solitary vice, diagnose it as arrested development, or praise it as a virtue of independent autoeroticism, each of these verdicts already assumes an autonomous self capable of engaging in autonomous sexuality. Analogously, Haldeman's emphasis on gay "becoming" implies that the gay male self constitutes itself by naming specific practices, and this inevitably includes sexual activities.

The transformation from straight to gay man that we witness in Haldeman's essays illustrates well the modernist quest for identity. But equally, Haldeman's self-set task to theologize the activities of the male body recalls—and perhaps repeats—the efforts of men in late antiquity to invent and model a new Christian masculinity.

Between Augustine and Freud stands not only Rousseau but also André Gide, a French man of the early twentieth century, who lived a married and gay life, practiced (colonizing) pederasty in Africa, and spoke openly about masturbation and other sexual and private intimacies in his journals and correspondences that fill many volumes. He also engaged freely in conversations with others. Roger Martin du Gard, for example, writes about a conversation he had with Gide in 1921: "Gide needs to empty himself out completely of sperm, and he reaches this state only after coming five, six, or even eight times in succession. . . . He can rarely come more than three times with the same person. When circumstances permit, he then finds himself a second person and comes the fourth and often fifth time . . . at the same time he urgently needs to ejaculate more in order to reach a point of satiation, with all the sperm emptied out. And normally he can only reach that final stage after he's gone home, by masturbation" (quoted in Segal 1998, 43–44).

A strange sort of kenosis: if there is such a thing as a radically anti-ascetic kenotic experience, we may find it in the modern hypersexuality of Gide.

Haldeman, as mentioned previously, does not tell us a coming-out story. He is not interested in a conversion narrative that, typically, recounts the moment when a gay man finally musters the courage to acknowledge who he has always *essentially* been. Instead, Haldeman tells a *coming-into* story (my words, not his). "Coming into" conveys more accurately the fluidity of masculine identities, pointing to reiterative performances (as Judith Butler would say) or to, as Haldeman says, practicing ritualized activities that go into making the male subject. And who does he become? Not generically "gay," but gay in multiple and particular ways. Haldeman moves from being a heterosexual man to becoming a gay "bottom" (not "top"). He has become, so to speak, a feminized, passive gay man—a sodomized man, as prejudiced and hostile voices might say. Not a man at all, really.

Haldeman, of course—and rightly so—resists such biased judgment. Staying true to his own experience, he reveals to the public multiple misconceptions of a sexual practice that is beset, at best, with misunderstandings and, at worst, provokes hostile reactions. He finds most language about male receptivity problematic on the grounds of the violence and ridicule it contains. He also criticizes the "top and bottom" terminology of the gay community as too static and stigmatizing. To be on the receptive side of male-male intercourse, the theologian writes, neither effeminates him nor renders him passive. "[M]y own sense of receptivity," he reports, "is not about being passive, but of fully participating in an act of mutual pleasuring. It is not abandoning my maleness, but about reinventing it" (2003, 223–224). Setting free the sexual and spiritual imagination, he turns his readers into witnesses of a male confessant's reinvention of the self.

Why not keep these sexual practices private? Why not limit them to the protective space of auricular confession? This study has repeatedly pointed out that the bravery to confess publicly is rooted in the retrospective view that male confessants assume when writing about their errant and delinquent old selves. In Haldeman's case, the presentness of his life seems to supplant the comfort that other confessants seek in retrospection. His own "becoming" is a not-yet-completed project, and the immediacy with which we, as readers, witness aspects of his intimate life renders him exceptionally vulnerable to criticism and ridicule, if not discrimination and social ostracism. Yet we come across the following sentence stashed away in the middle of a paragraph: "Over four years ago, in a flash of emotional and relational chaos, I found myself in an unexpected place of receptivity, a place where I now feel at home as I have felt in no other place in my life" (2003, 221). A flash of a fleshy experience—an epiphany of sorts after all? The reader does not learn more about this moment of lived intensity, but we can locate here a decisive event in Haldeman's life, a transformative sexual epiphany that also registers as a retrospective turn. After that "flash of chaos," Haldeman's practice of becoming a gay man changes radically. He finds himself in an unexpected new place—a sort of conversion after all. The revelatory moment of receptivity now offers him a grammar and vocabulary to talk about his new self.

From this new perspective—from this position of sexual and spiritual receptivity (and not from the position of "bottom," or from that of a passive, effeminized, or sodomized non-man)—he is able to name himself into being. Like Augustine after his conversion, Haldeman is finally arriving home. The found peace and comfort might be fragile: but then one must recall that Augustine's restless heart, too, never fully relaxes, even after finding rest in God. The bishop of late antiquity continued to struggle with the unruliness of his male member and his insatiable appetites long after his conversion. Augustine's commitment to a Christian male celibacy is never quite finalized, just as Haldeman's commitment to a Christian gay sexuality is not yet completed. Both men insist on the importance of practicing their newly embraced commitment on a daily basis: male celibacy and male receptivity. Seen in this light, the following thoughts could have been voiced by either man:

> When I am confessing not what I once was but what I am now, the benefit lies in this: I am making this confession not only before you with a secret exaltation and fear and with a secret grief touched by hope, but also in the ears of . . . my fellow citizens and pilgrims, some who have gone before, some who follow after, and some who are my companions in this life.[25]

Gay Hagiolatry

Haldeman's reflections on intimate sexual and erotic practices mirror the fluidity with which masculinities can be created and transformed in specific (postmodern) localities. No longer closeted away in a clandestine world of publicly unacknowledged desire (desire often rendered deviant and unspeakable), confessional scholarship, such as Haldeman's essays, audaciously explores the making of a gay self.

We find a similar audaciousness in Donald Boisvert's *Sanctity and Male Desire: A Gay Reading of Saints* (2004). As we shall see, Boisvert's gay male self is by far less fluid than Haldeman's. One reason for this difference lies in the fact that Boisvert addresses more directly a gay readership (hence, is comfortable with presenting a firm gay identity), whereas Haldeman— perhaps for reasons of his own biographical transformation—seems to have a wider audience in mind. A second reason has to do with the degree with which each of them identifies with his respective religious tradition. Haldeman is a theologian who thinks and writes out of his Protestant tradition, whereas Boisvert has distanced himself more deliberately from his Catholic upbringing.[26] The opening line in *Sanctity and Male Desire* reads, "I was raised Catholic" (note that he does not say, "I *am* Catholic"), and he calls himself "a gay scholar of religion" (2004, 7). Not identifying himself as a Catholic theologian does not, however, diminish his love for a tradition that continues to provide him with religious imagery charged with sacred and erotic power.

The difference between Haldeman's and Boisvert's approaches to the gay male body and to homosexual identity can be summarized thus: critical praxis versus fetishized iconicity. Whereas Haldeman emphasizes the lived dynamics of becoming, Boisvert focuses on saintly images. "I have examined the lives and imagery of a limited number of male saints, and I have recast them as gay icons" (2004, 207). Boisvert's iconic approach to saints, I will argue, relates to a desire more narrowly fixed on an idealized masculine gay body. What for Haldeman is an open-ended practice of becoming is, for Boisvert, a fetishized gazing.

Biographically, Boisvert traces his wish to read male saints through the perspective of gay desire back to his Catholic socialization: "While other boys may have been enthralled with sports cars or comic book figures, I was moved by the iconic image of the masculine saint" (2004, 7). Intellectually and mentally, he readied himself for this study for several years. In an article published four years before *Sanctity and Male Desire*, he already announces his infatuation: "I have arrived at a radically different, and far more sensible, understanding of my lifelong interest—obsession, I might add—with male saints. They are not really models of sanctity for me. They have been, in fact, secret lovers" (2000b, 18; see also 2000a).

In *Sanctity and Male Desire*, Boisvert mixes personal revelations with historical, phenomenological, and ethical musings, thus creating a rich tapestry of images, thought, and reminiscences that are often more suggestive in nature than systematically argued. Situating himself within a larger argument advanced by such scholars as Mark Jordan and Robert Goss, namely, that Roman Catholicism is simultaneously homophobic and "homoerotic and campy" (2004, 8), Boisvert explores the possibilities of desire with which iconic images of male saints can be invested. Loosely working within a Foucauldian framework, Boisvert unearths an embodied knowing of desire.[27]

The stories and visual representations of male saints, Boisvert argues, contain an eroticism that can be recovered from beneath a more repressive Catholic culture. As objects of veneration, saints exude a sensual quality. Devotees claim such sensuality through imitation (by adopting saints as exemplary models) and mediation (by engaging them as an intercessory force).

In either case, desire is at the center of veneration since the passionate and sensuous devotion to saints—often in tension with orthodoxy and scholasticism—speaks to the erotically charged dynamics between devotee and the object of admiration. "In intensely Catholic cultures," Boisvert writes, "[saints] are clothed and bathed, covered with flowers or dripping in bright red droplets of blood, gaudy and almost comical in their painted features, and lit by the reflective glow of a thousand votive candles" (2004, 19).

Boisvert invests male saints with gay erotic desire in two ways: first, by exploring the queerness of the saints themselves, and, second, by embracing male saints as eroticized objects. "I have been engaged in a process of 'queering' hagiography" (2004, 207).[28] Unapologetically, he presents a partisan view of sainthood. "It is difficult to understand the role and presence of the sacred in my life," he states in an earlier article, "if I don't first see it in homoerotic terms" (2000b, 18). His writings wish to speak to the gay community, affirming gay men who would like to remain within the affective and religious universe of (Catholic) Christianity and encouraging them to embrace proudly and boldly those dimensions of the tradition that give them spiritual sustenance without having to deny their erotic embodiedness. For this reason, he inserts into his texts his own erotic cravings for saintly male bodies, reflecting a style and method that strengthen and authenticate a gay male sanctity that knows no shaming.

> Saints are fully alive, fully self-determinant humans. Confessing, self-accepting men, men who witness to their own integrity and that of their gay brothers, can be saints in the making. . . . I and others have been every single one of those men at certain times in our lives, proud confessors in our own right. The confessing act, as with the act of martyrdom, is one of simple visionary courage. (2004, 191)

Not coincidentally, Boisvert ends each chapter with a short devotional prayer and hymn, casting the respective saint as a supporter and protector of Christian gay men. This mixing of devotional, confessional, and hagiographic styles makes *Sanctity and Male Desire* resemble, at times, a gay breviary.

Boisvert does not strive to prove his claims either historically or textually (not even intertextually) but relies on persuading his readers through a rhetoric of experience. Grounding his book in personal reminiscences, sexual reveries, and devotional reenvisionings is its strength and its weakness. Within a community of like-minded people, this approach might work well, but for readers who do not share the same erotic investment in devotional imagery, the heavy reliance on a rhetoric of experience is less persuasive. A heterosexual reader, for example, who is enlightened, amused, or provoked by the book, may remain intellectually and historically unsatisfied; a non-Catholic gay reader may be enchanted by the erotic(ized) language, but the passionate veneration of saints might remain utterly foreign to him.

My devoutly Catholic grandmother every so often opened the doors to the mysterious world of saints to me. These were special occasions in my childhood. She told stories of miraculous appearances of protective saints; she gently drew crosses with her finger on my forehead; she took me to incense-filled churches. Each time, I was overcome by a visual sensuality and tactile awe that I never experienced in my Protestant environment. Protestant church buildings in my hometown always exuded an air of functional sobriety, whereas the Catholic places I visited with my working-class grandma captivated me instantaneously. I entered a strangely titillating sacred space. Statues of Mary, of the pietà, of pierced saints, and of bloodied yet angelic-looking bodies exerted an irresistible pull toward veneration: furtive genuflections when I felt unobserved, quickly drawn crosses on the body with my finger, a stammered impromptu prayer in front of a saintly figure. Passages in Boisvert's book retrieve these early affections. When my father left behind his mother's devotion and converted to Protestantism, the Catholic religious universe became inaccessible and unfamiliar to me.

It would never occur to me, for example, to read my life through a hagiographic lens. "Lastly, there is in me," Boisvert writes, "love and affection about my own saints: a coming out with respect to religious and hagiographic fetishism; of how these beautiful, manly saints continue to inhabit my insides, gnaw at them, and fill them" (2004, 209). I could never write such words, not only because I do not share this fetishized desire but also because I was never taught to adopt the vita of a saint as a life model. Understanding my life hagiographically is not part of my religious imaginary. Even the short, disavowing autobiographical reference of another Catholic-socialized gay theologian is not part of my vocabulary: "God pulled me, carried me, and strengthened me to answer the call to become an intimate life partner. My story is certainly not hagiography, but it is woven with theological themes reflected throughout my writings and rooted in my life choices and practices" (Goss 2002, 3).

The erotic energy invested in saintly veneration offers coping mechanisms to (some)
Catholic men. Consider the Italian boy-saint Dominic Savio, who died in 1857 from
tuberculosis at age fifteen and was canonized in 1954: he served Boisvert in his boy-
hood as a "talisman against masturbation. . . . As a model of sanctity he was held up
as a shining example of bodily purity, especially for adolescent boys," a purity that "was
never actually spelled out or spoken" but correctly guessed anyhow. "As boys," Boisvert
continues, "we were always confessing our sins of masturbation, three, four, five times
a week. We were constantly reminded . . . that it was bad in the eyes of God, that we
were less 'manly' because of it. . . . My obsession and guilt with it were so extreme that
I actually developed a phobia about it. During my novitiate, the novice master sent me
for psychiatric consultation" (2004, 124, 128–130).

Boisvert's confessional reminiscence aims not so much at ridiculing Catholicism's
repressive attitude toward masturbation or its auricular confessional practice (though
Boisvert is surely critical of both) but at pointing to Dominic as an iconic materializa-
tion of internal bodily conflicts. The saint "was strong where I was weak . . . [and] I
still magically thought that Dominic's protected penis could save mine," he writes retro-
spectively about his adolescence. As an adult man, he understands that his "love affair
with, and devotion to, Saint Dominic Savio taught [him] about desire, about its inner
logic of want and need" (130).

I did not grow up with religious models of this kind. They are not part of my reli-
gious vocabulary. But in my body lingers, somewhere, a trace of hagiographic envy.

Boisvert does not make the reductionist claim that all male saints were gay,
although some "no doubt . . . were homosexual, as were other holy men from
the Judeo-Christian tradition" (2004, 193). But he makes another kind of
reductionist move when he ascribes to the saints a perfectly shaped, highly
eroticized male body. The imagined saintly body is repeatedly described as
"beautiful," "erotic," "titillating," "handsome," "bare-chested," "naked" or
"semi-naked," "muscular," "glorious," "ragged," and endowed with "perfection," "virile masculinity," and "masculine strength." In other words, the
saints of old appear in a body conforming to a contemporary (gay) norm
of male beauty.[29] Hints of age, illness, and deformity are mentioned only in
passing and do not elicit an eroticized response. "Mine is decidedly a fetish-
istic gaze," Boisvert confesses and, revealingly, adds: "If [Sebastian] were a

contemporary model strutting Calvin Klein underwear in some ad, the image would be equally arousing" (48).

The "gay male gym body," Halperin perceptively remarks, is "explicitly designed to be an erotic-turn-on" (1995, 117). Boisvert's saints mirror these body ideals. He describes, for example, Saint Sebastian, John the Baptist, and Francis Xavier in the following words:

> The almost naked body [of Saint Sebastian] is covered sensuously by a rippling piece of cloth, leaving his sinewy legs and chest exposed, while three golden arrows protrude almost lovingly from his chest, biceps, and thigh.

> But it is not a meek and mild Baptist that I seek, the gentle precursor of an equally vapid and girlish god. It is the energy and power of males that I crave and summon forth. It is brooding and callous indifference and beauty that I yearn for, the sharp pain of desire unfilled and despised, the burn in the pit of the stomach, the loins bursting to give forth their seed in fits of raw ecstasy. . . . The hairy Baptist is . . . a big Bear standing erect and proud, staring arrogantly down at you.

> [Francis Xavier's] iconography shows him as a classically dark and handsome Spaniard, young (he was only forty-six when he died), slim, and tall, almost a gay clone from the 1970s. (Boisvert 2004, 47, 64, 151)

When straight men and gay men fix their gaze equally on the muscled bodies of saints, their relations to these bodies differ significantly. Straight men would, in all likelihood, avert a sexually charged gazing. They would, in Halperin's words, "impose discretion on masculine self-display," requiring "that straight male beauty exhibit itself only casually or inadvertently." A gay gaze, however, would read into saints eroticized beauty ideals, such as the gay male gym body. Such bodies, "in their very solicitation of desire . . . deliberately flaunt the visual norms of straight masculinity" (Halperin 1995, 117). Both are particular ways of viewing, and the gay gaze is no more and no less biased than a conventional heterosexual reading that interprets these bodies as representing the virtues of purity and self-sacrifice. The entry point for my critique, then, is not the particular bias that Boisvert displays but a gazing that is fetishized, because it restricts the varieties of lived realities of men.

Devotional adoration as fetishism moves within an erotically charged religious imaginary that is static, not open. The fantasized ideal of a perfected and virile male body reflects a homonormative body,[30] a constructed body that appeals to a particular gay male gaze. It is not a vision based on the "imperfectible"[31] flesh of male bodies subject to the unforgivable force of impermanence but, indeed, an icon. Boisvert's body-positive, gay veneration of saints locks male beauty into a singular vision. His gay hagiolatry thus verges on gay idolatry.[32] Other imaginings—queer, gay, straight—thus fall to the wayside.

Other scholars committed to the critical study of masculinity and religion question such uniformity. Daniel Boyarin, an orthodox Jewish scholar, remarks that the "spectacular beauty" of the gay male gym body upholds a "standard for male beauty that is being practiced . . . [as] a certain form of muscular development." It "emphasizes the dimorphism of the gendered body and thus participates, to this extent, in the general cultural standard of masculinity rather than resisting it" (1997, xix). Boyarin, who links modern ideals of male beauty to traditions of Christian heroic masculinity, claims a Jewish alternative: the "feminized Jewish (colonized) male." This Jewish man "may be useful today, for 'he' may help us precisely today in our attempts to construct an alternative masculine subjectivity, one that will not have to rediscover such cultural archetypes as Iron Johns, knights, hairy men, and warriors within" (xiv). Against the promotion of a muscular Christian body, which *Sanctity and Male Desire* advances, there is "the pale, limp, and semiotically unaggressive 'nelly' or sissy male body," which "is not seen within this construct as beautiful or erotic at all" (xx).

Boyarin's sissified vision of a new Jewish masculinity stands in stark contrast to Boisvert's gaying of Christian saints. Such dissimilarity does not devalue what Boisvert is attempting to accomplish but it problematizes the singularity of his vision, which seems to strive more toward *sameness* than *difference*.[33] What is missing is a critical perspective toward one's own desire of appropriating saints and martyrs. We find such perspective in Haldeman's "critical praxis of masturbation" as well as in Boyarin's vision of "the Jewish male femme as a location and a critical praxis" (xiv),[34] but it remains underdeveloped in *Sanctity and Male Desire*.

Jewish male femmes, muscular gay saints, sparks of divinity in gay male receptivity: compared to these religious envisionings of alternative masculinities, I have nothing spectacular to offer. I am who I am because I am invested in other practices, often mundane and normative when weighed against the alternatives lived and imagined by men before and beside me. I don't even have spectacular muscles to offer. Despite several

attempts to join a gym and subject myself to the straight regimentation of muscle-tormenting machines, I never stayed long. Though I am not immune to the appeal of measuring progress by the weight one can stem, I've always felt distracted by the omnipresent mirrors in the gyms.

"I quit bodybuilding myself at age thirty-two," biblical scholar Stephen Moore reveals in God's Gym, *"because it was cutting too deeply into my research time. I set about building up my bibliography instead. The flesh began to peel away from my bones. I cut it into squares, stacked it in piles, and traded it for an assistant professorship" (1996, 75). We religious studies scholars may be "male femmes" after all! Perhaps I should read Samuel Fussel's* Muscle: Confessions of an Unlikely Bodybuilder *(1991) rather than Augustine's* Confessions *in order to widen my horizon of muscular possibilities.*

Boisvert includes a wider range of men's lives than his more limited reveries of a perfected gay male body, but his meditations on such figures as the Apostle Paul, Augustine, or Francis of Assisi do not carry the weight of his book. In the end, a singular vision of male beauty dominates, with the effect that *Sanctity and Male Desire* resembles gay hagiolatry more than queer discourse.

Talking Dirty

Two years after *Sanctity and Male Desire* appeared, Boisvert published an article in response to criticism that his original manuscript received after he had submitted it to a publishing house of a liberal Protestant denomination. This publisher insisted on revising and removing several controversial passages before acceptance. In "Talking Dirty About the Saints" (2006), Boisvert reflects on the recommendations of the press's reviewing committee. His response, which deconstructs several of the committee's objections, also reveals some flaws in his own confessional stance.

Sanctity and Male Desire, Boisvert writes in 2006, "tells my story":

> Not only is it a scholarly analysis with all that this implies in terms of academic discourse and cautious inference, but it is woven through with elements from my life: my Catholic life, and my gay life. The book centers on devotion to male saints . . . [and] from my experiences would hopefully come questions and insights for others—whether gay or not, Catholic or not—about the multiple and often unsuspected meanings of spiritual devotion and the hidden pleasures of hagiographic obsessions. (166)

Justifying his candid employment of graphic language as a "political choice" and "reclaiming without shame the homoerotic element in religious belief and practice" (2006, 166), Boisvert reasserts his earlier claim that "eroticism *is* our religion because for gay men, I believe, there is no other truly genuine way of being religious" (2000b, 10; emphasis in original). In his view, the reviewing committee's insistence on revising was grounded in two issues: first, theological and ecclesiastical anxieties about eroticizing religious figures ("bodily fluids and God do not mix well" [2006, 175]), and, second, explicit references to "gay erotic performances," which stirred the dread of the "polluting nature of queer desire" (173). Such queer messiness, Boisvert concedes, can trigger fear among nongay readers. "It is often not same-sex stuff in general that is necessarily problematic, but rather the fact that it is 'in your face,' that it is brought out into the light of day and celebrated. . . . Images of fellating, sodomized or poly-sexual saints may indeed be unnerving to some believers" (173, 174).

The details of Boisvert's arguments with and against the reviewing committee I need not rehearse here. What is worth asking, however, is whether his confessional scholarship crosses at times the line from self-reflective disclosure to uncritical self-exposure. Does his "in-your-face" declaration lock him into the immanence of exposure, thus revealing the large gap between modernity's (sometimes trifling) self-referentiality and Augustine's "not-yet-face-to-face" humility that opened the male soul to the realities of both interiority and transcendence? Depending on the sensitivities of individual readers, Boisvert's mixing of spirit and sperm might be considered either blasphemous or creatively evocative. But besides the taste and disposition of individuals, it is a lack of critical perspective that needs to be discussed. Similar to Leiris's confessional self-abasement, which crosses into voyeuristic self-loathing and the pornographic rendition of others (in his case, women), Boisvert's hagiolatry turns, at times, into a fetishized pornographic gazing.

In "Talking Dirty," Boisvert cites several of the controversial passages he had to remove, and I will quote two of them to make my point. The deleted portions that did not appear in the published version of *Sanctity and Male Desire* are italicized:

> The Bears celebrate hair: hair that is wild, hair that is everywhere and any-where, hair that glistens with sweat and sperm, *and that sticks to the roof of your mouth. I once had a lover whose preferred way of having sex with me was with me in him and his fingers tangled in my chest hair, pulling at it.* John the Baptist is nothing if not hairy.

The image of a young erect monk, his habit wide open, *penetrating a man or a woman, sometimes both*, touches upon a buried fantasy of mine: that of the handsome holy man ravishing me. (2006, 169–170; cf. *Sanctity and Male Desire*, 63, 121)

Whether deleting the italicized sentences makes much difference is debatable—after all, they only make explicit what is already implied. Still, the original version raises the question of the value of such explicitness. Strictly speaking, the deleted phrases have little to do with discovering "unsuspected meanings of spiritual devotion," which Boisvert declared the intention of his book (2006, 166). The confessional insertions of a private sex act and of a personal sexual fantasy do not shed much light on the veneration of saints. The intimate privacies evoked are not further explored for the meanings they might hold. One wonders, hence, whether they are included for no reason other than erotic titillation or, perhaps, provocation. "'Bad' gay man that I am, I simply could not resist pushing the envelope. I knew what I was doing, and I did it on purpose" (176). In the case of the penetrating monk, Boisvert deliberately aligns himself with "typical forms of anticlerical and antireligious discourse" (169; cf. 2004, 121), but he fails to call attention to the fact that charges of pornography have been part of modernity's disavowal of the church. Especially, images of penetrating monks belong to the staple of polemical anticlericalism, and the author does not exhibit awareness of the pornographic style of such language.[35] As a result, the singular vision of an idealized standard of gay beauty corresponds to a cessation of empathy toward the varieties of male sensitivities. Similar to Rousseau showing his naked butt and Leiris professing arbitrariness, Boisvert abandons the effort to demonstrate how such sexual exposures (the literal fantasy of the exposing monk; the mediated exposure of a private sex act) are spiritually and theologically valuable.

In light of these thoughts, the objections of the reviewing committee may have had less to do with the explicit descriptions of gay sexuality, as Boisvert argues. It is quite conceivable that the pornographic language itself was under dispute, independent of its gay or heterosexual content.

Passion for Jesus

A telling example of Boisvert's apologia is his defense of the gay eroticization of Christ. Devoting to the "Erotic Christ" a full chapter in *Sanctity and Male Desire*, he confesses that he seeks both the "saving blood of Christ" and the "sperm of Jesus": "I no doubt wanted the sperm of Jesus, the mark of his unfailing affection, to cover me and save me just as his holy blood did" (2004, 173). In a later passage, he is mesmerized by Michelangelo's "fully male, genitally endowed" sculpture of the *Risen Christ*, admiring "the muscular arms, thighs, and buttocks" of this "masculine beauty and perfection" (177). Two years later, in "Talking Dirty," he defends the devotional eroticization of the savior figure and asks whether "erotic desire [can] be part of the gaze one poses on the suffering, crucified Jesus" (2006, 175). His answer is, of course, in the affirmative. Surprisingly, though, he calls on an odd fellow for his defense: film director Mel Gibson.

> Though actor-director Mel Gibson and I may be worlds apart in terms of our politics and our beliefs, I do not think that his gaze on the suffering Jesus in his film *The Passion of the Christ* is substantially much different from mine. . . . The imagery we use, the language we select, the emotions we elicit are of the same cloth. When I saw Gibson's film, I was powerfully struck by how sensual, if not outright erotic, it was, particularly the flagellation scene. The film impressed me as one long, deliberate, intimate, slow-moving love-making session. . . . The defiantly straight Catholic film director can get off on the passion and suffering of his saviour, but the gay scholar of religion cannot express it in print. (Boisvert 2006, 176)

These reflections are written without a hint of irony. Rather than distancing himself from Gibson's hyperrealistic filmic presentation of a violent dismemberment, Boisvert conflates Gibson's blood-spilling scenes with gay images of the erotic Christ. Why would Boisvert want to equate a male eroticized gazing at messianic religious figures with an immensely profitable film that exploits the popular thirst for violent images? If anything, one should be happy about the difference, not lament it. The violence displayed in *The Passion of the Christ* is, after all, voyeuristic to the point of being pornographic, because it is so gratuitous and sensationalist. To cite Gibson's filmic focus on the violated male body in defense of the gay eroticized gaze on Jesus spotlights weaknesses in Boisvert's hagiographic project rather than strengthening it.

When I saw The Passion of the Christ *on the opening night at a local theater, the mixture of sadistic and masochistic suffering did not inspire me to what the Christian tradition knows as* imitatio Dei. *Instead, I was aesthetically and spiritually distressed*

over having been exposed to prolonged scenes of graphic violence. The strong visuals of this otherwise slow-moving film had the effect of keeping me fascinated yet detached. When I left the theater, I was speechless and stunned.

Public spectacles of violence immobilize. They rarely call us into action. Forced into the role of passive onlooker, I became a voyeur, not a witness. Witnessing implies an active and moral response, and Christians throughout the centuries have understood themselves as taking an active (and sometimes prophetic) stance toward the world by working against injustices and intervening when people's bodies and rights are violated. The fact that Gibson's The Passion of the Christ *ends with only the briefest filmic allusion to the resurrection is no surprise because it mirrors the religious and spiritual barrenness of Gibson's screen.*

Boisvert's citation of Gibson, especially his interpretation of the overdrawn torturing scene as a lovemaking session, is jarring. I have argued elsewhere (Krondorfer 2004b) that *The Passion of the Christ* is more iconography than theology; that is to say, it relies heavily on image rather than dialogue (that all actors in the film speak in Aramaic and Latin makes hardly any difference). It is the iconic quality of Gibson's film that must have attracted Boisvert. In Gibson's case, images of a violated and bloodied Jesus dominate the screen, a visual borrowing from late medieval and Renaissance paintings and a religious borrowing from popular piety (including the nineteenth-century visions of the German nun Anna Katharina Emmerich).[36] Gibson's borrowing, however, remains on the level of simulacra. In the end, his screen images have more in common with Hollywood's secular fondness for violent movies than with the theological world behind crucifixion scenes as depicted, for example, on the sixteenth-century altars by Matthias Grünewald.

A shared fondness for iconic saintly figures may be one way to understand Boisvert's fascination. Another reason might be the well-built male physique of the actor whom Gibson picked to play Jesus. Both Boisvert and Gibson share a singular vision of male beauty, although for different reasons. Whereas Boisvert is fixated on a gay male beauty ideal, Gibson uses a particular bodily aesthetic in the attempt to remasculinize Christianity. In *The Passion of the Christ*, it is a muscular white male body suffering on the cross. Gibson's choice can be interpreted as an ideological continuation of the Christian men's movement that began with the Victorian Muscular

Christianity and reappeared in the various guises of the Men's Forward and Religion Movement, the Promise Keepers, and, more recently, the God-Men.[37] The muscular body of Christ is put into the service of a paternalistic and patriarchal theology that tries to attract and reattach men to church and religious life. Matching the representation of Jesus' body to the current ideal of the male physique—tall, athletic, brawny, white, with a touch of stern gentleness—not only accommodates audience expectations but also seizes the religious and erotic imagination of men, both straight and gay. The overdrawn depiction of a suffering yet muscular Jesus remains manly even when he pleads for the viewer's pity and devotional empathy.

Gibson's filmic representation eerily parallels the iconic treatment of saintly male bodies in Boisvert's religious imagination, except that the latter is explicitly gay, and the former is supposedly straight. In Gibson's case, the visual display of the muscular martyrdom of a white man is played out against an apocalyptic background of otherness: Gibson's Christ does not inhabit a Jewish body, a dark-skinned body, or a black body. In Boisvert's case, the eroticized Jesus is a muscular Christian and is not imagined as a "feminized Jewish (colonized) male"—though, historically speaking, the Jesus of the Gospels was both Jewish and colonized.

At the turn of the century, Albert Schweitzer wrote in *The Quest of the Historical Jesus* that "there is no historical task which so reveals a man's true self as the writing of a Life of Jesus." His insight can be applied equally to Boisvert's imagined "erotic Christ" and Gibson's flagellated Jesus. "No vital force," Schweitzer continues, "comes into the [Jesus] figure unless a man breathes into it all the hate or the love of which he is capable. The stronger the love, or the stronger the hate, the more life-like is the figure which is produced" (1910, 4). Gibson and Boisvert breathe love and hate into their religious figures, and they use the means available to them to appeal to the contemporary tastes of their intended communities. As film director, Gibson breathes new life into the Jesus story through sadism veiled as devotional love; as a gay religious studies scholar, Boisvert breathes new life into Jesus through eroticism that borders on pornographic voyeurism. It would have been important for Boisvert to distance himself from styles of representations that "seize" the flesh—that is, in an extended sense, also a rape of the flesh (Latin *rapere*, "to seize").

In a review of *The Passion of the Christ*, the American Catholic commentator Gary Wills wonders aloud whether moviegoers are supposed to find a new love for Christianity or for "philoflagellationism."[38] In light of such sarcasm, Boisvert's remarks sound almost comical: "I was powerfully struck by how sensual, if not outright erotic, it was, particularly the flagellation scene" (2006, 176). In an odd reversal of the intended irony, Boisvert proves Wills's point. But rather than the love for flagellation, what is at stake here is a crisis of hegemonic masculinity. Gibson's filmic display of the "life-like" torture inflicted on Jesus' muscular white body appeals to the white man's fear of losing his masculine privileges. The simultaneous display of victimization and heroism, of humiliation and triumph—all of which are read into a messianically charged male body—elicits a passion that draws on real social fears. It also draws on the paucity of religious emotions in men and the concomitant fantasized aggrandizement (in the form of heroic suffering).

The "holy" passion that Gibson's film evokes seems peculiarly queer, since even straight men can indulge in and identify with the story of inflicted pain. *The Passion of the Christ* is, on the one hand, a conventional Jesus film and, on the other hand, a male rampage/male humiliation film in the Grand Guignol tradition.[39] The mixing of filmic genres allows a straight male gazing that is queer without threatening heteronormative masculinity. The affective dynamics oscillate between male humiliation and payback, male submission and ultimate triumph. Religious pathos is turned into digestible kitsch. In the end, Gibson's filmic hyperrealism of a tormented male messianic figure remains a secular fiction of a religious transfiguration—it elicits awe, dread, and comfort. Boisvert, in turn, may have produced his own version of religious kitsch.

The Eroticized Jesus and the Disembodied Christ

Besides Michelangelo's muscular and "fully male, genitally endowed" *Risen Christ*, which commands Boisvert's admiration, Jesus is also imagined as a "handsome man," "caring and attentive, sensitive yet principled," and working "bare-chested in the burning sun" (Boisvert 2004, 180). Both the perfected body and the crucified body appeal. The "handsomely glorious body of Jesus hung from the cross" (171) symbolizes the spiritual intimacy of a vulnerable masculinity. It is a body broken and violated, eliciting "strong feelings of comfort and passive submission, the male docile and compliant bottom" (170). In its brokenness, the body of Christ provides comfort for the brokenness of gay men's lives—lives that have been continually threatened by social rejection, the ravages of HIV/AIDS, and brute violence.

Lamenting the victimization of gays, however, is not the intention of Boisvert's confessiographic *Sanctity and Male Desire*. Rather, Boisvert aims at
restoring a life-affirming resource. In Christ, the once broken body promises
intimate communion; it is an instance of the "erotic grace" of "intimate
divine-human congress" (2004, 171).

> As gay men fix their tearful eyes on the crucified Jesus, infinitely desirable
> in his gashed and vulnerable beauty, they find themselves transfigured into
> his spiritual partners, and they can imagine themselves one in and with him,
> lovers in a dangerous time. . . . In embracing the broken body of Jesus, in all
> its precious parts, we also embrace and begin to heal our own broken and
> spurned bodies. . . . To enter a level of deep companionship with this Jesus
> implies an exchange of bodily fluids: ours, the saliva, tears, and occasional
> blood of our suppliant prayers; his, the redemptive blood, water, and semen
> of his sacred person. (2004, 171, 172, 175)

In this gay restorative vision, the eroticized Jesus is visualized as an icon
of a human body beautiful and muscular, yet vulnerable and broken, and
is remembered as a healing presence in the devotional practices of same-sex
eroticism. Eroticizing Jesus implies a willingness to free desire from restrictive and body-hostile norms, those regulations used by religious authorities
to prohibit, penalize, and despise same-sex love. "We [gay men] find Jesus
desirable, but, in turn, we find ourselves desirable in his sight" (2004, 172).
The confessional language Boisvert employs—and by "confessional" I mean
here both a statement of devotional faith and revelation of sexual intimacies—brings to the fore a reality that the heterosexist gaze does not want to
acknowledge. The "in-your-face" stance, hence, is not only a needed provocation but also the demonstration of a healthy confidence that gay religious
men have acquired over many years of difficult struggle.[40]

The rhetoric of experience, on which Boisvert's confessional gay devotion relies, has, however, its limits. Once it abandons critical perspectivity
that brings forth self-reflective disclosure, the indulgence in uncritical self-
exposure is prone to become flat. It flattens out the treacherously uneven
and bumpy road on which the male confessant in search of himself travels.
Depth becomes surface, like the mirrors of modern gyms, in which the
richly textured bodies of saints begin to look like the gay male gym beauty.
"An authentic gay male political identity therefore implies a struggle not
only against definitions of maleness and homosexuality as they are reiter-
ated and imposed in a heterosexist social discourse," Leo Bersani cautions,

"but also against those very same definitions so seductively and so faithfully reflected in those . . . male bodies that we carry within us as permanently renewable sources of excitement" (1988, 209). The deviant desire that Boisvert wishes to liberate from the shackles of an imposed heterosexist social discourse becomes bound again—this time by the seductively singular aesthetic vision of a gay male body.

A rhetoric of experience also flattens out the theological landscape. The positivist description of Jesus' male physique—presented without an impish twinkling of the eye—neglects to engage the depth of hermeneutical, historical, or biblical criticism that would assist in contextualizing the heavy emphasis on gay individuation as primarily a pleasure-seeking venture. To think the opposite, namely, that the body of Jesus, outside of devotional practice, may simply be inaccessible could be a helpful corrective. "We have no access to the body of the gendered Jew," writes Graham Ward. "So all those attempts to determine the sexuality of Jesus are simply more recent symptoms of the search for the historical Christ—which Schweitzer demonstrated was pointless at the beginning of this century" (1999, 177).

Because Ward presents a strong counterpoint to Boisvert's position, I need to introduce briefly his theological concerns. The differences between them will illustrate what is lacking theologically in a confessiographic text that, like *Sanctity and Male Desire*, relies heavily on a rhetoric of experience.

Ward, who is a representative of the new theological school of "radical orthodoxy,"[41] is, like Boisvert, interested in the intersection of desire and theology. Both authors explore the possible meanings that the body of Jesus as a gendered and sexed body can hold for people, but they arrive at radically different conclusions. The body of Christ, according to Ward, resists our human desire to sexualize him in particular ways. There is no unmediated access to his body because it has moved through a "series of displacements" that "continually refigure a masculine symbolics" (Ward 1999, 163). The Gospel stories, according to Ward, contain five scenes where the displacements of the body of Jesus are "dramatically performed: the transfiguration itself; the eucharistic supper; the crucifixion; the resurrection; and, finally, the ascension. Each of these scenes, in an ever-deepening way, problematize the sexed nature of Jesus's body and point towards an erotics far more comprehensive and yet informing the sexed and the sexual" (166). In other words, the continuous displacements supplant and transcend the particularity of Jesus' male-gendered, Jewish body, a process starting with his transfiguration and ending with his ascension. Those displacements do

not distance humans from the divine but call us into a different form of
participating in the promise of grace and restoration.

> In so far as in Christ human beings are restored to their pre-fallen splen-
> dor, the transfiguration scene on the Mount of Olives presents us with Jesus
> as the Second Adam. Not naked in any obvious sense, but nevertheless
> bathed in a certain translucence. What I am describing here as erotically
> charged is the way these manifestations of humankind glorified by God are
> attractive. They are incarnations of divine beauty and goodness, and as such
> they possess the power to attract, to draw us towards an embrace, a promise
> of grace. These disclosures establish economies of desire within which we are
> invited, if not incited, to participate. (Ward 1999, 166)

The naked beauty of Jesus and the nakedness to which we are restored
are, for Ward, very much within the economy of erotic desire (and not outside it). Yet such nakedness cannot be understood literally and is not bound
to a particular cultural aesthetics.

> Today's cult of the firm, hard, male physique, like the various cultural pur-
> suits it has fostered (body-building and dieting), is the result of certain
> conventions of masculinity which arose in Germany in the late eighteenth
> century—a masculinization modeled on classical sculpture. . . . We are at-
> tracted to the man [Jesus] and beyond him, so that the erotic economy does
> not flounder on questions of sexuality (i.e. is my attraction to this man as
> a man homoerotic, is my attraction to this man as a woman heterosexual?).
> . . . This economy of desire does not deny the possibility of a sexual ele-
> ment; it does not prevent or stand in critical judgment of a sexual element.
> It simply overflows the sexual such that we cannot, without creating a false
> and idolatrous picture of Christ, turn this man into an object for our sexual
> gratification. This man cannot be fetishized, because he exceeds appropria-
> tion. (Ward 1999, 166)

To particularize the body of Jesus and to project one's desire into this
body lead to a fetishized desire that can never be fulfilled. Such fetishization
limits the expansive vision of creation and redemption announced by Jesus
the Christ. By displacing the genderedness and ethnicity of Jesus, desire is
no longer limited to the needs of particular individuals or communities.

*Graham Ward, as I do, cautions against idolatry and fetishism. He does not specifi-
cally refer to* Sanctity and Male Desire *(his "Displaced Body of Jesus Christ" was
published five years earlier), but his criticism addresses the literalism of the gay devo-*

tional imagination. "I glance at . . . the almost naked, muscular man hanging on a wooden cross . . . [and] recognize his attractiveness as a powerful source of homoerotic longing" (Boisvert 2004, 168); "I imagined a naked Jesus as a muscular, handsome bearded man embracing me and became sexually aroused" (Goss 2002, 10); "I described [the gay Christ] . . . as a man on the cross completely naked with a cute face, well-developed 'pecs' and large penis, wearing an earring in his left ear" (Gorsline 1996, 136).[42] The gay image of Jesus is monovisually iconic.

Ward also serves as a corrective to my own iconic reticence. "Iconicity," he argues, "transcends physicality. It does not erase the physical but overwhelms it, drenching it with significance. The maleness of Christ is made complex and ambivalent, in the way that all things are made ambivalent as their symbolic possibilities are opened up by their liminality" (1999, 170). I am fond of the idea of iconicity opening up symbolic possibilities. Boisvert opens up new possibilities, and as long as his singular vision does not get totalized, I can appreciate it.

Then I think of Mel Gibson and I hesitate. Who knows how much of an iconoclast is somewhere buried in my soul—despite my professed love of images of all kinds.

Ward's radical orthodoxy is "radical" insofar as it does not shy away from a theological encounter with contemporary discourse on desire—from Sigmund Freud to Judith Butler. It is radically "orthodox" insofar as it relies on a neo-Augustinian and neo-Barthian vision of a Christianity that is the ground of all knowing and being, and hence always larger than any particular human expression.[43] The Gospel narratives, which testify to the transformation of Jesus to Christ through a series of displacements, contain the "good news" of a messianic body that does not operate outside human erotic desire but is always larger than the sexual and spiritual imagination of the contingent subject.

Boisvert, one could summarily say, eroticizes Jesus in order to search for a greater range of permissible sexual experiences; yet, because he theologically flattens the body of Jesus to carnal literalism,[44] he ultimately binds desire to a singular vision. Such is the fetishized gaze that Boisvert embraces, but Ward criticizes. Ward, on the other hand, frees Jesus from inscriptions of particular forms of masculinity and thus opens up gendered possibilities; yet, through the process of displacements, he ultimately ends up with a disembodied Christ. What remains is not a personal relation to a messianic figure but an engagement with that which remains after the ascension, after the "final displacement of the body of the gendered Jew" (1999, 175): the church.[45] "The Church now is the body of Christ, so to understand the body of Jesus we can only examine what the Church is and what it has to say concerning the nature of that body" (177).

For Boisvert and other gay theologians, Ward's conclusion cannot be good news. A disembodied Christ in the form of the church would be difficult to accept since it returns to where the trouble started. After all, it has been the church that too often denied a religious imaginary open to erotic possibilities. Why should the church be trusted now? How would one prevent the church as the new body of Christ from erasing yet again "the physical," "drenching it" with pleasure-negating, instead of pleasure-seeking, significance? (1999, 170). Ward's assertion of the "body of the Church as the erotic community" (177) is too tentative a promise for gay theologians aware of the struggles they have fought, and his theological optimism may lack the concreteness needed to name a gay self into being. Wouldn't it be more likely that the church imagined as an erotic community postponed yet again the gratification of particular cravings through a continuous series of their own theological displacements, consoling the faithful with the *eschaton*?

The theological tension between Ward's radical orthodoxy and Boisvert's unapologetically gay position cannot be solved here, but, in concluding, I would like to indicate a new direction that also brings us back to the multiplicity of confessional voices. It is the "nonfoundationalist stance" of Dale Martin, a scholar of biblical criticism, that will come to our assistance.

"Is it any wonder," Martin asks, seemingly agreeing with Boisvert, "that the gay imagination . . . [w]ith all this ambiguity surrounding Jesus' sexuality—whether in the popular imagination, the historical imagination, or the patristic imagination . . . can so easily find a Jesus for itself?" (2006, 99). Citing varied and contradictory evidence of the Gospels, Martin suggests that "Jesus is certainly not a normal man—not even a 'normal' *gay* man. He ends up again looking very singular—very queer" (100; emphasis in original). Most gay theologians, whether they identify with an essentialist gay or with a queer position, can consent to the view that Jesus was not a "normal man" and that he challenged heteronormative assumptions. Martin, however, is not really interested in defending Jesus as gay, queer, or straight. Like Ward and Schweitzer, he argues against any prescriptive portrayal. "As is the case with so many instances in all interpretation, how people interpret the sexuality of Jesus tells us more about the meaning of sex *for them* than for some 'real' Jesus freed from interpretation" (2006, 102; emphasis in original). Here, Martin seems to shift his support from gay theologies to radical orthodoxy: Jesus cannot be claimed by anyone's sexual yearning.

Martin takes yet another step:

> Christians have always made sense of their own sex and their very singular Savior. What makes my nonfoundationalist stance different from the foundationalism of modernism is my insistence that we can be no other way. We should learn from the facts of our contingency. . . . We have a right to think about the sex of Jesus, the sexuality of Jesus, the desires of Jesus, the singularity of Jesus. What none of us has a right to do . . . is to insist that he or she will supply *the* method of interpretation that will bring imagination to an end and silence the imaginations of others. (102; emphasis in original)

Martin makes clear in this paragraph that he rejects any totalizing singular view of Jesus. His nonfoundationalist stand thus creates a framework that can hold several positions—those of Boisvert and Ward included.

With this quotation, we have arrived at the end of this chapter. The non-foundationalism that Martin advocates allows male confessants, like Boisvert, to claim the singularity of Jesus as long as it is not restricted to *one* singular vision. It also offers a critical perspective from which to resist a fetishized gazing, thus providing space for Ward's position, too. Fetishization is—broadly speaking—equivalent to the *one* "method of interpretation" to which Martin objects. It is an object fixation, a narrowing of perspective that blends out other possibilities, and Ward's reluctance to sex Christ can be understood as a necessary antidote to confusing sameness and difference. Perspective that is warranted in the Otherness of the divine—that which is always more expansive than oneself—would be lost if clinging to sameness. The problem with radical orthodoxy, however, is that it does not acknowledge our human contingency and thus disavows the human need for investing religious figures with particular messianic hopes within the means available to people in specific contexts. Desire articulated in devotional confession needs to be truthful with respect to the particular confessant—it cannot be otherwise if it is to remain a confession. To be trustworthy, however, a confession of faith must also be respectful of the desire of other people.

Spirit and sperm: The confessional stance men take toward themselves, their bodies, and their religious traditions—whether Haldeman, Boisvert, Boyarin, Gibson, or Ward—is part of the dialectic relationship between the social reality of men's lives and the creative reality of men's religious and sexual imagination. In our contingency, we confess, we imagine, we critique. Acknowledging our contingency, we must attend audaciously to our unbounded imagination. Our imaginings may be flawed—they are flawed!—but imagine we must. Our critical interpretations may be faulty— they are faulty!—but interpret we must. Our confessional self-investigations may be imperfect—and they are imperfect, as we have seen throughout this study—but we are encouraged and empowered to confess. Confessants call on the imagination, religious and otherwise, in order to gain clarity on who they are, who they have been, and who they want to become.

CHAPTER 8

Outlook

The Power to Name Oneself into Being

In this book, I have traced how male confessants present, perform, and reflect upon themselves through the act of writing themselves into history—or, put differently, of writing themselves onto the (material) pages of history. Through a self-revealing process of the unmaking and remaking of the self, the male confessant names himself anew into being, preserving on paper and presenting to the public the afflictions of his soul and the resolution to his crisis.

I hope to have shown that confessiographies are not one-dimensional. The male confessant's investment in particular self-revelations and in particular choices of opening himself up to the public needs to be conceived as multivocal, manifold, densely enriched, ambiguous, and at times contradictory. The narrower the presentation of the self (such as Pohl's *Credo* and, to a smaller extent, Boisvert's fetishized gazing), the less trustworthy the testimony that the confessant left of himself; the deeper the presentation of the self (like Augustine and Perechodnik), the less solipsistic the male gazing. The religious imagination, I have argued, has the power to transcend the confines of the mirror's surface and can lead to an interiority in which the soul is naked in the face of an other. Herein lies perhaps the greatest promise of male confessions: to lay bare one's soul, to render the self vulnerable to the judgmental eye and ear of an other, and thus to empower oneself to live a life outside heteronormative regulations.

The unmaking and remaking of the male self, to which confessiographies testify, is never unambiguous and always incomplete. It is a creative dance between revealing and concealing, hiding and exposing, resisting and asserting, (re)membering and (dis)placing. It is also a dance between solipsistic self-absorption and divine transcendence, between narcissistic gazing and imagining Otherness, between fragmentation and searching for wholeness, between complicity and resilience. It is a dance between thoughtful disclosure of intimacy and reckless exposure of privacy.

At times, male confessants have taken advantage of the privileges bestowed on them by their cultural and religious surroundings, whether it is Augustine availing himself of the tacit benefits of being a free, male Roman citizen, or Oswald Pohl drawing on a cultural desire for national exculpation and political autonomy in order to seek clemency. At other times, male confessants struggle to maintain and claim subjectivity against the forces of history, as in the case of Calel Perechodnik, who is writing against annihilation, or of contemporary gay religious scholars, who affirm their lives against the forces of homophobia.

Confessiographies, whether resisting or accommodating, cannot escape from employing rhetorical devices and discursive strategies. I have paid attention particularly to the disavowal of moral agency, the disappearance of the particularity of the (heterosexual) male body, the displacement of the intimate (female) other, and the "becomingness" through sexual practices. At critical moments, narrative strategies conceal levels of moral agency even when asserting male subjectivity. Thus, the very project of self-revelation on which the male confessant has embarked is compromised. The retrospective tracing of the transformation into a new self (which attests to, renews, and revitalizes his subjectivity) is never innocent.

Such compromising is, on the one hand, inevitable, since every confessiography is necessarily incomplete. Even the modern search for total transparency—the project that Rousseau ambitiously started to pursue—is bound to fail. In the end, epistemological constraint, constriction of time and space, limitation of language, and the finiteness and contingency of the human condition work against a self capable of revealing itself in totality. The process of translating and transposing lived experience into narrated language is always subject to autobiographical choices, and every choice is a silencing, muting, and forgetting of other possibilities. Putting lived experiences into words invests meaning into these experiences. But even when multiple meanings are explored by the male confessant, the number of reflective spins he can give his life is limited. Each instance of meaning-making erases the lion's share of the unbounded richness of life's ambiguities and ambivalences. "We live and write on the tip of an iceberg, and there is a dimension of tragedy to our life and work that is ineliminable."[1] Given the inevitability of choice, the male confessant should not be blamed for the incompleteness of his testimony but appreciated for his efforts.

On the other hand, each confessiography must be judged and appraised for the choices its author made. What is left out? Whose voices are muted? Is the reader deliberately led astray or subtly seduced? Is the confessant hiding levels of complicity and culpability? Concealing and revealing are not exclusive operations—indeed, we need to conceive of them as dialectically and inextricably intertwined. But we can question the motives and motivations that lead to different degrees of eluding moral agency, and this, in turn, will affect the trustworthiness and credibility of a confessional text. The larger the discrepancy between male subjectivity and moral agency, the more cautious a reader should be about the seductive power of intimate confessions.

We can ask, for example, whether male confessants (re)constitute their subjectivity by operating solely within normative gender ideologies or whether they resist a hegemonic masculinity. Some of the texts we examined tend toward one or the other. Those confessants who write against the forces of history tend to be resistant, whereas those who write with the assuredness of history on their side tend to be complicit with normative ideologies. The lines between complicity and resistance, however, cannot be drawn with clarity. Augustine, for instance, makes use of the privileges bestowed upon him—as a matter of fact, he is largely blind to the privilege of being a man—yet he decides to reject benefits that his cultural milieu claims could be rightfully his (he could have become a respectable member of Milan's upper class). Like other Christian men before and after him, Augustine chooses an alternative path. Perechodnik, on the other hand, who has lost even the most basic human privilege, namely, the right to live, becomes complicit the moment he avails himself of the limited options he has as a Jewish man in order to increase the chances of his survival during genocidal assault.

Revealing their innermost selves, most male confessants are afraid of losing respect (usually from their peers) and wish to hold on to (moral and religious) respectability. We can think of Augustine's sinful self and Rousseau's debased self struggling between solitary pride and social need; we can recall Perechodnik's wounded self and Pohl's apologetic yet culpable self; or Broughton's androgynous self in awe of anything the body exerts and Haldeman's gay-becoming self. In one way or the other, all these male confessants speak of the fear of losing "face" and credibility. Aware of the risk of exposing themselves to the ridicule and scorn of other men and of depriving themselves of moral authority, they put countermeasures into operation in their texts. Should, for example, the disclosing of intimacy lead to the loss of respect among peers, then God and the ideal reader are imagined to understand the confessant correctly. Should the admission of trivialities, culpability, or sexual failure result in the loss of moral authority, then the transformed and remade self claims anew an improved moral expertise and respectability. These dynamics are discernible in Augustine's imaginary dialogue with a transcendent Other as well as in Perechodnik's self-effacing, imaginary dialogue with his dead wife from whom, in the face of his own impending death, he pleads for forgiveness and respect. We also find these dynamics in Pohl's effort to portray himself as a decent man who, through the detour of rendering himself a religiously devout man, feels compelled to adjust to the demands for a new masculinity in postwar Germany while, at the same time, stubbornly refusing to admit culpability. The need to maintain respect and respectability is also buried in Boisvert's "in-your-face" assertiveness of a gay identity against heteronormative understandings of religious imagery, as well as in Haldeman's attempt to read morality back into sexual practices that have been declared immoral by heterosexism and homophobia. Only with modernity's loss of a religious universe have some male confessants begun to mock the very notion of respectability itself, such as Leiris (and, in a limited way, Rousseau), whose self-portrayal as an abject self refuses to seek respect and empathy from the reader. Such a move renders a man radically vulnerable, making him look ridiculous in his unmanly disavowal of virtuous behavior. But loss of the religious imagination also comes with a loss of being in dialogue with an other. The solitary modern male subject remains relationally challenged.

Because confessiographies usually do not pay much heed to the political connotations of the intimate self, the critical reader must bring to bear upon such texts their larger political context. In this book, I moved from the personal in the early chapters to the political in the later chapters, only to return in the last chapter, and under new conditions, to the intimate dimension of the sexual and eroticized male body. I began, so to speak, with questions of self-referentiality and gradually widened the circle of relationality. Starting with the very private act of the male self looking into the mirror (Leiris, Augustine, Rousseau, Broughton), I pushed the argument all the way up to suggest that the labor of reconstituting a male identity that perceives itself under attack is as much part of modernity's state violence (Perechodnik) as it can become part of a larger effort of nation building (Pohl). I finally returned to the male body through the lens of the gay subject: the gay man names himself into being through sexual practices and with the help of an imagination that blends spiritual and erotic powers (Haldeman and Boisvert).

The political dimension of the intersection of masculinity, religion, and nation building, which I addressed briefly in my gender analysis of Pohl's *Credo*, is an issue that deserves a study of its own. Suffice it to say here that in particular times and places, religious efforts of remasculinization are related to the restructuring and reimagining of political communities, and that such processes usually take place under the banner of conservative and gender-restrictive value systems. This can be demonstrated for postwar Germany in the 1950s but applies equally to today's global rise of religious fundamentalism.[2] The insight that masculine ideals are modified in tandem with the creation of religious/moral and political/national communities provides a lens through which to study hegemonic and alternative masculinities in religious history.[3] Especially when established paradigms, authorities, or technologies lose their persuasive or coercive power, masculine identities become unstable, leading some men to confess their conflicted soul.

Such power shifts become visible when comparing the internal dynamics of confessional texts with the external dynamics of their political settings. Pohl, for example, shifts his ideological investment from Nazism to a conservative Catholicism. What, at first glance, appears to be a heart transformed, turns, at closer inspection, into a man clinging to power under a different rule. In Augustine's work we can trace coercive power, too: what in the *Confessions* is a genuine struggle to discover the freedom of a confessing self (freedom from dominion of false pleasures)—a struggle that implies a critique of Roman imperialism—turns, later in Augustine's life, into a growing reliance on imperial might to support his own hegemonic vision and to neutralize his theological enemies.[4]

The invention of new technologies also destabilizes gender identity and forces the self into new ways of managing itself. I briefly indicated such technology shifts by pointing to the invention of the printing press at the beginning of modernity and, correspondingly, to the emergence of private reading patterns. We can also see it in modern technologies of the self, such as psychoanalysis. Today, in the midst of the digital revolution, the Internet has become a prime medium that seduces, persuades, and compels people to disclose and expose their private lives to the public. The Internet—a hybrid between oral confession and confessiography—promises, on the one hand, the anonymity of a religious confessional by seducing people to address themselves to transpersonal confessors (such as impersonal cameras and home pages); on the other hand, the information shared always leaves a documented trace on the Net, like a written confession. What Internet confessants tend to forget and ignore is the seductive and coercive power that the new technology exerts. Having been promised the democratization of information access, people willfully suspend their critical judgment regarding the medium's anonymity, reliability, and credibility. Internet confessants open themselves up to no one in particular, yet the posting of digitalized intimacies is disseminated globally within seconds and stored in perpetuity. Neither anonymous nor trustworthy, the Internet is seductive because it rests on a delusional, yet effective fantasy.

A heart poured out in cyberspace might be nothing more than a cleverly concealed act of recitation and masquerading: high school students masquerading as violent pranksters, housewives as sexual insomniacs, sexual predators as compassionate friends, sex workers as domestic spouses. Intimate truth telling is processed in millions of bytes of information, presenting the confessant in fragmented, fictionalized, and fetishized ways. On the Net, there is seemingly no limit to phantasmic self-representation. But amid myriad acts of private intimacies, will we discover a person's true soul? No longer responsible to anyone but the impersonal technology of recording and downloading information, the self is freed from relational responsibility. With ever-stronger stimuli needed, intimate exposures are moved into the macabre, the lethal, and the obscene. In its digitalized shape, the soul's true self is a figment of the imagination.

"If the tongue and the heart are at odds, you are reciting, not testifying," Augustine said. Living in an age of innovative recitations, there is little patience left for a self's introspective journey: what counts is the entertainment value of the performances of the self. The totalizing access to intimate spaces, which digital technology makes possible, destroys the intimacy the confessant seeks. The modern individuated search of the confessing self disappears behind a thousand selves masquerading as unique subjects.

Compared to these trends, male confessiographies in the form of a book seem antiquated—and lamenting these changes nostalgic. I hope to have shown, though, that the power of the act of introspective writing creates and maintains a subjectivity that, however flawed and incomplete, has the potential of self-revelation and, importantly, self-evaluation. New technologies may create greater fluidity of gender categories and gender constructions, but they also create greater fictionalizations of gender. These fictional selves are no longer grounded in the material basis of perceiving oneself in relational interdependence but float in a space of nonrelational autonomy. The solitary self, which Rousseau equally feared and embraced at the beginning of modernity, has led to a dissolution of the self into digital bytes of information that can be consumed by no one and everyone simultaneously. It is a virtual consumption of the private body without flesh, a transubstantiation of a bodiless self—something that male confessants before the digital revolution could not have imagined.

.   .   .

Let me return, in the end, to the reader of male confessiographies. Being seduced by a text that allows us to peek into secretive places of the hearts and souls of other men is pleasurable. Seduction not only commands our ability to be pleasured but also commands our gullibility through which we become complicit. We become complicit when "believing too much." Seduced into giving the male confessant too much credit, we wish to believe his efforts of revealing himself truthfully. In this case, we become his empathetic co-confessant. We identify with his failures, wounds, risk taking, and longings for forgiveness. As gendered readers, we may also seek with him absolution, and we hope to regain, like the confessant with whom we identify, respect and respectability.

Confessional writings, however, may also fail to seduce, in which case we "believe too little." We cease being a sympathetic co-confessant and become, instead, a judgment-dispensing confessor. We are now free to condemn the confessant without granting him absolution. Having lost trust, we divest our mimetic desire and are now free to rebuff his moral authority and ridicule him.

Believing too much or believing too little: are these the only choices we have? A gender-conscious, critical reading protects us from falling blindly into either of these two polarizing options. Neither do we need to deny ourselves the pleasure of reading nor should we cut ourselves loose from the responsibility of exercising critical judgment. We need not be seduced to either undue praise or unfair condemnation. A wound described by a male confessant may be a self-pitying attempt at exculpating himself, but it may also constitute the only genuine means at his disposal of rendering himself vulnerable and speaking about himself intimately and truthfully. A critical reading that is conscious of the genderedness of the subject appraises male confessions as necessarily flawed yet courageous attempts at self-revelation and self-reflectivity. The confessiographic impulse is, after all, one way of naming oneself into being.

As consumers of intimacies, we are invited to participate in the introspective and retrospective journeys of confessants. We can respect them for their risk taking, but we have no obligation to imitate them. We may feel for them, identify with them, suffer with them, love them, get angry at them, or be bored by them.

We would also be well advised to remind ourselves of our differences from these men and to claim our own uniqueness.

Notes

Chapter 1

1. The quotations are appropriately referenced later.

2. Among the large body of scholarship on the history and practice of confessions, the following works are especially relevant: Brooks's *Troubling Confessions: Speaking Guilt in Law and Literature* (2000) examines the use of confessions in modern legal procedures against a rich historical and literary background; Tambling's *Confession: Sexuality, Sin, the Subject* (1990) emphasizes the emergence of the subject and discourses of sexuality as a result of a confessional culture; Tentler's *Sin and Confession on the Eve of the Reformation* (1977) offers an excellent historical study of religious confession from the early penitential practices to the highly developed practice of auricular confession prior to the sixteenth century; Foster's *Confession and Complicity in Narrative* (1987) traces the "confessional turn" in select literature and its implications for the reader; Senior's *In the Grip of Minos: Confessional Discourse in Dante, Corneille and Racine* (1994) takes a literary perspective on confessions and pays particular attention to the architectural manifestation of the confessional in the wake of the sixteenth-century Catholic Counter-Reformation; Coles's *Self/Power/Other* (1992) discusses the confessing self from the perspective of political philosophy and examines the implications of Augustine's interior soul searching and Foucault's critique of the soul as a discourse that imprisons the body. Foucault's *History of Sexuality* (1990) must be credited for raising the interest in confessional discourse with respect to the emergence of the self, to coercion, sexuality, and power.

3. See Bourdieu's theory of the masculine "habitus" in *Masculine Domination* (2001; first published in French, *La Domination masculine*, 1998).

4. The scholarly discussion on masculinity within the field of men's studies has correctly pointed to differences between, on the one hand, the multiple social practices of men of different backgrounds (sexual, ethnic, national, class, etc.) and, on the other, the legitimization of a dominant and normative masculine ideal that upholds the patriarchal order. The latter has been appropriately described as "hegemonic masculinity," a concept convincingly introduced by Connell (1995); see also Brod (1987); Brod and Kaufman (1994); West and Lay (2000); Gardiner (2002); Adams and Savran (2002). The term "heteronormativity" has been introduced by

queer studies, referring to a "set of norms that make heterosexuality seem natural and right and that organize homosexuality as its binary opposite. . . . As a result, the dominance of heterosexuality often operates unconsciously or in unmarked ways that make it particularly difficult to expose and dislodge" (Corber and Valocchi 2003, 4). For an overview of the influence of American men's studies on the German/European conceptualization of masculinity, see Stephan (2003).

5. "Men after all have written plenty about their subjectivity and power, but they have constantly universalized it at the same" (Middleton 1992, 3). Regarding the creation of gendered "fictions" based on exclusion of the lived reality of others, see, for example, Theweleit's chapter "Männliche Geburtsweisen" (Forms of Male Nativity/Generativity), where he voices a biting critique of continental philosophy that vehemently resists the inclusion of "female fertility," "birthing," and "motherhood" as categories of thought into their epistemologies: "Spricht man einen der Denk- oder Wissenschaftsherren auf diesen Mangel an, stellt man fest, sie wissen gar nicht, was gemeint ist, und wenn sie es doch zu verstehen meinen, halten sie es für einen Witz. . . . Und bleibt man dabei, daß sie doch hierher gehören und zwar *gerade* hierher, wird man in ihren Augen zu einem denkunfähigen Wesen . . . zu einer Art Frau, die keine Ahnung hat von den Geheimnissen des männlichen/philosophischen Diskurses" (2002, 6; emphasis in original). (Once one makes those men of thought and of science aware of such lack, one realizes, they are clueless. And when they think they understand, they assume it is a joke. . . . And if one insists that [women] have a place in [continental philosophy], and particularly here, then one turns in their eyes to a being incapable of any thought . . . into a kind of woman who has no idea about the secrets of the masculine/philosophical discourse.)

6. May and Bohman (1997) argue strongly that the social practice of men confessing sexual sins reinforces and reproduces patriarchal values. They also envision a progressive confessional practice in which a patriarchal male self can be transformed.

7. Butler suggests linking "reiteration" and "performance" as a way to describe the maintenance of gender identity: "the action of gender requires a performance that is *repeated*. The repetition is at once a reenactment and reexperiencing of a set of meanings already socially established; and it is the mundane and ritualized form of their legitimation" (1990, 140; emphasis in original). Elsewhere, Butler theorizes the linkage between the materiality of the body and the performativity of gender: "performativity must be understood not as a singular or deliberate 'act,' but, rather, as the reiterative and citational practice by which discourse produces the effects it names" (1993, 2).

8. On the issue of "moral space," which offers the self a chance of reorientation, see Taylor (1989, 25–52). In personal conversation, Stephen Boyd has pointed out that I am implicitly arguing for the ethical importance of creating a cultural space for male introspection.

9. See Krondorfer's *Critical Reader* (2009), which introduces the spectrum of scholarly accomplishments in the religious study of masculinities of the past decades. For the status of men's studies in religion as it took on a recognizable shape

in the mid-1990s, see Boyd, Longwood, and Muesse (1996); Krondorfer (1996); and Boyd (1995).

10. For a fuller argument about the importance of the phrase "critical men's studies in religion," see Krondorfer (2009, esp. the introduction).

11. Foucault's term *dispositif* refers to the inclusion of "nonlinguistic phenomena" in cultural analysis (Senior 1994, 6).

12. The so-called *Bekenntnisschriften* are of particular importance to Protestantism, such as the Augsburg Confession (*Confessio Augustana*, 1530) or the Book of Concord (*Konkordienbuch*, 1580), in which Lutheranism articulated and presented its creeds and doctrinal standards. "Male confessional writings" also differ from studies that analyze masculinity within organizations belonging to a particular religious tradition, such as Lisa Zwicker's "New Directions in Research on Masculinity and Confession" (2006), in which she investigates notions of masculinity in Catholic German fraternities; see also Blaschke (2008).

13. Within the field of autobiographical studies, there is an ongoing debate on what constitutes generic autobiography. James Olney, an important voice in this field, writes: "Although I have in the past written frequently about autobiography as a literary genre, I have never been very comfortable doing it. . . . I call the kind of writing I am looking at by various names—confessions, autobiography, memoirs, periautobiography. . . . What I like about the term 'periautobiography,' which would mean 'writing about or around oneself,' is precisely its indefinition and lack of generic rigor" (1998, 339–404). See also Marcus (1994, 294). Moseley concludes: "One consequence of the oceanic nature of the discourse surrounding autobiography has been that this discourse has slowly but surely lost its moorings in any generically recognizable category of writing" (2006, 3).

14. On confessional poetry, see Lerner (1987); Middlebrook (1993).

15. Desisting from defining "confessiography" as a genre is supported by recent debates about the fuzziness of autobiographies. See Olney, who argues against "generic rigor" (1998, 404).

16. See Krondorfer (1995); Krondorfer, Kellenbach, and Reck (2006); Kellenbach, Krondorfer, and Reck (2001).

17. See Tentler (1977). For some useful introduction to the history and practice of penitentials, see Payer (1984); Driscoll (1996). See Jordan (1997) for the role of penitentials in the "invention" of sodomy. For cultural and intellectual investigations into the history and role of the religious confessional, see Tambling (1990, 35–87); Senior (1994, 75–103); Brooks (2000, 88–112). Credited for the actual invention of the confessional (including instructions for its architectural design) is St. Charles Borromeo, bishop of Milan and a central figure at the Council of Trent (1545–1563).

18. Brooks (2000, 101) uses the terms "transindividual" and "impersonal" to describe the transferential dynamic in the confessional.

19. For a discussion of the implied coerciveness of confessional practices in religion and psychoanalysis, see Brooks (2000, 88–143). Tambling is less pessimistic about confessions and proposes differentiating coercive techniques from elements

of resistance within confessions. "To make distinctions between psychoanalysis and either religious or police confession, panoptical or clinical observations, seems vital. . . . It might be argued, then, that far from psychoanalysis colluding with forms of confessional knowledge, it has the capacity to put into question precisely the repressions and interdictions forming the basis of religious confession and of societal restraint" (1990, 179, 182).

20. St. John Nepumoc, for example, was put to death in 1383 for not revealing the confession of the queen of Bohemia (see Senior 1994, 100). Current changes in the laws of Western democracies try to soften those social agreements. Claiming the need to protect against terrorism, German lawmakers in 2007 began to discuss changes regarding the secrecy of doctor-patient conversations (the medical *sigillum*), while keeping religious confessional sacred; in the wake of 9/11, the U.S. government under the administration of George W. Bush moved toward the admissibility of coerced confession through torture and torture-resembling practices; see Danner (2004); Mayer (2008); Sands (2008).

21. Unless otherwise noted, I am using Henry Chadwick's translation of Augustine's *Confessions* (1992). I am omitting Chadwick's text insertions of the biblical references. For the Latin text, see O'Donnell (1992). Coles quotes this sentence from the 1942 translation of F. J. Sheed (Kansas City: Sheed, Andrews, and McMeel) as, "I have become a *question* to myself" (emphasis added); he interprets it as evidence of "the dawn of the hermeneutic self" (1992, 14).

22. "Introspection," Denise Riley writes, is "a means of getting beyond one's person to the universal reachable through that fierce concentration on the particular" (2005, 39).

23. On "confessional performances," see Payne (2008, 13–40). Gill argues that confession is a "ritualized technique for producing truth" (2006, 4), and Foucault calls it a "ritual of discourse" (1990, 61).

24. Other feminist critics have argued the opposite, namely, that the confessional mode as intimate speech is primarily a female genre; see Gammel (1999); Gill (2006, 1–10). For a brief overview, see Radstone (2007, 56–111).

25. In the "confessional relation" between speaker and listener, the "issue is not persuasion" but "seduction" (Foster 1987, 4).

26. "Conversion" is a particularly "seductive form of rhetoric and a unique ordering principle" (Riley 2004, 7).

27. "Memory work" is a working through the materials of "personal and collective memory" and assigns remembering a transformative quality (Radstone 2007, 197). For Kuhn, memory work is a form of inquiry that is "potentially interminable: at every turn . . . there is always something else to look into" (1995, 5).

28. On the interplay between verbal interrogation and the infliction of pain in coerced confessions (legal and religious), see Scarry (1985); Brooks (2000); Glucklich (2001).

29. *Confessions* (9.4.10). This rendering of the Latin text is quoted in Riley (2004, 24), who uses Pine-Coffin's 1961 translation of the *Confessions* (London: Penguin).

Chadwick translates the phrase more neutrally: "In the place where I had been angry with myself."

30. In *The Question of Lay Analysis*, Freud engages in a dialogue between himself as psychoanalyst and an imagined "Impartial Person" who is curious about psychoanalysis but also voices doubts. In this context the Impartial Person asks whether psychoanalysis does not follow the same "principle of Confession" as the Catholic Church, to which Freud replies: "Confession no doubt plays a part in analysis—as an introduction to it, we might say. But it is very far from constituting the essence of analysis or from explaining its effects. In Confession the sinner tells what he knows; in analysis the neurotic has to tell more. Nor have we heard that Confession has ever developed enough power to get rid of actual pathological symptoms" (1959, 189).

31. Given the proximity of confessions and conversions, it is no surprise that retrospection is a strong ordering principle in conversion narratives. "Conversion is the moment that motivates autobiographical production and provides a structure for a narrative of the self. Yet it also implies the self's dissolution into alterity. If conversion legitimates narrative retrospection by offering a unitary, even teleological, framework in which to cast the subject's history, it also threatens to expel the self from its textual edifice" (Riley 2004, 9; and 24–59 on Augustine's *Confessions*).

32. For biblical studies, see Anderson and Staley (1995); Staley (1995); Oldenhage (2000); Patte (1995); for American religion/Jewish studies, see Levitt (2007). Scholars of gay religious studies have more consistently inserted an intimate voice into their research than have their heterosexual colleagues (see Krondorfer 2007b).

33. Despite his strong argument for self-reflexive, confessional writing, Middleton himself "largely eschews personal writing" since, as he argues, "it is not yet possible to produce such writing and have it mesh with theoretical analysis" (1992, 22). My book is an attempt to move beyond this male reticence.

34. Moore adopts this definition from Nancy Miller (1991, 1).

35. See, for example, the creative arrangement of Derrida's autobiographical "circumfession," accompanying in small print, and at the bottom of each page, Bennington's analysis of his work (1993); see also Caputo (1997, 281–329). In "Stabat Mater" (1986), Julia Kristeva's personal voice is printed in boldface and inserted as separate columns.

Interlude: On Mirrors

1. The translation is mine. Though more prosaic in form, it highlights the meaning of Rilke's stanza. Herter offers a more poetic rendition: "Mirrors: never yet has anyone described / knowing what you are really like / You, interstices of time / filled as it were with nothing but sieve holes" (Rilke 1962).

2. Text cited in Hopkins (2007, 52). The collection of photographs was first published in 1934 as *Photographs by Man Ray 1920 Paris 1934*, and reprinted in 1979 (New York: Dover).

3. With this sentence, Foucault ends *The Order of Things* (1973, 387), in which he discusses modernity's operations of discursive knowledge. The French original (*Les

Mots et les choses) reads, "alors on peut bien parier que *l'homme* s'effacerait, comme à la limite de la mer un visage sable" (1966, 398; emphasis mine). *L'homme* can be translated as "man" or generically as "human" (or "Mensch" in the German translation, *Die Ordnung der Dinge* [1990, 462]).

Chapter 2

1. As a crude way of marking the difference, one could say that autobiography is about external achievements whereas confessions are about an interior search. In "Confessions and Autobiography," Spender writes: "One of these lives [of the autobiographer] is himself as others see him—his social or historical personality—the sum of his achievements, his appearances, his personal relationships. . . . But there is also himself known only to himself seen from the inside of his own existence" (1980, 116). Brenner argues that retrospection is a feature of autobiography in distinction to diaries: "The perspective in autobiography is mainly retrospective, whereas in diary it is contemporaneous" (1997, 120). I would argue that autobiographies, though clearly retrospective, differ from confessiographies in that the former can pursue contemporaneous utilitarian goals, while the latter is retrospective *and* introspective based on self-reflexivity and a transformative moment. On autobiography and confessions, see also Chapter 1, notes 13 and 15.

2. In late antiquity, a mother's milk had sacred and redemptive qualities. The nursing goddess Isis, for example, became the Christian icon of Maria *lactans*; see Corrington's "The Milk of Salvation" (1989).

3. For the expressiveness of Cieslak's body language, see the photo documentation in Grotowski (1969).

4. Augustine was well educated in the liberal arts of his time (he had read, among others, Cicero, Plotinus, Aristotle, and neo-Platonic philosophy), and the *Confessions* are also an intellectual reckoning with this tradition. But in the *Confessions* Augustine has rarely anything good to say about his teachers. They may have been learned and sophisticated but lacked depth and understanding. Sometimes, they were just pompous, and Augustine was repeatedly dissatisfied by them. The most memorable of those is the "eagerly awaited Faustus," a Manichean teacher: "When he came, I was delighted by the force and feeling he brought to his discourse and the fitting language which flowed with facility to clothe his ideas. . . . When I put forward some problems which troubled me, I quickly discovered him to be ignorant of the liberal arts other than grammar and literature" (5.6.11). In the end, no matter how learned a teacher or how sophisticated a philosophy, none would be able to compete with the wisdom of Scripture, the book Augustine loved most. See also Tambling (1990, 16; esp. chap. 1 ["I Have Become a Problem to Myself: Augustine Agonistes"]).

5. Only toward the end of his life—spurred by the sacking of Rome and the siege of Hippo by the northern invaders—did Augustine reconsider the significance of renewed Christian martyrdom (see Brown 1969, 287–298, 424–426, 431–432).

6. *L'Age d'homme* was to become the prologue of Leiris's four-volume work, *La Regle du jeu* (*The Rules of the Game*). Although the 1939 edition fell into oblivion,

the second printing of *L'Age d'homme* in 1946 gave it "almost instant notoriety" (Pilling 1981, 63).

7. On nostalgia, melancholy, and masculinity, see Radstone (2007, 159–191); Capps (1997); Enterline (1995).

8. Leiris underwent five years of psychoanalysis around the time of writing *Manhood* (see 1992, 157). He credits Freud in a 1961 interview (Pilling 1981, 64). Pilling also suggests that *Manhood* might be better understood as an "auto-analysis than an auto-biography" (64).

9. For the significance of the childhood self in modern autobiographies, and the temporal tension created by the confluence of "child self" and "adult self," see Moseley (2006, 8–11).

10. In Leiris's self-abasement might also be parody; see Hopkins's study on the Dadaist ironic/iconic reversals of masculinity, which views *Manhood* in the context of Duchamp (2007, 81–83).

11. Rousseau (1712–1778) wrote the *Confessions* between 1764 and 1776, to be published posthumously. Part I (Books 1–6) was first published in 1782, and part II (Books 7–12), a few years later; see Kelly (2001); Dent (1992, 55–62).

12. Rousseau's relation to religion is more complex than can be indicated here. See Grimsley, who concludes that "what [Rousseau] was as a living individual, what he imagined himself to be in moments of despair, exultation, or secret desire, and what he thought should be the universal basis of any valid religious outlook" did not form a "consistent whole" (1968, xiii).

13. Following Lejeune, Moseley argues that "for Rousseau, the ultimate criterion of sincerity is not that he be true to the 'Eternal Being,' but rather to 'the succession of feelings which have marked the development of my being'. . . . For Rousseau and for autobiographers who follow him, even Christian, it is the 'self' that assumes many of the functions traditionally assigned to God in Christian confessional literature" (2006, 7).

14. "Self-abnegation . . . constitutes revelation for Augustine but is a source of anxiety . . . for a writer such as Rousseau" (Renza 1908, 278; also Jackson 1992, 81).

15. "I showed to the girls . . . a sight more laughable rather than seductive" (Rousseau 1953, 91; also Brooks 2000, 49–51).

16. Unaware of gender implications, Spender claims that autobiography, which is "the story of one's life written by *himself*," rests on the "basic truth" that "I am alone in the universe" (1980, 115, 117; emphasis added). Spender, even though he does not say so, really has the modern male subject in mind.

17. See also Moore's mention of a modern peeing/potty episode and its relation to academic discourse and autobiographical intervention (1995, 21–25).

18. Paul de Man, to the contrary, argues that Rousseau's is "not primarily a confessional text" since "to confess is to overcome guilt and shame in the name of truth" (1979, 279). My study of confessiographies suggests a broader understanding of confession.

19. The "lessons of the *Confessions* is not that Jean-Jacques never did anything

morally wrong" but "that good people can have moral failings that lead them to misdeeds" (Kelly 2001, 313).

20. Rousseau's "desire for total transparency is linked to the ambition to confess entirely, to provide a seamless narrative of the inwardness as well as the exterior life story of a person" (Brooks 2000, 161).

21. For a different view, see Brée, who writes that of Leiris's four volumes, "*Manhood* comes closest to the traditional narrative model as analyzed by Philippe Lejeune" (1980, 203).

22. For emotions and memory, see Rousseau (1953, 20, 22). For an example of dissonance, see Rousseau's profound disorientation after he had wrongly accused the young girl Marion of stealing a ribbon (88). On the much-commented-upon "ribbon" episode, see Starobinski (2001, 370–381) and de Man (1979, chap. 12).

23. One needs to keep in mind, though, that Leiris underwent psychoanalysis (see note 8).

24. Especially Cranach's paintings of *Lucretia and Judith*; see Leiris (1992, 14).

25. Analyzing Leiris's new preface to the 1946 edition of *Manhood*, Pilling argues that Leiris "no longer conceives of himself in a kind of solipsistic vicious circle but rather in relation to the world at large" (1981, 67).

26. "Throughout the nineteenth and twentieth centuries, the confessional mode flourishes, and nearly always it promises revelation of the shameful, the abject, that which is normally covered over and repressed in polite or official social intercourse" (Brooks 2000, 73).

27. In my reading, *Manhood* undoes Spender's argument that "no one confesses to meanness, cowardice, vanity, pettiness: or at least not unless he is assured that his crime, instead of excluding him from humanity, brings him back into the moral fold" (1980, 121).

28. For the Internet's seductiveness, see the extraordinary success of Frank Warren's "secret posting," both in digital format (postsecret.blogspot.com; retrieved February 2009) and in print (2005). Several contributions in Sher and Vilens (2009) address the issue of suicide and the Internet.

29. Quoted in Tambling (1990, 40).

30. In the English edition, the 1946 preface is added as an afterword, "The Autobiographer as *Torero*" (1992, 153–164); see also Pilling (1981).

31. See Pilling (1981, 68). Tambling (1990, 21, 27) sees a similar agon at work in Augustine's *Confessions*, where Augustine shows that the personal agon of the confessant cannot be completed: "when you hear a man confessing, you know he is not free." Tambling also detects in the *Confessions* a contest between the "Pelagian and the Augustinian" model of understanding humans, with Augustine's pessimism winning the battle, and hence bringing to an end the ancient world and starting the Middle Ages.

32. Rousseau assigns different desires to men and women and, generally, a "subservient existence" of women to men (Dent 1992, 248–249). Cf. Tambling, who argues that Rousseau turns himself into a "sexual subject" in the *Confessions*, rendering himself "feminine" by describing his various submissive sexual encounters with

women and thus resisting the "male-based political nature of the sexual" (1990, 108–113; also Schwartz 1984; Kavanagh 1987).

33. For critical perspectives on the mythopoetic men's movement, see Clatterbaugh (1990); Messner (1997).

34. "Wholly reflected by the looking glass of the female body, the thinking subject no longer sees his mirror; nor does he see that his thought . . . rests on a fiction" (Rosi Braidotti, quoted in Marcus 1994, 219).

35. Tambling compares truth-telling speech to waste products: "The illusion is that speech is the speech of the subject . . . [that belongs] to the self, and may be examined as closely as other waste products of the body, themselves classified as defilement" (1990, 3).

36. The phrase comes from Kaufman's *Beyond Patriarchy* (1987).

Interlude: On Testimony

1. Philologist Joshua Katz argues that "the two senses of *testis* truly do stem from semantic split" and "not from accidental homophony" (1998, 191).

2. *Yarek*, which can mean "thigh," "loins," or "shaft," most certainly refers here to the sexual organ; see Katz (1998, 192–193); Eilberg-Schwartz (1994, 155; 1990, 169).

3. For different views, see Chapter 1, note 24.

Chapter 3

1. Tambling notes that "telling" about the self "in the past" sets up the expectation of "a death of the former self, a break between the past of narrative time and the now of writing" (1990, 19).

2. "A full confession would presumably require that a private knowledge be revealed in a way that would allow another to understand, judge, forgive, and perhaps even sympathize" (Foster 1987, 2).

3. Unlike Spender, I do not claim that there is "an outer objective life." Instead, the outer life is *perceived* to be objective by the introspective confessant. But I agree with Spender when he writes that "confessional autobiography may be the record of a transformation of errors by values; or it may be a search for values, or even attempt to justify the writer by an appeal to the lack of them" (1980, 121).

4. For Foucault (1990, 1999), confession, with its monastic origins, has played a central role in ordering civil and religious power in the West since the Middle Ages (1990). For a strong proponent of autobiography as a uniquely Western form, see Gusdorf (1980); Marcus (1994, 154–162); Ross-Bryant (1997, 84–86). For views critical of the idea of Western uniqueness, see Bruner (1993); Watson (1993).

5. I mentioned in Chapter 2 that Frye credits Augustine for inventing the "confession form" (1957, 307). See also Riley, who discusses whether the *Confessions* constitute the first coherent autobiography (2004, 24–26), citing both the contrary assessment of Vance, who wonders whether modern readers accept too eagerly the "myth of autobiography" with regard to Augustine's *Confessions*, and Pascal's affirmative view that "autobiography" as a European creation "begins with Augustine" (184, notes 2, 3); see also O'Donnell (2005).

6. "*Confessio* meant, for Augustine, 'accusation of oneself; praise of God'" (Brown 1969, 175).

7. Given the Christian roots of confession, one can argue about the compatibility of Perechodnik's work with this literary and religious tradition. The question of literary compatibility is muted insofar as my study deemphasizes the issue of genre in favor of a confessiographic *quality*. Also, as indicated in Chapter 1, the term "autobiography" itself has become fluid, with some critics suggesting that it should be replaced by "outlaw genres," such as "testimonial literature, oral narratives and ethnographies," or "autobiothanatography" (Marcus 1994, 294–296). Regarding religious difference, it can be observed that the term "confession" sits less easily within Judaism. However, Moseley in his study on East European Jewish autobiographical writings demonstrates the existence of confessional styles within Jewish literature. Repeatedly referencing Rousseau, Moseley cites several confessional instances, including Hasidic texts (2006, 185, 197, 253, 289, 313, 330, 335). See also the biography of Nahman of Bratslav (1772–1810), who was known for his confessional practice for initiating his disciples. "Seemingly so alien to Jewish practice . . . the rite of confession" was not "unique to Bratslav" but known among medieval "German-Jewish pietists" and the "literature of East European Jews" (Green 1979, 45–46, 60–61). On confessional self-incrimination, see Maimonides' ruling that "no man is to be declared guilty by his own admission" (quoted in Brooks 2000, 72).

8. Questions have been raised about the trustworthiness of Perechodnik's narrative, particularly as it relates to the English translation of the original Polish manuscript. Historian Steve Paulsson provides several examples of poor or misleading translations. For example, the Polish phrase *typ przecietnego inteligentego Zyda*, with which Perechodnik describes himself, is rendered into English as "a Jew of average intelligence." According to Paulsson, it should read "the type of an average intelligent Jew," or, more idiomatically, "an average member of the Jewish intelligentsia" (pers. comm., April 2008). As far as I can tell, however, these semantic and historical inaccuracies do not derail my argument in this chapter.

9. Quoted in Moseley (2006, 110, also 330; Berdichevsky's piece originally appeared in 1909). Perechodnik uses the Polish word *spowiedz* for confession, which, according to Paulsson, is an accurate translation (pers. comm., April 2008). The Polish American sociologist Orla-Bukowska adds that *spowiedz* refers to confession in the strict Roman Catholic sense, whereas *wyznanie* (not used in the original manuscript) would carry the connotation of "testimony," used in such cases as confessing one's love (pers. comm., April 2008). The use of *spowiedz* may indicate Perechodnik's intention to write for a Christian audience, having lost all hope for the survival of Polish Jews. This is, however, not a foregone conclusion, since deathbed confessions can be located within the context of Jewish religious and literary tropes. For a secular version of a Jewish confession, see Derrida's "Circumfession" (1993) and Caputo's interpretation of it (1997, 281–329).

10. Anetka is another name he uses for his wife.

11. Elizabeth Grosz, quoted in Marcus (1994, 218).

12. For the idea of making, unmaking, and remaking, see also Tambling, who

writes that "the first nine books [of Augustine's *Confessions*] seem to be that act of remaking, by recounting, remembering what has happened to him, as though trying to solidify the experience which belongs to the labile memory by textualizing it" (1990, 15). For the destructive and traumatizing effects of the unmaking of the self in the context of coerced confessions, particularly in political torture, see Scarry (1985).

13. "When I look in the mirror," Michael Kimmel reflects self-critically in an interview, "I see a human being—a white middle-class male," and "gender is invisible to me because that is where I am privileged. I am the norm. I believe that most men do not know they have a gender" (quoted in Middleton 1992, 11).

14. There are, of course, other absences (or "non-absences") in the *Confessions*, left out by Augustine himself and also overlooked by scholarship, as Elizabeth Clark argues. "'The gap and absence' on which I shall focus," she writes, "is the mysterious erasure of Donatists" (Augustine strongly opposed the popular Donatist church) as well as Augustine's "North African" identity (2005, 222).

15. Augustine warns that none of these delights, including the "custom of singing" (10.33.50), should "go to excess" because it would "produce mental fatigue" (10.34.53).

16. Augustine allows for limited cultural relativism in terms of nonbiological sources of pleasure: "variations in custom" exist due to a "mutually agreed convention of a city or nation" (3.8.15). Those cultural divergences, however, still go back to the fundamental source of human imperfection, due to, as he insists in the same pages, three "chief kinds of wickedness" (3.8.16): the lust for domination (power), lust of the eyes (beauty), and lust from sensuality (sexuality, food).

17. On the problem of nightly emissions in early Christianity, see Brakke (1995).

18. Some editions even omitted the last three books (11–13) of the *Confessions* because they were considered not to match the narrative unity of the first books (1–9). Kotzé provides a good overview of the discussion on the unity of the *Confessions* (2004); Tambling regards chapter 10 as a transitional chapter from autobiography to philosophy (1990, 14, 19); Lionnet strongly argues for the autobiographical integrity of the entire work (1989, 37). Given what I have said so far, it should be clear that I, too, perceive an integral and intended unity in the composition of the *Confessions*.

19. Augustine's construct of woman is a "projection on the external world of an inner and scary reality" (Lionnet 1989, 52; also Miles 1992; Power 1996; Kilgour 1990, 46–62).

20. Augustine, of course, is not the first to promote the virtue of celibacy, but he works within a tradition of patristic thought and early Christian gender experimentation. Ambrose, his theological mentor in Milan, had already advocated strongly for clerical celibacy; see Brown (1988); Ranke-Heineman (1990).

21. Perechodnik's attitudes toward faith and God are more complex than can be explored here (see also pages 39, 74, 78, 101, 153, 158).

22. The Hebrew means "God full of mercy"; it is the opening of the mourning prayer, recited after a funeral and on anniversaries of a death.

23. For a polemic attack on scholarship that combines Holocaust and gender studies, see Schoenfeld: "Between the Scylla of an academicized 'Holocaustology' and the Charybdis of a universalized victimology," the senior editor of *Commentary* writes, "the worst excesses of all on today's campuses are being committed . . . by the voguish hybrid known as gender studies" (1998, 44).

24. A gendered reading of Holocaust narratives has been applied to women's writing but rarely to men's writing. See Brenner (1997); Ofer and Weitzman (1998). Young (1988) addresses with much sensitivity the issue of violating survivor narratives.

25. For a short history of how the manuscript survived the war, how it subsequently found its way into the archives in Warsaw and Jerusalem (where it was read by a few historians), and how it was finally published (first in Polish in 1993, then in English in 1996), see the "Foreword" by Fox and the "Afterword" by Szapiro (Perechodnik 1996).

26. About the social makeup of the ghetto police, Perechodnik writes: "It is worth noting that the Jewish police had in its ranks the same number of lecturers, physicians, and engineers as it did illiterates" (1996, 69).

27. Brenner (1997, 119), who argues that "self-introspection" can be "a mode of resistance" (5).

28. Genia's letter is reprinted in Perechodnik (1996, 203–205). The Warsaw uprising refers here not to the Jewish ghetto revolt but to the Polish uprising in the summer of 1944.

29. Ezrahi argues that Holocaust literature engages only in "very few instances" in "relentless self-exposure" (1980, 64). Perechodnik's work, I believe, can be counted among them.

30. "We may assume that *Perechodnik's text comprises the truth*" (Szapiro 1996, 216; emphasis in original).

31. Szapiro (1996, 220), who mentions an example of a documented event that Perechodnik should have known of but does not mention.

32. Burrus argues that the *Confessions* are a replacing, devouring, consummating of his mother, his "unfinished business . . . present in all his beginning. . . . Writing the Life of a woman, he gives birth to his own Life" (2004, 77, 84). Lionnet writes that "Augustine re-creates himself" and the "result is his own book, the *Confessions*" (1989, 63).

33. On the problem of Augustine's anxiety over the circularity of his attempts at avoiding pride and vainglory, see Asher (1998).

34. On confession and resistance, see Tambling's conclusion (1990, 212).

35. According to Paulsson, the English translation of "recklessness" for the original Polish word *lekkomyslnosc* is wrong. Literally, it means "'light-mindedness'; it implies acting without stopping to think about the consequences, whereas 'recklessness' would imply that he knew the consequences and went ahead anyway." Paulsson suggests translating *lekkomyslnosc* more accurately as "thoughtlessness," "frivolity," or "irresponsibility" (pers. comm., April 2008).

36. These words are from a letter by Genia, written after the war (Perechodnik

1996, 204). Eighteen-year-old Genia was Perechodnik's short-term lover in his hiding place. I return to their relationship in Chapter 6.

Chapter 4

1. Wills suggests that the *Confessions* should be translated as "testimony," because this term "best covers [the] range of meanings for *confessio*" and matches more closely Augustine's "entire theology" (1999, xiv–xv).

2. "A past tense narrative thus has built into it the sense that it will reveal a lack, a failure, requiring a confession/conversion to end it, either in the past, or indeed in the act of telling" (Tambling 1990, 19); also Riley (2004, esp. chap. 2).

3. Schissler's *The Miracle Years* (2001) covers various cultural aspects of this period in West Germany. See Gabriel (1993) for the German situation of the Catholic Church in the 1950s. For a sociopolitical perspective on the 1950s as a new epoch, see Schwarz (1989).

4. All translations are mine. Because the authorship of *Credo* cannot be attributed to Pohl alone, I am citing this work throughout as *Credo* (listed in the References under Pohl).

5. For a detailed analysis of political cohorts as an instrument for understanding generational differences in relation to National Socialism and the Holocaust, see Krondorfer (2006, 31–66); Marcuse (2001, 291–296). The 1918ers were defined by their war enthusiasm in 1914 and, when Germany lost the war in 1918, by their disillusionment and anger.

6. There are slight divergences in the scholarly literature about the dates of Pohl's party membership. According to the best source, he joined the NSDAP (National Socialist German Workers Party) in 1923 (Schulte 2001, 33; he mentions that others have dated it to 1925 or 1929). Koch (1988, 69) and Posset (1993a, 22) date the NSDAP membership to 1926. Schulte mentions no date for joining the SA; Allen (2000, 396) writes that Pohl had been active in the SA since 1925; Koch (1988, 69) dates the SA membership to 1926; and Posset, to 1929 (1993a, 22). Pohl contributed to this confusion since he intentionally obscured some of his biographical data. To endear himself to Himmler, he described himself in 1932 as a "National Socialist before there even was National Socialism." But when in Allied custody after the war, he toned down his NS enthusiasm and portrayed himself as an administrator pressured by Himmler's recruitment efforts.

7. See Schulte (2001, esp. 44–45). For a detailed history of the Landsberg prisoners, including Pohl, and the various legal appeals and calls for clemency and amnesty, see Buscher (1989); Schwartz (1990).

8. For earlier publications on personal family history, see Krondorfer (1995, 2000, 2001, 2002b).

9. The abbreviation "A.D." after a professional title stands for *außer Dienst* (retired).

10. "mit kirchlicher Druckerlaubnis, München 7.7.50 / G. V. Nr. 6193."

11. For the mentality of the 1918ers, see Krondorfer (2006, 46–49). See also Niemöller's memoir, *Vom U-Boot zur Kanzel* (1934; *From a Submarine to the Pulpit*).

Like Pohl, Niemöller had joined the navy during the First World War. After the German defeat, he channeled his frustration into national-conservative causes. Later, Pastor Niemöller chose a path very different from Pohl's. His Christian-inspired, political opposition led to his imprisonment in a concentration camp. After 1945, Niemöller visited Allied internment camps to preach about confessing and repenting German guilt, but he also supported church efforts for political amnesty. See Kellenbach (2006, 246–252).

12. Steigmann-Gall summarizes the situation in 1936: "There was no directive from the party leadership ordering *Kirchenaustritt*; the evidence suggests that it arose as a spontaneous movement within the NSDAP. . . . In 1936 there came a flood, however, beginning with Himmler and Heydrich leaving the Catholic Church early that year" (2003, 219). Pohl, who left in 1936, echoes the historian's observation: "members of the SS were never ordered to leave the church. I am not familiar with any such order by Himmler" (*Credo*, 29).

13. The German terms *Kriegsverbrecher* (war criminal) and *Kriegsverurteilte* (those accused of war crimes) were highly politicized in postwar Germany. They were used to draw comparisons to alleged Allied war crimes or to express doubt over the Allied justice system. See Krondorfer (2004a, 64, esp. n. 7); Schulte (2001, 432).

14. In German, the title is "Im Schoß der alleinseligmachenden katholischen Kirche."

15. See Chapter 3, note 18.

16. Karl Adam's work *Das Wesen des Katholizismus* (1924; *The Nature of Catholicism*) is most often quoted in *Credo*, sometimes in long passages. It was Adam's most popular book, reprinted thirteen times until 1957. On Adam's NS complicity, see Scherzberg (2001). Other theologians occasionally quoted in *Credo* are Romano Guardini, the Swedish bishop Söderblom, the Protestant Heiler, Augustine, biblical verses, and briefly Goethe and Kant.

17. A line-by-line linguistic analysis and further historical research might detect with greater clarity the exact authorship of various passages; such detailed exegetical clarification would not, however, significantly change my interpretation of *Credo*. Other people in the church may have been involved in drafting *Credo*. Posset articulates this conjecture in a private correspondence with Katharina von Kellenbach (April 5, 2006) but does not provide further evidence. The auxiliary bishop of Munich, Johannes Neuhäusler, who "oversaw the spiritual affairs at Landsberg" (Buscher 1989, 93), embodied interests similar to those of Morgenschweis and Pohl. Neuhäusler tirelessly pushed U.S. High Commissioner John McCloy and others to grant clemency. "From 1948 to 1951, the auxiliary bishop intensively lobbied American authorities on behalf of convicted war criminals" and, starting in January 1951, this included "the last condemned [at Landsberg], among them Pohl and four leaders of the mobile killing squads" (Buscher 1989, 93, 96). See also Phayer (2000, 142–144).

18. "We think of confessions as preeminently first-person narratives—even though we know they may be the product of collaboration between confessant and confessor, analysand and analyst, suspect and interrogator" (Brooks 2000, 143). Augustine perceived his confessional writing as a true dialogue between himself and God,

but from a "postmetaphysical perspective" one can argue that the *Confessions* have a "distinctly monological quality," drowning out all other voices. "For those who reject Christian metaphysics," Coles writes, "Augustine's polyphony becomes . . . monotony" (1992, 172).

19. The German word for "conversion" is unambiguously *Bekehrung*. The term *Bekenntnis*, however, carries both the meaning of "confession" of sin and "profession" of faith. In the German original, the repeated usage of *Bekenntnis*, hence, leaves no doubt that *Credo* must be read in light of a Christian confession story.

20. Payne (2008) makes a compelling argument for the performative quality of public perpetrator confessions. Her case studies from South Africa and South America can be applied to the few "confessional performances" by Nazi perpetrators.

21. For Catholicism, see Löhr (1990); Gabriel (1993). For the Catholic rejection of modernism, see Kienzler (1996, 49–55); Remele (2005, 53–68); also Stegmann (1996), who reads Catholic antimodernism in light of fundamentalism. For the Protestant churches, see Hockenos (2004); Greschat (1990). See also Herzog (2005, 103–107).

22. For a short summary on the trials and German efforts for political amnesty and clemency, see Kellenbach (2001, 47–48). For Pohl, see Schulte (2001, 432). For the Catholic Church, see Phayer (2000, esp. 138–144). For detailed historical studies on the social, legal, and political dimensions, see Buscher (1989, 91–130); Frei (1999, 133–233); Schwartz (1990). During the late 1940s and early 1950s, the most important Protestant spokespersons for clemency were Hans Meiser (Munich), Theophil Wurm (Stuttgart), Otto Dibelius (Berlin), and Martin Niemöller; among Catholics, Cardinal Frings and auxiliary bishop Johannes Neuhäusler.

23. Retired Admiral Gottfried Hansen played an active role in West Germany's apologetic discourse, calling repeatedly for amnesty. During Christmas in 1950, he demanded a "general amnesty . . . for the so-called war criminals" (quoted in Frei 1999, 209).

24. The letter is dated June 5, 1951, and reprinted in a revisionist-conservative university bulletin, *Deutsche Hochschullehrer-Zeitung* (Jg. 11, 1/2 (1963): 25–26). The letter is also reprinted in Koch (1988, 159) but mistakenly dated as July 5, 1951 (Pohl was hanged on June 7). Koch's nonscholarly and often sensationalist work has to be treated cautiously with respect to the reliability of its sources, facile judgments, and the occasional inflammatory language. But it contains useful historical material.

25. Posset (1993b, 25). According to Posset, Morgenschweis continued his defensive attitude on behalf of accused Nazis long after 1951 in various lectures, articles, and letters to newspapers. Unfortunately, Posset does not properly identify his sources.

26. *Haltung* is a term rich with meaning, referring simultaneously to an inner attitude, one's overall attitude toward life/general view of life, and one's physical posture. It is the embodied expression of a person's moral, political, social, and religious interior. *Haltung* implies a principled attitude that moves a person beyond individual gratification to the point of self-sacrificial duty. It carries a certain emotional coldness and is often employed to portray military and conservative men.

Pre-1945 generational cohorts embraced it as a positive virtue; see Autsch (2000). Pohl uses the term several times in *Credo*, mostly to describe his straight and righteous attitude toward the prison conditions (39, 40, 46).

27. Although I am aware of the inelegance of this translation, it captures the awkwardness of the German original.

28. Like the English *intercourse*, the German word *Verkehr* (which means "traffic") can refer to social exchange/company as well as to sexual intercourse. Morgenschweis clearly uses it in the former sense, and I do not intend to insinuate any sexual impropriety.

29. He received the papal blessing by telegram in March 1951. The Vatican later explained that it had not known that Pohl was a Nazi criminal and that the benediction was given simply in response to a request for a member of the church who was dying. I am thankful to Katharina von Kellenbach for providing this information. She tracked down an English translation of an article on this issue (*Münchner Merkur*, March 28, 1951) at the National Archives in Silver Spring, Maryland (RG 549 USAEUR, Records of War Criminal Prison No. 1 at Landsberg, Records Related to Executed Prisoners, Jan. 2, 1946–June 7, 1951).

30. The awards and honors are listed in Posset (1993b, 26–27).

31. In a West German parliamentary debate in December 1950 about ending the American denazification program, a Social Democrat, who had been a prisoner of the Gestapo, protested against clemency calls for Pohl. Mockingly, he wondered how the "greatest murderer" in German history "suddenly found Christ," impressing visitors with "so-called repentance" (quoted in Frei 1999, 65).

32. Morgenschweis's reference to the collapse of an "anti-Christian power" is vague enough to point, narrowly, to the Nazi regime and, more broadly, to modernism itself.

33. Pohl's personal and professional devotion to Himmler was known at the time (Schulte 2001, 41). For the many private and professional layers of the relationship between Himmler and Pohl, see Koch (1988, 37–91).

34. See note 26.

35. The rhetorical situation suggests that the hateful other, who is juxtaposed to the reconciliatory Catholic convert, is the Jew. Morgenschweis himself never mentions Jews directly, just as *Credo* avoids any direct reference. But in letters from prison, Pohl repeatedly identifies his contemporary enemies as Jewish. During his Nuremberg incarceration, he writes that "an American officer (definitely a Jew), who apparently had to handle me 'psychologically,' appeared very often." In the same letter from 1948, he writes about "the blind hate and plain vindictiveness . . . of the prosecution, which was dominated by Jewish representatives" (reprinted in Koch 1988, 156, 158). Other interned Nazis made similar charges about the Jewishness of the American interrogators. For example, Rudolf Höß, the camp commandant of Auschwitz, writes in his memoirs about the conditions of Nuremberg in 1946: "Physically there was no problem, but more so were the mental and emotional effects. I cannot really blame the interrogators—they were all Jews. I was for all intents and purposes psychologically dissected. That's how

accurately they wanted to know everything—this was also done by Jews" (Höss 1996, 180).

36. "Pohl's statements in the postwar period give the impression that he moved from Kiel [his navy position] to the central SS-office in Munich reluctantly and only after persistent urging by Himmler. This version does not stand up to the facts" (Schulte 2001, 36). See also Allen (2000, 396).

37. The letter is dated June 1, 1948, and reprinted in *Deutsche Hochschullehrer-Zeitung* (Jg. 11, 1/2 (1963): 21–24); also reprinted in Koch (1988, 158).

38. Pohl uses the terms *Kreaturen* and *Geschöpf,* both of which are translated as "creature." In this passage, the word *Geschöpf* has a biblical-religious connotation and points to the divine origin of humans. The term *Kreaturen* is employed whenever Pohl speaks about his opponents, suggesting their more animalistic nature and weak character.

39. He blames "the disgusting quarreling within the evangelical churches" in the 1930s for his decision to become *gottgläubig* (*Credo,* 34)—listing the *Deutsche Christen* (Christians openly embracing Nazism; see Bergen 1996), the *Deutsche Glaubensbewegung* (a paganist movement appropriating Protestantism; see Steigmann-Gall 2003, 149–154; Nanko 1993), and the Confessing Church, which partially resisted Nazi ideology (Hockenos 2004, 15–41). Pohl accuses his former WVHA comrades, who appeared with him as witnesses and defendants at the Nuremberg trials, of being turncoats, scarecrows, lifeless dummies (43–44). "To the disgrace of the German nature it has to be said that a number of these dark and sad creatures played this miserable game in Nuremberg. . . . These creatures, who, according to the victors, were just as guilty as their incriminated German comrades, heedlessly sold their honor and conscience for a lentil dish [*Linsengericht*] in order to be released from the charges" (letter reprinted in *Deutsche Hochschullehrer-Zeitung* Jg. 11, 1/2 [1963]: 24; also Koch 1988, 157). The "lentil dish" refers to the biblical story of Esau selling his birthright to Jacob (Gen. 25:29–34).

40. Complaints about so-called professional witnesses (*Berufszeugen*) were often voiced against John McCloy and the U.S. High Commission for Germany; see Schwartz (1990, 384); Buscher (1989).

41. The German sentence "habe ich entschlossen einen Strich gezogen" echoes the widespread postwar German motto of *Schlussstrich ziehen* (drawing a final line), with which Germans expressed their desire to leave the past behind and start anew.

42. The disavowal of (Jewish) victims as credible witnesses for Pohl's actual crimes, and the typologizing of them as recalcitrant, negative witnesses to his reborn self must be seen in the long Christian tradition of Jews as "negative witnesses," which, according to Flannery (1965, 49), began with Augustine; see also Fasching (1992, 19, 71–73).

43. "It is as though the perpetrator, on finding himself in the midst of interpersonal proximity, reacts by going out of his way to instantly disengage himself from it. It is worth recalling that this is precisely the 'effort' Himmler sought to spare his SS personnel: he saw to it that proximity between perpetrator and victim not be permitted to arise in the first place" (Vetlesen 2005, 262).

44. The foregrounding of technical/logistical skills and simultaneous absence of thinking through the consequences of one's action are often commented on by readers of the more widely known memoir of Rudolf Höß. When, for example, Höß's career took him away from Auschwitz in 1943, he writes: "At first I was not happy about moving away because Auschwitz had become my life precisely because of the difficulties, the problems, and the many difficult duties" (1996, 165). Lifton is citing the example of an SS physician in Auschwitz who, after the war, recalls his duties in the following words: "The gas chambers were sufficient, you see, that was no problem. But the burning, right? The ovens broke down. And they [the corpses] had to be burned in a big heap. . . . The problem is really a large technical difficulty. . . . And then everyone contributed his knowledge of physics, about what might possibly be done differently" (1986, 177).

45. *Credo* wrongly attributes this biblical verse to Psalm 62. It is actually Psalm 63:1.

46. The *Hannoversche Presse* and *Christ und Welt*, respectively; quoted in Frei (1999, 232–233).

47. This is one of three definitions under the entry "confessor" in *Webster's II: New Riverside University Dictionary* (Boston: Houghton Mifflin, 1984).

48. In a 1948 letter, Pohl claims that he was pummeled and beaten in the early weeks after his arrest (reprinted in *Deutsche Hochschullehrer-Zeitung* Jg. 11, 1/2 [1963]: 21–24; also in Koch 1988, 154–158). In Koch's sensationalist retelling of these claims, the Allies have morphed into torturers: "Acid in his face, broken teeth—the arguments of the Allies were fantastic, especially the British proved to be masters of torture. Salt was poured into the bloody wounds, then razor blades cut up his face" (1988, 33). Pohl reports only a rough shaving: "[A guard] smeared some mixture onto my face, which burned like acid. . . . After I was thoroughly soaped, he scratched my face with a dull razor so recklessly that blood dripped onto my jacket" (quoted in Koch 1988, 155).

49. For a comparative perspective on perpetrator narratives, see Payne (2008); Gallagher (2002). Also Hülya Adak (2007), who studied memoirs of Turkish perpetrators of the Armenian genocide, esp. Talad Pasa's apologetic memoirs. Adak comes close to the notion of "disingenuousness" when analyzing historical and narrative manipulations. Suggesting "autobiographical void" (with reference to Lejeune's "autobiographical pact"), Adak describes the hide-and-seek game of the narrating "I" in perpetrator memoirs. "The reader is expected to participate in a different pact, of forgetting, or perhaps 'transcending' the authorial signature; annulling the pact of identity between the authorial signature and the narrator." The combination of passive voice and autobiographical void conceals the culpability of the narrator and replaces the autobiographical "I" with an "ideological I" (2007, 153, 158). For a different outcome of confessional writings by perpetrators, see Buchholz (2003, 2007), who examined the confessions of 969 Japanese war criminals in Chinese reeducation camps. The accused were repeatedly asked to put into writing their confession (between 1950 and 1956), but as long as they continued to conceal culpability, the drafts were returned to them. Only when a Japanese confession was

deemed complete (that is, full acknowledgment of the crimes committed) did the writing requirement stop and the prisoner was released. According to Buchholz, only one of the former 969 prisoners later recanted these confessional statements, whereas many engaged in the Japanese peace movement or published memoirs in which they acknowledged Japanese atrocities committed in China.

50. Kerner (1786–1862): "Mensch, bist du ganz verlassen / klag keinen Augenblick! / Da kannst du erst dich fassen / kannst geh'n in Gott zurück!"

Interlude: On Tears

1. For Assisi, see Cioran (1988, 37); for the desert fathers and monastic founders, see Benke (2002); Hunt (2004). Ignatius "boasts of 175 episodes of crying . . . in one forty-page stretch of [his] diary" (Lutz 1999, 48); Benke (2002, 287–288). For Dante, see Senior (1994). For the Renaissance, see Enterline (1995). For Derrida, see Derrida (1993, 9, 18–20, 38–40, 117–120) and Caputo (1997, 288–299; 2005, 3). For a general historical overview, see Lutz (1999).

2. For references to and quotations from Aristotle's *History of Animals* and William James's *Varieties of Religious Experience*, see Lutz (1999, 48, 176).

Chapter 5

1. According to Kavanagh, Rousseau's *writing* of the *Confessions* was motivated by his frustration about the impossibility of *speaking* about true friendship without it being mediated through social degradation. "Speaking in the presence of others means for Rousseau certain humiliation and self-parody" (1987, 31–32).

2. For Augustine, the impatience and envy that he registers already among infants—even when their needs are satisfied—are symptoms of the imperfection and fallenness of humanity. The human dependence on necessities, such as food, is a reminder of not yet residing in the City of God. The difference between the biological dependence on nourishment and the moral vice of greed is, hence, one of gradation, not an absolute.

3. Kotzé argues that Augustine's *Confessions* address primarily a Manichean audience, concluding that its "communicative purpose" is to target "an already-converted Christian audience and (increasingly towards the end) a Manichean audience" (2004, 251).

4. Tears, for Augustine, can be markers of authenticity; so, for example, the intellectual pleasure of reading the "Platonist books" does not bring him to tears, because "those pages do not contain the face of this devotion, *tears of confession*, your sacrifice, a troubled spirit, a contrite and humble spirit . . . [and] the cup of redemption." In contrast, the "sacred writings of your Spirit and especially the apostle Paul" are healing and "had a visceral effect on me as I read the least of your apostles [Paul]. I meditated upon your works and trembled" (7.21.27; emphasis added).

5. For an excellent study on the emergence of new Christian ideals of manliness in late antiquity, see Kuefler (2001).

6. For a brief explanation of the anatomical basis of tears, see Lutz (1999, 67–72).

7. For context and full text of the confession, see Assaf (2006). Rabbi Yitzhak

Nahum Twersky (1888–1942) is part of the Chernobyl Hasidic dynasty. In his confessional letter, he loathes the Hasidic world and goes through great pains to explain how much he wants to escape it. Moseley's (2006) extensive study of East European Jewish autobiographies does not mention Twersky.

8. Culbertson has extensively published on religion and masculinity (1992, 1996, 2002, 2007).

9. Burrus inserts her autobiographical voice when interpreting Augustine: "Augustine bends God's ear but seeks his mother's eyes. Frequently they are overflowing with tears: he is the son of her tears, her ever-breaking maternal waters. . . . You [Burrus] too have the gift of tears, my friend tells me. . . . My son teases me about weeping at movies. (And I wonder when it was that he stopped crying)" (2004, 89–90).

10. Tambling draws a parallel between the pairs of Augustine/Monica and Rousseau/Mme Warens (1990, 25).

11. The word *virile* contains the Latin root *vir* (man). Miles actually translates the phrase as "masculine faith" (1992, 90).

12. "The ninth book, which opens with a reference to the mother as a 'handmaid' . . . closes with her death, which also finishes the narrative of the *Confessions*: perhaps suggesting that biography closes with the removal of everything literal and material, in favour of the spiritual and intellectual" (Tambling 1990, 26).

13. This issue has been frequently noted. Because of the richness of the text, one can read Augustine against Augustine, just as Freud has been read against Freud. "Augustine was well aware of—and frightened by—the unpredictability and volatility of interpretation" (Miles 1992, 13). See also Derrida's "circumfession," which is an "intentional misreading or mis-leading of Augustine, carrying [him] down paths that Augustine himself will not travel" (Caputo and Scanlon 2005, 4).

14. Burrus's exploration (2008) on tears and ridicule in Augustine's *Confessions* and other confessional performances in late antiquity came too late to my attention to integrate here.

15. The sayings of the desert fathers are taken from Benedicta Ward's translation of the Latin collection *Verba Seniorum*. For a short introduction to the textual sources and to questions of transmission, see Ward (2003, xxix–xxxiii); White (1998, xi–liii).

16. The mythic story of Narcissus and Echo—with Narcissus condemned to fall in love with the water's reflection of his own image—is retold in Ovid's *Metamorphoses* (Book 3).

17. All quotations from the sayings of the desert fathers in Ward (2003, 12–18).

18. For a comparative religious study on tears, see Patton and Hawley (2005).

19. The Greek *penthos* adopted by the patristic tradition refers to individual and liturgical expressions of a sorrow related to God, not to earthly losses. It is a "heartfelt sorrow, expressed by actual tears, or a desire to weep, which is generated by and expressive of the mystery of divine participation." It is "other-oriented" (rather than oriented toward oneself) and "constitutes a participation in the economy of salvation" (Hunt 2004, 3, 15). Compunction is a divinely caused pricking of the heart,

soul, or conscience—a wounding of God that awakens "the consciousness of sin" (16) and leads to the sorrow and grief of *penthos*. For the early Christian East, see Hunt (2004); for Western Christianity up to the seventeenth century, see Benke (2002).

20. *De Compunctione*, quoted in Hunt (2004, 16).

21. For a translation, see Russell (1980, 114–115). Regarding translation and interpretation, I am relying on Masterson (2006).

22. Quoted in Masterson (2006, 217). Masterson shows that such understated brevity was odd even to ancient readers. Within ten years, Rufinus's Latin translation of the Greek text begins to embellish the original: "When Paul had seen with his own eyes his wife having sex with another man, saying not a thing to anyone he left the house. Driven by heartsickness, he gave himself [to wander] into the desert, where, while he was wandering agitatedly, he came to Antony's monastery" (227).

23. Masterson pushes this argument further by reading such displacement as homosocial bonding and homosexual desire. "Viewing Paul's new life with Antony as a sort of replication of prior married life leads, then, to questions about desire . . . suggest[ing] that perception of homosexual desire is possible in ancient reception of this text" (2006, 219–220).

24. "Yet it is not the woman, arbitrarily rejected, involuntarily losing her husband of thirteen years and the child of her body, that readers are urged to sympathize with, but Augustine" (Miles 1992, 78; also 2008, 127–148).

25. In the same paragraph, he repeats (6.13.23): "Nevertheless, pressure for the marriage continued, and the girl who was asked for was almost two years under the age of marriage" [i.e., the girl's age could have been as young as ten years].

26. See Jostein Gaarder's *Vita Brevis* (1997) for an imaginative reconstruction of the concubine's voice. In "Not Nameless but Unnamed," Miles imagines possible names for her but concludes that we must "respect her 'namelessness,' acknowledging that her subjectivity is indeed lost to us, elided in Augustine's text" (2008, 131).

27. My translation from German.

28. "The gaps, voids, and silences within Augustine's sexual discourse both stimulate readers' imagination and frustrate their curiosity" (Miles 1992, 74). Compare Augustine's belaboring of the minor incident of pear stealing to Paul de Man's analysis of Rousseau's self-accusing confession of stealing a "pink and silver colored ribbon" (1979, 279; esp. chap. 12). The juvenile stealing of a pear or a ribbon does not amount to a crime or attest to moral depravity, but both Augustine and Rousseau negotiate larger issues. At stake is, in Augustine's case, the human condition and, for Rousseau, the social order of relationships. "Once it is removed from its legitimate owner, the ribbon, being in itself devoid of meaning and function, can circulate symbolically as a pure signifier and become the articulating hinge in a chain of exchanges and possession" (de Man 1979, 283).

29. Interview in *L'Express* (1961; quoted in Pilling 1981, 65); see also Leiris (1992, 107, 131). Brée remarks that Leiris's early marriage "into the well-established Kahnweiler family" as well as his "deep" attachment to his wife "destroy his wish to see himself as a convention-breaking rebel or the outcast" (1980, 195, note 3). "In

Manhood . . . we catch sight of his childhood and adolescent world . . . and of his abortive love affairs . . . [but] rarely do we get a glimpse of married life. . . . Therefore the absence of any allusions—except fleetingly—to the most intimate relations in his life" (196–197, 206).

Chapter 6

1. Compunction, the piercing of the heart, is also known in Jewish confessiographies, though not to the theological extent as in Christianity. Berdichevsky writes that in Judaism, "confession is the breaking of the heart and the reckoning of man with his heart and soul. . . . [It] is not an ethical, but a poetic imperative toward vital and actual self-revelation" (quoted in Moseley 2006, 110). Hasidic stories and hagiographies speak of pious men weeping in response to overwhelming grief or joy (for example, at the death of a master/Tsaddiq, or when experiencing God's presence).

2. From *De dono perseverantiae*, quoted in Miles (1992, 47). Brown indicates the year 428 for this work (1969, 378).

3. In a self-conscious, ironic reversal—typical of postmodernism—Derrida imagines the "billions of others" who, together with his mother, will *never know* his writings (1993, 232). Such nostalgic regret—couched in the language of realistic assessment—still hides a male confessant's desire to be widely known.

4. "I reproached [my mother] for leaving me in this world," Derrida writes (1993, 271), echoing a son's age-old biblical lament: "Woe is me, my mother, that you bore me" (Jer. 15:10).

5. To spoon off the honey from the desert ground is itself a form of displaced or sublimated eroticism, since honey stands for male sexual desire. "We may also interpret Paul's [the Simple] ability to overcome the adhesive qualities of honey as an ability to transmute desire in spite of itself into something else; Paul dissolves dusty dirty desire for a wife (and/or for Antony) into a cleanly adhesive and sweetly pure obedience in the context of sublime homosociality" (2006, 222). Gregory of Nazianzus praises male friendship as finer than gold and sweeter "than honey, and drippings of the honeycomb" (quoted in Culbertson 1996, 154).

6. The chapter opens with the memory of a summer in 1913, when young Pohl stumbles across graves of German sailors killed by an indigenous uprising on this island.

7. The objects in the bottom half may symbolize obedience toward the state (sword) and the Enlightenment readings of Nietzsche and Voltaire (books), both of which led Pohl astray. Like Augustine, who abandons the Platonist books and the violent powers of the empire, Pohl leaves those influences behind as he moves toward a new cosmic reality, toward the sun. This image might refer to Constantine's legendary conversion to Christianity when, before a decisive battle, he looked at the sun and saw a cross. Sun and stars, however, might also represent the symbolic universe of neo-paganism, to which many high-ranking Nazis had subscribed. Possibly, the sword might represent Constantine's sword and the books Pohl's new Bible readings, assisting him in his move toward a new reality. However we interpret the symbolism of the depicted objects, the precise content of this new reality remains undetermined.

8. Pohl's 1936 departure was part of the wave of Nazis leaving the churches; see Chapter 4, note 12.

9. Eleonore contributed similar drawings to an article on Pohl in the popular weekly magazine *Quick* (March 11, 1951; see Schmitz-Köster 2007, 190–191); Koch (1988) also identifies her as the illustrator.

10. See Schmitz-Köster (2007); for the *Lebensborn*, see Lilienthal (2003).

11. For a study on the complicity of women, esp. women married to men in the SS, see Gudrun Schwarz (1997).

12. Pohl (*Credo*, 21) also mentions his disenchantment with the Gospels after reading Ernest Renan's *Das Leben Jesu* (1863). Renan's book created a sensation in the late nineteenth century, presenting the Gospels as legend rather than historical accounts (see Heschel 1998, 154–158).

13. The church "for Augustine is overwhelmingly maternal. Like Monica her yearning is ever for her erring children and, like Monica, she seeks them patiently but inexorably . . . motivated by the desire to convert the prodigal" (Power 1996, 92).

14. In German: "Da öffnete ich mein Herz dem katholischen Gefängnispfarrer. Hatte dieser wortgewaltige Gottesmann bis dahin durch seine aufrüttelnden Predigten den verkrusteten Glaubensboden gelockert, so säte er nun den Samen göttlicher Offenbarung in das saatgierige Land. . . . [I]n gewaltigem Strom überflutete mich die Frohe Botschaft, wie sie die alleinseligmachende katholische Kirche lehrt."

15. Such triangular relationships are an essential element of homosociality; see Sedgwick (1985). "In the triangle of two men and a woman, the attraction between two men must be taken at least as seriously" as between man and woman (Culbertson 1996, 160).

16. *Lebensraum* was one of the key concepts of Nazi ideology, arguing that Germany deserved more living space, especially in the East.

17. This subject deserves a treatment of its own; other testimonial writings left by NS perpetrators, like Rudolf Höß, Hans Frank, and Robert Ley, reveal similar religious rhetoric.

18. Brandt was hanged in the Landsberg prison on June 2, 1948.

19. Reprinted in *Deutsche Hochschullehrer-Zeitung* (Jg. 10/1 [1962]: 5–9). All quotations related to Brandt's letters are from this source.

20. Letter dated April 6, 1947. The awkwardness of the translation mirrors the style of the original.

21. Lonitzer's sermon is reprinted in *Deutsche Hochschullehrer-Zeitung* (Jg. 10/1 [1962]: 5–9).

22. For preliminary arguments of such research in the case of postwar Germany, see Herzog (2005); Moeller (1993); Krondorfer (2006, 2008a); Fehrenbach (1998).

Chapter 7

1. "Stonewall" refers to the 1969 riots between gay people and police in New York City; the resistance of large numbers of people harassed by police launched the gay rights movement.

2. See Krondorfer (2009; esp. introduction). Greater public visibility of gay

discourse within religious scholarship does not necessarily translate into accept-ability of individual gay theologians, who continue to experience job discrimina-tion; for brief personal accounts of career difficulties, see Goss (2002, xiv); Com-stock (1993, 5); Clark (1990).

3. See Clark, *Toward an Unapologetic Gay Liberation Theology* (1989), and Com-stock, *Gay Theology Without Apology* (1993).

4. Long, who advocates a strong "indigenous" gay theology within the "gay ghetto," voices a sharp critique of Clark's "gay feminism" and Goss's "queer" label-ing of gay discourse (1997, 278–279). Clark (1993), in turn, is skeptical of the gay ghetto mentality. Regarding "minoritizing" discourse, see Frantzen (1996); Kron-dorfer (2007b).

5. On transgression, see Goss (2002, 223–238); Gorsline (1996, 131).

6. See, for example, Robert Lockwood of the Catholic League: in a Web-based review of Jordan's *The Silence of Sodom* (2000), he sneers at the "ugly stuff that speaks more of the path Jordan has taken in life and his obsessions, rather than any kind of an honest view"; it is a "book of opinion—outrageous opinion—based on little more than the author's own fantasy life" (July 2000, http://www.catholic league.org/rer.php?topic=Book+Reviews&id=30; retrieved July 2009). Elsewhere I argue that such antagonism stems from a (perceived) threat to heterosexual identity (Krondorfer 2007b).

7. Note that not all personal insertions are confessional, such as talking about one's publications, career choices, or job discrimination.

8. Published respectively in Krondorfer (1996) and Ellison and Thorson-Smith (2003).

9. Haldeman teaches worship, liturgy, and ritual at a leading U.S. theological seminary.

10. Haldeman is aware of the risks of "permeability," both in the immediate sense of the physical and emotional harm of anal intercourse as well as in its medi-ated form of cultural rejections. "Culturally considered, the anus is a place of dirt and discomfort. By allowing another person to approach this part of your body, you risk giving offense and being rejected as dirty, smelly, and ugly" (2003, 226).

11. Already Boswell had pointed to the irrationality of these fears and the con-tradictions of homophobic arguments (1980, esp. introduction). See also Bersani (1988).

12. "Confessional gay" scholarship, like Haldeman's essays, is very much contrary to testimonies of the so-called ex-gay movement. The latter tries to reconvert (that is, sexually reorient) homosexuals. Organizations and individuals belonging to the ex-gay movement often rely on "reparative therapy," also known as "conversion therapy," which is explicitly religious in orientation and motivation. Evidence of success often comes in the form of personal testimonials of ex-gay people. Infor-mation on this movement as well as on its critics (like the ex-ex-gay movement) is readily available on the Internet.

13. For medieval Christian theologians, "*luxuria* came to be seen as the source of sinfulness in diverse acts, many of them having to do with the genitals . . . rang[ing]

from masturbation through same-sex copulation, bestiality, openmouthed kissing, touching of the genitals of another, touching one's own genitals without ejaculation, to showing one's penis to another" (Jordan 1997, 29, 104).

14. My translation from the German: "Die Wüste bildet . . . ein leeres kosmisches Therapiezimmer [das] für die Inszenierung der Seele offensteht. Sie ist purer Projektionsraum, in dem die Selbst- und Gotteserfahrung . . . zum Auftauchen gebracht werden kann."

15. For the devotional practices of women mystics, see Bynum (1987).

16. On the confessional/penitential literature regarding masturbation in the (late) Middle Ages, esp. Gerson's contribution, see Laqueur (2003, 160–161); Tentler (1977); McGuire (1996). Also see Jordan (1997, 46–47, 60, 102–106, 145), who mentions that *mollitia* (softness) was seen as a sexual act against nature and that "the monster of masturbation" was variously described as "the worst kind of incest" (102, 105). For general information on penitentials, see Payer (1984); Bossy (1975). See note 13.

17. For these and other terms, see Laqueur (2003; on Freud, 73, 360; on Voltaire, 42; on Rousseau, 235–236, 291).

18. Rousseau completed his *Confessions* "only a few years after the Swiss doctor, Samuel-Auguste-André-David Tissot, himself known to Rousseau," had published in 1758 *L'Onanisme*, itself based on an earlier eighteenth-century work by a cleric and medical quack, *Onania, or the heinous sin of self-pollution, and all its frightful consequences, in both sexes, considered* (Tambling 1990, 108; also Laqueur 2003, esp. chaps. 1, 3). Laqueur dates the publication of *Onania* to 1712. There is a general consensus that Tissot's work supplanted the earlier theological discourse on masturbation with medical discourse (see Tambling 1990, 108).

19. The privacy of the reading experience—the reading of books in solitude—gives birth to and produces "masturbatory fantasies," which, then, in turn, leads in the seventeenth century to Puritan confessional literature on masturbation (see Tambling 1990, 96–97). In literary studies, much is made of the moment of private reading between Paolo and Francesca in Dante's *Divine Comedy* (1321), indicating a change in the understanding of self and confessions; see Senior (1994); for a brief reference, also Tambling (1990, 96).

20. Virtual pornography, as a new addiction enjoyed predominantly by men, has potentially large-scale social consequences. Therapists see an increase in young men who have become incapable of engaging in actual relationships with intimate others because of their masturbatory practices in response to omnipresent pornographic Internet sites (personal conversation with Yvonne Maurer, director of therapy center in Zurich, May 2008).

21. Voltaire's anticlericalism, according to Laqueur, led him to blame "clerical celibacy" for "unnatural pleasures," such as masturbation. "[L]ike most of those who helped to invent modern masturbation," Laqueur concludes, Voltaire "cared about autoerotic sexuality because it was at odds with social and moral life as it ought to be lived" (2003, 42). See also Moseley (2006, 6): "Of primary significance, as has frequently been noted, is Rousseau's desacralisation of the religious confessional."

22. Rousseau's "dangerous supplement" is his autoerotic experience, which is practiced with anguish; see Derrida (1988); Laqueur (2003, 235–236, 291); Tambling (1990, 109). Moseley briefly mentions "dangerous supplement" (i.e., masturbation) in "Hebrew autobiographical discourse" (2006, 26). Marcus relates Rousseau's "dangerous supplement" to the act of writing itself (1994, 197).

23. Coming-out stories "end in the author's decision to make a (more or less) public declaration of his homosexuality. In this regard they are entirely typical of the flood of American gay autobiographies written in the last decade. They invite comparison with the conversion narratives that figure so prominently in the Western cultural tradition, from St. Augustine to Malcolm X" (Robinson 1999, xix). Gay religious studies scholars explicitly connect the gay coming-out experience to religious conversion; see Goss (2002, 19); Long (1997, 273–274). For samples of religious coming-out stories, see Bouldrey (1995); Schallenberger (1998).

24. One can, of course, read this transition more unfavorably, suggesting that Haldeman's liberal attitude toward solitary sex led him to become gay. Such a conclusion I leave to the homophobic mind.

25. I have already cited this passage by Augustine (10.4.6) at the end of Chapter 2.

26. Catholic and Protestant gay theologians, despite sharing similarities, differ in how they name their religious universe and their particular struggles. For openly gay Catholic theologians, see, for example, Goss (2002, esp. preface and chap. 1); Jordan (1997, ix, 2000, 2003). For Protestant gay theologians, see, for example, the works of Clark (1989, 1992); Comstock (1993).

27. "I have taken a look at a small selection of Catholic saints, and tried to read them as one might an encoded historical or ethnographic text, teasing the queer elements from the text, trying to 'read out,' or rather 'read in,' same-sex desire and affinity. I have argued that this process of 'unpeeling' is both advantageous and necessary" (Boisvert 2004, 201).

28. Devoting each chapter to one or two male saints, Boisvert introduces and reflects on such figures as the archangel Michael, Saint Sebastian, Paul and Augustine, Francis of Assisi, Damien and Peter Julian Eymard. One chapter is devoted to the "erotic Christ." In two concluding chapters he reflects more broadly on how to understand saints in a secularized, modern world and how to affirm gay male sanctity today.

29. On contemporary representations and images of the ideal male physique, see Dutton (1995); Doty (1996); Davis (1991); Lingis (1994); Halperin (1995, 115–119).

30. For a critique of both heteronormative and homonormative theologies, see Goss (2002, 228–229).

31. This is a deliberate reference to, and reversal of, Dutton's *The Perfectible Body* (1995).

32. "Our same-sex desire is ultimately the measure of our place in the world, and . . . this is a grand and noble thing. We are the creatures of a homoerotic god . . . [and] it calls forth authentic commitment and devotion in the cause of the holy, of the most perfectly and universally masculine" (Boisvert 2000b, 16).

33. Compare, for example, Castelli's approach to "martyrdom as a form of culture making" (2004, 4). Hers is not a confessional text, but she embeds her sophisticated argument in an autobiographical framework. Reflecting on gendered differences between boys and girls during their confirmation when adopting names of saints, she writes: "After all, the selection of one's saint was [for us girls] not a matter of locating someone whose story was decidedly similar to one's own. The saints' lives were not *our* lives; indeed, their *differences* were precisely the point" (3; emphasis in original).

34. "What I want is to produce a discursive catachresis, not a quick fix by a halakhic committee but a new thing in the world, the horizon of possibility for a militant, feminist, nonhomophobic, traditionalist—Orthodox—Judaism . . . in a world of memory, intimacy, and connectedness, a pleasure that I call *Jewissance*" (Boyarin 1997, xxiii).

35. Whether or not Boisvert is aware of the pornographic gaze, he certainly abstains from directly engaging the issue. Since he works with the rhetoric of experience, one can fault him for not showing all his cards.

36. See, for example, Garry Wills, "God in the Hands of Angry Sinners," *New York Review* (April 8, 2004): 68–74. For Gibson's inspiration by the German Catholic visionary Anna Katharina Emmerich (1774–1824), see Will Winkler, "Mad Man im Münsterland" (*Süddeutsche Zeitung*, Wochenend-Ausgabe, March 20, 2004); also Emmerich (2006); for scholarly criticism of Gibson's film, see Fredriksen (2006); Plate (2004); *Perspectives on the Passion of the Christ* (2004).

37. Elsewhere, I am developing a fuller argument of remasculinization (Krondorfer 2004b). On remasculinization and modern Christian men's movements, see Hall (1994); Kirkley (1996); Lippy (1997); Gill (1999, 2000); Kimmel (1996, 175–181); Culbertson (2007); Krondorfer (2008b).

38. Wills, "God in the Hands of Angry Sinners," 68.

39. The Grand Guignol tradition refers to forms of graphic horror entertainment. The name comes from the Grand Guignol (1897–1962) theater in Paris, which staged naturalistic horror shows (see Gordon 1997). The "male rampage film" is a subgenre of the action adventure film. I owe much of this information to Robin Bates. Perhaps a good label for the *The Passion of the Christ* would be "male humiliation, Grand Guignol Jesus film."

40. "I gladly confess that I have done all this with the firm intention of causing trouble: not to myself or to others, mind you, but to a hagiographic tradition that remains deaf to the bothersome complexities of human lives, ours and those of the saints themselves" (Boisvert 2004, 201).

41. "Radical orthodoxy" is a fairly recent, U.K.-based theological movement that is, in some ways, a crossing of Karl Barth and Jacques Lacan. It describes itself as a "theological project made possible by the self-conscious superficiality of today's secularism" and wants to "visit sites in which secularism has heavily invested—aesthetics, politics, sex, the body, personhood, visibility, space." It is strongly philosophical in outlook: "Where Barthianism can tend to the ploddingly exegetical, radical orthodoxy mingles exegesis, cultural reflection and philosophy in a complex but coherently executed *collage*" (Milbank, Pickstock, and Ward 1999, 1–2).

Routledge is publishing a series on radical orthodoxy, and there is already a critical rejoinder (Hankey and Hedley 2005).

42. In fairness, it needs to be said that the statements of Goss and Gorsline are retrospective reminiscences that do not reflect their current attitude. Gorsline is explicit about abandoning his earlier erotic imagination: "What is clear to me today is that there is no gay Christ but a queer Jesus—that is, a man who liked men and women sensually and who acted contrary to the gender, racial, and religious norms of his day" (1996, 136). Similar to Haldeman on gender justice, Gorsline reflects on the crucified body—his "homoeroticized gaze" toward images of Jesus—in order to encourage "fundamental social change. . . . I hope that the reappreciation of images of the embodied Jesus can help end violence among men" (126).

43. "And just how is it *radical*? Radical, first of all, in the sense of a return to patristic and medieval roots, and especially to the Augustinian vision of all knowledge as divine illumination. . . . Radical, second, in the sense of seeking to deploy this recovered vision systematically to criticize modern society, culture, politics, art, science and philosophy with an unprecedented boldness. . . . Underpinning, therefore, is the idea that every discipline must be framed by a theological perspective; otherwise these disciplines will define a zone apart from God, grounded literally in nothing" (Milbank, Pickstock, and Ward 1999, 2–3).

44. His theological simplification is also evidenced in the slippery use of the terms "Jesus" and "Christ." For example, the title "The Erotic *Christ*" does not reflect the chapter's almost exclusive focus on the body of *Jesus*. Whether and how Boisvert sees a difference between the Jesus in the Gospels and the post-ascension Christ of the developing church is not discussed. In his defense, one can argue that he adopts a mystical approach, like the medieval women mystics, wherein differences between Jesus as a companion and Christ as a sacramental reality are blurred and reconciled in ecstatic visions and devotional practices. Boisvert does not explicate these issues theoretically and hermeneutically.

45. On this central point, Ward can be criticized for reintroducing a supersessionist Christianity, since his displacement theology de-Judaizes Christianity in order to claim universality.

Chapter 8

1. Coles writes these words in the context of appraising Augustine's outlook on himself and the world. "We might attempt to read Augustine's errors *in a tragic mode* as the errors of a human being who, like all of us, submerged in the depths of being, could comprehend only a fraction of the proliferating strengths, weaknesses and meanings of his work. We live and write on the tip of an iceberg" (1992, 176). See also Ross-Bryant who—building upon Lyotard's insight that "men in all their claims to construct meaning, to speak the truth, are themselves only a patchwork"—sees multiplicity "at the heart of feminist models of autobiography" (1997, 86).

2. Regarding "remasculinization" in postwar Germany, see Chapter 6, note 22; in modern Christian men's movements, see Chapter 7, note 37; in religious fundamentalism, see Riesebrodt (1998, 2001).

3. Kuefler (2001) has demonstrated this for Christianity in late antiquity.

4. "Augustine is a penetrating critic of [Roman] imperialism, but he is perhaps implicated in an imperialism of his own . . . engender[ing] the increasing and ultimately singular hegemony of his Word in the future. . . . We know what this meant for the Donatists, Pelagians—and the pagans" (Coles 1992, 48, 52); see also E. Clark (2005). On Augustine and coercion, see Brown (1963, 1964).

References

Adak, Hülya. 2007. "Identifying the 'Internal Tumors' of World War I: Talat Pasa'nin Hatiralari [Tale Pasa's Memoirs], or the Travels of a Unionist Apologia into 'History.'" In *Räume des Selbst: Selbstzeugnisforschung transkulturell*, ed. Andreas Bähr, Peter Burschel, and Gabriele Jancke, 151–169. Cologne: Böhlau.

Adams, Rachel, and David Savran, eds. 2002. *The Masculinity Studies Reader*. Malden, U.K.: Blackwell.

Allen, Michael Thad. 2000. "Oswald Pohl: Chef der SS-Wirtschaftsunternehmen." In *Die SS-Elite unter dem Totenkopf: 30 Lebensläufe*, 394–407. Paderborn: Ferdinand Schöninger.

———. 2002. *The Business of Genocide: The SS, Slave Labor, and the Concentration Camps*. Chapel Hill: University of North Carolina Press.

Anderson, Benedict. 1983. *Imagined Communities*. London: Verso.

Anderson, Janice Capel, and Jeffrey L. Staley, eds. 1995. *Taking It Personally: Autobiographical Biblical Criticism*. Semeia 72. Atlanta, Ga.: Scholars Press.

Apel, Dora. 2002. *Memory Effects: The Holocaust and the Art of Secondary Witnessing*. New Brunswick, N.J.: Rutgers University Press.

Artaud, Antonin. 1958. *The Theatre and Its Double*. Trans. Mary Caroline Richards. New York: Grove Press.

Asher, Lyell. 1998. "The Dangerous Fruit of Augustine's *Confessions*." *Journal of the American Academy of Religion* 66/2 (Summer): 227–255.

Assaf, David. 2006. "'My Tiny, Ugly World': The Confession of Rabbi Yitzhak Nahum Twersky of Shpikov." *Contemporary Jewry* 26:1–34.

Athanasius. 1980. *The Life of Antony and the Letter to Marcellus*. Trans. Robert C. Gregg. New York: Paulist Press.

Augustine. 1992. *Confessions*. Trans. Henry Chadwick. Oxford: Oxford University Press.

Autsch, Sabiene. 2000. "Haltung und Generation: Überlegungen zu einem intermedialen Konzept." *Bios: Zeitschrift für Biographieforschung und Oral History* 13/2:163–180.

Barris, Chuck. 2002. *Confessions of a Dangerous Mind*. New York: Miramax.

Benke, Christoph. 2002. *Die Gabe der Tränen: Zur Tradition und Theologie eines vergessenen Kapitels der Glaubensgeschichte*. Würzburg: Echter.

Benthien, Claudia, and Inge Stephan, eds. 2003. *Männlichkeit als Maskerade: Kulturelle Inszenierungen vom Mittelalter bis zur Gegenwart*. Cologne: Böhlau.

Bergen, Doris L. 1996. *Twisted Cross: The German Christian Movement in the Third Reich*. Chapel Hill: University of North Carolina Press.

Bersani, Leo. 1988. "Is the Rectum a Grave?" In *AIDS: Cultural Analysis, Cultural Activism*, ed. Douglas Crimp, 197–222. Cambridge, Mass.: MIT Press.

Blaschke, Olaf. 2008. "Fältmarskalk Jesus Kristus: Religiös remaskulinisering i Tyskland." In *Kristen manlighet: Män och religion i en nordeuropeisk kontext 1840 till 1940*, ed. Yvonne Maria Werner, 23–50. Lund: Nordic Academic Press.

Bly, Robert. 1990. *Iron John: A Book About Men*. New York: Addison-Wesley.

Boisvert, Donald L. 2000a. *Out on Holy Ground: Meditations on Gay Men's Spirituality*. Cleveland, Ohio: Pilgrim.

———. 2000b. "Men, Muscles and Zombies: A Partial Response to Michelangelo Signorile." *Theology and Sexuality* 16 (March): 9–20.

———. 2004. *Sanctity and Male Desire: A Gay Reading of Male Saints*. Cleveland, Ohio: Pilgrim.

———. 2006. "Talking Dirty About the Saints: Storytelling and the Politics of Desire." *Theology and Sexuality* 12/2:165–180.

Bordo, Susan. 1993. "Reading the Male Body." *Michigan Quarterly Review* 32 (Fall): 696–737.

Bossy, John. 1975. "The Social History of Confession." *Transactions of the Royal Historical Society* 25:21–38.

Boswell, John. 1980. *Christianity, Social Tolerance, and Homosexuality: Gay People in Western Europe from the Beginning of the Christian Era to the Fourteenth Century*. Chicago: University of Chicago Press.

Bouldrey, Brian, ed. 1995. *Wrestling with the Angel: Faith and Religion in the Lives of Gay Men*. New York: Riverhead.

Bourdieu, Pierre. 2001. *Masculine Domination*. Stanford, Calif.: Stanford University Press. First published in French 1998.

Boyarin, Daniel. 1997. *The Rise of Heterosexuality and the Invention of the Jewish Man*. Berkeley: University of California Press.

Boyd, Stephen B. 1995. *The Men We Long to Be: Beyond Domination to a New Christian Understanding of Manhood*. San Francisco: HarperCollins.

Boyd, Stephen B., W. Merle Longwood, and Mark W. Muesse, eds. 1996. *Redeeming Men: Religion and Masculinities*. Louisville, Ky.: Westminster John Knox.

Brakke, David. 1995. "The Problematization of Nocturnal Emissions in Early Christian Syria, Egypt, and Gaul." *Journal of Early Christian Studies* 3/4:419–460.

Brée, Germaine. 1980. "Michel Leiris: Mazemaker." In *Autobiography: Essays Theoretical and Critical*, ed. James Olney, 194–206. Princeton, N.J.: Princeton University Press.

Brenner, Rachel Feldhay. 1997. *Writing as Resistance: Four Women Confronting the Holocaust*. University Park: Pennsylvania State University Press.

Breyfogle, Todd. 2003. "Book Three: 'No Changing nor Shadow.'" In *A Reader's*

Companion to Augustine's "Confessions," ed. Kim Paffenroth and Robert P. Kennedy, 35–52. Louisville, Ky.: Westminster John Knox.

Brod, Harry, ed. 1987. *The Making of Masculinities: The New Men's Studies.* London: Routledge.

Brod, Harry, and Michael Kaufman, eds. 1994. *Theorizing Masculinities.* Thousand Oaks, Calif.: Sage.

Brooks, Peter. 2000. *Troubling Confessions: Speaking Guilt in Law and Literature.* Chicago: University of Chicago Press.

Broughton, James. 1977. *The Androgyne Journal.* Oakland, Calif.: Scrimshaw Press.

Brown, Peter. 1963. "Religious Coercion in the Later Roman Empire: The Case of North Africa." *History* 48:283–305.

———. 1964. "St. Augustine's Attitude to Religious Coercion." *The Journal of Roman Studies* 54:107–116.

———. 1969. *Augustine of Hippo.* Berkeley: University of California Press.

———. 1988. *The Body and Society: Men, Women and Sexual Renunciation in Early Christianity.* New York: Columbia University Press.

Bruner, Jerome. 1993. "The Autobiographical Process." In *The Culture of Autobiography: Constructions of Self-Representation*, ed. Robert Folkenflik, 38–56. Stanford, Calif.: Stanford University Press.

Buchholz, Petra. 2003. *Schreiben und Erinnern: Über Selbstzeugnisse japanischer Kriegsteilnehmer.* Munich: Iudicium.

———. 2007. "Geständnisse japanischer Kriegsgefangener im geschlossenen Raum: Einsicht unter Zwang." In *Räume des Selbst: Selbstzeugnisforschung transkulturell*, ed. Andreas Bähr, Peter Burschel, and Gabriele Jancke, 197–216. Cologne: Böhlau.

Burrus, Virginia. 2004. *The Sex Lives of Saints: An Erotics of Ancient Hagiography.* Philadelphia: University of Pennsylvania Press.

———. 2008. *Saving Shame: Martyrs, Saints, and Other Abject Subjects.* Philadelphia: University of Pennsylvania Press.

Buscher, Frank M. 1989. *The U.S. War Crimes Trial Program in Germany, 1946–1955.* New York: Greenwood Press.

Butler, Judith. 1990. *Gender Trouble: Feminism and the Subversion of Identity.* New York: Routledge.

———. 1993. *Bodies That Matter: On the Discursive Limits of "Sex."* New York: Routledge.

Bynum, Caroline Walker. 1987. *Holy Feast, Holy Fast: The Religious Significance of Food to Medieval Women.* Berkeley: University of California Press.

Capps, Donald. 1997. *Men, Religion, and Melancholia: James, Otto, Jung, and Erikson.* New Haven, Conn.: Yale University Press.

———. 2003. "From Masturbation to Homosexuality: A Case of Displaced Moral Disapproval." *Pastoral Psychology* 51/4 (March): 249–272.

Capps, Donald, and James E. Dittes, eds. 1990. *The Hunger of the Heart: Reflections on the "Confessions" of Augustine.* West Lafayette, Ind.: Society for the Scientific Study of Religion, Monograph Series 8.

Caputo, John D. 1997. *The Prayers and Tears of Jacques Derrida: Religion Without Religion*. Bloomington: Indiana University Press.

Caputo, John D., and Michael J. Scanlon, eds. 2005. *Augustine and Postmodernism: Confessions and Circumfession*. Bloomington: Indiana University Press.

Card, Claudia. 2002. *The Atrocity Paradigm: A Theory of Evil*. Oxford: Oxford University Press.

Carrigan, Henry. 1991. "Shit, God, and Kitsch: The Role of the Body in Milan Kundera's *The Unbearable Lightness of Being*." Paper presented at the American Academy of Religion, November, Kansas City.

Castelli, Elizabeth A. 2004. *Martyrdom and Memory: Early Christian Culture Making*. New York: Columbia University Press.

Chambers, Ross. 1998. *Facing It: AIDS Diaries and the Death of the Author*. Ann Arbor: University of Michigan Press.

Cioran, E. M. 1988. *Von Tränen und von Heiligen*. Trans. from French by Verena von der Heyden-Rynsch. Frankfurt: Suhrkamp. Original appeared 1937 in Bucharest. English edition: 1995. *Tears and Saints*. Trans. Ilinca Zarifopol-Johnston. Chicago: University of Chicago Press.

Clark, Elizabeth A. 2005. "On Not Retracting the Unconfessed." In *Augustine and Postmodernism*, ed. John D. Caputo and Michael J. Scanlon, 222–243. Bloomington: Indiana University Press.

Clark, J. Michael. 1989. *A Place to Start: Toward an Unapologetic Gay Liberation Theology*. Dallas, Tex.: Monument Press.

———. 1990. *Diary of a Southern Queen: An HIV+ Vision Quest*. Dallas, Tex.: Monument Press.

———. 1992. *Masculine Socialization and Gay Liberation: A Conversation on the Work of James Nelson and Other Wise Friends*. Arlington, Tex.: The Liberal Press.

———. 1993. *Beyond Our Ghettos: Gay Theology in Ecological Perspective*. Cleveland, Ohio: Pilgrim.

———. 1994. "Men's Studies, Feminist Theology, and Gay Male Sexuality." In *Sexuality and the Sacred: Sources for Theological Reflection*, ed. James B. Nelson and Sandra P. Longfellow, 216–228. Louisville, Ky.: Westminster John Knox.

———. 1997. "Doing the Work of Love: I. Men's Studies at the Margins." *The Journal of Men's Studies* 5/4 (May): 315–331.

Clatterbaugh, Kenneth. 1990. *Contemporary Perspectives on Masculinity: Men, Women, and Politics in Modern Society*. Boulder, Colo.: Westview Press.

Coles, Romand. 1992. *Self/Power/Other: Political Theory and Dialogical Ethics*. Ithaca, N.Y.: Cornell University Press.

Comstock, Gary David. 1993. *Gay Theology Without Apology*. Cleveland, Ohio: Pilgrim.

Connell, Robert W. 1995. *Masculinities*. Berkeley: University of California Press.

Corber, Robert, and Stephen Valocchi, eds. 2003. *Queer Studies: An Interdisciplinary Reader*. Malden, U.K.: Blackwell.

Corrington, Gail Patterson. 1989. "The Milk of Salvation: Redemption by the

Mothers in Late Antiquity and Early Christianity." *Harvard Theological Review* 82/4:393–420.

Couser, Thomas G. 1979. *American Autobiography*. Amherst: University of Massachusetts Press.

Culbertson, Philip L. 1992. *New Adam: The Future of Male Spirituality*. Minneapolis, Minn.: Augsburg Fortress.

————. 1996. "Men and Christian Friendship." In *Men's Bodies, Men's Gods*, ed. Björn Krondorfer, 149–180. New York: New York University Press.

————. 1998. "Designing Men: Reading the Male Body as Text." *The Journal of Textual Reasoning* 7/1. Available at http://etext.virginia.edu/journals/tr/archive/volume7.

————. 2002. *The Spirituality of Men: 16 Christians Write About Their Faith*. Minneapolis, Minn.: Augsburg Fortress.

————. 2006. "Mothers and Their Golden Sons: Exploring a Theology of Narcissism." In *Religion and Sexuality: Passionate Debates*, ed. C. K. Robertson, 209–238. New York: Peter Lang.

————. 2007. "Christian Men's Movements." In *International Encyclopedia of Men and Masculinities*, ed. M. Flood, J. K. Gardiner, B. Pease, and K. Pringle, 65–67. London: Routledge.

Danner, Mark. 2004. *Torture and Truth: America, Abu Graib, and the War on Terror*. New York: New York Review of Books.

Davis, Melody. 1991. *The Male Nude in Contemporary Photography*. Philadelphia: Temple University Press.

Deak, Istvan. 1997. "Memories of Hell." *The New York Review* (June 26): 38–43.

de Man, Paul. 1979. *Allegories of Reading: Figural Language in Rousseau, Nietzsche, Rilke, and Proust*. New Haven, Conn.: Yale University Press.

Dent, N. J. H. 1992. *A Rousseau Dictionary*. Oxford: Blackwell.

Derrida, Jacques. 1988. ". . . That Dangerous Supplement . . ." In *Jean-Jacques Rousseau*, Modern Critical Views, ed. Harold Bloom, 39–64. New York: Chelsea House Publishers.

————. 1993. "Circumfession." In *Jacques Derrida*, by Geoffrey Bennington and Jacques Derrida, 3–315. Chicago: Chicago University Press.

————. 2005. "Composing 'Circumfession.'" In *Augustine and Postmodernism*, ed. John D. Caputo and Michael J. Scanlon, 19–27. Bloomington: Indiana University Press.

Doty, William G. 1996. "Baring the Flesh: Aspects of Contemporary Male Iconography." In *Men's Bodies, Men's Gods*, ed. Björn Krondorfer, 267–308. New York: New York University Press.

Driscoll, Michael S. 1996. "Penance in Transition: Popular Piety and Practice." In *Medieval Liturgy*, ed. Lizette Larson-Miller, 121–163. New York: Garland.

Driver, Tom F. 1977. *Patterns of Grace: Human Experience as Word of God*. San Francisco: Harper and Row.

Dutton, Kenneth. 1995. *The Perfectible Body: The Western Ideal of Male Physical Development*. New York: Continuum.

Eilberg-Schwartz, Howard. 1990. *The Savage in Judaism: An Anthropology of Israelite Religion and Ancient Judaism*. Bloomington: Indiana University Press.

———. 1994. *God's Phallus and Other Problems for Men and Monotheism*. Boston: Beacon Press.

Ellison, Marvin M., and Sylvia Thorson-Smith, eds. 2003. *Body and Soul: Rethinking Sexuality as Justice-Love*, ed. Marvin M. Ellison. Cleveland, Ohio: Pilgrim.

Emmerich, Anne Catherine. 2006. *The Dolorous Passion of Our Lord Jesus Christ*. Trans. Clemens Maria Bretano. With an introduction by E. Ann Matter. New York: Barnes and Noble.

Enterline, Lynn. 1995. *The Tears of Narcissus: Melancholia and Masculinity in Early Modern Writing*. Stanford, Calif.: Stanford University Press.

Erikson, Erik. 1962. *Young Man Luther: A Study in Psychoanalysis and History*. New York: W. W. Norton.

Ezrahi, Sidra DeKoven. 1980. *By Words Alone: The Holocaust in Literature*. Chicago: University of Chicago Press.

Fasching, Darrell J. 1992. *Narrative Theology After Auschwitz: From Alienation to Ethics*. Minneapolis, Minn.: Fortress Press.

Fehrenbach, Heike. 1998. "Rehabilitating Fatherland: Race and German Remasculinization." *Signs: Journal of Women in Culture and Society* 24/1:107–127.

Felman, Shoshana. 1993. *What Does a Woman Want? Reading and Sexual Difference*. Baltimore: Johns Hopkins University Press.

Ferrari, Leo C. 1977. "The Theme of the Prodigal Son in Augustine's *Confessions*." *Recherches Augustiniennes* 12:105–118.

Flannery, Edward. 1965. *Anguish of the Jews*. New York: Macmillan.

Folkenflik, Robert, ed. 1993. *The Culture of Autobiography: Constructions of Self-Representation*. Stanford, Calif.: Stanford University Press.

Foster, Dennis A. 1987. *Confession and Complicity in Narrative*. Cambridge: Cambridge University Press.

Foucault, Michel. 1973. *The Order of Things: An Archeology of the Human Sciences*. New York: Random House. First published 1966. *Les Mots et les choses: Une archéologie des sciences humaines*. Paris: Gallimard.

———. 1989. "Friendship as a Way of Life." In *Foucault Live: Interviews 1966–84*, ed. Sylvere Lotringer, trans. John Johnston, 203–209. New York: Semiotext(e).

———. 1990. *The History of Sexuality: An Introduction*. Vol. 1. New York: Vintage Books. First English publication 1978.

———. 1999. "The Battle for Chastity." In *Religion and Culture*, ed. and selected by Jeremy R. Carrette, trans. Anthony Forster, 188–197. New York: Routledge. First published in France 1982.

Frantzen, Alan. 1996. "Between the Lines: Queer Theory, the History of Homosexuality, and Anglo-Saxon Penitentials." *The Journal of Medieval and Early Modern Studies* 26/2 (Spring): 255–296.

Fredriksen, Paula, ed. 2006. *On "The Passion of the Christ": Exploring the Issues Raised by the Controversial Movie*. Berkeley: University of California Press.

Frei, Norbert. 1999. *Vergangenheitspolitik: Die Anfänge der Bundesrepublik und die NS-Vergangenheit.* Munich: Deutscher Taschenbuch Verlag.

Freud, Sigmund. [1900] 1958. *The Interpretation of Dreams.* In *The Standard Edition of the Complete Psychological Works,* vol. 4 (reprinted with corrections), trans. and general ed. James Strachey. London: Hogarth Press.

———. [1926] 1959. *The Question of Lay Analysis: Conversations with an Impartial Person.* In *The Standard Edition of the Complete Psychological Works,* vol. 20, trans. and general ed. James Strachey. London: Hogarth Press.

Friedrich, Jörg. 1994. *Die kalte Amnestie.* Munich: Piper Verlag.

Frye, Northrop. 1957. *Anatomy of Criticism.* Princeton, N.J.: Princeton University Press.

Fussel, Samuel. 1991. *Muscle: Confessions of an Unlikely Bodybuilder.* New York: Avon Books.

Gaarder, Jostein. 1997. *Vita Brevis: A Letter to St. Augustine.* Trans. Anne Born. London: Phoenix.

Gabriel, Karl. 1993. "Die Katholiken in den 50er Jahren: Restauration, Modernisierung und beginnende Auflösung eines konfessionellen Milieus." In *Modernisierung im Wiederaufbau: Die westdeutsche Gesellschaft der 50er Jahre,* ed. Axel Schildt and Arnold Sywottek, 418–432. Bonn: Dietz.

Gallagher, Susan V. 2002. *Truth and Reconciliation: The Confessional Mode in South African Literature.* Portsmouth, N.H.: Heinemann.

Gammel, Irene. 1999. *Confessional Politics: Women's Sexual Self-Representations in Life Writing and Popular Media.* Carbondale: Southern Illinois University Press.

Gardiner, Judith Kegan, ed. 2002. *Masculinity Studies & Feminist Theory: New Directions.* New York: Columbia University Press.

Gerzon, Mark. 1982. *A Choice of Heroes.* New York: Houghton Mifflin.

Gill, Jo, ed. 2006. *Modern Confessional Writing: New Critical Essays.* London: Routledge.

Gill, Sean. 1999. "Christian Manliness Unmanned: Some Problems and Challenges in the Study of Masculinity and Religion in Nineteenth- and Twentieth-Century Western Society." In *Is There a Future for Feminist Theology?* ed. Deborah F. Sawyer and Diane M. Collier, 160–172. Sheffield, U.K.: Sheffield Academic Press.

———. 2000. "*Ecce Homo*: Representations of Christ as the Model of Masculinity in Victorian Art and Lives of Jesus." In *Masculinity and Spirituality in Victorian Culture,* ed. Andrew Bradstock et al., 164–178. New York: St. Martin's Press.

Giordano, Ralph. 1990. *Die zweite Schuld oder Von der Last Deutscher zu sein.* Munich: Knaur.

Glucklich, Ariel. 2001. *Sacred Pain: Hurting the Body for the Sake of the Soul.* Oxford: Oxford University Press.

Gordon, Mel. 1997. *The Grand Guignol: Theatre of Fear and Terror.* Cambridge, Mass.: Da Capo Press.

Gorsline, Robin Hawley. 1996. "Facing the Body on the Cross: A Gay Man's

Reflections on Passion and Crucifixion." In *Men's Bodies, Men's Gods*, ed. Björn Krondorfer, 125–145. New York: New York University Press.

Goss, Robert E. 2002. *Queering Christ: Beyond Jesus Acted Up*. Cleveland, Ohio: Pilgrim.

Green, Arthur. 1979. *Tormented Master: A Life of Rabbi Nahman Bratslav*. University, Ala.: University of Alabama Press.

Greschat, Martin. 1990. "'Rechristianisierung' und 'Säkularisierung': Anmerkungen zu einem europäischen interkonfessionellen Interpretationsmodell." In *Christentum und politische Verantwortung: Kirchen im Nachkriegsdeutschland*, ed. Jochen-Christoph Kaiser and Anselm Doering-Manteuffel, 1–24. Stuttgart: Kohlhammer.

Griffith, R. Marie. 2004. *Born Again Bodies: Flesh and Spirit in American Christianity*. California Studies in Food and Culture, 12. Berkeley: University of California Press.

Grimsley, Ronald. 1968. *Rousseau and the Religious Quest*. Oxford: Clarendon Press.

Grotowski, Jerzy. 1969. *Towards a Poor Theatre*. New York: Simon and Schuster.

Gusdorf, Georges. 1980. "Conditions and Limits of Autobiography." In *Autobiography: Essays Theoretical and Critical*, ed. James Olney, 28–48. Princeton, N.J.: Princeton University Press.

Haldeman, Scott. 1996. "Bringing Good News to the Body: Masturbation and Male Identity." In *Men's Bodies, Men's Gods*, ed. Björn Krondorfer, 111–124. New York: New York University Press.

———. 2003. "Receptivity and Revelation: A Spirituality of Gay Male Sex." In *Body and Soul: Rethinking Sexuality as Justice-Love*, ed. Marvin M. Ellison and Sylvia Thorson-Smith, 218–231. Cleveland, Ohio: Pilgrim.

Hall, Donald, ed. 1994. *Muscular Christianity: Embodying the Victorian Age*. Cambridge: Cambridge University Press.

Halperin, David M. 1995. *Saint Foucault: Towards a Gay Hagiography*. Oxford: Oxford University Press.

Hankey, Wayne J., and Douglas Hedley, eds. 2005. *Deconstructing Radical Orthodoxy: Postmodern Theology, Rhetoric and Truth*. Aldershot, U.K.: Ashgate.

Hartle, Ann. 1983. *The Modern Self in Rousseau's "Confessions": A Reply to St. Augustine*. Notre Dame, Ind.: University of Notre Dame Press.

Hawkins, Anne Hunsaker. 1990. "St. Augustine: Archetypes of Family." In *The Hunger of the Heart: Reflections on the "Confessions" of Augustine*, ed. Donald Capps and James E. Dittes, 237–254. West Lafayette, Ind.: Society for the Scientific Study of Religion, Monograph Series 8.

Herzog, Dagmar. 2005. *Sex After Fascism: Memory and Morality in Twentieth-Century Germany*. Princeton, N.J.: Princeton University Press.

Heschel, Susannah. 1998. *Abraham Geiger and the Jewish Jesus*. Chicago: University of Chicago Press.

Hockenos, Matthew D. 2004. *A Church Divided: German Protestants Confront the Nazi Past*. Bloomington: Indiana University Press.

Hogan, Rebecca. 1991. "Engendered Autobiographies: The Diary as a Feminine Form." In *Autobiography and Questions of Gender*, ed. Shirley Neuman, 95–107. London: Frank Cass.

Hopkins, David. 2007. *Dada's Boys: Masculinity After Duchamp*. New Haven, Conn.: Yale University Press.

Höss, Rudolph. 1996. *Death Dealer: The Memoirs of the SS Kommandant at Auschwitz*. Ed. Steven Paskuly. Trans. Andrew Pollinger. New York: Da Capo Press.

Hunt, Hannah. 2004. *Joy-Bearing Grief: Tears of Contrition in the Writings of the Early Syrian and Byzantine Fathers*. Leiden, The Netherlands: Brill.

Jackson, Susan K. 1992. *Rousseau's Occasional Autobiographies*. Columbus: Ohio State University Press.

Jaspers, Karl. 1947. *The Question of German Guilt*. Trans. E. B. Ashton. New York: Dial Press. First published 1946. *Die Schuldfrage*. Heidelberg: L. Schneider.

Jordan, Mark D. 1997. *The Invention of Sodomy in Christian Theology*. Chicago: University of Chicago Press.

———. 2000. *The Silence of Sodom: Homosexuality in Modern Catholicism*. Chicago: University of Chicago Press.

———. 2003. *Telling Truth in Church: Scandal, Flesh, and Christian Speech*. Boston: Beacon.

Jung, C. G. 1973. *Memories, Dreams, Reflections*. Trans. Richard Winston and Clara Winston. New York: Pantheon.

Katz, Joshua T. 1998. "Testimonia Ritus Italici: Male Genitalia, Solemn Declarations, and the New Latin Sound Law." *Harvard Studies in Classical Philology* 98:183–217.

Kaufman, Michael, ed. 1987. *Beyond Patriarchy: Essays by Men on Pleasure, Power, and Change*. New York: Oxford University Press.

Kavanagh, Thomas M. 1987. *Writing the Truth: Authority and Desire in Rousseau*. Berkeley: University of California Press.

Keen, Sam. 1991. *Fire in the Belly: On Being a Man*. New York: Bantam.

Kellenbach, Katharina von. 2001. "Theologische Rede von Schuld und Vergebung als Täterschutz." In *Von Gott reden im Land der Täter: Theologische Stimmen der dritten Generation seit der Shoah*, ed. Katharina von Kellenbach, Björn Krondorfer, and Norbert Reck, 46–67. Darmstadt: Wissenschaftliche Buchgesellschaft.

———. 2006. "Schuld und Vergebung: Zur deutschen Praxis christlicher Versöhnung." In *Mit Blick auf die Täter: Fragen an die deutsche Theologie nach 1945*, by Björn Krondorfer, Katharina von Kellenbach, and Norbert Reck, 227–313. Gütersloh: Gütersloher Verlagshaus.

Kellenbach, Katharina von, Björn Krondorfer, and Norbert Reck, eds. 2001. *Von Gott reden im Land der Täter: Theologische Stimmen der dritten Generation seit der Shoah*. Darmstadt: Wissenschaftlicher Buchverlag.

Kelly, Christopher. 2001. "Rousseau's *Confessions*." In *The Cambridge Companion to Rousseau*, ed. Patrick Riley, 302–328. Cambridge: Cambridge University Press.

Kienzler, Klaus. 1996. *Der religiöse Fundamentalismus: Christentum, Judentum, Islam*. Munich: C. H. Beck.

Kilgour, Maggie. 1990. *From Communion to Cannibalism: An Anatomy of Metaphors of Incorporation*. Princeton, N.J.: Princeton University Press.

Kimmel, Michael. 1996. *Manhood in America: A Cultural History*. New York: Free Press.

Kirkley, Evelyn A. 1996. "Is It Manly to Be Christian? The Debate in Victorian and Modern America." In *Redeeming Men: Religion and Masculinities*, ed. Stephen B. Boyd, W. Merle Longwood, and Mark W. Muesse, 80–88. Louisville, Ky.: Westminster John Knox.

Kleßmann, Christoph. 1993. "Kontinuitäten und Veränderungen im protestantischen Milieu." In *Modernisierung im Wiederaufbau: Die westdeutsche Gesellschaft der 50er Jahre*, ed. Axel Schildt and Arnold Sywottek, 403–417. Bonn: Dietz.

Koch, Peter-Ferdinand, ed. 1988. *Himmlers Graue Emminenz: Oswald Pohl und das Wirtschaftsverwaltungshauptamt der SS*. Hamburg: Facta Oblita.

Kotzé, Annemaré. 2004. *Augustine's "Confessions": Communicative Purpose and Audience*. Leiden, The Netherlands: Brill.

Kristeva, Julia. 1986. "Stabat Mater." In *The Kristeva Reader*, ed. Toril Moi, 160–186. New York: Columbia University Press.

Krondorfer, Björn. 1995. *Remembrance and Reconciliation: Encounters Between Young Jews and Germans*. New Haven, Conn.: Yale University Press.

———, ed. 1996. *Men's Bodies, Men's Gods: Male Identities in a (Post-)Christian Culture*. New York: New York University Press.

———. 2000. "Afterword." In *My Father's Testament: Memoir of a Jewish Teenager, 1938–1945*, by Edward Gastfriend. Ed. with an afterword by Björn Krondorfer, 173–187. Philadelphia: Temple University Press.

———. 2001. "At Ratner's Kosher Restaurant." In *Second Generation Voices: Reflections by Children of Holocaust Survivors and Perpetrators*, ed. Alan Berger and Naomi Berger, 258–269. Syracuse, N.Y.: Syracuse University Press.

———. 2002a. "Revealing the Non-Absent Male Body: Confessions of an African Bishop and a Jewish Ghetto Policeman." In *Revealing Male Bodies*, ed. Nancy Tuana et al., 245–268. Bloomington: Indiana University Press.

———. 2002b. "Eine Reise gegen das Schweigen." In *Das Vermächtnis annehmen: Kulturelle und biographische Zugänge zum Holocaust: Beiträge aus den USA und Deutschland*, ed. Brigitte Huhnke and Björn Krondorfer, 315–344. Giessen: Psychosozial Verlag.

———. 2004a. "Theological Innocence and Family History in the Land of Perpetrators: German Theologians After the Shoah." *Harvard Theological Review* 97/1 (January): 61–82.

———. 2004b. "Mel Gibson's Alter Ego: A Male Passion for Violence." *Cross-Currents* 54/1 (Spring): 16–21.

———. 2006. "Nationalsozialismus und Holocaust in Autobiographien protestantischer Theologen." In *Mit Blick auf die Täter: Fragen an die deutsche The-*

ologie nach 1945, by Björn Krondorfer, Katharina von Kellenbach, and Norbert Reck, 23–170. Gütersloh: Gütersloher Verlagshaus.

———. 2007a. "World Religions, Christianity." In *International Encyclopedia of Men and Masculinities*, ed. M. Flood, J. K. Gardiner, B. Pease, and K. Pringle, 658–660. London: Routledge.

———. 2007b. "Who's Afraid of Gay Theology? Men's Studies, Gay Scholars and Heterosexual Silence." *Theology & Sexuality* 13/3:257–274.

———. 2008a. "Protestantische Theologenautobiographien und Vergangenheits-bewältigung: Helmut Thielicke als Beispiel für einen nachkriegsdeutschen Leidensdiskurs." In *Vergangenheitsbewältigung im französischen Katholizismus und deutschen Protestantismus*, ed. Lucia Scherzberg, 203–222. Paderborn: Ferdinand Schöningh.

———. 2008b. "Eunuchen oder Viagra? Frühchristliche Männlichkeitsideale als zeitgenössische Irritation." In *Theologie und Geschlecht: Dialoge Querbeet*, ed. Heike Walz and David Plüss, 57–71. Münster: LIT.

———. 2008c. "Is Forgetting Reprehensible? Holocaust Remembrance and the Task of Oblivion." *Journal of Religious Ethics* 36/2:233–267.

———, ed. 2009. *Men and Masculinities in Christianity and Judaism: A Critical Reader*. London: SCM-Press.

Krondorfer, Björn, and Philip Culbertson. 2004. "Men Studies in Religion." In *Encyclopedia of Religion*, vol. 9, 2nd ed., ed. Lindsay Jones, 5861–5866. Detroit, Mich.: Macmillan.

Krondorfer, Björn, Katharina von Kellenbach, and Norbert Reck. 2006. *Mit Blick auf die Täter: Fragen an die deutsche Theologie nach 1945*. Gütersloh: Gütersloher Verlagshaus.

Kuefler, Mathew. 2001. *The Manly Eunuch: Masculinity, Gender Ambiguity, and Christian Ideology in Late Antiquity*. Chicago: University of Chicago Press.

———, ed. 2006. *The Boswell Thesis: Essays on Christianity, Social Tolerance and Homosexuality*. Chicago: University of Chicago Press.

Kuhn, Annette. 1995. *Family Secrets: Acts of Memory and Imagination*. London: Verso.

Kundera, Milan. 1984. *The Unbearable Lightness of Being*. Trans. Michael Henry Heim. New York: Harper and Row.

Laqueur, Thomas W. 2003. *Solitary Sex: A Cultural History of Masturbation*. New York: Zone Books.

Lee, John H. 1987. *The Flying Boy: Healing the Wounded Man*. Deerfield Beach, Fla.: Health Communications.

Leiris, Michel. 1992. *Manhood: A Journey from Childhood into the Fierce Order of Virility*. Trans. Richard Howard. Chicago: University of Chicago Press.

Lejeune, Philippe. 1989. *On Autobiography*. Ed. Paul John Eakin. Trans. Katherine Leary. Minneapolis: University of Minnesota Press.

Lerner, Laurence. 1987. "What Is Confessional Poetry?" *Critical Quarterly* 29/2:46–66.

Levitt, Laura. 2007. *American Jewish Loss After the Holocaust.* New York: New York University Press.

Lifton, Robert Jay. 1986. *The Nazi Doctors: Medical Killing and the Psychology of Genocide.* New York: Basic Books.

Lilienthal, Georg. 2003. *Der Lebensborn e. V.: Ein Instrument nationalsozialistischer Rassenpolitik.* 2nd ed. Frankfurt: Fischer.

Lingis, Alphonso. 1994. *Foreign Bodies.* New York: Routledge.

Lionnet, Françoise. 1989. *Autobiographical Voices: Race, Gender, Self-Portraiture.* Ithaca, N.Y.: Cornell University Press.

Lippy, Charles H. 1997. "Miles to Go: Promise Keepers in Historical and Cultural Context." *Soundings* 80/2–3 (Summer/Fall): 289–304.

Löhr, Wolfgang. 1990. "Rechristianisierungsvorstellungen im deutschen Katholizismus, 1945–1948." In *Christentum und politische Verantwortung: Kirchen im Nachkriegsdeutschland,* ed. Jochen-Christoph Kaiser and Anselm Doering-Manteuffel, 25–41. Stuttgart: Kohlhammer.

Long, Ronald E. 1997. "The Sacrality of Male Beauty and Homosex: A Neglected Factor in the Understanding of Contemporary Gay Reality." In *Que(e)rying Religion: A Critical Anthology,* ed. Gary D. Comstock and Susan E. Henking, 266–281. New York: Continuum.

Luther, Martin. 1962. *Luther's Works.* Vol. 55. Ed. Walther I. Brandt. Gen. ed. Helmut T. Lehmann. Philadelphia: Fortress Press.

Lutz, Tom. 1999. *Crying: The Natural and Cultural History of Tears.* New York: W. W. Norton.

Marcus, Laura. 1994. *Auto/biographical Discourses: Theory, Criticism, Practice.* Manchester, U.K.: Manchester University Press.

Marcuse, Harold. 2001. *Legacies of Dachau: The Use and Abuse of a Concentration Camp, 1933–2001.* Cambridge: Cambridge University Press.

Martin, Dale B. 2006. *Sex and the Single Savior: Gender and Sexuality in Biblical Interpretation.* Louisville, Ky.: Westminster John Knox.

Marx, Anthony. 2003. *Faith in Nation: Exclusionary Origins of Nationalism.* Oxford: Oxford University Press.

Masterson, Mark. 2006. "Impossible Translation: Antony and Paul the Simple in the *Historia Monachorum.*" In *The Boswell Thesis: Essays on Christianity, Social Tolerance and Homosexuality,* ed. Mathew Kuefler, 215–235. Chicago: University of Chicago Press.

May, Larry, and James Bohman. 1997. "Sexuality, Masculinity, and Confession." *Hypatia* 12/1 (Winter): 138–154.

Mayer, Jane. 2008. *The Dark Side: The Inside Story of How the War on Terror Turned into a War on American Ideals.* New York: Doubleday.

McGuire, Brian Patrick. 1996. "Education, Confession, and the Pious Fraud: Jean Gerson and Late Medieval Change." *American Benedictine Review* 47/3 (September): 316–338.

Meeks, Wayne A. 1993. *The Origins of Christian Morality: The First Two Centuries.* New Haven, Conn.: Yale University Press.

Messner, Michael A. 1997. *Politics of Masculinities: Men in Movements.* Thousand Oaks, Calif.: Sage Publications.

Middlebrook, Diane W. 1993. "What Was Confessional Poetry?" In *The Columbia History of American Poetry*, ed. J. Parini and B. C. Millier, 632–649. New York: Columbia University Press.

Middleton, Peter. 1992. *The Inward Gaze: Masculinity and Subjectivity in Modern Culture.* London: Routledge.

Milbank, John, Catherine Pickstock, and Graham Ward, eds. 1999. *Radical Orthodoxy: A New Theology.* London: Routledge.

Miles, Margaret R. 1992. *Desire and Delight: A New Reading of Augustine's "Confessions."* New York: Crossroad.

———. 2008. *Rereading Historical Theology: Before, During, and After Augustine.* Eugene, Ore.: Cascade Books.

Miller, Nancy K. 1991. *Getting Personal: Feminist Occasions and Other Autobiographical Acts.* New York: Routledge.

Moeller, Robert G. 1993. *Protecting Motherhood: Woman and the Family in the Politics of Postwar West Germany.* Berkeley: University of California Press.

———. 2001. *War Stories: The Search for a Usable Past in the Federal Republic of Germany.* Berkeley: University of California Press.

Moltmann, Jürgen. 1992. *The Spirit of Life: A Universal Affirmation.* Trans. Margaret Kohl. Minneapolis, Minn.: Fortress Press.

Moore, Stephen D. 1995. "True Confessions and Weird Obsessions: Autobiographical Interventions in Literary and Biblical Studies." In *Taking It Personally: Autobiographical Biblical Criticism*, Semeia 72, ed. Janice Capel Anderson and Jeffrey L. Staley, 19–43. Atlanta, Ga.: Scholars Press.

———. 1996. *God's Gym: Divine Male Bodies of the Bible.* New York: Routledge.

Morris, Leslie. 2003. "Berlin Elegies: Absence, Postmemory, and Art After Auschwitz." In *Image and Remembrance: Representation and the Holocaust*, ed. Shelly Hornstein and Florence Jacobowitz, 288–304. Bloomington: Indiana University Press.

Moseley, Marcus. 2006. *Being for Myself Alone: Origins of Jewish Autobiography.* Stanford, Calif.: Stanford University Press.

Mosse, George L. 1996. *The Image of Man: The Creation of Modern Masculinity.* New York: Oxford University Press.

Nanko, Ulrich. 1993. *Die Deutsche Glaubensbewegung: Eine historische und soziologische Untersuchung.* Marburg: Diagonal Verlag.

Neuman, Shirley. 1991. "Autobiography, Bodies, Manhood." In *Autobiography and Questions of Gender*, ed. Shirley Neuman, 137–165. London: Frank Cass.

Niemöller, Martin. 1934. *Vom U-Boot zur Kanzel.* Berlin: Martin Warneck.

O'Donnell, James J. 1992. *Augustine: Confessions.* 3 vols. Oxford: Oxford University Press.

———. 2005. "Augustine's Unconfessions." In *Augustine and Postmodernism*, ed. John D. Caputo and Michael J. Scanlon, 212–221. Bloomington: Indiana University Press.

Ofer, Dalia, and Lenore J. Weitzman, eds. 1998. *Women in the Holocaust.* New Haven, Conn.: Yale University Press.

Oldenhage, Tania. 2000. *Parables of Our Time: Rereading New Testament Scholarship After the Holocaust.* New York: Oxford University Press.

Olney, James, ed. 1980. *Autobiography: Essays Theoretical and Critical.* Princeton, N.J.: Princeton University Press.

———. 1998. *Memory and Narrative: The Weave of Life-Writing.* Chicago: University of Chicago Press.

Paffenroth, Kim. 2003. "Book Nine: The Emotional Heart of the *Confessions.*" In *A Reader's Companion to Augustine's "Confessions,"* ed. Kim Paffenroth and Robert P. Kennedy, 137–154. Louisville, Ky.: Westminster John Knox.

Paffenroth, Kim, and Robert P. Kennedy, eds. 2003. *A Reader's Companion to Augustine's "Confessions."* Louisville, Ky.: Westminster John Knox.

Patte, Daniel. 1995. "Acknowledging the Contextual Character of Male, European-American Critical Exegeses: An Androcritical Perspective." In *Reading from This Place,* ed. Fernando Segovia and Mary Ann Tolbert, 1:35–55. Minneapolis, Minn.: Fortress Press.

Patton, Kimberly C., and John S. Hawley, eds. 2005. *Holy Tears: Weeping in the Religious Imagination.* Princeton, N.J.: Princeton University Press.

Payer, Pierre J. 1984. *Sex and the Penitentials.* Toronto: University of Toronto Press.

Payne, Leigh A. 2008. *Unsettling Accounts: Neither Truth nor Reconciliation in Confessions of State Violence.* Durham, N.C.: Duke University Press.

Perechodnik, Calel. 1996. *Am I a Murderer? Testament of a Jewish Ghetto Policeman.* Ed. and trans. Frank Fox. Boulder, Colo.: Westview Press.

Perspectives on The Passion of the Christ: Religious Thinkers and Writers Explore the Issues Raised by the Controversial Movie. 2004. New York: Miramax.

Phayer, Michael. 2000. *The Catholic Church and the Holocaust, 1930–1965.* Bloomington: Indiana University Press.

Pilling, John. 1981. *Autobiography and Imagination: Studies in Self-Scrutiny.* London: Routledge.

Plate, Brent S., ed. 2004. *Re-viewing "The Passion": Mel Gibson's Film and Its Critics.* New York: Palgrave Macmillan.

Pohl, Oswald. 1950. *Credo: Mein Weg zu Gott.* Landshut: Alois Girnth.

Porter, Roger J. 1991. "Figuration and Disfigurement: Herculine Barbin and the Autobiography of the Body." In *Autobiography and Questions of Gender,* ed. Shirley Neuman, 122–136. London: Frank Cass.

Posset, Anton. 1993a. "Der Priester und der SS-General: Die Bekehrungsgeschichte des Oswald Pohl." *Landsberger Hefte* 1:20–24.

———. 1993b. "Kronzeuge Morgenschweis: Wahrheit, Legendenbildung und Geschichtsverfälschung." *Landsberger Hefte* 1:25–29.

Power, Kim. 1996. *Veiled Desire: Augustine on Women.* New York: Continuum.

Radstone, Susannah. 2007. *The Sexual Politics of Time: Confession, Nostalgia, Memory.* London: Routledge.

Rank, Otto. 1971. *The Double: A Psychoanalytic Study*. Trans. Harry Tucker. Chapel Hill: University of North Carolina Press.

Ranke-Heineman, Uta. 1990. *Eunuchs for the Kingdom of Heaven: Women, Sexuality, and the Catholic Church*. New York: Doubleday.

Remele, Kurt. 2005. "Katholischer Fundamentalismus: Unterscheidungen—Erklärungen—Anfragen." In *Religiöser Fundamentalismus: Vom Kolonialismus zur Globalisierung*, ed. Clemens Six, Martin Riesebrodt, and Siegfried Haas, 53–68. Innsbruck: Studienverlag.

Renza, Louis A. 1980. "The Veto of the Imagination: A Theory of Autobiography." In *Autobiography: Essays Theoretical and Critical*, ed. James Olney, 268–295. Princeton, N.J.: Princeton University Press.

Riesebrodt, Martin. 1998. *Pious Passion: The Emergence of Modern Fundamentalism in the United States and Iran*. Berkeley: University of California Press.

———. 2001. *Die Rückkehr der Religionen: Fundamentalismus und der Kampf der Kulturen*. 2nd ed. Munich: Beck.

Riley, Denise. 2005. *Impersonal Passion: Language as Affect*. Durham, N.C.: Duke University Press.

Riley, Patrick. 2004. *Character and Conversion in Autobiography: Augustine, Montaigne, Descartes, Rousseau, and Sartre*. Charlottesville: University of Virginia Press.

Rilke, Rainer Maria. 1962. *Sonnets to Orpheus*. Trans. M. D. Herter Norton. New York: W. W. Norton.

Robbins, Jill. 1983. "Reading Scripture: Prodigal Son and Elder Brother: The Example of Augustine's *Confessions*." *Genre* 16:317–334.

Robinson, Paul. 1999. *Gay Lives: Homosexual Autobiography from John Addington Symonds to Paul Monette*. Chicago: University of Chicago Press.

Ross-Bryant, Lynn. 1997. "The Self in Nature: Four American Autobiographies." *Soundings* 80/1 (Spring): 83–104.

Rousseau, Jean-Jacques. 1953. *The Confessions*. Trans. J. M. Cohen. New York: Penguin.

Russell, Norman. 1980. *The Lives of the Desert Fathers: The "Historia Monarchorum in Aegypto."* London: Mowbray.

Sands, Philippe. 2008. *Torture Team: Rumsfeld's Memo and the Betrayal of American Values*. New York: Palgrave Macmillan.

Scarry, Elaine. 1985. *The Body in Pain: The Making and Unmaking of the World*. New York: Oxford University Press.

Schallenberger, David. 1998. *Reclaiming the Spirit: Gay Men and Lesbians Come to Terms with Religion*. New Brunswick, N.J.: Rutgers University Press.

Scherzberg, Lucia. 2001. *Kirchenreform mit Hilfe des Nationalsozialismus: Karl Adam als kontextueller Theologe*. Darmstadt: Wissenschaftliche Buchgesellschaft.

Schissler, Hanna, ed. 2001a. *The Miracle Years: A Cultural History of West Germany, 1949–1968*. Princeton, N.J.: Princeton University Press.

———. 2001b. "'Normalization' as Project: Some Thoughts on Gender Relations in West Germany During the 1950s." In *The Miracle Years*, ed. Hanna Schissler, 359–375. Princeton, N.J.: Princeton University Press.

Schmitz-Köster, Dorothee. 2007. *Kind L 364: Eine Lebensborn-Familiengeschichte.* Berlin: Rowohlt.

Schneider, Laurel C. 2000. "Homosexuality, Queer Theory, and Christian Theology." *Religious Studies Review* 26/1 (January): 3–12.

Schoenfeld, Gabriel. 1998. "Auschwitz and the Professors." *Commentary* 105/6 (June): 42–46.

Schulte, Jan Erik. 2001. *Zwangsarbeit und Vernichtung: Das Wirtschaftsimperium der SS. Oswald Pohl und das SS-Wirtschafts-Verwaltungshauptamt 1933–1945.* Paderborn: Ferdinand Schöningh.

Schwartz, Joel. 1984. *The Sexual Politics of Jean-Jacques Rousseau.* Chicago: University of Chicago Press.

Schwartz, Thomas Alan. 1990. "Die Begnadigung deutscher Kriegsverbrecher: John J. McCloy und die Häftlinge von Landsberg." *Vierteljahreshefte für Zeitgeschichte* 38:375–414.

Schwarz, Gudrun. 1997. *Eine Frau an seiner Seite: Ehefrauen in der "SS-Sippengemeinschaft."* Hamburg: Hamburger Edition.

Schwarz, Hans-Peter. 1989. "Die Fünfziger Jahre als Epochenzäsur." In *Wege in die Zeitgeschichte*, ed. Jürgen Heideking, Gerhard Hufnagel, and Fran Knipping, 473–496. Berlin: Walter de Gruyter.

Schweitzer, Albert. 1910. *The Quest of the Historical Jesus: A Critical Study of Its Progress from Reimarus to Wrede.* Trans. W. Montgomery. New York: Macmillan.

Sedgwick, Eve Kosofsky. 1985. *Between Men: English Literature and Male Homosocial Desire.* New York: Columbia University Press.

Segal, Naomi. 1998. *André Gide: Pederasty and Pedagogy.* Oxford: Clarendon Press.

Senior, Matthew. 1994. *In the Grip of Minos: Confessional Discourse in Dante, Corneille, and Racine.* Columbus: Ohio State University Press.

Shaw, Teresa M. 1998. *The Burden of the Flesh: Fasting and Sexuality in Early Christianity.* Minneapolis, Minn.: Fortress Press.

Sher, Leo, and Alexander Vilens, eds. 2009. *Internet and Suicide.* Hauppauge, N.Y.: Nova.

Sloterdijk, Peter. 1993. *Weltfremdheit.* Frankfurt: Suhrkamp.

Smith, Sidonie. 1993. *Subjectivity, Identity, and the Body.* Bloomington: Indiana University Press.

Sontag, Susan. 1992. "Foreword." In *Manhood*, by Michel Leiris. Chicago: University of Chicago Press. First published 1964. "Michel Leiris' Manhood." In *Against Interpretation.* New York: Farrar, Straus and Giroux.

Spencer, Daniel T. 2004. "Lesbian and Gay Theologies." In *Handbook of U.S. Theologies of Liberation*, 264–273. St. Louis, Mo.: Chalice Press.

Spender, Stephen. 1980. "Confessions and Autobiography." In *Autobiography: Essays Theoretical and Critical*, ed. James Olney, 115–122. Princeton, N.J.: Princeton University Press. First published 1962 in Spender, *The Making of a Poem*.

Staley, Jeffrey L. 1995. *Reading with a Passion: Rhetoric, Autobiography, and the American West in the Gospel of John*. New York: Continuum.

Starobinski, Jean. 2001. "The Motto *Vitam impendere vero* and the Question of Lying." In *The Cambridge Companion to Rousseau*, ed. Patrick Riley, 365–396. Cambridge: Cambridge University Press.

Stegmann, Franz Josef. 1996. "Integralismus." In *Lexikon für Theologie und Kirche*, vol. 6, ed. Walter Kasper. Freiburg im Breisgau: Herder.

Steigmann-Gall, Richard. 2003. *The Holy Reich: Nazi Conceptions of Christianity, 1919–1945*. Cambridge: Cambridge University Press.

Stephan, Inge. 2003. "Im toten Winkel: Die Neuentdeckung des 'ersten Geschlechts' durch *men's studies* und Männlichkeitsforschung." In *Männlichkeit als Maskerade: Kulturelle Inszenierungen vom Mittelalter bis zur Gegenwart*, ed. Claudia Benthien and Inge Stephan, 11–35. Cologne: Böhlau.

Stone, Ken. 1997. "Biblical Interpretation as a Technology of the Self: Gay Men and the Ethics of Reading." *Semeia* 77:139–155.

Szapiro, Paweł. 1996. "Afterword (from the Polish Edition)." In *Am I a Murderer?* by Calel Perechodnik, 213–225. Boulder, Colo.: Westview Press.

Tambling, Jeremy. 1990. *Confession: Sexuality, Sin, the Subject*. Manchester, U.K.: Manchester University Press.

Taylor, Charles. 1989. *Sources of the Self: The Making of Modern Identity*. Cambridge, Mass.: Harvard University Press.

Tentler, Thomas N. 1977. *Sin and Confession on the Eve of the Reformation*. Princeton, N.J.: Princeton University Press.

Theweleit, Klaus. 2002. "Männliche Geburtsweisen: Der männliche Körper als Institutionenkörper." In *Masculinities—Maskulinitäten: Mythos—Realität— Repräsentation—Rollendruck*, ed. Therese Steffen, 2–27. Stuttgart: Metzler.

Veeser, Aram H., ed. 1996. *Confessions of the Critics*. New York: Routledge.

Vetlesen, Arne Johan. 2005. *Evil and Human Agency: Understanding Collective Evil-doing*. Cambridge: Cambridge University Press.

Vollnhals, Clemens. 1992. "Die Hypothek des Nationalprotestantismus: Entnazi-fizierung und Strafverfolgung von NS-Verbrechen nach 1945." *Geschichte und Gesellschaft* 18/1:51–69.

Ward, Benedicta, trans. 2003. *The Desert Fathers: Sayings of the Early Christian Monks*. London: Penguin.

Ward, Graham. 1999. "Bodies: The Displaced Body of Jesus Christ." In *Radical Orthodoxy: A New Theology*, ed. John Milbank, Catherine Pickstock, and Graham Ward, 163–181. Routledge: London.

Warren, Frank. 2005. *PostSecret: Extraordinary Confessions from Ordinary Lives*. New York: William Morrow.

Watson, Julia. 1993. "Toward an Anti-metaphysics of Autobiography." In *The Culture of Autobiography: Constructions of Self-Representation*, ed. Robert Folkenflik, 57–79. Stanford, Calif.: Stanford University Press.

West, Russell, and Frank Lay, eds. 2000. *Subverting Masculinity: Hegemonic and Alternative Versions of Masculinity in Contemporary Culture*. Amsterdam: Rodopi.

White, Carolinne, ed. and trans. 1998. *Early Christian Lives*. London: Penguin.

Wills, Garry. 1999. *Saint Augustine*. New York: Viking.

Young, James E. 1988. *Writing and Rewriting the Holocaust: Narrative and the Consequences of Interpretation*. Bloomington: Indiana University Press.

———. 2000. *At Memory's Edge: After-Images of the Holocaust in Contemporary Art and Architecture*. New Haven, Conn.: Yale University Press.

Zwicker, Lisa F. 2006. "New Directions in Research on Masculinity and Confession." *Kirchliche Zeitgeschichte/Contemporary Church History* 19/2:315–335.

Index

Abraham, 72

absent presence, 80, 162, 170

absolution, 13–14, 16, 19, 77, 237

abuse, 61, 127, 155–156. *See also* self-abuse

Adak, Hülya, 256*n*49

Adam, 81, 100, 152, 155, 226

Adam, Karl, 109, 252*n*16

Adeodatus (son of Augustine), 86–88, 95, 132, 158–159

Ambrose, 249*n*20

Am I a Murderer? (Perechodnik), 76–77, 89, 96, 162, 166, 169

amnesty, 110, 115, 125–126, 129, 252*n*11, 253*nn*22–23

Anderson, Benedict, 189

Androgyne Journal, The, 66–68

androgynous, 66–68, 190, 234

annihilation, 24, 89–90, 108, 111, 121, 125, 161–162, 189, 232. *See also* Nazi, annihilate

antisemitism, 79, 90, 122, 189

Anthony (Antony), 38–40, 153–156, 163, 169, 183, 200

antiquity. *See* late antiquity

anus/anal, 56, 63–68, 262*n*10; experience, 66; intercourse, 195, 262*n*10; permeability, 196, 206; phase, 66; process, 70; region 50. *See also* rectum

anus mundi, 63, 68

anxiety (male), 23, 27, 46–47, 54, 59, 62–63, 68, 85, 127, 138, 144, 150, 153, 158–159, 183, 185, 191, 197–198, 202–204, 218, 250*n*33

apologetic, 103, 106, 113, 118, 129, 192, 235, 253*n*23

arbitrariness, 50, 54, 56–57, 219

Aristotle, 50, 133

Arsenius, 154

Artaud, Antonin, 38

ascetic (male), 38, 41, 46, 67, 154; body, 38, 40; discipline 38–40; life, 39; practice, 40, 200

asceticism, 36; radical, 40

Asher, Lyell, 55, 75

Assaf, David, 144, 148, 167, 190

Assisi, Francis of, 133, 217

Athanasius, 38, 40, 154

Augustine, passim; Antony and, 39–40, 153–154; conversion and, 31, 40–41, 104, 155; Fall and, 81–82, 84, 197; father of, 151–152; friend of, 141–142; God and, 12, 16, 23, 32, 36, 39–44, 55, 70–71, 75–76, 78–79, 81–83, 85–88, 96–99, 100, 104, 136, 139–145, 148, 151–153, 155, 158, 169–170, 179–180, 183, 197, 199, 210; 252*m*18; human condition, 259*n*28; lover of (female partner), 70, 83–84, 86–87, 93, 95–96, 98, 157–159, 161, 163, 165, 168, 259*n*26; mirror and, 29–31, 41–43, 60, 70; mother of, 37, 41–42, 60–61, 83, 88, 95, 132–133, 139–152, 154–155, 157, 163, 168–169, 179–180, 183, 190; nightly emission, 82; radical reflexivity, 40; as role model, 32; sickness and, 15–16, 32, 44; son of, 70, 87, 96, 132–133, 157, 159. *See also* Adeodatus; *Confessions* (Augustine); Monica; Patricius

authenticity, 9–10, 15, 19, 26, 45, 74, 103, 110, 127, 129–130, 191, 195, 224, 257*n*4; penitence and, 89; self-disclosure and, 26. *See also* confession

autobiography, 9–10, 24, 18, 20, 35, 51–52, 58, 72, 75, 106, 108–109, 119, 132–133, 176, 178, 191, 193, 206, 232, 241*nn*13,15, 244*m*1, 247*nn*3–5; 248*n*7, 266*n*1; compulsion 29; disclosure, 28; feminine, 18; feminist criticism, 80; framework, 265*n*33; insertion, 25, 109, 194; integrity, 249*m*18; itinerary, 50; Jewish, 248*n*7, narration, 20; performance, 26; prose, 49; reference, 213; reminiscence, 186; revelation, 51, 97; style, 46, 54; voice, 6, 26; void, 256*n*49. *See also* gay, autobiography

banality, 25, 27. *See also* triviality

Barris, Chuck, 51

becomingness, 207, 232

Belzec (death camp), 145

Berdichevsky, Michah Yosef, 77, 260*n*1

Bersani, Leo, 224

birth (birthing), 32, 40, 42, 62, 69, 95, 138, 163, 177, 182, 240*n*5, 250*n*32. *See also* confession, as birth; rebirth

blushing (blush), 38, 50, 78. *See also* shame
Bly, Robert, 61
body (male), 22, 24–26, 30–31, 37, 39, 42–57,
    59, 63–69, 80, 83, 88–91, 93–94, 153, 163, 166,
    169, 190–191, 195–197, 199, 208, 212, 214,
    215–216, 220, 222–225; boundary of, 38, 139;
    Christian, 85, 216; dry, 67, 69, 153; erotic/
    eroticized, 11, 191, 195, 200, 214, 234; fatherly,
    93; female, 63, 170; gendered, 22, 80–81, 85,
    89, 92, 216, 225; God's, 169; heterosexual,
    22, 52, 69, 80, 232; homonormative, 215;
    intimate, 42, 138, 194; Jewish, 79, 85, 89–90,
    92, 98, 222, 225; language of, 37; masculine,
    61, 211; maternal, 150, 170; messianic, 223,
    227; mirrored, 50–51, 190; mother's, 61;
    muscular, 67, 214, 216, 221–224, 227; negative
    presence of, 89; non-absent, 75, 78, 80–84,
    88–89, 92, 95; normative, 69, 80, 84; queer,
    67; sexual, 235; textual, 138. *See also* ascetic;
    embodiment; gay
body of Jesus Christ, 64, 222–228
Boisvert, Donald, 2, 191, 193, 210–226, 228–229,
    231, 234–235, 264n28
Boswell, John, 262n11
Boyarin, Daniel, 216, 229
Brandt, Karl, 185–187
Brée, Germaine, 50
Brenner, Rachel Feldhay, 244m1
Brooks, Peter, 8, 10, 13–14, 46–47, 136, 203,
    239n2
Broughton, James, 66–68, 190–191, 234–235
Brown, Peter, 41, 151, 181
Brüning, Eleonore von (wife of Pohl), 170–171,
    176–179, 182–185, 188
Buchholz, Petra, 256n49
Burrus, Virginia, 21, 24–25, 60, 124, 132, 143,
    146–147, 153, 181, 250n32, 258n9
Buscher, Frank, 253m17
Butler, Judith, 227, 240n7

cannibalism/istic, 162, 169
Capps, Donald, 205
Caputo, John, 36
Card, Claudia, 125
Carthage, 140, 142, 144, 180
Castelli, Elizabeth, 265n33
castrate, 72
celibacy, 60, 71, 82, 85, 95, 99, 140, 184, 192, 210,
    249n20, 263n21
child, 37, 45, 47–48, 62–63, 65–66, 68, 70, 77,
    79, 86–88, 91–96, 98, 113, 115, 124, 135–136,
    138, 142–143, 146–147, 152, 158, 163–164,
    177–178, 182, 187, 204
childbirth, 63. *See also* pregnancy
childhood, 43–46, 53, 56, 66, 77, 123, 149, 179,
    213, 245n9
Christ, 107, 112, 121, 123, 126, 129, 131, 141, 152,
    176, 186, 219–220, 222–229, 254n31, 266nn42,

44; erotic, 219–220, 222, 264n28, 266n44. See
    also *Queering Christ*
Christian: anti-, 102, 116, 185; attitude, 201;
    confessiography, 101, 130; East, 154–155;
    economy of redemption, 101, 198; faith, 41,
    95, 100, 123, 171; forgiveness, 117–118; gay
    sexuality, 210; hymn, 59; man, 37–38, 40,
    76, 79, 81, 148, 154, 210, 212, 222, 233; men's
    movement, 37, 221; muscular, 222 (*see also*
    muscular Christianity); new masculine ideal,
    140; new self, 31; spiritual child, 96; symbol/
    symbolism, 66, 171; teaching, 203; tradition,
    6, 193, 214, 220, 255n42. *See also* body;
    church; confession; confessional; masculinity
Christianity, 4, 7–9, 11–12, 17, 37, 41, 101,
    104–105, 107, 121, 127, 153, 183, 185–188,
    199, 203, 212, 221–223, 227, 260nn1, 5, 7;
    supersessionist, 266n45. *See also* church
Chrysostom, John, 155
church, 8, 36–37, 64–65, 101–102, 105–106, 122,
    127, 129, 143, 158, 171, 179, 181, 185, 195, 219,
    222, 228, 252nn11–12; as body of Christ, 228;
    Catholic, 106, 108–112, 114, 116, 121, 127, 176,
    181–182, 185, 188, 243; Confessing, 255n39;
    Donatist, 249m14; Mother, 170, 176, 179,
    181–182; Protestant, 108, 122, 171, 213; and
    Rousseau, 47
church father, 16, 63, 137, 154–155. *See also* desert
    father; saint
Cioran, E. M., 158–159
circumfession, 73, 132–133, 243n35, 248n9, 258n13
Clark, J. Michael, 192–194
clemency, 105, 110–111, 116, 120, 126, 128–129,
    183, 187, 232, 252n17, 252n22, 254n31
co-confessant, 16, 237
Coles, Romand, 14, 17, 239n2, 253n18
colonized (man), 63, 69, 79, 216, 222
complicity, 11, 19–20, 22, 28, 91, 106, 112, 114,
    122, 147, 177, 184, 188, 232–233, 237, 252m16
compunction, 154–156, 258n19, 260m1
Comstock, Gary, 193
concupiscentia, 62
confessant (male), 7, 10, 12–15, 19, 22, 24–25, 27,
    33–35, 48, 57–58, 60, 68–69, 72, 81, 95–96,
    109–110, 112–113, 122–123, 125, 128–130, 132–
    136, 138–139, 147, 161, 178, 183, 188, 190–191,
    206, 209, 224, 229–234, 237
confessare, 35
confessio fidei et laudis, 75, 100
confessio peccati, 75, 100
confessiography, 8–11, 14–17, 19, 21, 24–25, 31,
    35, 57, 59, 63, 68, 72, 74–75, 79–80, 98, 101,
    129–130, 135–137, 156, 161, 178, 190, 194, 223,
    225, 231–234, 236–237; form of, 128; fragment
    of, 193, 199; impulse, 238; quality of, 10, 191,
    248n7. *See also* Christian; Jewish
confession: auricular (oral) 9, 12–15, 109, 137,
    153, 163–164, 209, 214, 236; authentic, 103;

as birth, 138, 182; Christian, 31, 94, 100, 101, 103, 109, 248*n*7; in Christianity, 4, 7–8, 11–12, 75, 77, 99, 103, 109, 204, 248*n*7; coerced (coercive), 2, 8, 22, 27, 57, 113, 156, 236, 241*m*9, 249*m*12; deathbed, 11, 77–79, 84–85, 87, 89–91, 96–97, 122, 162, 248*n*9; devotional, 213, 224, 229; dialogical, 11–12, 14, 109–110, 252*m*18; as gendered activity, 7, 72; heard, 141; Internet, 236; intimate self-disclosure, 3, 15, 58, 232; Jewish, 248*nn*7, 9; mode of self-examination, 2–3, 8, 22, 24; modernist, 147, 159, 198; monastic roots/origin, 6, 247*n*4; monological, 11–12, 14, 16, 59, 253*m*18; private, 137; public, 2, 89–90, 136–137, 147 (*see also* public; testimony); read, 141; as rebirth, 95; self-aggrandizement, 18; spiritual, 79, 102, 115, 117; total self-disclosure, 15 (*see also* transparency, total)

confessional: act, 98; convention, 109; Christian, 103, 109, 245*m*3; culture, 13, 57; diary, 22; discourse, 17, 80, 84; document, 189; effort 44; form, 103; fragment, 144, 147; genre, 170; insertion, 219; language, 224; letter, 144, 148; manuscript, 138; mode, 194; narrative, 7, 29, 94, 104, 150, 171, 177, 183; performance, 17, 110, 119, 242*n*23, 253*n*20, 258*n*14; practice, 147; rhetoric, 136; scholarship, 210, 218; self-incrimination, 248*n*7; television 57; theology, 203; voice, 26, 156, 228

confessional (religious), 7–9, 12–14, 57, 94, 101, 103, 109, 136–137, 236, 263*n*21. *See also* penitential

Confessions (Augustine), 6, 11–12, 15–17, 20, 29, 31–32, 36, 39–44, 46, 55, 60, 70, 75–76, 79, 81–84, 87, 94–97, 99–100, 104, 109, 114, 124, 129, 132–133, 136–137, 139–141, 151, 155, 164, 166, 169–170, 179–180, 197, 199, 217, 235

Confessions (Rousseau), 46–48, 50, 52, 60, 124, 136, 199

confessor, 12–13, 16, 109–113, 115, 117–118, 123, 127–128, 136, 176, 178, 182, 185, 187–188, 202, 212, 236–237, 263*m*18

consumption, 9–10, 15, 153, 162, 178, 237

conversion, 1–2, 11, 24, 31, 35, 40, 44, 60, 70, 74, 79, 101–104, 106, 109–114, 116, 124, 127, 149, 155, 176, 178, 181, 183, 185, 187–189, 206, 208–210, 243*n*31

convert, 30, 74, 82, 116, 121–122, 142, 150–151, 179, 180, 188–189

Corinthians (Paul's letter to), 30, 64, 101, 204

Council of Trent, 12, 241*m*17

courage, 24, 41–42, 45, 47, 50, 55, 58, 65, 68, 77, 94, 166, 185, 208, 212

credibility gap, 129

Credo (Pohl), 101, 103–114, 116–131, 136, 161, 170–176, 179–180, 182–183, 185, 187–189, 231, 235, 252*m*17

Culbertson, Philip, 5–6, 144–148, 163, 180, 194; mother of, 145–147, 163

culpability, 11, 21–22, 93–94, 97, 103, 106, 112, 116–117, 119–120, 122–123, 125, 127, 129–130, 161, 176–177, 183–184, 188, 190, 233–234, 256*n*49

danger, 14–15, 24, 36, 57–60, 62, 80, 111, 134, 146, 183, 193, 203

"dangerous supplement," 202, 204

Dante Alighieri, 133

Deak, Istvan, 92

De Confesione Mollitiei (Gerson), 201

De Man, Paul, 259*n*28

Derrida, Jacques, 17, 45, 132–133, 143, 146, 243*n*35, 248*n*9, 258*m*13, 260*nn*3–4; mother of, 132, 146, 260*n*1

desert father, 11, 39–40, 67, 133, 153–154, 200. *See also* church father; Egyptian desert

desert saint/monk, 40–41, 183–184. *See also* saint

desubjectification, 91

detachment, 22, 46, 191

Dineson, Jacob, 144

disembodied, 29, 51–52, 162, 180, 223, 227–228

displacement/displaced, 66, 135, 138, 146, 156, 162, 170, 178, 204, 225–228, 231–232, 260*n*5. *See also* theology

divine: beauty, 226; consolation, 150, 155; design, 75; embrace, 169; energy, 66; eros, 159; freedom, 199; grace, 101–102, 200; love, 121, 129, 156; mandate, 38; mercy, 71, 154; nourishment, 95, 145, 162; partner, 12; perspective, 36–37, 43, 76; power, 13–41; promise of redemption, 197; refuge, 130; safety net, 47; sorrow, 155; vitality, 121. *See also* father; gaze

drag: identity, 146; performance, 147, 150

Driver, Tom, 52–54, 56, 64, 190

Duchamp, Marcel, 31

Egyptian desert, 39, 153–155, 169. *See also* desert father

Eilberg-Schwartz, Howard, 66

Eisenhower (General), 111

el mole rachamim, 87

emasculanization, 145, 150

embodiment, 24, 35, 39, 65, 190, 194, 196, 212; communion as, 200; knowing of desire as, 211; male 6–7, 88, 94, 153, 196; national, 115; revelation as, 52; sacred, 203; self, 17, 29, 51, 68, 81, 83, 85, 98, 195; spirituality as, 68; theology, 194. *See also* body

emission. *See* nocturnal emission; sperm

Emmerich, Anna Katharina, 221

Enlightenment, 33, 42, 204, 260*n*5; pre-, 102

Enterline, Lynn, 44

erection, 53, 195–197

Evagrius, 154

Eve, 81

exculpation, 232, 238. *See also* self-exculpation

exposure, 47, 102, 198, 218–219, 232, 236. *See also* self-exposure

extermination. *See* annihilation

Ezrahi, Sidra DeKoven, 92

face-to-face (encounter, conversation), 7, 15, 29–32, 40, 44, 138, 160, 196, 218

fantasy, 2, 51, 59–60, 63–65, 145, 159, 169, 190, 204, 206, 219, 236, 263*n*19

father, 68, 88, 92, 114, 123, 143, 152, 207; of all, 141, 152; divine, 150; of orphans, 151; spiritual, 112, 151; *See also* Augustine; church father; desert father; Perechodnik; Pohl; Rule of the Father; Twersky

fatherland, 120, 123, 185

Felman, Shoshana, 18–19

female: absence of subjectivity, 20, 177–178, 183; actress, 154; anatomy, 63; biography, 25; collaborative support, 177; companion, 22, 137, 155, 157–159, 161, 169, 178, 182–183; deity, 149; despair, 150; ecclesia, 181; erasure, 137, 178; face, 61; figure, 170, 178; frequency, 61; gaze, 188; gender, 62; intimate other, 232; power, 149, 188; presence, 183; reader, 19; sex, 204; subject 20; subjectivity, 25; voice, 25. *See also* body; wife; woman

femininity, 25; existence and, 18; sea as, 62; soul and, 61. *See also* autobiography

feminism, 27, 62, 192, 202, 205; criticism and, 5, 80, 83; pro-, 177; theory and, 5. *See also* autobiography

feminization/feminized, 54, 63, 128–129, 182–183, 185, 187–188, 209, 216, 222

fetishism, 211, 213, 215, 226, 229, 236. *See also* gaze

Flannery, Edward, 255*n*42

flesh, 37–39, 53–54, 82, 140, 190–191, 197, 199, 216–217, 22, 237; banality of, 25; gift of God, 199; goodness of, 201, 203; performance of the, 190

flesh-and-blood, 180; conversation, 138; daughter, 96; people, 136; woman, 204

forgiveness, 53, 78–79, 117–118, 131, 162, 198–199, 234, 237

Foster, Dennis, 11, 19, 239*n*2

Foucault, Michel, 6, 9–10, 16, 32, 98, 206–207, 239*n*2, 247*n*4

Fourth Lateran Council, 12

Frank, Fox, 77

Frei, Norbert, 114

Freud, Sigmund, 23–24, 27, 43, 47, 55, 202–203, 205, 208, 227, 243*n*30

Friedrich, Jörg, 115

friendship, 166, 257*n*1, 260*n*5

Frye, Northrop, 48

Fussell, Samuel, 217

gay, 145, 147, 190–230 passim, 261*n*2, 264*n*28, 266*n*42; autobiography, 191, 206, 264*n*23; beauty, 219; body, 63, 211, 217, 225; bottom/top, 208–209, 223; breviary, 212; confessional scholarship, 194; desire, 211–212; gaze, 215; ghetto, 193; habitus, 193; icon, 211 (*see also* icon); identity, 146, 193, 200, 207, 210, 234; male gym body, 215–26, 224; man 27, 191, 194, 198, 209, 212, 215, 218, 223; reader, 213; receptivity, 197, 200, 205–206, 209–210, 216; religious scholar, 192, 194, 198, 211, 220, 232, 264*n*23; religious studies, 193, 222; self, 207–208, 210, 228, 234; sexual desire, 198; sexuality, 196, 210, 219; son, 146; theologian, 11, 193, 200, 228. *See also* homoeroticism; homosexuality; same sex

gay theology, 192–193, 198, 229, 264*n*26

gaze/gazing, 16, 51, 54, 111, 171, 215, 220; act of, 30; apprehensive, 141; disembodied 51; divine, 52; eroticized, 220; female 188; fetishized/fetishistic, 211, 214–215, 218, 227, 229, 231; gay, 215; heterosexist, 224; homoeroticized, 266*n*42; introspective, 23–24; inward, 40; male, 68, 223; narcissistic, 31, 232; pornographic, 218, 265*n*35; private, 44; public, 44, 137; retrospective, 24; self-, 45, 52, 54, 200; sexually charged, 215; solipsistic 43, 63, 231; woman, 50; voyeuristic, 44

gender, 1–28 passim; activity, 72; belief system and, 39; blindness, 80, 88 159; desire, 81; difference, 133; fictionalization of, 237; identity, 235, 240*n*7; imagery, 163, 182; Jew and, 225, 228; perspective and, 4, 48; performance and, 17; reading and, 3–4, 11, 20, 25, 32, 237, 250*n*24; rhetoric, 3, 8, 189; subject, 32, 81, 88, 93; subtext and, 170. *See also* body

Genia (Perechodnik's lover), 91, 162–170

Germany, 79, 103, 105, 108, 114–115, 119–120, 123, 179, 184, 188–189, 226; postwar, 37, 76, 101, 110, 112, 115, 149, 189, 234–235, 252*n*13

Gerson, Jean, 57, 201

Gerzon, Mark, 62

Gibson, Mel, 133, 220–223, 227, 229

Gide, André, 46, 208

Gill, Jo, 147

Giordano, Ralph, 115

God, 2, 30, 38, 43, 47, 53, 55, 64, 68, 70–71, 79, 82, 85, 88, 100–104, 109, 111–114, 118, 122, 124–125, 128–131, 153–154, 156, 158, 164, 169, 186, 197, 199–201, 210, 213–214, 218, 226, 234; defecating, 64–66, 190; as figure of speech, 16; image of, 66; is dead, 17; possibilities of, 66, 199; plaything of, 75; presence of, 96. *See also* Augustine; divine; Perechodnik; Pohl; Rousseau; Twersky

God's Phallus, 66

golden son, 146–147, 150, 183,

Golgotha, 77, 127

Göring, Hermann, 105

Gorsline, Robin Hawley, 227, 266*n*42
Gospel, 52–53, 104, 130, 222, 225, 227–228, 261*n*12, 266*n*44
Goss, Robert, 193–194, 211, 213, 227, 266*n*42
gottgläubig, 105, 107–108, 171, 179, 255*n*39
Grand Guignol, 223, 265*n*39
Gregory, 25, 133, 153, 260*n*5
grief, 71, 88, 94, 132, 135, 137–144, 146, 149, 151–152, 154, 158, 184, 210, 259*n*19, 260*n*1
Grotowski, Jerzy, 38
Grünewald, Matthias, 221
Gruyter, Walter de, 177
guilt, 2, 61, 78–79, 83, 93–94, 101, 108, 114–120, 122–124, 129–131, 145, 148, 176–177, 184, 202, 214, 252*n*11; collective, 114; personal, 114, 122–123
Gusdorf, Georges, 52

hagiographer, 12, 112–115, 124, 138, 154, 182, 185–186
hagiography/hagiographic, 25, 155, 212–213; accounts, 11, 156–157; ambition, 112–113; envy, 214; frame, 118; intervention, 121; lens, 213; obsession, 217; project, 220; style, 212
hagiolatry, 217–218
Haldeman, Scott, 191, 194–211, 216, 229, 234–235
Halperin, David, 215
Haltung, 112, 117, 253*n*26
Hansen, Gottfried, 111, 253*n*12
Hasid/Hasidic, 11, 144–145, 148, 167, 169, 258*n*7, 260*n*1. *See also* Jew; Jewish
healing, 53, 58, 102, 150, 156, 225. *See also* self-healing
heart, 3, 22–23, 41, 47, 59, 62, 77–78, 84, 87–88, 98, 104, 109, 111, 129–130, 132, 138–139, 141–142, 144, 151–152, 154–157, 162, 167–170, 182, 210, 235–237, 258*n*19, 260*n*1
hegemony, 85, 134, 267*n*4; religious discourse and, 193; vision of, 235. *See also* masculinity
hermeneutics of suspicion, 19
Herrenmensch, 102, 184
Herzog, Dagmar, 184–185, 189
Hess, Rudolf, 105
Hesse, Hermann, 36
heteronormativity, 4, 6, 223, 228, 232, 234
heterosexism, 224, 225, 234
heterosexuality, 22, 27, 52, 54, 56, 63–66, 69, 80, 183, 187, 191–193, 196–198, 204, 206, 208, 213, 215, 226
Heydrich, Reinhard, 108, 252*n*12
Himmler, Heinrich, 105, 107–108, 116, 119, 170, 251*n*6, 252*n*12, 254*n*33
Historia Monachorum, 155
Hitler, Adolf, 105
Hockenos, Matthew, 118
Hogan, Rebecca, 73
Holocaust (Shoah), 11, 76–79, 81, 87–90, 97, 102, 118, 250*n*24

holy: actor, 38–39; blood, 2, 220; duty, 112; ground, 52; love, 40; man, 214, 219; passion, 223; spirit, 64
homoeroticism, 66, 198, 211–212, 218, 226–227, 266*n*42. *See also* gay
homonormativity, 215
homophobia, 63, 193, 198, 211, 232, 234, 262*n*11, 264*n*24. *See also* imagination
homosexuality, 183, 187, 195, 198, 205–207, 211, 214, 224, 259*n*23, 264*n*23. *See also* gay
homosociality, 182–183, 185, 187, 191, 259*n*23, 260*n*5
horde of brothers, 47, 152
Höß, Rudolf, 254*n*35, 256*n*44
humility, 71, 140, 188, 218
hunger, 91, 163, 166, 169, 195; popular 103; spiritual, 60
Hunt, Hannah, 154, 258*n*19

icon/iconic, 11, 51, 211, 216, 224, 227; images, 211; materialization, 214; quality, 221; reticence, 227; reversal, 245*n*10; saintly figures, 221; treatment, 222
iconography, 211, 215, 221, 227
idiot (*idios*), 47
idolatry, 216, 226
Ignatius of Loyola, 133
imaginary, 14–15, 95, 137; erotic, 199; horizon, 3. *See also* religious imaginary; sexual, imaginary
imagination, 162, 196, 229–230, 235–236; act of, 135; cultural, 170; devotional, 227; direct speech, 136; erotic, 202, 222, 266*n*42; gay, 226–228; historical, 228; homophobic, 64; literary, 157; patristic, 228; poetic, 29; popular, 103, 228; pornographic, 60; reader's, 55, 159, 259*n*28; sexual, 209, 227, 230; spiritual, 209, 227; theological, 194, 204. *See also* religious imagination
imperialism (Roman), 235
imperial religion, 41
impotence, 42, 56, 59, 72, 184, 188
intercourse, 112; anal, 195, 262*n*10; erotic, 138; heterosexual, 196, 204; male-male, 209; sexual, 72, 254*n*28; spiritual, 138; verbal, 138
interiority, 7, 10, 16, 23, 218, 231
intertextuality, 7
intimacy, 6–7, 10, 15, 32–33, 35–37, 55–56, 59, 70, 112, 136, 144, 146, 156, 194, 197, 207–208, 223, 234, 236, 238; body-affirmative, 191; communion and, 223; conversation and, 16, 196; digitalized, 236; discourse, 59; "divine-human congress," 224; exchange, 190; fabric, 191; familiar, 136; feeling, 46; fragment of, 83; life, 5, 137, 146, 193, 209; male-male, 182, 191, 207; memory and, 57; partner, 136; privacy and, 219; relational, 39, 191; relationship, 60; reflections, 147; (self-)revelation, 6, 41, 193; self and, 2, 5, 7, 10, 32–33, 56, 234; space, 236;

intimacy (*continued*)
  thought of, 62; truth-telling and, 236; voice
    of, 11. *See also* body; mimetic intimacy;
    sexual, intimacy
intimate other, 7, 13, 22, 57, 59, 70, 112, 133, 135–
  136, 138–139, 143, 152, 155–156, 158–159, 161,
  170, 178, 183, 190, 232, 263*n*20. *See also* other
introspection, 16, 22, 24, 41–42, 72, 74–75, 91,
  191, 237, 247*n*3; mode of, 10; journey of, 23,
  236, 238; search of, 110. *See also* gaze

Jacob, 53, 72
Jackson, Susan, 73
James, William, 133
Jaspers, Karl, 114
Jerome, 25, 153
Jesus, 2, 64, 186, 199–200, 219–229, 266*nn*42,
  44; as gendered Jew, 225, 228; queer, 228,
  266*n*42
Jew/Jewish people, 11, 77–79, 85, 88–94, 99, 105,
  108, 111, 118, 121, 168, 222, 225, 254*n*35, 255*n*42
Jewish: alternative to masculinity, 216;
  autobiography, 248*n*7; body, 79, 85, 89–90,
  92, 98, 222, 225; child, 91; confessiography,
  260*n*1; culture, 77, 90; dead fetus, 96;
  Eucharistic meal, 169; gendered, 228; girl,
  167; heart, 162; male femme, 222; man,
  63, 66, 77, 88–89, 98, 167, 216, 222, 233;
  masculinity, 216; notion of repentance
  (*teshuva*), 75, 162; sign of, 90; tradition, 6, 92;
  woman, 167. *See also* confession, deathbed;
  confession, Jewish; Hasidic
John the Baptist, 215, 218
Jordan, Mark, 195, 211
Judaism, 11, 77
Jung, C. G, 64–65, 190–191

Kavanagh, Thomas, 203
Katz, Joshua, 72
Keen, Sam, 62, 69
Kellenbach, Katharina von, 118, 252*n*17, 253*n*22,
  254*n*29
kenosis, 199–200
Klein, Calvin, 215
Klimakos, John, 154
Kimmel, Michael, 249*n*13
Kuhn, Annette, 242*n*27
Kundera, Milan, 66

Landsberg am Lech (War Crime Prison), 104–
  106, 108, 117, 127, 176, 185–186
Laqueur, Thomas, 195, 201, 203–205, 263*n*21
late antiquity, 12, 29, 33, 37, 107, 147, 200–201,
  203, 210
Lebensborn, 177
Lee, John, 58, 61
Leiris, Michel, 1–2, 11, 31, 42–47, 49–54, 56–60,
  70, 72–73, 132, 134, 136, 159–161, 163, 190, 199,

205, 218–219, 234–235; and psychoanalysis,
  245*n*8; wife of, 159, 163, 259*n*29. *See also*
  Manhood
Lejeune, Philippe, 49, 58, 256*n*49
Lifton, Robert Jay, 256*n*44
Lionnet, Françoise, 74–75, 79, 83
Long, Ronald, 192, 194
Lonitzer (pastor), 186–187
Luther, Martin, 52, 64, 68
Lutz, Tom, 133–134, 141
luxuria, 199, 262*n*13

Macarius, 153–154
Maimonides, 248*n*7
male: anatomy, 82; beauty, 192, 215–217, 221;
  difference, 4; entitlement, 188; posturing, 24.
  See also anxiety; body; embodiment; gaze;
  manliness; masculinity
male-male: embrace, 187; enclosure, 182;
  intercourse, 209; intimacy, 191, 207; intimate
  exchange, 182; penetration, 197. *See also*
  same-sex
Manhood (Leiris), 42–43, 45, 49–52, 56–58, 73,
  132, 159, 161, 199, 260*n*29
manliness, 5, 134, 182, 184–188, 213–214, 222;
  character and, 106; defiance and, 186; façade
  of, 128; reputation of, 188. *See also* male;
  masculinity
Martin, Dale, 228–229
Martin du Gard, Roger, 208
martyr, 12, 38, 41, 126–127, 216
martyrdom, 127, 212, 222
martyrology, 102, 126
Mary (virgin), 181, 213
Marx, Anthony, 189
masculinity, 3, 5, 20, 26, 54, 62, 128, 134,
  183–184, 188–189, 191, 194, 214–216, 223,
  225, 235, 239*n*4, 241*n*12; assertion of, 188;
  autobiography and, 51; beauty and, 214, 220;
  Christian, 140, 208, 216; Dadaist, 245*n*10;
  embattled, 187–189; enlightened, 177; faith
  and, 258*n*11; German, 184, 188, 226, 234;
  healthy, 134; hegemonic, 4, 223, 233, 235,
  239*n*4; heroic, 216; heteronormative, 223;
  ideal of, 85, 140, 235; identity and, 208,
  235; Jewish, 216; martial, 183; negated, 61;
  normative, 4–5, 39, 239*n*4; phallocentric,
  196; privilege of, 223; protagonist, 20; role,
  6; saint and, 211; self and, 140, 165; self-
  display, 216; stoic, 134; strength of, 149,
  214; subjectivity and, 216; supremacist,
  186; symbolics of, 225. *See also* body; male;
  manliness; masquerade
masculinization, 189, 226. *See also*
  remasculinization
masquerade/mask, 5, 19, 23, 184, 236–237
Masterson, Mark, 155–156, 259*n*23
masturbation, 54, 195–197, 199, 201–208,

214, 263*nn*13–14, 19, 20, 21; critical praxis of, 201–202, 207, 216. *See also* self-abuse; solitary sex

maternal, 61, 83, 151; care, 151; clutch/hold, 143–144; compassion, 143; control, 152; influence, 168; nourishment, 145; piety, 180–181; typology, 179; wrath, 148. *See also* body; tears

McCloy, John, 115, 252*n*17, 255*n*40

medieval age, 12, 37, 57, 63, 112, 134, 154, 200, 202, 221, 248*n*7, 262*n*13, 266*n*44

melancholy, 81, 94, 133,

memory work, 21, 242*n*27

"Men Before the Mirror," 31, 52

men's movement, 61, 177; Christian, 37, 265*n*37; mythopoetic 61. *See also* Promise Keepers; Muscular Christianity

men's studies in religion, 5, 241*n*10

metanoia, 75. *See also* repentance

Michelangelo, 66, 220, 223

Middleton, Peter, 26, 240*n*5, 243*n*33

Milan, 39, 41, 98, 140, 144, 157, 163, 180, 233, 241*n*17, 249*n*20

Miles, Margaret, 20, 41, 55, 81, 159, 258*n*11, 259*n*28

milk: of God, 83, 169; human, 37; mother, 37, 41, 44, 95, 145, 169, 190, 244*n*2

mimetic desire, 145–147, 237

mimetic intimacy, 145, 150

mirror, 20, 26, 29–33, 35, 41–47, 50–52, 60–61, 70, 74, 79–80, 140, 217, 224, 231, 235

misogynist, 50, 201

modernism, 1–2, 16, 102, 110, 134, 147, 198–199, 205, 229, 254*n*31; obsession and, 56; project of, 56; quest for identity and, 208. *See also* confession

modernity, 1, 9, 39, 42, 46, 52, 99, 102, 133, 199, 201, 204, 207, 218–219, 236–237

Moltmann, Jürgen, 124

Monica (Augustine's mother), 60, 88, 95, 141–144, 146, 148–152, 155, 157, 179–181

monk, 112, 154, 200, 219. *See also* desert father; saint

Moore, Stephen, 26, 217

moral: act, 22; ambiguity, 94; anguish, 91; authority, 74, 128, 188, 234, 237; backbone, 88, 187; balance, 118; choice, 85, 89, 92; corruption, 180; crisis, 179; decency 131; demarcations, 11; depravity, 259*n*28; dilemma, 94; disapproval, 295; discourse, 118; exoneration, 125; expectation, 74; expertise, 234; failure, 77–78, 85, 108, 115, 120, 122–123, 136; fortitude, 118; freedom, 85; gain, 86; high ground, 119; improvement, 84; integrity, 110; lesson, 55; order, 116; personality, 52; point, 178; reckoning, 101–102; reflection, 22; response, 221; responsibility, 104, 126, 163; risk, 58; space, 5, 240*n*8; self, 21, 106; sincerity, 171; structure, 74; system, 74;

teaching, 179; verdict, 122; voice, 188; witness, 11. *See also* moral agency

moral agency, 21–22, 75, 81, 85, 88, 92, 94, 119, 125, 128, 157, 164, 177, 191, 232–233

morality, 74, 79, 85–86, 114–115, 118, 126–128, 234; inquisitorial 13; medical, 205

Morgenschweis, Karl, 106, 109–113, 115–118, 121, 127–131, 176, 178–179, 182, 185–188, 252*n*17, 254*n*35

Moseley, Marcus, 46, 97, 248*n*7

Mosse, George, 188

mother, 60–62, 65, 69, 83, 93, 95, 123, 132–133, 136, 142–143, 146–149, 152, 154, 178, 181; archetypal, 61, 179; Aryan, 177; biological, 182; breast of 42; idealized, 147; ideal Roman, 181; natural, 150, 181–182. *See also* Augustine; church; Culbertson; Derrida; milk; Perechodnik; Pohl; Twersky

Muscular Christianity, 222

mystic, 6, 95, 154–155

nakedness, 47, 65, 122, 129, 136, 214–215, 219, 226–227, 231

narcissism, 51, 54, 61, 68–69, 147, 153, 162, 168, 199, 201–202; comfort and, 152; meditation and, 35; longing and, 35; pride of, 142. *See also* gaze

narrative: choice, 147; control, 19, 170; convention, 129; loss, 136; significance, 162

nation, 114–115, 162, 186, 188–189, 235; building, 161, 182, 189, 235; cohesion and, 189; consciousness of, 189; democratic, 115–116, 189; emerging, 188–189; German, 188; humiliation and, 118; identification, 105; martyr and, 126; reintegration of, 114; trauma and, 149

National Socialism (NSDAP), 101–102, 105–107, 113, 116, 119, 122–123, 171, 177, 183, 188

Nazi, 116, 118, 123, 131, 170, 260*n*5; aesthetics, 176; annihilate, 77, 79, 89–90; assault/ onslaught, 85, 88; attitude, 185; bureaucracy, 123; category, 108; comrade, 122, 187; convicts, 114–115; crime, 108, 112, 188; criminal, 187; encroachment on Jewish body, 85; era, 179; ideology, 79, 104–105, 108, 114, 183, 186; leadership, 126; monster, 103; occupation, 76, 90; perpetrator, 11, 22, 101–103, 106, 112–118, 124, 128, 161, 170, 184–185; persuasion, 177; presence 97; propaganda, 171; representation, 177; policy, 84, 189; regime, 116, 120, 123, 128; rouge, 106; terror, 105, 108. *See also* war criminal

Nazism, 110, 185, 189, 235

Neuhäusler, Johannes, 252*n*17, 253*n*22

Neuman, Shirley, 51, 59

Niemöller, Martin, 252*n*11, 253*n*22

Nietzsche, Friedrich, 180

nocturnal/nightly emission, 82, 84–85. *See also* sperm

normative: behavior, 8; claim, 155; control, 200; expectation, 75; ideal, 239; ideology, 63, 233; model, 100; perspective, 4; practice, 216; voice, 32; world, 191. *See also* body; masculinity

nostalgia, 43, 139, 237; perspective of, 35; regret and, 260*n*3

nourishment, 42,71, 95, 138, 145, 147, 162, 169–170, 182, 200

Nuremberg trials, 105, 111, 116–117, 255*n*39, 254*n*35

O'Donnell, James, 75

Olney, James, 241*n*13

original sin, 81–82, 84, 117

orthodoxy. *See* religious, orthodoxy; radical orthodoxy

Ostia, 95, 144, 150, 181

ostracism (social), 15, 47, 209

other: external, 135–136; internal, 135–136, 139. *See also* intimate other

Otwock (ghetto), 77, 90, 92, 94

Paffenroth, Kim, 181

Passion of Christ, 131

Passion of the Christ, The (Gibson), 220–223

paternalism, 62, 106, 177; rule of, 152

patriarchy, 35, 222, 239*n*4, 240*n*6; post-, 70, 177

Patricius (father of Augustine), 151–152

Paul (apostle), 30, 43, 64, 217, 257*n*4, 264*n*28

Paul the Simple, 155–157, 161, 163, 169, 182–184, 260*n*5; wife of, 156, 161, 169, 183

Paulsson, Steve, 248*nn*8–9, 250*n*35

Payne, Leigh, 110, 115, 253*n*30

penetration, 197, 206; male-male, 197

penis, 63, 66–67, 151, 195–196, 203, 227. *See also* phallus

penitential, 9, 12, 201, 204, 239*n*2, 241*n*17, 263*n*16. *See also* confessional (religious)

penthos, 154–155, 162, 258*n*19

Perechodnik, Calel, 1–2, 11, 75–80, 84–99, 117, 119, 122, 136, 138, 161–167, 169, 189, 191, 231–235; Anorek and, 167–168; daughter of (Aluska/Athalie), 77–78, 85–89, 93, 96, 162, 164; father of, 166, 168; God and, 86, 94; lover of (Genia), 162–163, 168; mother of, 166–168; wife of (Anna/Anka), 76–78, 85–90, 92, 96, 162–164, 166, 169–170, 182, 234. See also *Am I a Murderer?*

performance, 17–18, 26, 33, 147, 150, 194, 240*n*7; confessional, 17, 110, 119, 242*n*23, 253*n*20, 258*n*14; eccentric, 41; gay erotic, 218; of the flesh, 190; of the self, 236; of the soul, 200; reiterative, 4, 208

perpetrator, 87, 89–90, 92, 101, 109–110, 112, 114, 116, 118, 124–126, 128–130, 176, 182, 187. *See also* Nazi, perpetrator

phallus, 53, 55, 67–68, 159, 196, 203. *See also* penis

"philoflagellationism," 223

piety, 60, 107, 140, 142, 145, 150, 169, 179–181, 221

Pilling, John, 159

pleasure, 9, 19, 21, 24, 37, 39, 55, 57, 59–60, 62–64, 66–67, 71, 79, 81–82, 84, 96, 98, 102, 124, 137, 140–141, 159, 164–165, 195, 197, 199, 201–205, 207, 209, 217, 225, 228, 235, 237–238, 257*n*4, 263*n*21

Pohl, Oswald, 1–2, 11, 101, 103–131, 136, 138, 161, 170–171, 177–189, 191, 231–232, 234–235, 252*nn*12, 17, 254*n*33, 256*n*48, 260*n*5, 261*n*12; children, 178; father, 178; first wife, 178; God and, 104, 106–109, 112–113, 116–118, 121, 124, 127, 129–131, 176, 181–182; mother, 107, 170, 179–182; Nazi party membership, 251*n*6; siblings, 178; wife, 170, 176, 178–179, 183, 187, 189. *See also* Brüning; *Credo*; victim

politics/political: 6, 54, 62, 105, 114, 118, 123, 125, 129, 134, 218, 220, 234–235; amnesty, 110,125, 129; autonomy, 232; choice, 115; climate, 115; cohort, 113, 188, 251*n*5; community, 235; context, 35, 234; dimension, 101, 235; discourse, 101; document, 103; drivel, 185; identity, 192, 224; ideology 122; morality, 118; musing, 106; networking, 193; opportunism, 122; opposition, 252*n*11; oppression, 35, 134; order, 134; philosophy, 239*n*2; rhetoric, 176; self-interest, 125; setting, 235; sexual, 202; torture, 27, 249*n*12; transformation, 35; transition, 189; will, 79

Ponticianus, 39–41

pornographer, 56

pornography, 2, 201, 218–220, 222, 263*n*20; imagery and, 198; language and, 219; material of, 9; non-, 196; whispers, 9. *See also* gaze; imagination

Porter, Roger, 50

power, 8, 13–15, 32, 41–43, 84, 100, 102, 116, 120, 123, 134, 137, 145, 155, 185, 188, 215, 226, 231, 233–237; and beauty, 81–82, 84; coercive, 113, 235–236; deception, 31; divine, 13, 41; erotic, 211; of faith, 102; female, 149, 188; generative, 95, 182; God's, 36, 79, 83, 97, 100; magical, 13; mythic, 148; reconciliatory, 125; of religion, 28; restorative, 13; of testicles, 72; therapeutic, 151; transformational, 123; transcendent, 96; of witches, 63

Power, Kim, 95, 181

pregnancy, 95, 163, 177. *See also* childbirth

pride, 107, 125, 144, 193; abusive, 102; false, 97; narcissistic, 142; solitary, 234

prodigal son, 111–112, 114–116, 118, 126, 182, 185

Promise Keepers, 222

psychoanalysis, 9–10, 13, 202, 236. *See also* Leiris

publicity/public, 2, 13–14, 16, 34–35, 38, 41, 44–45, 49, 56–58, 101, 109–110, 128, 133, 136–137, 139, 146, 191–193, 199, 205, 209, 231; acclaim,

58; access, 65; arena, 44; audience 59; award, 115; consumption, 10, 15, 178; declaration, 14; devotional, 229; discourse 58–59, 83; eye, 128–130, 136; hearing, 7, 17; honor, 57; hostile, 13; image, 178; noncompassionate, 13; other, 14; performance, 33; reception, 153; recognition, 16, 129; scrutiny, 129, 137, 177, 193–194; self-disclosure, 32; spectacle, 221; speech, 203; transparency, 56; view, 70; visibility, 192, 261*n*2; voice, 18. *See also* confession; gaze; testimony; witness

queer, 27, 184, 212, 216, 218, 223, 228, 240*n*4, 262*n*4; desire, 218; discourse, 217; hagiography, 212; Jesus, 228, 266*n*42; love, 199–200; religious scholarship, 192; voice, 192. *See also* body
Queering Christ (Goss), 193–194
Quest of the Historical Jesus, The (Schweitzer), 222

radical orthodoxy, 225, 227–229, 265*n*41
Radstone, Susannah, 207, 242*n*27
rapture, 30, 95–96, 154
Ray, Man, 31, 134
reader: contemporary, 7, 16–17, 25, 136; critical, 97, 103, 194, 234; cynical, 122; desire of, 19; disobedient, 81, 83, 89; empathetic 56, 92; experience of, 137; female, 19; hostile, 147, 153; human, 32; ideal, 16, 27, 70, 97, 135, 146, 234; imagined, 14, 76, 147; judgment of, 136; male, 18–19, 56; modern, 41, 61; obedient, 81, 83, 88; reception of, 153; reluctant, 153; sympathetic 56, 70, 73–74, 135; unknown, 147. *See also* imagination
rebirth, 79, 82–83, 88, 95, 97, 148, 178. *See also* birth; confession
receptivity, 187. *See also* gay; spiritual
reckleckness, 77, 98, 122, 232, 250*n*35
reconciliation, 101, 117–118
rectum, 66. *See also* anus
redemption, 3, 40, 44, 53–54, 66, 79, 98, 101, 122, 169, 197–199, 226
Reformation, 9, 12; Counter-, 8
relationality, 68, 191, 201, 203, 235
religious: discourse, 106, 189; imagery, 211, 234; imaginary, 3, 8, 16, 24, 191, 195, 213, 215, 228; orthodoxy, 3, 212; rhetoric, 103, 170, 189
religious imagination, 2–5, 13, 39, 66, 101, 188, 191, 194, 222, 230–231, 234
remasculinization, 129, 188, 221, 235, 265*n*37
Renaissance, 9, 52, 133, 221
Renan, Ernest, 261*n*12
repentance, 48, 75, 101, 117, 122, 155, 206, 254*n*31.
  See also *metanoia; teshuva*
resistance, 8, 11, 26, 31, 89–91, 127, 192, 233
respect/respectability, 47, 51, 64, 108–113, 115, 188, 233–234, 237, 266*n*42

restlessness, 41, 52, 98, 109, 140, 142, 149, 176, 180, 210
restoration, 13, 80, 132, 224, 226; German, period of, 103
retrospection, 24, 59, 72, 94, 97, 197, 206, 209, 232, 243*n*31; 244*n*1, 266*n*42; journey of, 238; mode of, 10; narration and, 21; presentation of, 137; turn of, 209. *See also* gaze
revelation, 27, 41, 46, 51–51, 56, 78, 98, 102, 182, 193, 197, 206–207, 211, 224. *See also* self-revelation
revenge, 76, 86, 90, 92, 96, 136, 139, 162, 169, rhetoric of experience, 212–213, 224–225
ridicule, 7, 15, 41, 48, 52, 55, 58, 60, 68, 100, 136, 140, 153, 185–186, 209, 234, 237
Riley, Patrick, 243*n*31, 247*n*5
Rilke, Rainer Maria, 29–30, 32–33, 35
Risen Christ (Michelangelo), 220, 223
risk, 7, 15, 19, 49, 54, 58–60, 68, 97–98, 100, 185, 194, 234, 237–238
Robinson, Paul, 206
Roman Empire, 76, 85, 140
Romantics, 8
Rome, 140, 144, 148, 154, 244*n*5
Rousseau, Jean-Jacques, 1–2, 11, 33, 36, 46–50, 52, 55–57, 59–60, 77, 124, 136, 139, 164, 190, 202–205, 207–208, 219, 232, 234–235, 237, 259*n*28, 263*nn*18, 21; as feminine, 246*n*32; God and, 46, 52, 245*n*13; relation to religion, 234, 245*n*12; women and, 204, 246*n*32. See also *Confessions* (Rousseau)
Rule of the Father, 134, 141, 150, 152, 183
rupture, 10, 96, 98, 132–133
Russell, Norman, 163
sacrifice, 39, 67, 98, 112, 126, 142, 148, 167. *See also* self-sacrifice
saint, 12, 24, 38, 112, 134, 139, 155, 158, 184, 211–219, 224, 264*n*28, 265*n*33. *See also* desert father; monk; Savio; Sebastian; woman
salvation, 52–54, 79, 82, 95, 121, 148–149
same-sex: activity, 183; allegation, 183; copulation, 263*n*13; eroticism, 224; love, 224; pleasure 64; stuff, 218. *See also* gay; homosexuality; male-male

Savio, Dominic, 214
Schaumann, Ruth, 130
Schmitz-Köster, Dorothee, 170, 176
Schutzstaffel (SS, Defense Corps), 105, 106–108, 116–117, 119, 122, 125, 171, 177, 185
Schwarz, Hans Peter, 114
Schweitzer, Albert, 222, 225, 228
Sebastian (Saint), 214–215, 264*n*28
secularism, 9, 13, 64, 102, 110, 162, 180, 203, 221, 223, 248*n*9
seduction, 18–20, 22, 72–74, 121, 147, 225, 233, 236–238

self-: abasement/abasing, 47, 218; absorption, 3, 27, 232; abuse, 195, 202 (*see also* abuse; masturbation); accusation (accusatory), 73, 95, 162, 259*n*28; aggrandizement, 18; alienation, 133; analysis, 44; awareness, 46; centered/centeredness, 43, 46–47, 161, 204; congratulating, 70; conscious/consciousness, 42–43, 202; contained, 68; deceiving, 35; definition, 14; deprecating, 96; destruction, 57; diagnosed, 41; disclosure, 26, 170, 194; discovery, 41; disempowerment, 188; distancing, 80, 94, 161; effacement/effacing, 15, 83, 95–96, 122, 136; embrace, 191; erasure, 3, 15, 130, 167; evaluation, 237–238; examination, 2–3, 8, 10–12, 22–24, 102, 138, 178; exculpation, 19; exoneration, 114; exposure, 26, 47, 50, 57, 67, 92, 218, 224; expression, 8; feminization, 128; forgiveness, 131; gaze/gazing, 45, 52, 54, 200 (*see also* gaze); glorification, 203; healing, 102 (*see also* healing); humiliation, 57; interested, 2, 158; interrogation, 21, 122; investigation, 230; knowledge, 152; loathing, 49, 63, 78–79, 95, 218; love, 196, 202, 205; mockery, 73; pitying, 18, 27, 35, 27, 11, 124, 126–129, 139, 157, 238; pleasure (pleasurable), 68, 197, 203; pollution, 202; possessiveness, 204; present, 18; preservation, 73; protectiveness, 195; purification, 101; questioning, 106; referentiality, 218, 235, 238; reflection/reflective, 5, 22, 48, 63, 218, 224; reflexivity (double), 147; rehabilitation, 114–115; representation, 8; revelation, 6, 17–18, 56, 58, 75, 81, 97, 125, 163, 231–232, 237–238; sacrifice/sacrificial, 39, 126–127, 168, 179, 215; scrutiny/scrutinizing, 16, 26, 42, 83, 95; shattering, 18; sufficient, 67, 69, 207; touching, 80, 161; understanding, 44; victimization, 128–129

semen. *See* sperm

Senior, Matthew, 8, 13, 239*n*2

sexual: activity, 60, 192, 195, 202, 208; affair, 162; agency, 164; allusions, 159; attraction, 165; awakening, 54; behavior, 179; body, 200; comfort, 195; conservatism, 179; conversion, 35; desire, 6, 86, 163, 191, 194, 260*n*5; drive, 38; economy, 151; embarrassment, 60; epiphany, 209; escapade, 159; ethics, 54; experience, 194, 227; exposure, 11; face, 165; failure, 234 (*see also* impotence); fantasy, 204, 219; fluids, 200; gratification, 226; guilt, 61; imaginary, 195, 204; impotence, 59; impropriety, 124, 254*n*28; intimacy, 207, 224; liberation 24, 57; licentiousness, 179; life, 60, 159; lust, 62; morals, 162; optimism, 203; penetration, 159 (*see also* penetration); politics, 6, 202; practice, 6, 192, 194–196, 199–202, 209–210, 232, 234–235; predator, 165, 236; preference, 192; prowess, 59;

relation, 72, 86, 134; reveries, 212; secret, 9; self, 152; self-restraint, 199; sign, 151; urge, 163; violation, 64; vocabulary, 202, 205; yearning, 166, 229. *See also* intercourse; theology

sexuality, 6, 20, 24, 60, 81–82, 86, 179, 194, 196, 201–203, 207, 210, 225, 228–229; autoerotic, 202, 263*n*21 (*see also* masturbation); hyper, 208. *See also* gay; heterosexuality; homosexuality

shame/shameful, 1–2, 10, 18, 23, 63, 18, 40, 47–50, 57, 60, 63, 65–67, 70, 78, 100–102, 127, 153, 180, 196, 198, 212, 218. *See also* blush

shamelessness/shameless, 50, 74, 89

sigillum, 11, 13–16, 153

sin, 2, 12–13, 37, 42, 46, 48, 52–53, 57, 73, 75, 80, 86–88, 100, 103, 109, 117, 121–124, 128, 130, 141, 152, 158, 199, 202–203, 214. *See also* original sin

sinfulness, 19, 47, 180–181, 197–200

sinner, 2–3, 12–14, 24, 31, 57, 74, 82, 89, 93, 100–104, 109, 11, 113–114, 117, 125, 128–129, 181, 187, 234

Sloterdijk, Peter, 200

sodomy, 183, 195, 209, 218

solipsism, 14, 31, 36, 51, 190, 202, 204, 232; circling of, 16, 43; operation of, 69; perspective of, 42. *See also* gazing

solitary: act of writing, 14, 59; confinement, 111; contact 41; discourse, 138; ego 67; existence, 39; journey, 67; pride, 234; self, 47, 52, 237; sex, 199, 201–203, 205, 207 (*see also* masturbation; self-abuse); subject, 234; subjectivity, 203; vice, 204, 207

solitude, 45–46, 57, 67, 184, 203, 263*n*19

son of tears. *See* tears

Sontag, Susan, 46, 50–51, 57

sorrow, 44, 77, 1320134, 141–142, 151, 154–155, 162, 169, 258*n*19

soul, 52, 77, 83, 86, 102–104, 123, 129–130, 138, 144–145, 152, 154–156, 176–177, 180, 182, 184, 191, 197, 200, 202, 218, 227, 232, 235; aching, 145; afflicted, 144, 148, 190, 231; corrupt, 90; crisis, 104; feminine, 61; naked, 231; performance of, 200; pierced, 154; transparency, 191; true, 236; work, 190

Spender, Stephen, 47, 73–74, 244*n*1, 247*n*3

sperm (semen), 2, 46, 83–84, 200, 208, 218, 220, 224, 229

spirituality/spiritual, 3, 6, 12, 32, 35, 37, 39, 53, 55, 61–62, 64–70, 80, 83–84, 95, 99, 102, 117, 121, 125, 133, 140, 142, 148–149, 152, 154–155, 178–179, 181–182, 187, 193–194, 199–201, 223–224, 234; adventure, 67; barrenness, 221; body, 11; child, 95–96; conversion, 35, 39; crisis, 61; deadness, 143; depth, 22; desire, 181; devotion, 217, 219; discipline, 153, 156; ecstasy, 181; fatherhood; 152; freedom, 85;

health, 16; homecoming, 108, 176; hunger, 60; impregnation, 182; insemination, 182, 185; integrity, 118; journey, 156; joy, 159; life, 53, 154–155; machismo, 39; master, 155; mother, 179, 181; nourishment, 169; pas de deux, 110; paucity, 36; possibility, 38, 66, 199; progress, 95; quest/search, 67, 69; rebirth, 82–83, 88, 95, 97, 178; receptivity, 209; sustenance, 40, 212; tears, 152; theatricality, 38; trajectory, 155, 171; transformation, 70, 100, 178, 182, 206; transience, 15; truth, 108; union, 95; virility, 140; voice, 6; writing, 5. *See also* confession; father; imagination; intercourse

subjectivity, 4, 17–18, 20–22, 25, 30, 46, 75, 170, 177–178, 189, 203, 216, 232–233, 237, 240*n*5. *See also* female

Stallone, Sylvester, 133

Steigmann-Gall, Richard, 252*n*12

Stone, Ken, 207

Sylvanus, 154

symbiosis: bind of, 143; dilemma of, 144; relationship and, 141, 144, 148; tie of, 145

Szapiro, Pawel, 89–90, 92

Tambling, Jeremy, 9, 14, 147, 239*n*2, 241*n*19, 246*n*32

tears, 24, 58, 77, 87, 131–134, 135, 137–143, 149–155, 157–158, 168, 224, 257*n*4; agony of, 139; coercion and, 140; false, 139; gift of, 139, 155, 158; grief of, 141; hermeneutic of, 155; maternal, 139, 142–143, 148, 152, 168, 183; "mother of tears" (Chrysostom), 155; private, 140; son of, 143, 147, 150, 154. *See also* weeping

Tentler, Thomas, 239*n*2

teshuva, 75, 162. *See also* repentance

testicles (*testis*), 72–73

testimony, 2, 6, 11, 15, 18, 21, 35, 41, 72, 75–76, 85, 94–95, 100, 103, 110, 112, 129, 132, 137, 168, 170, 182, 188–189, 193, 231, 233, 251*m*1; public, 15, 71, 101, 110–111, 113, 137

textless text, 147–148, 180

Thagaste, 140, 142

theater, 38, 53, 140, 220–221; of cruelty, 38; poor, 38–39

theatricality, 38

theology/theological, 27, 36–37, 52–54, 66, 84–85, 117–118, 122, 155, 162, 194, 221–222, 225; admonition, 203; anxiety, 218; bathtub, 52–54; bracket, 66, 68; certainty, 55; concern, 225; confessional, 203; debate, 205; displacement, 228, 266*n*45; embodied, 194; encounter, 227; enemy, 235; framework, 54, 106, 111, 154; justification, 54; landscape, 225; language, 199; meditation, 200; mirror, 52; musing, 106, 120; optimism, 228; paradigm, 204; perspective, 54; possibility, 53; project, 53; reasoning, 118; reference, 109, 200; reflection, 53, 55, 192–194, 205; sexual, 6, 193, 200;

tension, 228; theme, 213; truth, 102; value, 103, 199; world, 221. *See also* gay theology; imagination

Theweleit, Klaus, 240*n*5

torture, 12, 22, 27, 59, 223, 249*n*12, 256*n*48

transcendence, 70, 75, 218, 232

transformation, 1, 5, 9–10, 24, 35, 41, 70, 95, 100, 101–104, 118, 122–123, 127, 129, 156, 178, 182–183, 187, 191, 194, 197, 206–209, 210, 227, 232, 247*n*3

transparency, 56, 191; total, 136, 232

transpersonal, 236; entity, 13; listener, 15; other, 14

trauma, 13, 18, 149, 156, 162, 169–170, 183, 189

Treblinka (death camp), 77, 84, 86

triviality, 26, 43, 49, 53, 55–57, 78, 114, 119, 136, 140, 159, 178, 190, 200, 234. *See also* banality

truth/truthfulness, 8, 10, 13, 15–16, 35, 48, 56, 58, 74, 92, 94, 98, 108, 110–111, 113, 157, 180, 190, 229, 237–238

Twersky, Yitzhak Nahum, 144–145, 148, 167, 169, 190, 258*n*7; father of, 145; God and; 145; mother of, 145, 148

vainglory. *See* vanity

Valentinus (gnostic), 64

vanity/vainglory, 19, 23, 29, 31, 52, 54–55, 70–71, 97, 100, 197, 250*n*33

Vetlesen, Arne Johan, 119, 125–126

victim, 11, 84, 116, 118, 187; of Holocaust/Shoah, 87, 89–90, 108, 118, 122, 125–127, 131, 176, 189, 255*n*42; of torture, 27; Perechodnik as, 92; Pohl as, 108, 116, 128, 176

victimization, 108, 223–224. *See also* self-victimization

virginity, 164

Voltaire, 180, 202, 204, 263*n*21

voyeurism, 44, 51, 218, 220, 222; curiosity and, 55; desire of, 102; expectation of, 159. *See also* gaze

vulnerability, 3–4, 60, 67, 72, 94, 97, 101, 103, 125, 130, 135–136, 153, 165, 193, 200, 206, 209, 223–224, 232, 234, 238

war, 11, 54, 89, 96, 102, 118, 120, 123–124, 128, 149, 162, 177–178, 184–185; cosmic, 102; god of, 203; Great War (World War One), 104–107, 128, 171, 183, 251*n*5, 252*m*11

war criminal: Japanese, 256*n*49; Nazi, 1, 101, 105, 108, 110, 252*nn*13,17. *See also* Nazi, criminal

Ward, Benedicta, 153

Ward, Graham, 225–229

Warhol, Andy, 17

Warsaw, 91–92, 98, 144, 162, 165–167, 250*n*25

weep/weeping, 132–134, 139–144, 149–150, 152–154, 157–158, 168, 185; coerced, 139; false, 154; spiritual, 155 (*see also* penthos); womanish, 153–154. *See also* tears

wife (spouse), 2, 13, 59–60, 65, 69, 79, 135, 138, 135–136, 138, 159, 169, 178, 197–198, 204, 206, 234. *See also* Augustine; Leiris; Paul the Simple; Perechodnik; Pohl
Willis, Bruce, 133
Wills, Gary, 100, 130, 222–223, 251*n*1
Wirtschafts-Verwaltungshauptamt (WVHA), 105, 116, 119, 122, 125–127, 131, 187, 255*n*39
witness, 21, 29, 31, 72, 76, 83, 96, 98, 125, 137, 209, 221, 255*nn*39–40; moral, 11; negative, 255*n*42; public, 11, 35, 72, 100, 138, 147
woman, 17–19, 38, 51, 60–63, 65, 69, 72, 80, 83, 92, 132–134, 137, 144, 150, 153, 158–159, 162–163, 168, 178, 180, 183, 187–189, 218; archetypal, 63, 179; body 53, 63; disgust of, 42; erotic partner, 60, 84, 140; as fiction, 147; fictive construct, 83, 161, 177; invisible, 84, 161; medieval saint, 200; menstruating 50, 63; misogynist, 49, 133; mythological, 63; mystic, 154, 266*n*44; as screen, 60; spirit, 67; subjectivity, 189
womanish, 154, 183; Christians as, 186; man, 153, 185
womanist, 192
wound/woundedness, 18, 23, 51, 53, 57–59, 61, 63, 135, 137–138, 144, 146, 138, 152, 154–158, 166, 234, 237–238

Xavier, Francis, 215

yarek, 72
Young, James, 76